Paul H. Ray, Ph.D.,

and

Sherry Ruth Anderson, Ph.D.

creatives

 THREE RIVERS PRESS · NEW YORK

Grateful acknowledgment is made to the following for permission to reprint previously published material:

T. S. Eliot. Excerpt from "East Coker," in *Four Quartets,* copyright © 1940 by T. S. Eliot and renewed 1968 by Esme Valerie Eliot. Reprinted by permission of Harcourt, Inc.

Susan Griffin. From "This Earth, What She Is to Me" by Susan Griffin, from *Woman and Nature: The Roaring Inside Her* by Susan Griffin. Copyright © 1978 by Susan Griffin. Reprinted with permission of Sierra Club Books.

Audre Lorde. Excerpt from "Sister Outsider" by Audre Lorde, copyright © 1984. Reprinted by permission of the Crossing Press, Freedom, California 95076.

Joanna Macy. Excerpt from Elizabeth Roberts and Elias Amidon, eds., *Prayers for a Thousand Years.* Reprinted by permission of the author.

John Moyne and Coleman Barks. Quatrain 91 from *Open Secret: Versions of Rumi.* Originally published by Threshold Books. Reprinted by permission of Threshold Books.

Alice Walker. "We Have a Beautiful Mother," from *Her Blue Body Everything We Know: Earthling Poems 1965–1990,* copyright © 1991 by Alice Walker. Reprinted by permission of Harcourt, Inc.

Published by Three Rivers Press, New York, New York. Member of the Crown Publishing Group. Random House, Inc. New York, Toronto, London, Sydney, Auckland www.randomhouse.com
THREE RIVERS PRESS is a registered trademark and the Three Rivers Press colophon is a trademark of Random House, Inc.
Originally published in hardcover by Harmony Books in 2000.

Printed in the United States of America

DESIGN BY LYNNE AMFT

Library of Congress Cataloging-in-Publication Data
Ray, Paul H.
The cultural creatives : how 50 million people are changing the world / Paul H. Ray, Sherry Ruth Anderson.
1. Culture.   2. United States—Social life and customs—20th century.
3. Creative ability—United States.   4. Social change—United States.   5. Subculture—United States.
6. Social values—United States.   I. Anderson, Sherry Ruth.   II. Title.
HM831 .R39   2000
306—dc21   00-038293

ISBN 978-0-609-80845-0

17

First Paperback Edition

We dedicate this book
with gratitude to those who have walked ahead of us:

Willis Harman · *Marion Woodman* · *Jeanne Hay*

and with blessings to those who will come after us:

Spike, Catherine, and Jake Anderson · *Andrea Chandler*
and Larissa Odell

acknowledgments

Many thoughtful and deeply committed social activists, teachers, artists, and change agents, as well as businesspeople, journalists, therapists, and others took time from the great demands of their lives to contribute to this book. Not everyone we spoke with is quoted directly in the following pages, but each one helped to deepen our understanding of the new phenomenon that is the Cultural Creatives.

The people we interviewed included Catherine Allport, Ray C. Anderson, Spike Anderson, Doug Burck, Margery Anderson Clive, Mark Clive, Carol Collopy, Raymond Davi, Dixon T. De Leña, Vicki and Romeo Di Benedetto, Abbe Don, William Drayton, Riane Eisler, Mary Ford, Tracy Gary, Marilyn Ginsberg, Andrew Gold, Dr. Iris Gold, Rabbi Shefa Gold, Vijali Hamilton, Molly Hanchey, Professor Vincent G. Harding, Willis Harman, Jane Helsey, Frank C. Hider, Laure Katz, Dr. Steven Katz, Will Keepin, Kevin W. Kelley, Fran Korten, Barbara Kresse, Joseph Kresse, Peter Levine, Bernard Lietaer, Anne Kerr Linden, David Loye, Marc Luyckx, Sr. Miriam Therese MacGillis, Joanna Macy, Sandra Mardigian, Dominique Mazeaud, Paul E. Milne, Patte B. Mitchell, David Mueller, Wayne Muller, Anne Firth Murray, Ruben F. W. Nelson, Richard Rathbun, Maureen Redl, Elisabet Sahtouris, Glen Schneider, Robert Stilger, Don Thompson, Celia Thompson-Taupin, Dirk Velten, Marion Weber, Dr. Mariquita West, and Mark D. Youngblood.

Alison Stevens and Brooke Warrick at American LIVES, Inc., provided moral and financial support all along and good cheer in the face of Paul's frequent absences. Many of the insights about the cognitive style and purchase patterns of the Cultural Creatives came from Brooke's qualitative research over the years, and Brooke had a large role in developing the original survey questionnaires that started us on the path to identifying the Cultural Creatives.

Important funding for a baseline study on the Cultural Creatives was provided by the Fetzer Institute of Kalamazoo, Michigan, with sponsorship from the Institute of Noetic Sciences. We wish to thank Rob Lehman and Tom Callanan of the Fetzer Institute, and Wink Franklin and Tom Hurley of the Institute of Noetic Sciences for their support.

No one writes a book alone, but we have been blessed with the suggestions, resources, and unflagging support of very good friends: Palden Alioto, Rosanne Anonni and Richard Hunt, Joan Bieder, Jalaja Bonheim, Wilma Cliff, Patricia Hopkins, Jeanine Mamary, Gay Luce and David Patten, Sara and Tom Hurley, and our Thursday Salon—Philip and Manuela Dunn,

Noelle and Claude Poncelet, Leonard Joy, Bernard Lietaer, Peter Russell, and Barbara and Maurice Zilber.

Betty Karr typed our transcripts, cheered us on, and was a stalwart in an often chaotic process. Sara Van Gelder and Robert Stilger read early portions of the manuscript, and Bernard Lietaer read the whole of it, with astute and very helpful comments. Our agent, Ned Leavitt, was the demanding taskmaster we greatly needed, and we are immensely grateful to him. Philip and Manuela Dunn of the Book Laboratory gave us a good start on the book. And finally our editor, Patty Gift, publisher, Linda Loewenthal, production editor, Camille Smith, and the support staff at Harmony Books have been the kindest midwives any authors could wish for.

contents

preface   xi

are you a cultural creative?   xiv

part one   introducing the cultural creatives
1

chapter one   who are the cultural creatives?
7

chapter two   becoming a cultural creative
43

chapter three   the three americas
65

part two   a creation story
97

chapter four   challenging the codes
107

chapter five   turning green
139

chapter six   waking up
169

chapter seven   a great current of change
205

part three   maps for the journey
231

chapter eight   into the between
235

chapter nine   caterpillar, chrysalis, butterfly
263

chapter ten   a wisdom for our time
287

chapter eleven   inventing a new culture
315

epilogue   the ten thousand mirrors
343

appendix a   survey results   *349*
notes   *351*
index   *363*

preface

We had a good time writing this book together. This surprised everyone we know. They asked: Are you divorced yet? Are you still talking to each other? In fact we were worried too. We wondered how in the world we were going to reconcile our two voices and different professional backgrounds to tell the story of a very big new baby on the cultural scene. Paul's background as a macrosociologist concerned with the evolution of culture was not an obvious fit with Sherry's perspective as a psychologist focusing on the qualities of inner experience. But the story we wanted to tell seemed to need both the big picture and the intimate details of people's lives, as well as a blending of other opposites: masculine and feminine, science and spirituality, consciousness and social action. Each time we thought in terms of these opposites, we found ourselves ridiculously hemmed in. To write this book, we had to meet outside the old categories, beyond the walls that divide and restrict new ways of thinking. The convergence of social movements and consciousness, the odd and creative mixtures of business and personal growth, sustainable development and feminism and health—these and many more new solutions to old problems demanded that we, too, be open to wholly new possibilities.

Amid all this openness, there was one foundation we could count on: the thirteen years of research on values and lifestyles that Paul had been doing with his company, American LIVES, Inc. Over that time, surveys and focus groups showed, month after month, year after year, that an important new subculture was emerging. In the early 1990s, after years of surveys by American LIVES, Paul named this new group the Cultural Creatives because they are literally creating a new culture in America. We have been able to draw upon reliable research findings from what were cumulatively more than 100,000 responses to questionnaires and hundreds of focus groups. We also have been able to rely on the results of two big baseline studies of the role of values in American life. In January of 1995, Paul designed and analyzed a national survey on the role of transformational values in American life, sponsored by the Fetzer Institute and the Institute of Noetic Sciences. In January of 1999, Paul helped to design and analyze a study of the role of values and concerns for ecological sustainability in American life, sponsored by the Environmental Protection Agency and the President's Council on Sustainable Development.

Once the big surveys and focus group data were in, the picture of an emerging subculture was clear. But who were the people? Where did they come from, and where are they likely to go? Sherry came in at this point, bringing her experience in the personal dimension and the feminine perspective. Her book with Patricia Hopkins on women's spiritual development, *The Feminine Face of God,* provided the groundwork for our interest in the Cultural Creatives' stories in this book. We agreed to use in-depth interviews for the intimate wisdom they can reveal about values and meaning in people's lives. Together we interviewed about sixty people—artists, activists, elders, businesspeople, teachers—anyone we thought was part of the robust group we wanted to describe. And, like many of the people we interviewed, we read hundreds of books that helped us to map the new territory the Cultural Creatives are traversing.

We didn't anticipate how much the Cultural Creatives' story would begin to take shape once the personal stories were added to the large-scale studies and focus group results. That is where the fun (and a few wrestling matches, too) began. Our hope is that what we have begun, with the generosity and great patience of the people we interviewed, will awaken Cultural Creatives' interest in themselves. We imagine them meeting and talking together, laughing and arguing, and very likely disagreeing with some or much of what we've said about them. We believe that their self-awareness as a culture will help us all, help our civilization to develop the fresh solutions that we need so urgently now. In this book, we're able to offer strong empirical evidence for the major change in our culture predicted by hundreds of writers over the past fifty years. The evidence is even more surprising than the futurists imagined. Furthermore, in the last few years, other researchers have been finding results very much like the ones we report in this volume. Their studies start independently from different places and data and yet arrive at very similar conclusions. The conclusions correspond to one another precisely because all of us are looking at values and culture.

Interested readers may want to compare our depiction of the personal values of Cultural Creatives to Don Edward Beck and Christopher C. Cowan's insightful book connecting values changes with stages of cultural and personality development, *Spiral Dynamics: Mastering Values, Leadership and Change* (1996), and to Brian P. Hall's skillful analysis of values in stages of personal and organizational development, *Values Shift: A Guide to Personal and Organizational Transformation* (1995). Our picture of the role of values in environmental issues is closely matched by the data presented by Willett Kempton, James S. Boster, and Jennifer A. Hartley in *Environmental Values in American Culture* (1997). The sense we have of a major change of worldviews and values is shown by Ronald Inglehart to be happening to some degree all around the planet in *Culture Shift in Advanced Industrial Society* (1990) and *Modernization and Postmodernization: Cultural, Economic and Political Change in 43 Societies* (1997), and by Paul R. Abramson and Ronald Inglehart in *Value Change in Global Perspective* (1995). Our sense of the immense importance that new social movements have had in shaping the emerging values of the emerging global era is strongly paralleled by the evidence and theories presented by Alberto Melucci in *Challenging Codes: Collective Action in the Information Age* (1996) and Manuel Castells in *The Power of Identity*, volume 2 of *The Information Age: Economy, Society and Culture* (1997).[1]

Each of the book's three parts does a different kind of work. Part One describes the Cultural Creatives and contrasts them to the other two major subcultures in Western life. It shows both their "big picture," from thirteen years of surveys and focus groups, and their intimate personal stories, from our in-depth interviews. We show both how individuals changed their personal lives and how Cultural Creatives emerged in American history. This phenomenon can only be understood as part of a huge change in Western culture, on the time scale of centuries.

Part Two is an origins story. Cultural Creatives are the common constituency of the social and consciousness movements. There has been a great convergence of all the movements' constituencies into a common worldview. They were both creators and products of a massive cultural education process that led most Westerners to adopt a new worldview. Crucial was the "reframing" of dozens of areas of social life by all the new social movements and consciousness trends that have been quietly growing since the Sixties. Much of the more recent growth has been invisible to the national media. We retell and reframe that movement history, with more personal stories, because few know the many facets of it. The movements were far more successful in changing our culture and worldviews than in changing our politics, however.

Part Three gives the implications for our emerging future. It tells a news story for our times, at both personal and societal levels, giving new maps to help grasp the gigantic transformational change process in which we find ourselves. This new story is more challenging—and vastly more hopeful—than most of us would have guessed. A whole new culture is emerging, with a greater promise than most of us have dared to dream.

For those readers who are in a hurry, the key arguments are in Chapters One to Four, Seven, and Eleven. To focus on the solid evidence, be sure to read the pages accompanying the charts and boxes. If you are interested in personal stories, you'll find Chapters Two, Six, Nine, and Ten valuable.

We hope that the evidence and the stories presented here will support the Cultural Creatives to grow into the promise they carry, not just for themselves but for the sake of all of us, and for the seventh generation.

PAUL H. RAY AND SHERRY RUTH ANDERSON
San Rafael, CA
www.culturalcreatives.org

are you a cultural creative?

Check the boxes of statements you agree with. If you agree with 10 or more, you probably are one—and a higher score increases the odds. You are likely to be a Cultural Creative if you . . .

❑ 1. love nature and are deeply concerned about its destruction

❑ 2. are strongly aware of the problems of the whole planet (global warming, destruction of rain forests, overpopulation, lack of ecological sustainability, exploitation of people in poorer countries) and want to see more action on them, such as limiting economic growth

❑ 3. would pay more taxes or pay more for consumer goods if you knew the money would go to clean up the environment and to stop global warming

❑ 4. give a lot of importance to developing and maintaining your relationships

❑ 5. give a lot of importance to helping other people and bringing out their unique gifts

❑ 6. volunteer for one or more good causes

❑ 7. care intensely about both psychological and spiritual development

❑ 8. see spirituality or religion as important in your life but are also concerned about the role of the Religious Right in politics

❑ 9. want more equality for women at work, and more women leaders in business and politics

❑ 10. are concerned about violence and the abuse of women and children around the world

❑ 11. want our politics and government spending to put more emphasis on children's education and well-being, on rebuilding our neighborhoods and communities, and on creating an ecologically sustainable future

❑ 12. are unhappy with both the left and the right in politics and want to find a new way that is not in the mushy middle

❑ 13. tend to be rather optimistic about our future and distrust the cynical and pessimistic view that is given by the media

❑ 14. want to be involved in creating a new and better way of life in our country

❑ 15. are concerned about what the big corporations are doing in the name of making more profits: downsizing, creating environmental problems, and exploiting poorer countries

❑ 16. have your finances and spending under control and are not concerned about overspending

❑ 17. dislike all the emphasis in modern culture on success and "making it," on getting and spending, on wealth and luxury goods

❑ 18. like people and places that are exotic and foreign, and like experiencing and learning about other ways of life

part one

introducing the
cultural creatives

IMAGINE A COUNTRY the size of France suddenly sprouting in the middle of the United States. It is immensely rich in culture, with new ways of life, values, and worldviews. It has its own heroes and its own vision for the future. Think how curious we all would be, how interested to discover who these people are and where they have come from. In Washington and on the Sunday morning news shows, politicians would certainly have strong opinions about what it all means, and pundits would be expressing their views with their usual certainty. Businesses would be planning strategies to market to this population, and political groups would be exploring alliances. The media, of course, would be blazing with first-person interviews and inside stories of the new arrivals, instead of the latest Beltway scandals.

Now imagine something different. There is a new country, just as big and just as rich in culture, but no one sees it. It takes shape silently and almost invisibly, as if flown in under radar in the dark of night. But it's not from somewhere else. This new country is decidedly American. And unlike the first image, it is emerging not only in the cornfields of Iowa but on the streets of the Bronx, all across the country from Seattle to St. Augustine. It is showing up wherever you'd least expect it: in your brother's living room and your sister's backyard, in women's circles and demonstrations to protect the redwoods, in offices and churches and online communities, coffee shops and bookstores, hiking trails and corporate boardrooms.

SHAPING A NEW CULTURE

This new country and its people are the subject of this book. We report thirteen years of survey research on more than 100,000 Americans, hundreds of focus groups, and about sixty in-depth interviews that reveal the emergence of an entire subculture of Americans. Their distinctive beliefs and values are shown in the self-scoring questionnaire on page xiv. The underlying themes express serious ecological and planetary perspectives, emphasis on relationships and women's point of view, commitment to spirituality and psychological development, disaffection with the large institutions of modern life, including both left and right in politics, and rejection of materialism and status display.

Since the 1960s, 26 percent of the adults in the United States—50 million people—have made a comprehensive shift in their worldview, values, and way of life—their *culture*, in short. These creative, optimistic millions are at the leading edge of several kinds of cultural change, deeply affecting not only their own lives but our larger society as well. We call them the Cultural Creatives because, innovation by innovation, they are shaping a new kind of American culture for the twenty-first century.

One useful way to view the idea of "culture" is as a large repertoire of solutions for the problems and passions that people consider important in each time period. So these are the people who are creating many of the surprising new cultural solutions required for the time ahead. In the chapters that follow, we tell their stories and the story of how they are changing our world.

A LONG-ANTICIPATED MOMENT

When we say that a quarter of all Americans have taken on a whole new worldview, we are pointing to a major development in our civilization. Changing a worldview literally means changing what you think is real. Some closely related changes contribute to and follow from changes in worldview: changes in values, your fundamental life priorities; changes in lifestyle, the way you spend your time and money; and changes in livelihood, how you make that money in the first place.

As recently as the early 1960s, less than 5 percent of the population was engaged in making these momentous changes—too few to measure in surveys. In just over a generation, that proportion grew steadily to 26 percent. That may not sound like much in this age of nanoseconds, but on the timescale of whole civilizations where major developments are measured in centuries, it is shockingly quick. And it's not only the speed of this emergence that is stunning. Its extent is catching even the most alert observers by surprise. Officials of the European Union, hearing of the numbers of Cultural Creatives in the United States, launched a related survey in each of their fifteen countries in September 1997. To their amazement, the evidence suggested that there are at least as many Cultural Creatives across Europe as we reported in the United States.

Visionaries and futurists have been predicting a change of this magnitude for well over two decades. Our research suggests that this long-anticipated cultural moment may have arrived. The evidence is not only in the numbers from our survey questionnaires but in the everyday lives of the people behind those numbers. The sheer size of the Cultural Creative population is already affecting the way Americans do business and politics. They are the drivers of the demand that we go beyond environmental regulation to real ecological sustainability, to change our entire way of life accordingly. They demand authenticity—at home, in the stores, at work, and in politics. They support women's issues in many areas of life. They insist on seeing the big picture in news stories and ads. This is already influencing the marketplace and public life. Because Cultural Creatives are not yet aware of themselves as a collective body, they do not recognize how powerful their voices could be. And if the rest of us are blind to the paradoxical gifts that their awakening brings, then we may well be left wondering where all the changes are coming from.

This book aims to sharpen our collective awareness with an in-depth look into who the Cultural Creatives are and what their emergence means for them and for all of us. Whether you are a Cultural Creative or share an office, a home, or a bed with one, or whether you simply want to create new projects or do business with Cultural Creatives, you'll discover what differences their presence will make in your life.

chapter one

who are the cultural creatives?

t o spot a change in the shape of American culture, you have to go far beyond opinions and attitudes, because these shift as quickly as a summer wind. You have to dive down into the values and worldviews that shape people's lives—the deep structure that shifts gradually, over decades or generations. Once you catch sight of these deep changes and track them, you can discover a lot about what matters most to people and how they will act. Values are the best single predictor of real behavior.

Cultural Creatives have changed their substrate of values, and they may be reshaping it in our larger culture as well. Because our research has focused on Americans' values since the 1980s, we've been able to discover the emergence of this remarkably large—and so far hidden—subculture. We've learned who they are and what they feel connected to, what has meaning for them and what doesn't, what they choose to act on and what they refuse to support with their time, energy, and money.

Let's turn now to an overview of these values, to see where the Cultural Creatives put their priorities once they've taken care of the basics of making a living and looking out for their loved ones.

AUTHENTICITY

Cultural Creatives are the ones who invented the current interest in personal authenticity in America. Authenticity means that your actions are consistent with what you believe and what you say. The people in this new subculture prefer to learn new information and to get involved in ways that feel most authentic to them. Almost always, this preference involves direct personal experience in addition to intellectual ways of knowing. It shows up in how they receive information, how they form their impressions, and how they decide what is real and important. They distrust presentations that rely on bullet points that march to the bottom line, in part because these kinds of presentations are so often manipulative and make it harder to come to conclusions that are personally relevant. They like first-person accounts, and they dislike journalistic styles that claim to be completely objective and that focus only on externals. And they are especially sensitive to what they regard as slick, meaningless hype in advertising.

Brooke Warrick of American LIVES has led more focus groups with Cultural Creatives than anyone, and he calls their radar for authenticity "scanning for the coin of the real." This distinctive cognitive style, he notes, relies on two apparently contradictory ways of perceiving. On the one hand, Cultural Creatives emphasize personal experience: "Tell me what it was like for you." And they do love telling each other their experiences, even their whole life stories. On the other hand, they take a wide synoptic view of "the big picture," often extending to the whole planet. They synthesize many bits and fragments of information from the media to make their own big picture, often using the perspective of whole systems and ecology. And they're just as passionate about that personal, up-close feeling as they are about the condition of the planet.

Here's an example of what you are likely to hear when a focus group of Cultural Creatives is asked to comment on ads. In this case, it was a focus group in the Seattle area, and the ads were from several of the major oil companies. After looking at an array of storyboards on the wall, one young woman's deception-detectors were on full alert. "I'm sorry," she objected. "These ads about saving turtles and moose are just laughable. Throughout the century, the oil companies have been hindering cleaner technology. You could look at the question of a more fuel efficient car or the question of alternative fuels, and usually when you read through the news stories, there is an oil company in there somewhere holding things up, doing something in the background to stop the development of clean air technology."

The man sitting next to her agreed. "It's easy for the big oil companies to say they're going to support a wildlife sanctuary, but if you could get the line item on their legal fees, you would find that their lobbying efforts against clean air legislation and also their legal bills to fight clean air legislation make the wildlife sanctuary seem like a penny compared to a million dollars. Not to mention how much they're spending on ads to tell us about the wildlife sanctuary."

ENGAGED ACTION AND WHOLE PROCESS LEARNING

The kind of learning that Cultural Creatives like is intimate, engaged knowledge that is imbued with the rich, visceral, sensory stuff of life. The kind of action that especially appeals to them is what Margaret Mead called "whole process," where they can be part of creating something from the beginning, middle, end, and through to the new beginning. They would agree with educator Jean Houston, one of the early Cultural Creatives, that "the world is too complex for linear analytic thinking now. To be smart in the global village means thinking with your stomach, thinking rhythmically, thinking organically, thinking in terms of yourself as an interwoven piece of nature."[1]

When it comes to giving money and time, Cultural Creatives want to be engaged in the whole process of a project, and they want to be personally involved. The Sacred Grove, a project in which some six hundred women are purchasing an old-growth redwood forest in Humboldt County, California, is a case in point. We spoke with Catherine Allport, one of the project's founders, when the forest was well on its way to being preserved in a land trust. "We've created something for the seventh generation," Catherine told us. "It's small, but there is something about knowing we have done this that is very powerful. It's not an idea. It's not a theory. We've actually done it. And our vision is to be able to do this one, and another one, and do one somewhere else, and keep this growing. Because the vision of the Sacred Grove is not just this one location but other sacred groves as well. It has been very empowering."

We asked her what it is that inspires so many hundreds of women to stay with the process, sending in quarterly donations of $10 to $500 over a five-year period. She reflected for a while, then said, "Every woman who has been to the forest takes it into herself in a personal way and builds a relationship with it. So what happens is little but it's big." She went on to say, "It seems so important that preserving this forest grove—it's only fourteen acres, after all—is little to begin with, and personal. Because if it isn't personally real, then the grounding isn't there to see you through over the long term. This is how something that's genuine starts."

IDEALISM AND ACTIVISM

Direct personal experience is also important to Cultural Creatives in the projects they create and give their time and money to support. They expect to follow through on their values with personal action. Many are convinced that if they are not engaged, their convictions are "just talk." They express more idealism and altruism, and less cynicism, than other Americans. Sixty-five percent say "having your work make a contribution to society" is very or extremely important. Fifty-four percent say "wanting to be involved in creating a better society" is very or extremely important.

And their actions line up with these values: 75 percent of them are involved in volunteering, compared to 60 percent of the rest of Americans. They also spend a median of four hours a month in volunteer activities compared with a national average of one hour a month. Everything we have studied about their behavior says they do indeed walk their talk. And if they change their minds about what really does matter, they make quite an effort to change their talk and their walk, too. One of the most dramatic stories we know about this kind of thoroughgoing change is what happened to a soft-spoken southerner named Ray C. Anderson.

When Ray Anderson, CEO of Interface, Inc., the largest commercial carpet firm in the world, was to give an environmental vision for his company, he sweated for three weeks over what to say. The reason was simple. He didn't have a vision or even much interest in the topic. "Frankly, all I knew was comply, comply, comply," he told us. And that can and often does mean being "as bad as the law allows." By serendipity, someone sent him a copy of Paul Hawken's *The Ecology of Commerce.* "Reading that book was like someone threw a spear through my heart," he said. "I wasn't halfway through it when I felt a powerful sense of urgency and knew exactly what I was going to say. As I wrote that speech, I knew we were headed way beyond compliance."

His first order of business was to turn his own company, with its manufacturing sites spread across four different continents, into a "restorative enterprise," not merely recycling their waste materials but returning to the Earth more than they took out. To do this, Ray and his associates in 110 countries are reimagining and redesigning everything they do, including the way in which they define their business. Over the first five years of this effort, Interface invested $25 million in waste reduction and saved a whopping $122 million. Recognizing the magnitude of the challenge, Ray hopes to see his company become completely sustainable within twenty years, taking nothing from the Earth and doing no harm to the biosphere.

The second order of business was helping other companies have the same kind of success. By the beginning of 1998, Ray was traveling almost constantly, giving more than a hundred speeches a year to associates and businesses and environmental groups around the world. He's interested in creating "the next industrial revolution." Business is the largest, wealthiest, most pervasive institution on the Earth, Ray tells his listeners, and it's responsible for most of the damage to the environment. "We're a major part of the problem," he says. "Unless we become part of the solution, it's over, and our great-grandchildren won't have a world worth living in."

GLOBALISM AND ECOLOGY

Cultural Creatives like to get a synoptic view—they want to see all the parts spread out side by side and trace the interconnections. Whenever they read a book, get information on-line, or watch TV, they want the big picture, and they are powerfully attuned to the importance of whole systems. They are good at synthesizing from very disparate, fragmented pieces of information. That's why they are the people most concerned about the condition of our global ecology and the well-being of the people of the planet. Cultural Creatives are the key opinion leaders of the growing movement beyond ordinary environmental concerns to a concern for ecology and for making a new way of life sustainable over the long run. Eighty-one percent of Cultural Creatives say that they are very or extremely concerned about "problems of the global environment: global warming, destruction of rain forests, destruction of species, loss of the ozone layer." Seventy-eight percent say, "Americans need to consume a much smaller proportion of the world's resources." Seventy-three percent see "living in harmony with the Earth" as very or extremely important. And 68 percent say, "We need to develop a whole new way of life for ecological sustainability."

One of the best stories we know about Cultural Creatives holding the big picture and creating a powerful new solution to an ecological problem is what happened with the hypercar. Creating a hypercar means making the car of the future with today's aerospace technologies. Here's the strategy: use either hydrogen fuel cells for electric power, or a gasoline-electric hybrid engine; use flywheels to store energy when it brakes and use that for acceleration; cut the weight in half by using carbon fiber materials, like those used for airplanes and Indy racecars; and make the surface slick for ultralow drag. At 110 to 190 miles per gallon of gas, you could drive coast to coast on a single tank of gas. That would result in vast savings of oil and gasoline. Its air pollution is next to nothing. The same technology is good not only for cars but for trains, buses, and even powered bicycles. Implementing it should make a major contribution to stopping global warming. Whoever owns that intellectual property should make a fortune, right?

Instead, its key developers were Cultural Creatives at the Rocky Mountain Institute, and they did the unthinkable. *They gave it away.* They gave away the entire intellectual property on the hypercar to whoever could develop it, because they were interested in saving the planet, not in making a bundle. In this way, they generated unprecedented marketplace competition among many potential hypercar makers. Refusing to maximize their own profits, they stayed centered in their own values and created an unstoppable momentum that is leading to an ecologically and socially responsible innovation. The first hypercar is expected to come to market around the year 2001. Its proud manufacturer may not even be a metal-bending auto company but one of the high-tech aerospace or electronics companies—who prosper by the perpetual motion of "next generation products" that come every couple of years—and would not at all mind doing well by doing good.

THE IMPORTANCE OF WOMEN

What politicians often refer to as "women's issues" are a key to understanding Cultural Creatives. They see women's ways of knowing as valid: feeling empathy and sympathy for others, taking the viewpoint of the one who speaks, seeing personal experiences and first-person stories as important ways of learning, and embracing an ethic of caring. They are distressed about violence and the abuse of women and children, and they want more good childcare facilities and far more attention on children's needs and education. They have strong concerns about the well-being of families and want to improve caring relationships in all areas of life, private and public. Eighty-nine percent say "the caring quality of your relationships with people" is very or extremely important to their lives. Seventy-nine percent are very or extremely concerned "that women and men don't get equal pay for equal work." Sixty-four percent agree that "women should never have to return to their traditional roles in society." And

58 percent are very or extremely concerned "that more women should be top leaders in business and government."

In all of the Cultural Creatives' concerns, women are leading the way. They are taking what were once considered personal issues, issues to be discussed at home and in friendship groups, and bringing them directly into public view. And they want to see women in leadership roles. Not surprisingly, 60 percent of Cultural Creatives are women. And here's a surprise: the dramatic gender gap in values and meanings that shows up so regularly in surveys does not hold for Cultural Creatives. Quite simply, both male and female Cultural Creatives embrace what are usually designated "women's issues" and "women's values." This result is strikingly different from the gender gap found in other American subcultures.

One of the many Cultural Creative cultural innovations for women was developed by a charismatic dynamo in her fifties named Tracy Gary. "I wanted to build a series of nests for people with shared values to work together," she told us when we interviewed her in San Francisco. She started by creating seven small nonprofit organizations, a house for battered women, and in 1978, the first locally based women's foundation in the United States.

Each time she applied for funding, mainstream foundations and banks turned her down. When no one would fund La Casa, the women's shelter, Tracy mortgaged her own home for the down payment. When it was time to start a foundation that would be run by women and fund their projects, she put $25,000 on the table and found six others who would do the same. "We were audacious, fired with a sense of urgency," she says. "With the Women's Foundation, we committed ourselves to raise $300,000 within a year. It was ridiculous. I was twenty-seven—way too young to know what I was doing— and when I started, I didn't know five people who had more than $1,000 to put in. But after a year I did. And there was an inner push, a cultural and moral longing to build the kind of community we all wanted to live and work in."

By the time we spoke with Tracy in 1997, she had helped create ninety foundations across the United States. We asked what kept her so committed over all these years. "I really want democracy to work," she replied without hesitating. "I like what my country stands for. But one of the links that was missing in this democracy was the voices of women. In helping to create the Women's Funding Movement, as it is now called, I wanted to seed environments where women could listen to each other and grow into a greater confidence about what we intuitively know we need and what our communities need." She paused for a moment, reflecting, "It's not just about money, you know. It's about values. What are we really trying to achieve? What's the expression of our values that we can pass on with our money?"

Like so many other Cultural Creatives, Tracy told us that her forays into new cultural territory do not spring from any dry sense of obligation. "It's not like I have this poster over my bed telling me to do something for my country," she said. "It's more like I keep coming into relationship with people I think are incredibly talented and I want to bring forth their talents. Each time I'm with a group of people who come forward to envision a different kind of society, who take time to feel and pray and consider the long-term purpose of what we're doing, there is a kind of resonance, a tonality that shows up viscerally for me. It tells me that doing this work is a blessing or grace. It says, 'You're in the right place. Roll up your sleeves and go deeper.'"

TWO WINGS OF THE CULTURAL CREATIVES

There are two kinds of Cultural Creatives, and they differ in the intensity of their values and beliefs—and often in the extent to which they put their values into action. The Core group is the creative leading edge of the subculture, consisting of about 24 million people, just under half of the Cultural Creatives. A huge proportion of published writers, artists, musicians, psychotherapists, environmentalists, feminists, alternative health care providers, and other professionals are in this group. These are the more educated, leading-edge thinkers. They combine a serious concern for their inner lives with a strong penchant for social activism, including a commitment to a sustainable future. All Cultural Creatives have "green" values—concerns for the ecology and the well-being of the whole planet—but the Core group is far more intense and activist about them. In addition, the Core group has strong values of personal growth and spirituality that are much less important to the other Cultural Creatives. And, not incidentally, twice as many women as men are in this group. This is very much about the values of women becoming more important in American life.

The values and social concerns of the second group, the Green Cultural Creatives, are more secular and extroverted; they tend to follow the opinions of the Core group. Their values are centered on the environment, relationships, and social issues, and they often regard nature as sacred. Although they are only "green," and not as concerned with the inner life as the Core group, that doesn't mean they are more green. They show just an average interest in other kinds of spirituality and in psychology and person-centered values. On the whole, they tend to have a conventional religious outlook. Their world-views are less thought out than those of the Core group, and their values are often more pragmatic and less intensely held—in part because they are less educated and include fewer activists than the Core group. There are 26 million Greens, just over half of the subculture. There are about equal numbers of men and women in this wing—a ratio of 47 to 53, close to the national ratio of 48 to 52.

ALTRUISM, SELF-ACTUALIZATION, AND SPIRITUALITY

Cultural Creatives have a well-developed social conscience and a sturdy but guarded optimism about the future. The Core group is the more active half, concerned about both social justice and the development of an inner life. Contrary to the conventional wisdom, these concerns are not mutually exclusive, for their sense of the sacred includes personal growth, service to others, and social activism. Strikingly, the stronger their values and beliefs about altruism, self-actualization, and spirituality, the more likely they are to be interested in social action and social transformation. The Core group are frequent users, and often the practitioners, of alternative health care. A huge 91 percent consider "helping other people" to be very or extremely important. Similarly, 89 percent believe that "every person has a unique gift to offer," 82 percent want to develop more self-awareness, and 58 percent see "discovering new things about yourself" as very or extremely important. The 26 million Green Cultural Creatives, the less active group, do not differ from the general population on these measures.

As we'll see, Core Cultural Creatives are combining their interests in social justice, inner development, and spirituality in many ways, but one of the most interesting stories takes place in the forested foothills of Tennessee. The addicted and disturbed kids who come to Peninsula Village have been bumped again and again through acute treatment centers and halfway houses and onto the street. By the time they get to the Village, their life is on the line. "When you decide to come here," the founder, Patte Mitchell, told us, "you know that if you don't make it this time, you'll probably end up back on the streets, in jail or dead."

As a society, we're pretty much at a loss to find solutions for the self-destruction of our teens. In two generations, the suicide rate for adolescents has tripled, and the murder rate has soared. The grisly statistics in our morning papers attest to our failure. Agency programs that are heralded as successes routinely send seven or eight out of ten adolescents back to drugs or alcohol, to treatment centers, prisons, or the street. Peninsula Village turns these proportions upside down. Eight out of ten of its graduates return to school and find jobs, and do not go back on drugs.[2]

Why? What's happening at this outpost in Tennessee that takes America's "lost" adolescents and turns them around? And what does that have to do with altruism, self-actualization, and spirituality? Just about everything. A yearlong program takes young people through the traditional stages of a Native American vision quest: leaving the old life, crossing a threshold into the unknown, and integrating what they have learned so they help to heal their communities. The map for their journey is a medicine wheel, which lays out the challenges ahead. And perhaps most important, there is a community of peers and elders who want with all their hearts to see those who set out on the journey make it all the way through to a new beginning.

"It's not playtime," Patte Mitchell says. "When you decide to spend the next year or so of your life on a vision quest, you're setting out on a grave and difficult journey. When I designed the Village, I saw that the children needed a way of life they could take with them into the world. And I knew it had to be something that made physical and spiritual sense to them. The kids tell us that when they finish the vision quest program and start to get into trouble, they know what to do. They lay out the stones of the medicine wheel, and they remember how to sit for a while and look at their own doubt and fear. They know how to descend into the dark of their own feelings and how to reconnect with a sense of balance. This tells them who to trust outside themselves, what they need to let go of, and what they need to keep. They know that if they let go of something big, they're going to feel emptiness. And they know how, when they're ready, to move to the place of prayer."

We asked her what we could learn from her program's successes. "I think that what technology has taken from kids is knowing the naturalness of things. They don't notice sunrise, high noon, sunset, midnight. They need living images to be anchored in their bodies, so they can be anchored into life and can trust their connection to each other and to the great round of Being. We have this place inside that's meant to be fed with imagination and rich images, but with these kids there's a vacuum, and they are bereft. The modern world gives them nothing they really need. So what we try to do at the Village is give them a way to get both inner support and community support for their life's journey. And they learn that they have to give to others as well as get, that like the wounded healer who becomes the shaman, they have great gifts after all, and a contribution to make in this life."

WHAT THEY REJECT

It is revealing to see what Cultural Creatives want to replace in conventional American life. They are disenchanted with "owning more stuff," materialism, greed, me-firstism, status display, glaring social inequalities of race and class, society's failure to care adequately for elders, women, and children, and the hedonism and cynicism that pass for realism in modern society. They also reject the intolerance and narrowness of social conservatives and the Religious Right. They are critical of almost every big institution in modern society, including both corporations and government.

They reject narrow analyses and are sick of fragmentary and superficial glosses in the media that don't depict what they see, or explain what they know from their own direct experience. One middle-aged woman told us, "Over and over, the messages I care about, the really intelligent solutions, are not carried by the mainstream or even the alternative media." They want descriptions and explanations that include both the big picture and their own and others' personal experiences. For Cultural Creatives, reality includes heart and mind, personal and public, individual and community. They would agree passionately with John Leonard's question in *Smoke and Mirrors:* How is it that our cultural mirrors got so distorted and so mean?[3]

CHANGING A WORLDVIEW

When Cultural Creatives change their values, a change in worldview is never far behind. Your worldview is the content of everything you believe is *real*—God, the economy, technology, the planet, how things work, how you should work and play, your relationship with your beloved—and everything you value. For some, their worldview shifts first and their priorities come later. For others, it happens in reverse order. Most often, there is a mix of the two strategies, with values and worldview shifting alternately, influencing each other.

Worldview changes don't happen often—or we'd be like teenagers heaving this way and that on Disney World's Space Mountain Ride. Most of us change our worldview only once in our lifetime, if we do it at all, because it changes virtually everything in our consciousness. When you make this shift, you change your sense of who you are and who you are related to, what you are willing to see and how you interpret it, your priorities for action and for the way you want to live. Regardless of whether you leave your home, change your job, or switch your career path, if your worldview changes, it changes everything.

The stories below are a sample of how Cultural Creatives feel as they shift what is true and important to them.

You're walking up the hill with your friend as he tells you what has been happening to him since he left his position as a psychology department head at a big HMO last year. Private practice has been slow, he confides, and with devastating openness, he proceeds to tell you how his confident shell of authority and competence has been crumbling over the last several months. That's both the good news and the bad news, he says with a wry smile. On the one hand, he goes to parties and doesn't know how to present himself anymore. On the other, he feels nearer to some inner core of himself. Oh, and one more thing, he says, with wonder: "I'm not sure, but at the edge of consciousness new ideas are peeking through, possibilities I never considered before." And then he stops walking and turns to look at you. "It's so damned hard to let this happen," he says. "I feel like I should launch some aggressive marketing plan for myself. But I can't think of who or what I'd market. I feel like I'm some kind of seed that's been planted, but I haven't the faintest idea of what kind I am or when I'm going to sprout—if I'm going to sprout at all."

•   •   •

You're at a wedding reception and the couple sitting to your right is telling you how they have both taken time off work—some "time out of time," they call it. He's a handsome Irishman who has worked for eighteen years as education director at a respected foundation, and his wife is a graceful Texan who ran a small publishing company. While she's cut back to half time, her husband has left work completely. They're spending their savings. "I've been taking long walks, playing with my son, reading. I have no idea what's next," he tells you. He's beaming, evidently at ease with this process. "The hardest part is my old friends and colleagues. They keep asking, 'Well, what are you going to do *next*?' as if I'm making them terrifically uncomfortable by not knowing."

Six months later, you hear that he has become the director of a new kind of nonprofit consulting firm, working with community groups and developing alliances between activists and businesses. No one has tried this before, and it took several months of interviews before he and the group decided they were a fit. "You should see him these days," a mutual friend confides. "His spirit's soaring, he's relaxed, and he's actually eager for the day to begin. I never guessed I'd see him like this."

• • •

Your favorite niece leaves a message on your answering machine with the cryptic announcement, "We need to talk." You invite her to lunch. After a pleasant meal with small talk, she says, "Last week I went on my first silent retreat. Eight days." The retreat was led by two rabbis over the Jewish High Holidays, in the mountains above Santa Cruz. There is no question that she has slowed down, she tells you, but something more intriguing is happening. "I feel almost transparent, as if I've emerged brand new and rather delicate from a thick cocoon of cotton batting I've been wrapped in all my life. And in the most ordinary moments, joy catches me by surprise." She smiles, and you notice how clear her eyes are. "The only thing is," she says, "I don't feel I can talk to my coworkers or my friends about this. When I told them I was going to be in silence for eight days, they practically screamed in horror."

You think of her work as a multimedia artist in the depths of Silicon Valley, at the cutting edge of the world of high-tech start-ups. "As an artist, I know what it is to hang out in the empty spaces," she says. "I know I have to wait and let the work unfold in its own way. But when it comes to trusting the empty spaces in my own personal life . . ." She throws up her hands. "I never learned that. I'm afraid that thirty-six is too late to start. I wonder if I can stand to stay with the process when none of my friends even know what I'm talking about. I'm not sure I can handle the loneliness."

ORDINARY PEOPLE

As we traveled across the country and sat in living rooms and offices and churches listening to stories like these, we found ourselves thinking of women meticulously patching calico and velvet into quilts, and fishermen patiently mending their nets at the end of the day. Cultural Creatives are like this. As they step away from the mainstream assumptions and values of modern culture, they are piecing together a life they passionately care about. If you ask them, they'll probably tell you that it's a slow and awkward process. In the midst of a society with compartmentalized values, they are doing what they can to weave a coherent and integrated life. They don't claim to have all the answers. Picking and choosing what matters most to them, each one is trying to create a new synthesis of value and meaning.

The educator Parker Palmer says that movements begin when people refuse to live divided lives. This is what is happening with Cultural Creatives. Many of them are going through major life transitions as they look for ways to live the values they have come to believe in. Some stay stuck. Others appear to be stuck in unpromising situations for a long while but then come out shining, to the amazement of their friends and colleagues. What Cultural Creatives have in common is not their success in navigating the cultural crossover, nor their personalities, intelligence, religion, or ethnic origin. They are simply ordinary people who share a culture of values and worldview and, to some extent, a lifestyle.

Nevertheless, as you read the stories in this book, many of the Cultural Creatives may seem remarkable to you. They seem remarkable to us, too. We've pondered this, wondering how much we've idealized them, and how much they've painted especially flattering portraits of themselves. Both of these biases are possible, of course, and we can only hope that they are not too significant. We did not intend to pick out extraordinary exemplars. We simply were looking for people who were living from the values we've described above, not just talking about them. With a few exceptions, we steered away from the famous paragons and teachers because we wanted to hear about the struggles and difficulties of being a Cultural Creative as well as their ideals and creative solutions. Still, most of the stories you'll read here are not "ordinary."

The reason, we think, involves what it takes to develop and follow values that are decidedly different from those of the dominant culture. Almost everyone who sets out to do this and stays with it for any period of time is going to have a problem: they will have to find a way to live those values or else lie to themselves.

It is not an easy choice. Many Cultural Creatives go back and forth, trying to convince themselves that they shouldn't care as much as they do, imploring themselves to please just fit in and not be so difficult. If they're lucky, they lose this battle. In time, they learn to seek their own counsel, to abide by what they believe to be most important and act on that.

People who go through this process of discovering their own truth and learning to trust it develop certain qualities. Perseverance. An impatience with hype. A capacity for self-reflection. These qualities are threaded through many of the Cultural Creatives' stories. Another one is openness: not the kind of openness that flaps with every wind, but an open-mindedness that seems natural when you trust yourself enough to listen to others and not lose your sense of direction. Mary Ford, an activist in her forties, spoke to us about that openness. "When you start working for change," she said, "people are going to call you all kinds of names. You have to be willing to be called those names. You have to have a definition of self that's bigger than their definitions, that's grounded in how connected we all are to each other." And you have to keep an open mind, she said, "because none of us is an end point in ourselves. The whole world is an open system, all of life is open and changing, and there's sure not one right way for change to happen."

Mary has been working for change since she was a teenager. She's a psychologist, the mother of an eight-year-old, and a soloist in a world-class interfaith gospel choir. Her husband, Rob Lewis, is a high school math and science teacher who is crazy about kids. And about math and science (and basketball). It's a mix that makes him willing to teach eight A.M. advanced calculus classes and work weekends with a few colleagues, plotting ways to tempt their students into loving science, too. In short, Mary and Rob are two "ordinary" Cultural Creatives exploring and looking for ways to live their values.

Prathia Hall is looking for that, too. A former leader of the Student Nonviolent Coordinating Committee in the 1960s, she spoke to Vincent Harding's class at the Iliff School of Theology in 1997, recalling her indelible early experience. "So many times at these demonstrations, behind the young men who were doing the slugging, there would be women with children, their faces contorted with hatred. Veins bulging, bloodred, twisted with hate. When I look into the face of that, it is easy not to hate. It is in my self-interest not to become what I see."[4]

Is there a distinction between ordinary and extraordinary Cultural Creatives? How do we draw it? Do the times make one person and not another exceptional? Should we separate Mary Ford and Rob Lewis from Prathia Hall? We could not make such divisions. Each story we tell here has the uniqueness of an individual's life and something significant that is shared with millions of Cultural Creatives. We hope that you will take whatever has value for you from these ordinary, extraordinary people.

IT'S NOT "THE DEMOGRAPHICS"

Most surveys are content to classify people by demographic categories: male or female, black or white, white collar or blue collar, income, education. It's familiar and easy to do. But those conventional categories show only a thin slice of people's lives. The research findings we report here do not reflect "the demographics." Rather, our research is values research, which leads directly to a rich and many-dimensional description of what Americans are up to—and why. This new subculture is considerably more than a demographic category. It's an immense new cohort of Americans who are very much like one another—and very different from other Americans—in their perspective on the world and in their fundamental life priorities.

Cultural Creatives are not what you might expect: you cannot reduce them to a few neat demographic categories. They are no more likely to be baby boomers than are most Americans. Contrary to the conventional wisdom, their values cannot be accounted for by their age, or their "generation." They live all over the country, not just California. They are no more liberal or conservative than most Americans, and in fact many reject the idea that "left or right" describes them. They are simply not homogeneous demographically.

As mainstream Americans in most respects, the Cultural Creatives have a very wide range of incomes, from the lower middle class to the rich, but few very poor and few very rich. Their average income is somewhat above the national average, but that doesn't mean much—it's the wide range and diversity of incomes that are important. The same is true of age, for their age profile is that of the whole country, with two exceptions: in any given year, there are slightly fewer Cultural Creatives aged 18 to 24, primarily because young adults seem to be still firming up what their values are. And there are far fewer of them among the elderly, age 70 and over, apparently because that population's values were firmly fixed by the time the 1960s came along. In terms of occupation and education, the Cultural Creatives are a diverse group, though there are a few more professionals and college-educated people among them. When we say that demographics don't define the Cultural Creatives, we mean that their demographics are not very different from those of the country as a whole.

Many Cultural Creatives do the everyday work of modern culture: they are accountants and social workers, waitresses and computer programmers, hair stylists and lawyers and chiropractors and truck drivers, photographers and gardeners. Some Cultural Creatives are explorers of physical reality—scientists working on leading-edge research in quantum theory, evolution biology, new forms of economics and theories of living systems. Others are explorers of the psyche and society—artists who are social activists for the environment, schoolteachers who are teaching origins in terms of the history of the earth. Still others are social activists who speak and organize from a perspective of saving the planet or empowering groups who have been marginalized by mainstream politics.

The term *demographics* also commonly refers to religion. The large majority of Cultural Creatives are very mainstream in their religious beliefs and affiliations. Even though most nonstandard believers in Eastern religions and new spirituality are Cultural Creatives, they are still a small minority of this new subculture. A fair number of Cultural Creatives even belong to religious conservative denominations, but they have other values and lifestyles that match the rest of the subculture. After all is said and done, except for fundamentalists, most Americans have religious beliefs that don't correspond that strongly to their nominal religious affiliation. Cultural Creatives are Christians, Jews, Muslims, Buddhists, Christian Scientists, and agnostics, and only a very few fit a New Age description. In fact, the vast majority of them would reject a New Age label for themselves.

"WHERE ARE ALL THE GOOD MEN?"

Only one demographic statistic stands out about the Cultural Creatives: 60 percent of them are women. In the Core group, the proportion rises to about 67 percent, or two-thirds. The way women formulate issues of caring, family life, children, education, relationships, and responsibility for others is reflected in Cultural Creatives' values and beliefs. Women's ways of valuing are finally coming out of the private domain into public life. That's the good news. The bad news is that there are not enough men to go around.

Our friend Carolyn is visiting from Boston, and once again she's complaining about a too-familiar problem that faces many women Cultural Creatives: "Where are all the good men?" An outgoing, attractive woman in her fifties, Carolyn certainly looks as if she should not have the least bit of trouble attracting male attention if she wants it. She wants it, she tells us, but the pickings are slim. And she wonders if she's done something wrong in her life.

"Will you stop psychologizing about it?" Paul bursts out. "It's not about you, and it's not your fault." He's shouting a little, which isn't the least bit necessary since he has Carolyn's rapt attention.

"There's an objective scarcity of men who fit your values and lifestyle," he explains. "Core Cultural Creatives like you are two-thirds women. It's like being in a tribe with too few eligible mates. So long as you'll settle only for men who are like you, with your perspective and your values, it's going to feel like there's a scarcity of *good* men."

"Oh, fine," she retorts. "So where are all the others hiding out?"

"I guess they're playing with their techno-toys and are caught up with the bottom line and getting ahead. Your values of personal growth, spirituality, and ecology might show up way down on their list. In your social class, more men are Moderns. Too many women are inclined to blame themselves when they don't find the partners they want. But what can you do? The fact is that women are leading the way here. The new cultural developments and new values are coming mostly from them."

She looks at him despairingly.

"And men are lagging somewhat," Paul adds weakly.

"Yes, they do grow up slower than we do, don't they?" She laughs lightly. "Well, I'm certainly glad to hear it's not my fault!"

It's hard not to hear the catch in her voice.

CONTENDERS FOR THE MAINSTREAM

Cultural Creatives are one of three large subcultures in America, but as far as our public discourse is concerned, there are only two. Moderns and Traditionals are the ones we recognize. Half a century ago, they were in fact the only ones. It was a matter of either-or, one set of values versus another: city or country, cosmopolitan or local, secular or pious, hip or square; style and efficiency versus character and reliability; debonair Cary Grant versus solid Jimmy Stewart; the cool glamour of Lauren Bacall versus the wholesome June Allyson; modern and materialistic versus socially conservative and pious; promoting aggressive change versus preserving simpler ways of life. Moderns encompassed both business conservatives and liberals, both capital and labor, as well as the socialists, fascists, and communists. All of these groups were committed to material progress and big-city ways. Traditionals included northern union members and southern segregationists, Bible Belt fundamentalists and ethnic Catholics (Irish, Italian, Polish, Hispanic), for all of these diverse groups were cultural conservatives in their own way. The jostling and competition between the two giant subcultures is a familiar story, told and retold in a hundred ways.

(In the "Values and Beliefs" chart on pages 28–29, you can get a quick sense of the differences in values across the three subcultures.)

Introducing the Moderns

How can we describe to you just under half of the American population, so richly diverse that it includes both liberals and conservatives and nearly all income levels from poor to rich? This is the dominant subculture of Modernism. Read *Time, The New York Times, The Wall Street Journal, Business Week, Forbes,* or *USA Today,* and you will get the official ideology laid out in detail, day after day. It's the culture we see at all levels of government, in the military, and in the courts. It's the normal culture found in the office towers and factories of big business; in banks and the stock market; in university science labs and high-tech firms; in hospitals and most doctors' offices; in mainline churches and synagogues; in the "best" schools and colleges. It's the culture of professional football, basketball, and baseball leagues; chain stores and malls; most TV programs; and most "mainstream" magazine and newspaper articles.

The standards we take for granted, the rules we live by, are made by and for Moderns. Their worldview is so all-encompassing and their viewpoint so much presupposed that most Moderns can't see any alternatives. As of 1999, this group was about 48 percent of the American population, or 93 million out of a total of about 193 million adults. They have the same diversity in age and education levels as the rest of the country. Unlike the Cultural Creatives, who are more women than men, there are more men among the Moderns. Their median family income in 1995 was $42,500 per year. They include not only conventional factory and office workers but the technological creatives of American culture, such as engineers and doctors, as well as businesspeople.

What is distinctive about the Modern subculture? It's not just what they value at home, in their neighborhoods, or in church, but what they believe at work and when they're shopping. In many ways, the economy dominates what's distinctive about their lives. In fact, it is their belief in a technological economy that is reshaping the face of the globe. The Moderns' perspective is the taken-for-granted perspective of those who belong to the dominant culture. It's a whole system of beliefs that says, "This is *obviously* how it is." In the practical workaday world, it is, "This is simply what works, the only way to do it." Or, "It's the latest and greatest development."

Moderns create status differences between "those who know how" and those who don't. It's the American version of class differences, but in this version you identify with the winners in life's competition, whether you are a winner yourself or just a wannabe. Much of this attitude includes a sure, and at times contemptuous, dismissal of other viewpoints and ways of life. The implication is that anyone who "doesn't know how" is somehow inferior.

This habit infuriates people of other cultures, especially America's Traditionals. But in fact most dominant cultures reject other ways of life, and it's not surprising that Moderns do it, too. Since Modernism *is* the dominant culture of America, its believers are only required to learn and stick with a well-established approach to life, hard and competitive though it may be. In this vein, what's "modern" is simply what's good, approved, efficient, and worthy of praise, the latest and most stylish, the most competitive and profitable. These evaluations are not even open to discussion.

This emphasis on "what's modern" as the latest and greatest can lead us to suppose that if something is a few decades or a few centuries old, then it couldn't possibly be modern. It's bound to be passé, "so over, so yesterday!" And such flippant dismissals are just what you hear from young Moderns today. But in fact, Modernism is a venerable matron of a culture that is at least five hundred years old. Urban Americans have been Moderns since before the American Revolution, and many of *their* ancestors were Moderns, too.

WHAT DO MODERNS BELIEVE?

When the Modern age was in the process of being invented around the time of the Renaissance, most people were bound by the particular loyalties of family, clan, community, and religion. What was good for the group, or what was defined as good by the Church, was good. As Moderns fought their way into power, they invented a host of universal principles to create a better world. We are the beneficiaries.

Universal principles cut right across group loyalties and are intended to apply to all humans. They include greater equality among persons, personal freedom, justice, civil rights (for example, freedom of speech, religion, and assembly, and fair trials), representative and deliberative democracy, equality before the law—and applying those principles to real people and situations. The struggles since the 1960s for civil rights and for women's rights were classic examples of actually living out those principles. To their credit, Moderns tend to believe in these universal principles more intensely than Traditionals.

And as we shall see, Cultural Creatives are the ones most likely to enliven these principles with new approaches.

Moderns embrace many of the virtues and values that nearly all Americans embrace: being honest, the importance of family and education, a belief in God, a fair day's pay for a fair day's work. Those common values might help define American culture against those of other societies, or Western versus non-Western culture, but since they are not distinguished among the three subcultures, we won't pursue them here.

The simplest way to understand today's Moderns is to see that they are the people who accept the commercialized urban-industrial world as the obvious right way to live. They're not looking for alternatives. They're adapting to the contemporary world by assuming, rather than reasoning about, what's important, especially those values linked to economic and public life.

Here are some values that are distinctive for Moderns and suggest their ideology. Not every Modern embraces all of them, of course. But what's most important for them is:
- Making or having a lot of money
- Climbing the ladder of success with measurable steps toward one's goals
- "Looking good" or being stylish
- "When the going gets tough, the tough go shopping"
- Having lots of choices (as a consumer, as a voter, or on the job)
- Being on top of the latest trends, styles, and innovations (as a consumer or on the job)
- Supporting economic and technological progress at the national level
- Rejecting the values and concerns of native peoples, rural people, Traditionals, New Agers, religious mystics

Many Moderns also share unspoken assumptions about "what works" that the other subcultures may not share. These presumptions can drive both Traditionals and Cultural Creatives up the wall (often not for the same reasons):
- It's flaky to be concerned about your inner or spiritual life.
- You have a right to be entertained by the media.
- Your body is pretty much like a machine.
- Most organizations lend themselves to machine analogies.
- Either big business knows best, or big government knows best.
- Bigger is better.
- Time is money.
- What gets measured gets done.

Values and Beliefs Among
the Three Subcultures

△ Traditionals ▪ Moderns ● Cultural creatives

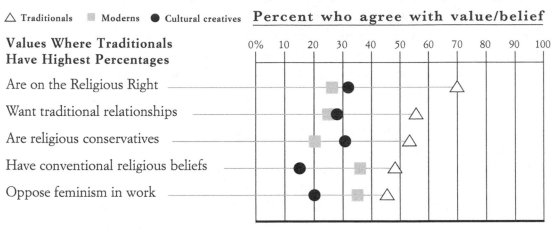

Percent who agree with value/belief

Values Where Traditionals Have Highest Percentages

0% 10 20 30 40 50 60 70 80 90 100

Are on the Religious Right

Want traditional relationships

Are religious conservatives

Have conventional religious beliefs

Oppose feminism in work

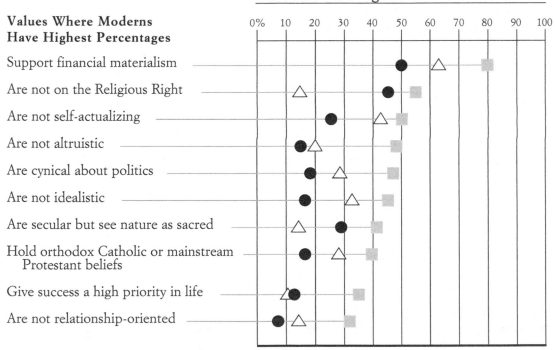

Percent who agree with value/belief

Values Where Moderns Have Highest Percentages

0% 10 20 30 40 50 60 70 80 90 100

Support financial materialism

Are not on the Religious Right

Are not self-actualizing

Are not altruistic

Are cynical about politics

Are not idealistic

Are secular but see nature as sacred

Hold orthodox Catholic or mainstream Protestant beliefs

Give success a high priority in life

Are not relationship-oriented

Each value is a scale that combines several questionnaire items to make it more reliable. Percentages are those who agree with the value, leaving out "neutral" middle and "disagree" responses. A value given as "Are not" is the percentage who disagree with it, leaving out "neutral" and "agree." Sample size = 1,036 adults. Values surveys cannot be applied to children, so the sample is of the 190 million adults in the United States. The date of this survey was December 1994/ January 1995.

Values and Beliefs Among the Three Subcultures

Percent who agree with value/belief

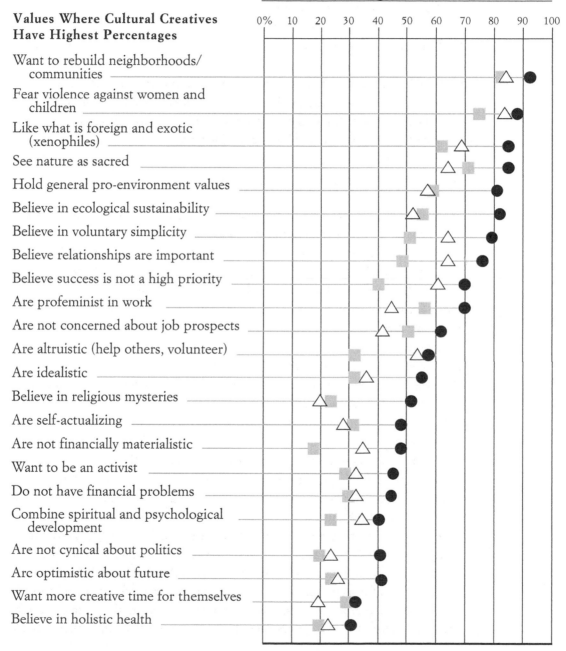

Values Where Cultural Creatives Have Highest Percentages

Want to rebuild neighborhoods/communities

Fear violence against women and children

Like what is foreign and exotic (xenophiles)

See nature as sacred

Hold general pro-environment values

Believe in ecological sustainability

Believe in voluntary simplicity

Believe relationships are important

Believe success is not a high priority

Are profeminist in work

Are not concerned about job prospects

Are altruistic (help others, volunteer)

Are idealistic

Believe in religious mysteries

Are self-actualizing

Are not financially materialistic

Want to be an activist

Do not have financial problems

Combine spiritual and psychological development

Are not cynical about politics

Are optimistic about future

Want more creative time for themselves

Believe in holistic health

- Setting goals is very important and effective, and so are measures of goal attainment.
- Analyzing things into their parts is the best way to solve problems.
- Science and engineering are the models for truth.
- Being "in control" is a top priority at work.
- Efficiency and speed are top priorities.
- The mainstream media's awe for and sense of importance of the very rich is about right.
- It makes sense to compartmentalize your life into very discrete and separate spheres: work, family, socializing, making love, education, politics, religion. It's a very complete kind of compartmentalization, covering what you do and believe, and what you value.

WHO'S A TRADITIONAL AND WHAT DOES THAT MEAN?

In a very real sense, everybody understands what Modernism is because its ideology is laid out for us in mainstream TV and newspapers every day. But most of us are less clear about Traditionals. The extent of their influence in the media is much debated. David Frum, a former writer for *The Wall Street Journal*'s polemical right-wing editorial page, describes the media's lack of empathy for conservative points of view: "Most reporters, when covering the rise of the Religious Right, can make no human connection with these people," he says. "They see them as dangerous." But for every conservative complaint that the mainstream media are too liberal, there is a corresponding sense of unease from Moderns. One *Business Week* writer complained, for example, that the right wing's talk shows and cable TV channels and desktop newsletters "empower fringe groups and magnify their unchecked rage."[5]

But who are the Traditionals? Surely Rush Limbaugh and Oliver North are not adequate spokesmen for this significant subculture. Do they live in small towns or rural areas, or mostly in the South? Are they always part of the Religious Right? Are they the ones the pundits call social conservatives? Are they Protestant fundamentalists, or do some Catholics and Jews qualify, too?

The answer is, they are some of all of the above. As of 1999, Traditionals were 24.5 percent of the U.S. population, or 48 million adults. *Traditionalism,* as we use the word, is not a thin category or a handy label to stick on someone. It is shorthand for a complex cultural conservatism and refers to a real subculture of shared values and familiar customs, rich with the details of life. America's cultural conservatives include more variety than the other subcultures might think. Many Traditionals are not white-bread Republicans but elderly New Deal Democrats, Reagan Democrats, and old-time union people as well as social conservatives in politics. There are more ethnic Catholics, uneducated people, and people from small towns and rural areas among the Traditionals than in the other subcultures. Those with strong religious feelings tend to be Catholics, Mormons, fundamentalists, or evangelical Protestants. Many are African American or Hispanic American. This subculture is not primarily about politics. It's about beliefs, ways of life, and personal identity.

Traditionals' views do not translate cleanly into the political positions laid out by the press and the politicians. They can be culturally conservative on some issues and liberal or centrist on others. They are just as likely to disagree with many Moral Majority and Christian Coalition social conservative stances as they are to agree. Many observers are surprised to find that large numbers of Traditionals are strongly pro-environment, for example. Some are even pro-choice but are culturally conservative in other ways.

Perhaps what's most surprising about this group is their general lack of interest in politics, contrary to the claims of the Religious Right. They're so uninterested in detailed ideological positions that political operatives must do handstands to try to say they support some political position or other. Most have low incomes and a high school education or less, and they don't vote. Their lives are caught up with just getting by in life.

The social conservative political agenda is supported by only about half of the Traditionals. About 70 percent are religious conservatives who oppose abortion, but after that the consensus disappears. They are led by a small subgroup of affluent Traditionals who are both business conservatives and cultural conservatives. These "double conservatives" have outsize voices in the Christian Coalition and the social conservative wing of the Republican Party. But they are only about 8 percent of the population, or 15 million adults.

Here's a short list of the values and beliefs that do define Traditionals:

- Patriarchs should again dominate family life.
- *Feminism* is a swearword.
- Men need to keep their traditional roles and women need to keep theirs.
- Family, church, and community are where you belong.
- The conservative version of their own particular religious traditions must be upheld.
- Customary and familiar ways of life should be maintained.
- It's important to regulate sex—pornography, teen sex, extramarital sex—and abortion.

- Men should be proud to serve their country in the military.
- All the guidance you need for your life can be found in the Bible.
- Country and small-town life is more virtuous than big-city or suburban life.
- Our country needs to do more to support virtuous behavior.
- Preserving civil liberties is less important than restricting immoral behavior.
- Freedom to carry arms is essential.
- Foreigners are not welcome.

Many Traditionals are pro-environment and anti–big business. They are outraged about the destruction of the world they remember, both its natural areas and their former small-town way of life. Some take a Main Street small-business stance against the Wall Street big-business ethic, and some have the traditional working-class resentment of big, rich corporations.

After listening to many Traditionals, it seems to us that there is a Traditional psychology. First, Traditionals fend off an intrusive modern world that they don't fully understand: sex-and-violence-loaded movies and TV programs, government agencies, big banks and insurance companies, the phone company. Because much of what they have to offer is not rewarded in modern life, they're also fending off a world they can't succeed in. They generally want black-and-white categories that offer a feeling of certainty. Finally, they look for ways of life that are comforting and familiar repetitions of their youth.

Most Traditionals, as they react against a rapidly changing and uncertain modern world, try to avoid complex situations and ideas. Demographically they are older, poorer, and less educated than other Americans. Their average age is mid-fifties. Their 1995 median family income was only $23,750 per year, partly because so many are retirees. As the older Traditionals die, they are not being replaced by nearly as many younger ones, so it is a population in slow decline over time. Quite a few young Traditionals become Moderns. Around World War II, about 50 percent of Americans were Traditionals, but now they are just under 25 percent. Population projections show a continuing decline.

THE ILLUSION OF SUCCESS

If the Traditionals are losing ground, how can they claim to be winning? Since they don't believe in scientific polling, they use other indicators of success. One is conservative religious programming. They see far more of this on TV than they used to, and they can tune in to many conservative radio stations, because the Religious Right has created several TV networks and thousands of radio stations. So even while elderly Traditionals are dying and are not being replaced by younger ones, Traditionals can seem to be omnipresent.

Another indicator they use is membership in a church or denomination. While particular megachurches and conservative denominations may be ballooning, this gives no accurate information about the whole population of Traditionals, for many do not have church memberships or are not in those denominations. Finally, there's lying. In 1999 an exposé by *The New York Times* showed that the main offices of the Christian Coalition had been pretending to reporters that they had more staff than they really did, and that they had kept a million or more obsolete names or names of the deceased in their computer files to puff up their apparent importance. It now appears that their members were never as numerous as claimed.

HEALING THE CULTURE WARS

Two worlds of meaning—Modern and Traditional—have coexisted uncomfortably in our nation since its founding. Their relationship has been like a long-burning family quarrel and has been called the "culture wars." At the threshold of the twenty-first century, the Cultural Creatives represent a third alternative. Their roots lie in the two earlier cultures, but their branches reach well beyond them. Their new world of meaning offers the opportunity to heal the wounds of the culture wars.

Each of the three subcultures has its own perspective on the fundamental priorities of American society: what a good life is, what is really important, why we are here, what we are living for, and what kind of country America should be, now and in the future. Each has a contribution to make to the emerging culture of the twenty-first century, but some considerable healing must also take place. For one thing, each subculture must stop dismissing the others as inferior, bad, and wrong simply because their values are different. And second, they need to see that this era is at least as much about cultural innovation as it is about decline and decay of established cultural forms.

LIFESTYLES OF THE CULTURAL CREATIVES

Placing the emerging new subculture in the context of the other two makes it easier to understand how much work must be done to piece together a different way of life. Cultural Creatives are different in almost everything that concerns lifestyle: the things they buy, the kind of stores and shopping experiences they choose, the media they listen to, the way their houses look inside and out, their demand for authenticity in their everyday lives, and the criteria by which they tell what's important and what's bogus.

Most Cultural Creatives are astonished to find that many other people live just the way they do. They believe that they have developed their lifestyle all by themselves. And usually they have, but they are not alone in the choices that they make. From dozens of surveys and hundreds of focus groups that American LIVES has conducted from 1986 through 1999, we know that Cultural Creatives choose a way of life that's distinct from that of other mainstream Americans.

The box on pages 35–37 shows some distinguishing characteristics of these lifestyle choices. If you are wondering whether you are a Cultural Creative, you can determine whether they match your own. Look at the overall pattern, and you'll see that most Cultural Creatives live day to day in a somewhat alienating Modern environment. This is not the way that they ideally would live in a culture they had made themselves.

Please allow us to emphasize what we are *not* saying. We are *not* saying that *all* Cultural Creatives do everything listed in the box. To do that, they'd have to be quite affluent, but Cultural Creatives range in income from lower middle class to wealthy. Many find their incomes don't allow them to do all they might like to. Furthermore, they are *not* people who define their lives in terms of consumption. Many Cultural Creatives are very uncomfortable at being described as "consumers," because they feel this elevates a minor part of their lives to more importance than they care to give it. Focusing on what they buy and how they live, they would complain, reflects the needs of the businesses that want to sell them things. In fact, a minority of Cultural Creatives are strongly in favor of voluntary simplicity and would not spend money on "consuming so much stuff."

What we *are* saying is: If and when Cultural Creatives engage in an activity, or buy something, this list shows what they prefer. The lifestyle findings show how they approach shopping and deciding what to put in their houses, as thoughtful readers, as careful consumers. It's an experiential, authentic, and holistic style.

- **Books and radio:** Cultural Creatives buy more books and magazines, listen to more radio, including classical music and NPR, and watch less television than any other group. About half of them are regular book buyers, far more than the general public. They are literate, discriminating, and dislike most of what is on TV. They demand good information and have exceptionally good deception-detectors for ads and for misleading corporate or political claims. They are particularly unhappy with the quality of TV news.

- **Arts and culture:** Most CCs are aggressive consumers of the arts and culture. They actively go out and get involved in it. They are much more likely than most Americans to be involved in the arts as amateurs or pros, and they are more likely to write books and articles and to go to meetings and workshops about creative endeavors.

- **Stories, "whole process," and systems:** CCs appreciate good stories and want views of the "whole process" of whatever they are reading, from cereal boxes to product descriptions to magazine articles. They like a systems overview: they want to know where a product came from, how it was made, who made it, and what will happen to it when they are finished with it. They hate to read mail or articles that come in bullet points and race to the bottom line (unless they are very time pressed and don't care much about the topic). They also want symbols that go deep, and more than most Americans, they actively dislike advertising and children's TV.

- **Desire for authenticity:** CCs are the ones who brought the criterion of "authenticity" to the marketplace. They lead the consumer rebellion against things that are "plastic," fake, imitation, poorly made, throwaway, cliché, or high fashion. If they buy something in a traditional style, they want it to be authentically traditional; Smith and Hawken garden tools speak to this desire for authenticity, as does much of the natural foods industry.

- **Careful consumers:** CCs are the kind of people who buy and use *Consumer Reports* on most consumer durable goods, like appliances, cars, and consumer electronics. For the most part, they are the careful, well-informed shoppers who do not buy on impulse. They are likely to research a purchase first and are practically the only consumers who regularly read labels.

- **Soft innovation:** CCs are *not the technology innovators* who buy the latest and greatest in computers, and many are just getting onto the Internet. But they are *at the leading edge of many cultural innovations.* They tend to be innovators and opinion leaders for some knowledge-intensive products, including magazines, fine foods, wines, and boutique beers.

- **The foodies:** CCs are the "foodies"—people who like to talk about food (before *and* after), experiment with new kinds of food, cook with friends, eat out a lot, do gourmet and ethnic cooking, and try natural foods and health foods.

- **Home:** Home is important to CCs, but they buy fewer new houses than most people of their income level, finding that new houses are not usually designed with them in mind. So they buy resale houses and fix them up the way they want. They don't like status-display homes with impressive entrances, columns, and gables: theirs are more inward-looking and hidden from the street by fences, trees, and shrubbery. They tend to prefer established neighborhoods with a lot of trees and privacy, and they want to stay far away from tract houses in treeless suburbs.

- **Authentic styling in homes:** CCs' preferences for home styling are all-embracing, including authentic New England saltbox, authentic Georgian, authentic Frank Lloyd Wright, authentic desert adobe, and authentic contemporary Californian. What's good, as far as CCs are concerned, is a building that fits into its proper place on the land. They want access to nature, walking and biking paths, ecological preservation, historic preservation, and master-planned communities that show a way to re-create community.

- **The nest:** When CCs buy a home, they want it to be a "nest." It should have a lot of privacy externally and private spaces within, including the buffering of children's space from adult spaces, and with lots of interesting nooks and niches. They are more likely to live out of the living room and not bother with a family room. They are far more likely to have a home office and to have converted a bedroom, den, or family room into one.

- **Interior decoration:** CCs are typically eclectic decorators, with a lot of original art and craft pieces around the house. Many seem to think a house is not properly decorated without a lot of books. The house that can't be seen from the street should be personalized to show on the inside who they are. Status display happens *inside* the house, not outside, though it is not blatant: it is display of personal good taste and creative sense of style. CCs would not buy a single decorator style for the whole house.

- **Cars:** CCs are far more likely to want safety and fuel economy in a midprice car. If they could also get an ecologically sound, high-mileage, recyclable car, they'd snap it up. If ever the auto industry were to provide the car they want, it would perhaps be a gas-electric hybrid or one with fuel cells. Volvos appeal to many CCs, as do well-made Japanese cars. They loathe the process at car dealerships even more than most. A car like the Saturn with its fixed price and top dealer service is designed for CCs.

- **Vacation travel:** CCs define the leading edge of vacation travel that is exotic, adventuresome without (too much) danger, educational, experiential, authentic, altruistic, and/or spiritual. They like tours of temples in India, tours of the back country where tourists don't go, ecotourism, photo safaris, fantasy baseball camps, save-the-baby-seals vacations, help-rebuild-a-Mayan-village vacations. They don't go for package tours, fancy resorts, or cruises.

- **Experiential consumers:** Many CCs are the prototypical consumers of the experience industry, which offers an intense/enlightening/enlivening experience rather than a particular product. Examples include weekend workshops, spiritual gatherings, personal growth experiences, experiential vacations, the vacation-as-spiritual-tour, or the vacation-as-self-discovery. The providers of these services have to be CCs too, or they can't do it authentically (the kiss of death), and so one sometimes gets the impression that everyone is taking in everyone else's wash—or workshop.

- **Holistic everything:** CCs are the prototypical innovators in, and consumers of, personal growth psychotherapy, alternative health care, and natural foods. What ties these interests together is a belief in holistic health: body, mind, and spirit are to be unified. CCs are forever sorting out the weird from the innovative. Some CCs are those whom unsympathetic physicians describe as the "worried well," who monitor every twitch and pain and bowel movement with minutely detailed attention. Perhaps for this reason, they spend more on alternative health care and regular health care even though most are fairly healthy. They may live longer because they do at least some kinds of preventive medicine—in contrast to the modern executive pattern of treating the body like a machine that you feed, exercise, vitaminize, and otherwise ignore until it breaks down.

SIGNPOSTS IN THE THREE SUBCULTURES

When you travel to a new place, one way to learn about the local culture is to read the signposts: look at the books in the stores, watch the TV programs, identify the local heroes and heroines, see who makes news. We can tell a lot about cultures from what they pay attention to, whom they admire, who is an esteemed leader, and who is merely a celebrity.

The "Leaders and Celebrities" table following is a partial "who's who" listing of key figures who represent the values of each of the three cultural streams. It's intended to be taken lightly. Each line presents comparable figures drawn from politics, religion, literature, psychology, philosophy, art and performance, television, or business. But this table could be a little misleading unless we know

leaders and celebrities from the three subcultures

Traditionals	Moderns	Cultural Creatives

POLITICAL AND RELIGIOUS FIGURES

Traditionals	Moderns	Cultural Creatives
Jimmy Carter	George H. W. Bush	Tony Blair
Jesse Helms	Ted Kennedy	Barbara Boxer
Orrin Hatch	Trent Lott	Václav Havel
Pope John Paul II	Cardinal Joseph Bernardin	Pope John XXIII
Billy Graham	Norman Vincent Peale	Martin Luther King, Jr.
Mother Teresa	Archbishop Desmond Tutu	The Dalai Lama

LITERARY FIGURES

Traditionals	Moderns	Cultural Creatives
Flannery O'Connor	Mary McCarthy	Isabel Allende
Carl Sandburg	e. e. cummings	Gary Snyder
Marianne Moore	Sylvia Plath	Adrienne Rich
J.R.R. Tolkien	Isaac Asimov	Arthur C. Clarke
C. S. Lewis	Ernest Hemingway	Doris Lessing
Malcolm Muggeridge	Margaret Atwood	Annie Dillard

PSYCHOLOGISTS AND PHILOSOPHERS

Traditionals	Moderns	Cultural Creatives
M. Scott Peck	B. F. Skinner	Abraham Maslow
Eric Voegelin	Bertrand Russell	Ken Wilber

ARTISTS AND PERFORMERS

Traditionals	Moderns	Cultural Creatives
Mary Cassatt	Barbara Hepworth	Georgia O'Keeffe
Norman Rockwell	Pablo Picasso	Marc Chagall
Pablo Casals	Vladimir Horowitz	Yo-Yo Ma
Dolly Parton	Madonna	Enya
Louis Armstrong	Dave Brubeck	Keith Jarrett
Lucille Ball	Woody Allen	Robin Williams
John Wayne	Harrison Ford	Robert Redford
Doris Day	Joan Crawford	Katharine Hepburn
John Ford	Alfred Hitchcock	George Lucas

TV PERSONALITIES

Traditionals	Moderns	Cultural Creatives
Pat Robertson	Jay Leno	Bill Moyers

BUSINESSPEOPLE

Traditionals	Moderns	Cultural Creatives
H. L. Hunt	Bill Gates	Anita Roddick

why those people are admired, influential, and celebrated. So you may also want to withhold judgment as to *why* these people are named as Traditionals, Moderns, or Cultural Creatives. This list should seem much clearer after reading the next chapters, when you have seen where Cultural Creatives have come from and the kind of world they are helping to build. If you disagree with our list, well, feel free to make up your own.

THE PROMISE OF THE CULTURAL CREATIVES

The Cultural Creatives are a coherent subculture—except for one essential thing: they are missing self-awareness as a whole people. We said initially that they are like a nation that emerged overnight. No one is more surprised to hear about this than the Cultural Creatives themselves. As we traveled around the country, we asked them, "How many other Americans do you suppose have values like yours?" Almost always they quietly pulled in their energy and shrugged or laughed in embarrassment, as if the answer were so obvious, it needn't be spoken. "Not very many," they'd say. If we pressed for a number, some said 5 percent. Others ventured 10 percent, then hurriedly took it back, sure they'd wildly overestimated their own importance. Most of them think that their worldview, values, lifestyle, and goals for the future are shared by only a few of their friends. They have little notion that there are 50 million of them. They do not know that they have the potential to shape the life of twenty-first-century America.

Like an audience in a theater, Cultural Creatives all look in the same direction. They read the same books and share the same values and come to similar conclusions—but rarely do they turn toward one another. They have not yet formed a sense of "us" as a collective identity; nor do they have a collective image of themselves. It is as if they have had no mirror large and true enough to show them their own face.

When 50 million people think they are almost alone, it is because what they believe, and what they are struggling with, is not being reflected in the culture at large. They do not often find their values voiced in the workplace or political arenas, in television or the popular press. Author Thomas Moore named this problem when he said, "Deep in American life lies a dormant soul, almost obliterated by politicians and the media that consider it too lowly and weak for serious attention." Many of the millions who lead a soul-oriented life, he suggested, feel isolated in their convictions. "They see a national persona of hype, ambition, narcissism, and materialism. Their values seem vulnerable and soft in comparison, their voices quiet." As a nation, he noted, "we hardly know they exist."[6]

NEW SOCIAL INVENTIONS

Cultural Creatives are at the leading edge of some of the most interesting developments in American culture. When they look at modern life with their distinct perspective, they see an antique system that is noisily, chaotically shaking itself to pieces. They want a cultural "new deal," a chance to remake their lives and our institutions around deeper values. By doing so, they may be developing a culture that will sustain us and our children's children over the long term.

When we think of "inventions," we usually think of hard-edged, high-gloss, high-tech developments in industry, motivated by the desire to make a pile of money. But Cultural Creatives' *social* inventions are often soft-edged, forgoing potentially massive profits for greater social benefit. Cultural Creatives are setting off a wave of social inventions today. Most are "not news" in the eyes of the media, even though some are likely to change major aspects of society.

REASONS FOR HOPE

Every time we meet with a group of Cultural Creatives in a seminar or focus group, we are fascinated by what we find. To borrow a phrase from the women's movement, they "hear each other into speech," expressing thoughts and feelings they seem never to have spoken publicly. It's fun to watch them, to see their faces light up and their evident ease with each other. Clearly, they find such meetings enlivening, because they routinely generate an abundance of new ideas and strategies for solving local, national, and even global problems.

The promise these energetic millions carry is impressive. They could open the way to a rich array of new cultural solutions. The risk of mutual recognition is that they will simply join in a happy exercise in identity politics, enjoying and congratulating each other on their excellent shared tastes. The critical question is this: Once they discover their common values, will they work together to implement them? The stakes are high for all of us.

EXPLORING A NEW COUNTRY

"You know," Badger said to Weasel, "I have heard wondrous rumors of these Inuit people, but you are the first person I've heard tell a story about them who had himself been among them. You make me marvel at the strangeness of the world. That strangeness, the intriguing life of another people, it is a crucial thing, I think, to know."

BARRY LOPEZ, *Crow and Weasel*[7]

When we travel to a new country, we feel an almost irresistible impulse to smooth over the strangeness, the distinct particularity of the people we meet. We slip seamlessly into supposing they are just like ourselves, and we forget to marvel at the differences. It's not until we have dwelt in the new country long enough to be shocked, repeatedly, at the wrongness of our assumptions that we begin to notice the crucial things we have missed. If you have been sailing smoothly on the vast ocean of Modernism all your life, you may encounter the Cultural Creatives this way. They loom like some massive continent directly ahead. How could you not prefer a nice little island or tidy peninsula—something manageable that fits in with the world you've gotten used to?

Even if you are a Cultural Creative yourself, meeting 50 million others all at once can be extremely disconcerting. Some Jews say they feel this perplexity on their first visit to Israel, while second- and third-generation Irish, Japanese, and Cubans often say the same about encountering their own people in their home country. It is moving and at the same time bewildering to find yourself among people who are as familiar as your own face in the mirror, who make the same gestures and have the same body type as your aunts and uncles and cousins. But with Cultural Creatives, it is not your ethnic family you're encountering, but something far more surprising—a tribe of millions of *cultural* relatives with the same values and worldview and life priorities you thought you'd invented virtually by yourself.

So whatever subculture you come from, whether you are a Modern or Traditional or a Cultural Creative, as you meet the Cultural Creatives in the pages that follow, you probably will feel some of the fascination and discomfort of a stranger in a strange land. In order to meet them, you'll need time and a variety of vantage points. To understand why the Cultural Creatives are emerging now, you'll need a long view, one reaching back to the 1960s. And to understand them, you'll need to get close enough to hear their stories, or there will be nothing to connect your heart to theirs. Finally, you'll need to take some wide-angle views, or you won't fathom how many of them are already gathering together to create new social solutions and build intricate networks in the United States and around the world.

One mystery, of course, is: Where did they all come from? How could so many Cultural Creatives sprout up overnight from nowhere? The short answer is that they've been growing for a long time, from seeds planted over the last two generations, in soil prepared over centuries. The longer answer can be unfolded through the stories of individuals who have gradually changed their values and, in many cases, their lives; through the sweeping changes that have shaped Western civilization since the Renaissance; and through something that we all thought we knew only too well—the history of the last four decades. For those few visionaries who expected a great and sudden transformation, the Cultural Creatives are surprisingly late. For the rest of us who saw the surface events but not the gestating process beneath, they are a surprise, period.

Our approach in Chapter Two will be to trace the lives of women and men who have become Cultural Creatives. In Chapter Three, we'll step back to look for the changes that were set in motion by the successes and failures of the modern era. And that will bring us to Part II, where we will see the most direct influence on the birth of the Cultural Creatives: the powerful cultural movements of the latter half of the twentieth century.

There are two good reasons for examining where this new group has come from. First, the changes that produced them affect all of us. And second, those streams of change are coming together now, flowing into a confluence that seems to be creating a great current of change for our civilization. In Part III, we'll be exploring how the Cultural Creatives may be a carrier wave for that great change, bringing a new kind of culture for the twenty-first century.

Throughout the book, we use personal interviews, historical perspectives, and social analyses to give you both the close-up and the long view. To help you see the big picture, we provide tables and graphs. (If you're allergic to these, feel free to skip over them.) To give close-ups, we provide individual stories. In a sense, everything in the following pages is a story: the story of the Cultural Creatives, telling how they were born and who they are now and what they are becoming. But it is also the story of how the Cultural Creatives are contributing to the emergence of a new cultural supersystem that cuts across national boundaries, a culture that may replace Modernism in the new millennium.

The stories of the Cultural Creatives are true stories of what it's like to create a new, meaningful way of life in the midst of an old way that is declining and destructive. Toward the end of *Crow and Weasel,* Barry Lopez's luminous fable of a quest to an unknown land, a wise old female Badger explains that telling true stories of where you've been and what you've seen is how people care for each other. "Sometimes," Badger says, "a person needs a story more than food to stay alive."[8] We think we are in a time like that now, as we face the tipping point where one civilization is ending and the new one is not yet in sight. We offer these stories of Cultural Creatives as food for our common journey.

chapter two

becoming a
cultural creative

You have set sail on another ocean
without star or compass
going where the argument leads
shattering the certainties of centuries.

JANET KALVEN, *"Respectable Outlaw"* [1]

like mariners of old, Cultural Creatives have sailed beyond the familiar horizon. Their old maps are useless, the landmarks are gone, and even the North Star is unrecognizable in the new sky. Almost always, as they depart from the Modern or Traditional culture in which they were raised, they feel a loss of mooring as an old self begins to drop away. On the surface, the departure can be as simple as sitting on the floor of your living room watching television in 1968. As you stare at the screen, you see Chicago police clubbing protesters who look a lot like you. The protesters are screaming, "The whole world is watching!" And suddenly you are crying, and for maybe the first time in your life, you cannot bear to sit back and watch.

The departure may be the first time you see the whole Earth from space. Or perhaps a personal and intimate cataclysm—cancer, the death of a child, a loss of work that you loved—suddenly catapults you far beyond the old sense of self. One middle-aged woman explained, "Leaving the old story behind doesn't necessarily mean that *you* leave anything; sometimes someone leaves you. Nor does it necessarily mean that anyone actually goes any-where, because after all is said and done, what is left—or lost—is not a rela-tionship or a place or even a context. What is left is a consciousness that once felt secure, had categories to fit things into, and knew who it was. And what replaces this sureness is not knowing. And openness. And something unspeak-ably, and sometimes almost unbearably, new."[2]

Once this process is under way, openness and not-knowing become your constant companions. At times the journey feels awkward or perilous: you're asking questions that everyone wishes would go away; you don't know how to put into words what you're searching for; you're wondering just how big an idiot you really are for leaving what felt sure and safe and comfortable. And at times, the freshness and exhilaration of setting out for new territory are pure pleasure. But whether it's a joy or a trial, the departure from the old worldview and values is fundamentally an inner departure. You do not necessarily leave your home or your work or your family physically. The change is above all a change in consciousness: who do you leave behind and who do you become as you make your way toward a new kind of life?

When tens of millions of people make such choices in the space of a few decades, we are witnessing not simply a mass of personal departures but an exo-dus at the level of culture itself. Again, it is a matter of consciousness: a con-scious change of mind and heart, a shift in the collective identity of a people.

With its mix of personal and cultural, private and public consequences, becoming a Cultural Creative is a multileveled, complex, and frequently bewil-dering experience. A personal choice that seems to have relevance only to you and your immediate family and friends can have cultural ramifications beyond anything you've imagined, simply because so many others like you are making a similar choice. And as these millions go beyond their familiar life horizons, they seem to be heading in the same direction. In this chapter, we'll trace the steps in the apparently personal process of becoming a Cultural Creative.

A FORMER SLEEPWALKER

The futurist Willis Harman was surely a Cultural Creative—one of the earliest. Born at the end of World War I, he grew up believing that science was the unquestioned authority about the nature of reality. He studied engineering and, after serving in the navy in World War II, taught at Stanford University for twenty years, becoming a systems analyst along the way. When we interviewed him in 1995, he divided his life between that early period—"when I was a sleep-walker"—and what happened next.

The decisive event was a two-week retreat in 1954 among the northern California redwoods. A Stanford law professor was offering what was supposed to be a "nonreligious discussion of ethics and life principles." It turned out to be a lot more. Long before the era of encounter groups and sensitivity training, the participants were introduced to extended meditations with soft classical music in the background, drawing with their left hand, and sharing at length what they felt most deeply about. The young engineering professor was intrigued and delighted at times, but he was also upset. "I felt I'd been tricked, because if I'd known what was likely to happen to me there, I probably would never have gone." What was most appalling was that the law professor "revealed that he thought there was something to psychic phenomena and the power of prayer. I felt that someone with his education ought to know that science had disproved those hypotheses long ago."

Despite his sense of betrayal, Willis was astonished to find that he burst into tears on the final day of the retreat, as he tried to describe what he had gotten from it all. The sobbing, he told us, had more to do with joy than with sadness, "but I couldn't for the life of me give a good explanation of what lay behind it. It was as though some part of me was signaling that it was about time I got my life off dead center. Clearly, there were aspects of life they never told me about in school."

For the next four decades, Willis Harman tried to find out about those aspects. He embarked on a second career as a researcher and futurist at Stanford Research Institute (now SRI International), helping government and business do strategic planning on a very wide range of practical policy issues. Over those years, he said, he came to understand very clearly that we are living through a period of fundamental transformation. It is hard to consider him what he considers himself: a most ordinary person. At the age of sixty, he began his third career: he accepted the invitation of astronaut Edgar Mitchell to found an institute "to expand the knowledge and potentials of the mind" for the well-being of the planet. Willis became the first president of the Institute of Noetic Sciences, whose name was taken from the Greek word *nous,* meaning "higher consciousness." Its purpose was to research that consciousness, and to explore all the levels of body, mind, and soul.

Finally, Willis was immersed in the topic he'd been searching for all those years—the critical aspects of being human. It took him so long to reach this point in his life, he told us, because he was a slow learner. He wasn't, but his sense of frustration was understandable. Before the 1960s, hardly anyone worried about such questions. "It was a heavy time," he told us, "because you knew that a new kind of knowledge was coming into the world and that you had the choice to be part of it. But at the same time, we feared knowing ourselves. Part of it was the fact that there wasn't any support in the culture." Even as such a wealth of knowledge lies within us untouched, he said, "we look at a thin slice of reality and convince ourselves somehow that this is all there is."

The issue of cultural support is crucial. In the 1950s there was no cultural support for exploring what Willis called "that wealth within us." Very few groups of budding Cultural Creatives existed where one could raise questions and compare experiences. The few groups in places like New York's Greenwich Village and the North Beach in San Francisco were soon flooded with unwanted publicity and unfortunate posturing by new celebrities. Few answers seemed available, and few trustworthy guides knew what to do or how to do it. Strange as it is to contemplate today, there were few books and practically no bookstores where you could even read about what Abraham Maslow was to call "the further realms of human nature." The new ways of knowing oneself and uncovering the unspoken assumptions of the culture at large had not yet been invented. Women's consciousness-raising circles, encounter groups, psychedelic experiments, ashrams, and retreat centers; meditation and yoga and martial arts practices; and the powerful new social movements were not available until the 1960s and 1970s. It would take about twenty years before a critical mass would emerge that could support a wholly new era of social learning, experimentation, and change.

CREATING A NEW LIFE PATH

At some point in their lives, most people who become Cultural Creatives let go of what once felt sure and safe and comfortable and venture onto a new life path. Whether their leave-taking is exhilarating or anxiety-provoking, sorrowful or determined, they are likely to encounter loneliness and a kind of primal fear of "being cut from the herd. Of being separated, unloved, uncared for."[3] Because they have no idea that many others have already set out ahead of them, or are walking nearby, they'll have a sense of marginality.

Reliably, obstructions rise up to meet them, especially the social codes that everyone knows but nobody talks about. Seeking their own way, asking their own questions, brings them nose to nose with the unexamined assumptions of their friends and employers and family. And their own childhood hopes and expectations come up for reexamination.

Cultural Creatives discover that changing their life path is like learning to speak a foreign language. You simply have no idea how many unspoken rules there are until you start stumbling over them. And because you don't know how many others are creating new life paths too, you don't realize that your new choices are shared by a whole subculture of others.

CHANGING THE DREAM OF SUCCESS

Earlier in human history, in slow-changing traditional societies buffered from outside influences, people's lives usually expressed and fulfilled what they believed and valued. People didn't say to each other, as they do today, "I feel so fake." Or empty, or depressed. Their lives flowed rather directly along the paths laid out by their understanding of the world, and it all made sense. But as the modern world emerged, the pace of change accelerated. With the rise of scientific and technological worldviews, and with the movement of people to cities to participate in the market economy, life paths diverged more and more from what people valued. The writer and preacher Matthew Fox points to this split in his impassioned complaint that "we almost all practice idolatry in the modern world because the God we're worshipping in church on Sunday mornings is not the one we believe in our hearts."[4]

Ray Davi, a former executive in the New York fashion industry and now a professional mentor living in Carmel, California, told us, "I had no problem with work, but quality work was getting more difficult to accomplish. People were getting angry faster. There was more noise in the way, more advertising, more hype, more confusion in getting things down the pipeline. I was always on, never quiet. The only balance I could have as a person was to get the hell out of the race. I needed some new reference points.

"I ended up going through an enlightenment where I learned that one does not have to be busy or control things to be okay. Some things take care of themselves. We have so many diversions from what really matters. We think, 'Oh, if I do that, I'll be successful. If I do that, I'll stand out. I'll be happy.' But what good is that when we have lost the passion for life? You have to know what it means to be true to your inner self, your soul. To get in touch with that and throw the other trappings out the door."

Modernism lays out a dream that most of us take to be a promise. If you follow the yellow brick road to success, you will end up with the good life: the diploma, the job, the house, the cars, the promotion or the stock options or both, the children, their education and their accomplishments. But this road is really not so much a life path as a career path. The guideposts to success are really signs to the marketplace. When you wake up to the fact that the path you are following is not the one you believe in your heart, you've taken the first step to becoming a Cultural Creative.

THE INNER DEPARTURE: THE FIRST STEP

Stepping out of the old culture's entrancement can start in childhood, when you see through a lie that all the grown-ups seem to believe. Molly Ivins, the shrewd and wickedly funny Texas journalist, left home in just this way. She calls it "how come I came out so strange." Even though she was "properly reared" by a right-wing family in East Texas, she writes, "I believe all Southern liberals come from the same starting point—race." But she spotted the lie in the culture's story: "If you grew up white before the civil rights movement anywhere in the South, all grown-ups lied. They'd tell you stuff like, 'Don't drink out of the colored fountain, dear, it's dirty.'" But as any clear-eyed five-year-old could see, "in the white part of town, the white fountain was always covered with chewing gum and the marks of grubby kids' paws, and the colored fountain was always clean." No contest, Molly Ivins says. "Children can be horribly logical. . . . Once you figure out they are lying to you about race, you start to question everything."[5]

For most Cultural Creatives, however, the Inner Departure starts later in life. Dominique Mazeaud had been an ambitious young art curator "happily working my way up the world of the New York galleries during the 1970s," she told us, and "at the same time I was working my way down into my soul. I was asking, 'Who am I? What am I here for?' Nobody I knew was talking about such things, so I kept the questions to myself. But all the time I was looking for answers because as much as I loved working with the masters of abstract expressionism and pop art, everywhere I looked I found insecurity and devastation. I concluded that something essential was missing, and I thought to myself, every period of history has had its own way of expressing the spiritual in art. I'm going to help find our way."

Whether your inner departure is sparked by something you saw on TV or in the morning paper, or by a personal shock and loss; whether it started in childhood or in the middle of your life or at retirement—at some point the previously accepted explanation of how things came to be the way they are doesn't satisfy you anymore. So although it is difficult to leave the old story, eventually everyone who becomes a Cultural Creative finds it impossible to stay. The old story is no longer invisible but inescapable and everywhere.

The teacher in Daniel Quinn's *Ishmael,* who happens to be a large silverbacked gorilla, explains this phenomenon to his student: "Once you learn to discern the voice of Mother Culture humming in the background, telling her story over and over again to the people of your culture, you'll never stop being conscious of it. Wherever you go for the rest of your life, you'll be tempted to say to the people around you, 'How can you listen to this stuff and not recognize it for what it is?'" As the student protests that it's a little hard to believe there *is* such a story, the gorilla "close[s] his eyes gently in an indulgent smile. 'Belief is not required. Once you know this story, you'll hear it everywhere . . . and you'll be astonished that the people around you don't take it in.'"[6]

When you can hear the incessant humming of the dominant culture's story, you step across the invisible threshold. In fact, you have already crossed the threshold and are heading into new territory. At this juncture, you have completed the Inner Departure, the first step in becoming a Cultural Creative. On the outside, nothing may have changed. But inside, your loyalty to the old worldview is like Swiss cheese. And instead of filling in the holes like a good member of the old culture, you're enlarging them. You're opening to new ways of seeing, to evidence that the old ideals are flawed or broken beyond repair—including some or all of the old ideals about yourself.

The change takes many forms. Perhaps you saw through the myth that what is modern is always better. Or you may have had a spiritual experience of connection to the Earth. Or read the scientific evidence of global warming and the destruction of fields, forests, and oceans—and wondered if your children will live in a desert. In American LIVES' 1998 study conducted for the Environmental Protection Agency, we held focus groups with Cultural Creatives and others who held strong pro-environment views. The first question we asked was what kind of future they expected for their children. To our surprise, almost without exception, participants in all nine focus groups across the country said the same thing: They had seen the decline of the planet over the last generation, and they expected that decline to continue. They were all terribly worried that their children and grandchildren would inherit a world far worse than our own.

SETTING OUT: THE SECOND STEP

The next step is actually to set out toward a new way of life. How you take this step—through your heart or your mind; intentionally or inadvertently—is utterly individual. The one thing you can be sure about is that this step is not predictable. Certainly, it was not something that Joe Kresse had planned.

By the time we met Joe and his wife, Barbara, just before Joe's sixtieth birthday, their thirty-year commitment to spiritual growth and social action was well known in their Silicon Valley community. One spring evening in 1997, we dined with Joe and Barbara and several of their friends in the Foundation for Global Community, an organization of several thousand members. An impressive mix of social action, ecological awareness, and Earth-centered spirituality comes through the foundation's seminars and magazine, and we hoped to learn in depth about the volunteers who worked behind the scenes.

Joe, a trustee of the foundation, began by saying, "Looking back at my life, there was no clue that I would be interested in anything outside the mainstream." Everyone at the table nodded in agreement, and later, most of them would echo these words as they told their own stories. Joe continued, "I attended a Catholic high school, and that's when I left the Church for good. All the stories I heard didn't make sense. Plus the guilt. The Church was really into guilt in the 1950s, and any teenager is going to do something that's not in line."

He paused and looked around. "Was I pulled to something more profound?" He burst out laughing and looked directly across the table at his friend Richard Rathbun. "Richard and I were into cars—riding around with our friends in my '50 Ford or Richard's Olds convertible." Richard beamed, as we pictured these two middle-aged men as rowdy teenagers gunning their low-riding cars through the once-sleepy streets of Palo Alto. Then Joe stopped laughing. "Once I threw the Catholic version of reality out," he said, "I had nothing to replace it with." Taking a quick sip of coffee, he went on. "I was born in New York City and had a completely normal kind of upbringing. My father was a successful businessman, and my mother was preoccupied with civilizing my three brothers and me. Neither was religious at all, so the larger questions weren't around me. What we talked about was eating with the right fork and going on vacation."

When Joe went to Stanford, he told us, "I went nuts. It's almost impossible to flunk out there, but I almost managed to do it. After a boys' high school with no drinking and no sex, and then coming to a place with no restrictions—wow! I joined the animal house fraternity, and it took me till my senior year to realize that if I didn't do something . . ."

During his senior year, he said, he started to grow up. After a stint in the navy, Joe went back to Stanford for business school and from there took a job at one of the top accounting firms in the country. Within four years, he had

THE CULTURAL CREATIVES

everything he had ever dreamed of. "By the time I was thirty, I distinctly remember thinking: 'Okay, I've got my career, I've got my wife, I've got my house, and I've got a child. Now what?'"

He didn't know. "I knew I could get more of the same, but there was no big thing out there calling me. I didn't have a clue what to do, nor did I think there was anything I could do."

But a door opened when a colleague invited Joe to a meeting of a group called Creative Initiative (a precursor of the Foundation for Global Community). Joe took a chance and got involved. "I was fascinated, because they were talking about the larger issues. I sort of pulled Barbara along, and after a while we went to a weeklong seminar. It was a life-changing experience. When I look back on that week, I can see that it answered questions I didn't know I had been asking, questions like 'How does this all work? Why am I here? Is there any logic to all of this?'

"In high school, when I threw the Catholic version of reality out, it left a hole. I didn't recognize that hole until I finally heard a description of God, religion, and life that made rational sense. When I could hook into understanding how human experience had developed religions in the first place, I wanted to keep learning and keep asking questions and inquiring. The books I read from then on were all about psychology and religion—Joseph Campbell's *Hero with a Thousand Faces,* Teilhard's *Phenomenon of Man.* A whole world opened up that I didn't know I was interested in. It was immensely satisfying and appealing."

Joe Kresse's mental doorway opened with questions he didn't know he'd had. Over the next several years, those questions pulled him along until his inner life was changing as well. He delved into psychology and started a daily meditation practice. In time, he and Barbara evolved a simpler lifestyle. He continued to work and move higher up the corporate ladder, but his life priorities had changed. At fifty, he left the accounting firm: "I was fortunate enough to retire early because we never spent very much money, never had a desire to spend it. Spending a lot of money wasn't going to get us anything anyway. Now I work at the foundation full time as a volunteer, and that's great. It's something I love to do."

He rocked back in his chair as he said this, took a long sip of coffee, and seemed to turn in toward himself for a while. Then he looked at each of us around the table, with something between amusement and tenderness crossing his face. "When I think of where I would be today without this whole exploration that Barbara and I have been involved in—when I think in terms of our relationship, and the way we've brought up our kids, and what it has meant in business, and how I've fit my work into my life as a whole—I see it has affected everything. If I hadn't opened up to those deep questions, I'd probably be a really successful businessperson *without* a wife and *without* a lot of friends. I'd probably be starting to wonder now that I'm almost sixty, where'd I miss the boat?"

A HEART PATH

What causes people to depart from Modernism? The short answer is: anything that makes them question the givens. Certainly that's how it happened for Joe Kresse. But there are other paths as well. One comes from the heart, or what is left of the heart when who you thought you were and what you thought your life was about is burned away. This is the path that opened for Sandra Mardigian.

We first met Sandra at a talk Paul was giving about Cultural Creatives. Following a discussion, a petite woman with curly blond hair raised her hand. "Can you become a Cultural Creative through the death of someone you love?" she asked. A silence entered the room then, as if some interior space had suddenly been hollowed out. "Yes," Paul replied. "Yes, of course."

Several months later we asked Sandra and her partner, Doug Burck, to spend an evening with us because we realized that we did not understand what she had meant by her question but very much wanted to. As Sandra told her story, we learned that becoming a Cultural Creative can be a path of the heart.

"If I trace a fine thread back to my childhood," Sandra said, "I come to Summit, New Jersey. My family lived on a lovely acre of property bordering a forest with clear streams and wild rhododendron, azaleas, violets, jack-in-the-pulpit. I loved being out there even when it snowed. It was a whole world for me, and it grounded my life in some fundamental way. My mother was very fearful, and my sisters were much younger than I, so all during my growing-up years, I played alone and learned to rely on my own judgment."

Sandra's life in high school was one of "busy, cheerful partying with dances every weekend." For the shy, rather solitary girl, it was a happy time. "I had a place there," she told us, "more than I ever had in my family, and it was wonderful for me." College was more of the same. Sandra found her courses easy and "the social life just glorious." At the end of her junior year, she married and left school, as did many young women in the 1950s.

She had four children in five years. The most significant thing that happened in her life, she told us, was losing one of those children to cancer when he was five years old. "I don't talk about this very easily," she said, looking down and speaking very quietly, "but it was pivotal for me. It changed my life—jelled it in a profound way. I have an image that comes to mind about that time. It's of a white fire roaring through my life and burning out what was superficial, frivolous, and unimportant and leaving a core of . . . I don't think there's any other word for it than *love*. A core of love. It's hard to convey what that means."

The years that followed were sadly predictable. The heartbreak of their son's death created an unbridgeable chasm for Sandra and her husband, and they divorced. She went back to college and got a teaching credential. "It was the only kind of work I could imagine doing, because of the hours, while I was taking care of my young children."

After several years of teaching, Sandra reconnected with Doug, an old college friend. "He came along and whisked us off to a new life. He was a wonderful gift to my family because of his fun-loving, adventuresome approach to life. For my children, it was a marvelous thing to have him in the family in their teenage years. He brought an experience from his years in the Peace Corps that none of us would have had."

Kenya was one of the places they visited frequently, and eventually they spent a year there in the 1980s. "The more I got to know the African people," Sandra told us, "the more I respected them, and the more I started looking for ways to facilitate what they needed." She began to meet with development experts. "I tried to understand what works and what doesn't, what violates the spirit and dignity of people and what doesn't. At that time, recognition of those violations was just dawning on agency people. They were beginning to see how colonialism had helped materially but had been very demeaning spiritually."

When the family returned to the States, Sandra began raising money to help one of the villages where they had lived. In the process, she created one of hundreds of citizen efforts to form new kinds of partnership communities: "Together the villagers decided what they most needed. They let me know, and I would raise the funds, which were very minimal because the people did all the labor themselves. We built a school and a dispensary and organized some cooperatives and some groups for young men so they could play soccer and earn a little money making bricks. Just about every kind of thing we could think of together, we did." By the late 1980s, Sandra was working with a school for biointensive small-scale agriculture. What appealed to her, she said, was its powerful leverage not just for productive agriculture but for developing creative leaders who could teach many others.

Why do we say that hers was a path of heart? Because it was love that burned away the inessential and led Sandra to the purposeful, joyful life she lives today. At the end of our evening together, she reflected, "They are doing it with so little, you know—just with what they have within themselves. When I see this, I see what is possible for all of us, and I feel connected with something . . . I guess the word is *divine*. I would say this connection has become my life purpose—to seek that quality of being human, encounter it, and hopefully promote it."

THE THIRD STEP: CONFRONTING THE CRITICS

When Cultural Creatives set out on a new life path, they are subject to critics— inner and outer—because they have no sure notion where they'll end up. They *can't* know. As the poet Antonio Machado put it, the path they're on is made by walking.

Cultural Creatives are especially vulnerable to uncertainty and criticism because of their stance in life: they are more open-minded than most Traditionals, and they take their values more seriously than most Moderns. So they listen to criticism, probably too carefully. As a result of this uncertainty, their images of success and standards of value tend to unconsciously blend Modernism, Traditionalism, and their own experience. Fortunately, this is changing as Cultural Creatives develop their own discussion and writing circles, salons (in living rooms and cyberspace), and gathering places where they can have frank and wide-ranging conversations with others who share their values.

A second source of vulnerability is the fact that Cultural Creatives are challenging the social codes of the dominant culture. Sooner or later they are bound to bump up against some very unhappy representatives of that culture. At such times, it helps immeasurably to have a community, as Joe Kresse did, or some understanding friends. If, like Sandra Mardigian, you have been catapulted out of the old worldview by a tragedy that everyone can recognize, your friends may understand. But regardless of whether you have companions to ease the way, the old culture will not greet your separation warmly. Worse yet, you'll repeatedly meet an internalized version of the old culture, the Inner Critic. If your external critics seize upon the same complaints as your Inner Critic, it can be a real stopper.

Few Cultural Creatives are as feisty as five-year-old Molly Ivins, who questioned everything once she spotted the lie in the old culture's story. Rather, when the cultural matrix they depended on turns out to be surrounded by barbed-wire fences designed to keep them on home pasture, they find themselves perplexed or furious and not quite clear why. We'll look at three of the critics' favorite techniques: distorted mirrors, silence, and denial.

DISTORTED MIRRORS

When the person creating a new life path is a widely admired scion of mainstream culture, the public media are likely to react with disdain and cynicism. Composer Richard Danielpour had been "leaping ahead of a promising pack" of other American classical musicians, it was said, when he spoke openly about his creative process to a music critic in 1998. Danielpour is "easy to ridicule," the reviewer complained, because he speaks of the creative process "in such spiritual, eccentric, even loopy terms" that he "invites mockery." Cultural Creatives would probably find this assessment shockingly wrong. The composer's words seem reflective and honest. "Where is the music received from?" he asks, then replies, "Where do your dreams come from? Composing is like being in a waking dream. To me, the 'where' is not important."[7]

Another occasional victim of the press's distorted mirrors is rock star Bruce Springsteen. In a 1996 interview in *The New York Times,* he spoke about feeling isolated in his convictions. He had started to write songs, he explained, so people would know who he was. And he trusted that if he let his audience know him, he would find others who cared about the things that mattered to him. "I very consciously set out to develop an audience that was about more than buying records," he said. "I set out to find an audience that would be a reflection of some imagined community I had in my head, that lived according to the values in my music and shared a similar set of ideals."[8]

The popular press reacted to Springsteen with puzzlement and irritation. They said that in writing lyrics about San Diego street kids and Mexican farm workers and millworkers in Youngstown, Ohio, he had become pretentious. They wished he would get back to what he knew. "Shh. Artist at work," the British rock magazine *Q* sneered.

Consider the cumulative effect of reading reviews and critiques like these. An occasional mocking journalist or reporter is not likely to affect the reader, and after a while contemptuous language becomes background noise, and you want to know what else was said. But the accrued effect of this kind of distorted mirroring is a muffling or muting of voices that would speak of spiritual values and inner-directedness. Privately, without even thinking about it, Cultural Creatives decide that if they want to get along in the wider world, they had better keep quiet about what really matters to them.

Dixon de Leña is a management consultant who has worked for twenty years with some of America's largest companies. He has a stunning capacity to say what everyone is thinking and nobody is saying—a talent he may have learned in his early confrontations with the domineering patriarch of his large Filipino clan. He's especially distressed at how hard it is for Westerners to speak about what they value.

"We are allowed to talk about the wrong things in our culture," he told us one evening. "We're silent about the things that matter the deepest to us. We're public about our hairdos, clothing, cars, and that stuff. I think it ought to be reversed. I think people should shut up about their clothing, cars, houses, and how much they make, and be public about the things that matter to them."

Like what? we asked him. Hopes and dreams, he told us. Values. "At the beginning, when I work with an organization to acknowledge who people are and the value they bring, it's considered to be a grating and unreasonable discussion," he said. "It's unreasonable because it's going against the mainstream. Unreasonable as related to 'insane, irrational.' To keep bringing up these themes in meeting after meeting, to keep saying what you see as possible in a thousand different ways, to stand for something unequivocally—all these are considered unreasonable ways of being in our modern world.

"In the beginning," he went on, "the men and women who can bring up these themes and take these stands are seen as absolute jerks, outside the box. They grate on everybody's nerves. Later on, the aftermath of the story is, 'Thank goodness they had the courage to stand up. What visionaries they are.'" He looked at us and shrugged. "It's almost always like that. It's just grating to people in the old culture when you talk about dreams."

Canadian futurist Ruben F. W. Nelson also spoke to us about the muting of people's deepest concerns. It happens not only in corporate boardrooms, he said, but at the highest levels of government. "I am stunned by how many people tell me, when the door is closed, in effect, 'Look, I'm supposed to be in charge here, but basically what we're doing outruns our theory. We have no theory to guide us.' Whether it's in economics or health care or education, confusion is growing. It's not yet visible enough in most places to be a clear signal, but one of the ways I read it is in the general cynicism in society. I think most of us know about this turmoil, and we're afraid to talk about it. In a sense, we've got a funny kind of open secret, where we all know that we've got some very hard moral, intellectual, spiritual homework to do together, but nobody wants to say so."

Denial

Not talking about the things that are most important is one way to try to keep turmoil at bay. The fact that it doesn't work in the long run does not seem to be enough of a reason to stop. It usually takes an outsider to unmask the denial and name what everyone is pretending isn't there. The child who loudly demands to know why the king is parading naked through the streets is one of our best-known stories about this process.

Daniel Quinn's gorilla-teacher, Ishmael, is a modern-day equivalent of that perspicacious child. Ishmael instructs his nameless human student, "According to your maps, the world of thought . . . ends at the border of your culture, and if you venture beyond that border, you simply fall off the edge of the world." And then he promises, "Tomorrow, we'll screw up our courage and cross that border. And as you'll see, we will not fall off the edge of the world. We'll just find ourselves in new territory."[9] The media guru Marshall McLuhan said the same thing more tersely: Once you can see the boundaries of your environment, they are no longer the boundaries of your environment.

A child, a gorilla, a professional student of culture—anyone who does not have the lenses of the dominant culture screwed in tight has the potential to describe what the culture is blind to. Perhaps this is why Oren Lyons, Peacekeeper of the Iroquois–Six Nations Confederacy, was invited to Davos, Switzerland, in 1996 to address the prominent government leaders, corporate CEOs, bankers, financiers, and entrepreneurs who gather at that mountain ski resort every January. Asked to give his perspective on the financial community's role in the present world situation, Chief Lyons responded with an indelible image: "I see you all as jockeys, and your companies are the horses you ride. You're beating your horses on in a race, but now you can see that you are racing toward a stone wall. You see some of those ahead of you smashing into the wall, but you don't turn around or even pause. You're beating your horses on anyway as fast as you can."

Elisabet Sahtouris, who attended this conference, couldn't get Chief Lyons's speech out of her mind. Several months later in Rio de Janeiro, when she was invited to tea at the home of a banker she had met at Davos, she had a chance to pursue the questions that had been worrying her. "I asked my host how he saw the world economic situation from his position as one of the leading bankers of Brazil," she told us. "He said that frankly it looked as though we were all going over the edge of a cliff. I caught my breath and asked if his colleagues felt the same way. He confirmed that they did. I asked him then whether he—or they—were interested in discussing alternatives. He said there was nothing to be done. Finally I tried one last question: How do you reconcile this inaction with the fact of being a grandfather? He turned his eyes away. 'Don't ask me that,' he said. 'I can't bear to think about it.'"

Distorted mirrors, silence about what matters, denial—all of these are barriers to honest discussion about what doesn't work in our modern world. They hide the truth and keep us from seeing clearly what is not working, and why, and what can be done about it. To the extent that Cultural Creatives have let go of their allegiance to Modernism's values, they are able to peer through the distortions better than most of us. But the barriers affect them, too, muffling their voices and silencing their objections.

THE FOURTH STEP: TURNING YOUR VALUES INTO A NEW WAY OF LIFE

How do Cultural Creatives turn their values into a new way of life? There's no single way to do this, no party line or dogma, no formula for success. It's not like solving a little problem in optimizing your financial returns, or getting voters to believe you one more time. Nobody's an expert here. To outside observers, the territory that lies before Cultural Creatives must seem like a cliff thousands of miles long fronting on absolutely nothing—empty space. Yet at tens of thousands of points on the edge of that frontier, innovators are creating solid new ground, extending the known world into the unknown. A key element in such innovation is the ability to think outside the box.

CREATING OUTSIDE THE BOX

Several of the Cultural Creatives we interviewed described Mark Youngblood as a "leading-edge thinker." They said he was a kind of Houdini who helped unlock the usual triple locks and chains of modern bureaucracy. At our first meeting, we repeated this description to Mark and asked, "How did you get so good at thinking outside the box? Did your whole high school graduating class think the way you do?"

He laughed out loud and looked at us appraisingly, as if wondering how much to say. Apparently he decided to plunge right in. "From my earliest memory I thought differently," he told us. "I felt like an alien my whole life, yet I look so mainstream. I don't wear Birkenstocks, I don't have a long ponytail, and I don't even identify with that sort of look, and yet I've always thought sideways."

He got kicked out of Sunday school for "being a smart aleck," he said, but what he had wanted was to be able to follow what the teachers were saying about Jesus, to understand how it could be true. "Clearly they had never thought about the questions I was raising but were mindlessly passing the story on. It was okay with me for it to be true, but I wanted more. I needed to explore how it could be possible." He walked away from Christianity and looked for his own spiritual path—and found it in a wonderfully unlikely way: through the Boy Scouts. While camping overnight, talking around the fire, river rafting—it was easy, he said, to find God everywhere. Not in churches or buildings, but all through the natural world.

The next step seemed easy, too. He would simply become a park ranger, and then wherever he went, he would be in the presence of that spacious freedom and sacredness. But the forestry program at his college had stringent rules about what students could and couldn't believe, could and couldn't argue with. The earnest would-be ranger was outraged. "I found out that you never get to think. You don't get to change things. You get moved around to wherever in hell they want you to be—they could send you to Timbuktu. I thought that would starve my need for creative expression, and I bailed out."

And that began what Mark calls "the lie." Determined to fit in somewhere, to be part of the dream of success that all his friends were following, he became an accountant. Telling us the story, he said, "I went insane. I became an account keeper—went into a big oil company, of all things. Here I'm a nature enthusiast, and I join the most exploitative industry you can be in, an oil, gas, and coal company!"

How does this happen? We think we know what matters to us. We have our compass in hand, a moral connectedness and conscience, a sense of clear contact with what is essential. And then a disappointment happens, and suddenly our orientation disappears, and we become accountants. Years later we may look back and realize that our orientation needed a lot more exploration and testing before it could be robust. After losing our orientation, we may have a kind of psychic numbing. Thought splits off from feeling, soul from action, and we end up far from what we loved. Suddenly we're off on a new trajectory, barely able to remember the old one.

"I started playing the game big-time," Mark recalled. "I was very successful because I was very aggressive. I still thought differently, and that let me see some things my MBA peers did not." He became an accounting supervisor, the youngest ever in the company. And then, at twenty-eight, intending to make "scads of money," he left to start his own company.

As Mark talked about this period of his life, he seemed awed that he could have poured so much energy into something he had no love for. "I spent a year developing the new company. I did it for the money. I had absolutely no passion for it. I hated it. I thought I had died. I'm a gregarious person, and here I was all by myself doing this thing, using up all my savings, all my money, and when it got time to roll it out, I didn't know anything about sales and marketing. I hadn't really involved anybody. It was going to fail, and I had never failed at anything in my life. A year after my divorce, I'm now failing in my business, too. I had become my job, my income, and my income-making potential, and now that self was collapsing."

It got worse afterward, he told us. His body began to shut down as waves of anxiety broke over him. He was unable to eat. His heart went into ventricular contractions, sending him to the hospital three times. "If you could have seen my energy, it would have been radiating, 'Danger Will Robinson, this guy is about to melt down here!'"

And then finally, he let go. "I went into this deep state. I utterly surrendered everything. I just quit. I had an epiphany. What happened in this deep state was a flash of white light. In an instant I was filled with joy, filled with love and well-being, and I sat up, ate three bowls of oatmeal, called my parents, and said, 'I'm canning the company. I'm going to find a job. Can you come up here and be with me? I'm in a bad place.'"

Sitting in a boardroom in downtown Dallas with this immaculately dressed, athletic-looking man in 1998, we could still get a whiff of the terror, and the surrender, that had blown his life open some twenty years earlier. Over the years, Mark's headstrong youthful brilliance got tempered as he slowly found his way to what he really wanted from his life. There were a number of jobs, some with prestigious firms and others with high-tech start-ups, a new marriage, and an intensive one-man study program that he launched by going through the shelves of his local bookstore. He joined the Indian mystic Paramahansa Yogananda's organization (the Self Realization Fellowship) and did all its studies, delved into Buddhism and Taoism, and then turned to the new sciences of quantum physics and chaos theory and evolution biology. "I was an addict," he told us, "reading everything I could find that would help me understand who I was and where I was going."

He was "becoming sane again," he said. He studied psychology for a while, thinking that it might be a new career. And then quite fortuitously, he was asked to write a book on large-scale, whole-system transformation in organizations.

Eating the Chocolate Elephant, he called it, somewhat whimsically, not expecting much of a response. "Suddenly, the phone's ringing off the wall. 'Loved your book,' people were saying. 'Can you consult on it?'" Finally, he said, he could see his path: "It was unfolding right in front of me."

Shortly after that, Mark started his own company. It was thrilling, he says, "stepping into the uncertainty. Because you're letting flow what's already there." Now he carries this perspective to organizations with a creative intelligence and sense of adventure.

We asked how his ideas actually work in a high-tech business. He told us about a company he advises that is struggling to stay ahead in cellular phones, pagers, satellite technologies, and a host of other innovations in telecommunications. "Lots and lots of industries in this field are beginning to blur together," he explained, "and suddenly it's hard to say where one starts and the other ends. Companies are faced not only with trying to renew and save themselves but with the fact that their whole industry could disappear overnight."

The old viewpoints don't work here, he said, because the models of business competition are turned upside down. Instead of pushing ahead with blinders on to eliminate your competition, you need to recognize that you're now in a complex field of relationships that works much more like an ecosystem than a battlefield. "Can you succeed if your chief competitor fails?" he asks his clients. Often they can't, since if their strongest competitor fails, the industry itself can be weakened and swallowed up by companies offering a related technology.

As a result, Mark says, the old definition of success doesn't work here. It's too single-focused, too narrow. "What we need to see in this industry is that we have to help our competitors stay alive and viable. When they are healthy, the whole system is healthy, and we are healthier, too. This is an astonishing realization because it means that the goal of classical management—the profit-making-machine goal—is too limited and too small." The larger goal, in terms of the big picture, is the health of the whole interconnected system, and it calls for executives who act more like ecologists than generals.

Mark's love for the natural world came full circle into his more inclusive—and sometimes shockingly innovative—view of success. It's a whole-systems perspective, interdependent and dynamic, more like an ecosystem than a battlefield. It's a view he learned over decades as he brought more and more of himself—his inquisitive, creative self that wanted to see the whole picture and its complex interconnections—to the problems of the modern marketplace.

Like Mark Youngblood, people who become Cultural Creatives look for the big picture. It's an organic perspective that is well suited to life in our complex, interconnected world. There are different ways to look for the big picture. Some Cultural Creatives construct and revise their own, in an ever-elaborating synthesis. They alternate between two ways of knowing. First, they scan their environment very broadly for what is new and interesting, then they go into detail on a topic, drilling deeply. Then they go back to scanning, for the next thing that interests them.

Chip Hider is like this. A Texan, he has spent a good many of his fifty-five years scanning and synthesizing as he developed a rich array of projects that promote cultural exchange—everything from bringing eleven-year-olds from Dallas to play basketball with Mexican youngsters, to founding a thriving Sister Cities project with Riga, Latvia. He is also a tax lawyer who, as he puts it, "likes to kind of observe things, check them out cautiously, get the overall picture of what works and how it works before I plunge in." One of his friends complained, "Chip, you're like an inchworm, very cautious."

"I didn't particularly like that image," Chip admitted. "It sounded so slow!" But his combination of heartfelt and analytical approaches serves him well in picking and choosing which projects to take on, just as it helps him sort out what makes sense as he reads the morning newspaper. Like many Cultural Creatives who are continually cobbling together their own big picture, Chip is an active reader and a careful consumer.

For other Cultural Creatives, the fourth step is more passionate. Francisco X. Alarcón is a poet who lives in the Mission District of San Francisco, and he began creating his own poetic linkages because he found he couldn't live without them. Born in Los Angeles in 1954, he came from generations who regularly moved back and forth across the Mexican border. "This is my own conflict, belonging to two cultures," Alarcón explains in Kenny Ausubel's *Restoring the Earth: Visionary Solutions from the Bioneers.*[10] "The border is right here, inside me."

Alarcón found himself constantly pulled into cultural narrows: "It didn't make any difference if I was in Guadalajara studying with upper-class Mexicans or at Stanford. They all had a disdain for mestizos and dark-skinned people. I have very dark skin and am the most Indian-like of my family." Alarcón's experiences, as he would be the first to acknowledge, are not unique, but what he does with them is. He takes what did not fit into the old cultural forms—his mixed cultures—and heals and honors it with truth. Calling on his Indian and Hispanic ancestry, he founded the magazine *El Tecolote Literario (The Literary Owl)*. The magazine, like his poetry, is written in Nahuatl, Spanish, and English.

In bringing the fragments of his own life into relationship, he extends his understanding to all Americans. "Somehow we have this separation in the West," he says. "We have body and soul, self and nature, and a mythology based on an ego that is individual, that is not connected with anything else." As a Nahuatl whose ancestors found their connectedness in every hill and plant and animal, he sees "an America coming that will be more humane, a reconciliation." As a mestizo poet, he writes not for a single country but for an America that stretches from Alaska to Patagonia. And on behalf of all people, he affirms, "I recognize myself as a complete being who is connected with the wholeness."

A PASSION FOR THE INTERCONNECTEDNESS OF LIFE

By the time they reach the fourth step, most Cultural Creatives are not only looking for the big picture, they're tracing underlying interconnections and relationships. This process inevitably leads to developing an ardent concern for the living system that holds us all—planet Earth. Ecological concerns inform most Cultural Creatives' choices, including what products they buy, the movements they support, and the life choices they make.

Evolutionary biologist Elisabet Sahtouris expresses her concern for the Earth in many ways, but especially when she teaches children. She invites them to imagine what it would be like to do world politics in their own bodies. "It would look something like this," she says. "You have raw material blood cells coming up in the marrow of all the bones in your body. The blood cells are swept up to these northern industrial organs—the heart-lung system—where the blood is purified and oxygen is added and you now have a useful product. So suppose the heart distribution center announces that the body price for blood today is so much, who wants? And the blood is shipped off to those organs that can afford it, and you chuck the rest out as surplus."

She asks: "Does this make sense? Is this a viable economics for a living system? You can see that it would kill the body to do economics that way because some of the parts of the body that couldn't afford the blood would now be starving and dying off. This is exactly what we see, of course, in the human world. We exploit some parts of humanity to the benefit of other parts. But that doesn't make sense, and it cannot work in a living system. If your body decided to value the heart over the liver, or tried to turn the heart into a liver or something like that, we just couldn't function. But that is the kind of crazy thing we're doing as humans!"

IF YOU UNDERSTAND THE PROCESS . . .

In the end, there can be no step-by-step description of how to become a Cultural Creative. It is a process of culture-making with tens of millions of people doing it in their own ways. Since they are part of a subculture that cannot yet see itself, these millions of Cultural Creatives do not know what a potential they carry for our common future.

Miriam MacGillis, a Dominican sister who founded Genesis Farm in Caldwell, New Jersey, tells a story that makes clear why this matters. An old woman in the Middle East planted a date: "When you plant a date, you know you'll never eat from the date tree," Miriam says, "because it takes about eighty years to grow roots deep enough to go to the scarce water. The date trees get so buffeted in that time by windstorms and droughts that for the most part, the tree looks like it's dying. If you didn't understand its process, you could easily cut it down. But if you understand the process, you can make the commitment. You have to have an image of what will happen. Once you do, it makes all the difference."

This is how it is for all of us now. Cultural Creatives especially need a picture of what they are doing and what it means. To bring a new kind of culture to life, they need to be able to stay the course. And they need to know where they have come from and where, as a collective body, they can go.

Perhaps it is true, as Václav Havel observes, that the modern age has already ended. But if it has, how could we tell? Will new maps be sold on every streetcorner? Hardly. As we shall see, we are in the midst of a transition. Mapmakers must be content with seeing the new territory from afar—which means their maps will have serious limits. Still, all clues are helpful when you're scouting beyond the known boundaries. In Chapter Three, we will examine the historical context of the birth of the Cultural Creatives: the culture wars between Moderns and Traditionals.

chapter three

the
three americas

"Politics itself has failed. And politics has failed because of the collapse of the culture," Paul Weyrich, an architect of right-wing strategies, wrote in 1999 in a widely quoted public letter following President Clinton's impeachment. The culture we are living in, Weyrich claimed, is becoming "an ever-wider sewer."[1] His voice was extreme, but other prominent conservatives have also worried aloud about a general moral decline in American culture. Henry Hyde, the House Judiciary Committee chairman who led the prosecution team against Mr. Clinton, told senators toward the end of the trial, "I wonder if, after this culture war is over . . . an America will survive that will be worth fighting to defend."[2]

The increasingly favorable ratings the public gave Mr. Clinton throughout the scandal were a direct affront to conservatives' fervently held conviction that they were "the moral majority." Over the months leading to the president's impeachment and subsequent acquittal by the Senate, only 23 to 28 percent of Americans supported the conservatives' position. In the spring of 1999, the press began to refer to them as the "moral minority." But let's consider their claim. Has our culture become a moral sludge pot, as Weyrich insists? Is there actually some embattled minority that is much more moral than the rest of the country, while the remaining majority is "slouching towards Gomorrah," as former judge Robert Bork puts it?[3]

Nothing could be further from the truth, according to the evidence. Most Americans have grown in the range and intelligence of their moral convictions over the last thirty years. If anything, our moral standards have risen. At the beginning of a new century, most Americans are living in a more complex, nuanced, and mature moral world than ever before. This conclusion takes into account both moral principles and personal relationships, the abstract and the particular, and looks beyond conventional conservative issues like abortion and sexuality to ethical questions in medicine, biotechnology, and the workplace, and to the ethics of destroying rain forests and introducing strange genes into agriculture. Many newspapers and weekly newsmagazines have run articles exploring these issues. In short, the certainties of the past are subjected to almost daily pondering of what is fair and just. As Americans ask new moral questions, we are finding new answers, answers that leave the moral concerns of people like Weyrich and Hyde looking small and pinched.

In fact, since the 1960s, we Americans have added more moral values than ever before, including many that were once considered purely women's concerns. To name some of the most important, there is serious interest in and concern for:

- the well-being and fair treatment of women, children, and people of color
- caring relationships in everyday life
- preserving the earth
- the sacredness of nature
- the evils of nuclear armaments
- inner experience, both psychological and spiritual
- personal responsibility, as opposed to childlike obedience to religious doctrines or moral rules

Clearly, most Americans today have a larger number and a wider variety of moral concerns than ever before.

A MACROVIEW

The Cultural Creatives did not materialize from some eternal cornfield in Iowa, near Kevin Costner's field of dreams. On the contrary, they walked into a scene that was a lot more like Madison Square Garden on the night of a heavyweight brawl. Two powerful subcultures were already contending in the arena, the Moderns and Traditionals. And the fight was, and is, a struggle to define America.

At this point, we'll need to take a cultural macroview and see America through a high-altitude lens. Viewed from up close, this so-called fight of the century could appear to be just another political battle, or a series of individual wrangles over single issues: abortion, school vouchers that allow public money in religious schools, multiculturalism, school prayer, child care, affirmative action and quotas, funding for the arts, gay rights, pornography, the status of women, the meaning of "pro-family," and sex, drugs, and graft in the lives of various politicians. If we view the culture war from too close a perspective, we'll be missing the big picture, because a culture war is not about individual issues and it's not just about politics.

The fight the Cultural Creatives walked in on is basically about who will define our social reality, and whose values will be the official values of our culture. It is a no-holds-barred match over who has the moral authority to decide how Americans live, both in public and in private. As sociologist James Davison Hunter points out in *Culture Wars,* the idea of cultural conflict may sound abstract, but nothing less than a way of life is at stake. And because that conflict is fundamentally a struggle for power, a lot of factors enter in, including "money (a great deal of it), reputation, livelihood, and a considerable array of other resources." When all is said and done, Hunter insists, the culture war is "ultimately about the struggle for domination."[4]

To get a sense of how visceral this conflict can be, and how trapped our vision is in our own cultural boxes, conjure up for a moment some public figure you love to hate—Rush Limbaugh, Arianna Huffington, Ross Perot, Bill Clinton, Howard Stern, Camille Paglia, Richard Gere, Sam Donaldson, or some other sabbath gasbag—and you can just feel the culture wars working on you.

In this chapter, we'll look at how the cultural stances of the Moderns and Traditionals are shaping the American definition of what is real. But where once there were only two Americas, now there are three. The entry of the third America, the Cultural Creatives, is changing the two-sided win-lose culture wars into a new game for all of us.

RANCOR IN YOUR LIVING ROOM AND YOUR MAILBOX

At the beginning of the 1990s, the Miami-based rap group 2 Live Crew put out *As Nasty As They Wanna Be,* an album that contained more than two hundred uses of *fuck* and countless descriptions of male and female genitals. The Beastie Boys and other groups mimed masturbation onstage. Ozzy Osbourne sang of the "suicide solution." In 1999, a nasty kid with bleached-blond hair hit the upper reaches of the charts with a rap album that tossed out lines like "By the way, when you see my dad, tell him I slit his throat in a dream I had."

Traditional groups consider most rap music "mind pollution and body pollution." A lawyer for the conservative American Family Association said, "This stuff is so toxic and so dangerous . . . that it shouldn't be allowed to be sold to anybody or by anybody." Modern critics, on the other hand, call rap music "a vibrant manifestation . . . of the larger folklore of the streets," a way "to transcend the tensions . . . of the communities it speaks to."[5]

Rap music is just one issue in the larger controversy. Films, magazines, television shows, newspapers, artworks of all kinds, and video games, as well as health care, education, law, and politics—all are daily arenas in which the culture war between Moderns and Traditionals is being fought.

Both sides denounce censorship of their views. The editors of the conservative magazine *Chronicles of Culture* complain in a fund-raising letter to their subscribers that much of contemporary censorship "employs the powerful weapons of *ridicule* and *condescension* to stifle the voices of millions of Americans, like you, who still cherish our traditional values." But Traditionals are at least as rancorous as they accuse Moderns of being. The same fund-raising letter goes on to denounce "profane books, depraved movies, and decadent art . . . drug-sodden entertainers, America-hating educators, and appeasement-obsessed legislators."[6] The mutual disdain and contempt manifests not just in attitudes but in grim and zealous confrontations at the entrances to women's health clinics, on hospital boards, in museum and foundation committees, in the courts, and—to the exasperation of most Americans—in the antics of politicians and the lobbyists who buy access to them with large campaign contributions.

The rhetoric makes the culture war sound like a struggle between good versus evil (in the view of the Traditionals) or rational versus simple-minded (in the view of the Moderns), but there are good people on both sides. The brawls fought with ideologically loaded sound bites make news week by week, but most Americans are much less extreme in their positions than the attackers and defenders on each side. "On all sides, the contenders are generally sincere, thoughtful, and well meaning," James Hunter observes, "but they operate with fundamentally opposing visions of the meaning of America: what it has been, what it is, and what it should be."[7]

VALUES RELATIVISM AND VALUES PLURALISM

In battle cries that resound through the daily press, Traditional ideologues claim that America has descended into a shallow, permissive period of *values relativism.* This terminology is used by people who are convinced that they have an exclusive claim on the truth, and they apply it to anyone whose values are different from theirs. It says unmistakably, *We live in a homogeneous society, and immoral people are destroying it by watering down and/or polluting the God-given moral absolutes we must all live by.* In the worst-case scenario, society collapses into an "anything goes" amoral confusion. Many Traditionals believe that this is where we are right now.

This belief is not new. The Religious Right has been attacking the values relativism of Moderns for more than two hundred years. Washington, Jefferson, Hamilton, Lincoln, and Franklin Roosevelt—whoever spoke up for diverse people living side by side with mutual toleration, acceptance, and appreciation of differences was seen as a threat to the moral order. But there's a liberal counterpart term: America has always had a lot more *values pluralism* than Traditionals like to admit. Since *The Federalist Papers,* since Tocqueville's *Democracy in America,* and especially since the great immigrations from central and eastern Europe and from Asia, we have long rubbed up against one another's values and moral systems. Contrary to conservative myth, diversity has strengthened American democracy. Exponents of values pluralism, however, go on to say that those on the other side are bigots and idiots.

In fact, both pluralism and relativism are part political philosophy, part myth. Contrary to conservative myth, there was never a time when all Americans agreed on what constitutes proper morality or "who's a good American." And contrary to liberal myth, we haven't been a tossed salad with all the lettuce and tomatoes and sprouts lying happily side by side. Rather, the American heritage has been that we're a fractious, contentious, intolerant, and pluralistic bunch.

Historically, the big values conflicts grew out of fights over religious doctrine. From about 1650 to 1950, our cultural quarrels were focused on religious hatreds and distrusts among Protestants, Catholics, and Jews. Ethnic feuds took second place, but they too were bitter and suspicious. First it was the Anglo-Saxon stock against the Irish and the Germans, then those groups against the Poles and Italians; and those of European ancestry were always against whoever was racially different: Asians, African Americans, Native Americans, and Hispanics. Still other struggles were organized around country versus city, racists versus the more tolerant, and South versus North, all going back to the early 1800s. Baneful animosities were carried over from "the old country" to the United States and took a long time to die out.

The good news is that since the 1960s, most purely religious and ethnic hatreds have relaxed or disappeared entirely. American racism, though still pervasive, is less virulent than in the past and no longer legal. People of goodwill have pretty much had their prayers answered. The bad news is that, since the turmoil of the 1960s, Traditionals of all different stripes have made common cause with one another against the Moderns. Agreeing on a number of issues, they are focusing their fervent opposition against people of their own religion and ethnicity. And Moderns have tended to line up on the other side.

THE MODERNS

Did you ever see Saul Steinberg's map of America, the one that first appeared on the cover of *The New Yorker* and was often reproduced as a poster? Manhattan's West Side occupies most of the foreground, with the Hudson River just about as wide as the Midwest; there's not even a little furrow of dirt for the Rockies, and only a tiny bump for L.A. off to the left. The Pacific Ocean is about as wide as Tenth Avenue, and a line on the far horizon represents China, Japan, and Russia. At one level this map perfectly epitomizes the provincialism and smugness of many New Yorkers. But on another level it summarizes the ethnocentrism of the larger Modern culture.

Being in Modernism is like being in midtown Manhattan. The buildings are huge, so you can't see very far, and the activities and signs are so engrossing that you could easily believe that there's nowhere else in the world. New Jersey is definitely a foreign country. And Iowa? Fuhgeddaboudit.

In the terms of Steinberg's map, everything that happens must be translated into Manhattanese. This is how it is for Modernism, too. From within the Modern worldview, it is almost impossible to encounter another culture sympathetically and on its own terms. Instead, every new and different worldview or ideology is treated as if it were just another street in Manhattan, or maybe a funny little bump off to one side of the picture.

Today's Modern imagery and worldview has nineteenth-century roots in European intellectualism and in U.S. urbanism and industrialism. Modern culture originally emerged five hundred years ago in Europe, and over the past three centuries, it has had important roots in the urban merchant classes and the creators of the modern economy, in the rise of the modern state and armies, and in the successes of scientists, technologists, and intellectuals. It invented our contemporary world, reshaping almost every place on the planet to meet its needs. (What we call Modernism in the arts started in the late nineteenth and early twentieth centuries.) Today's business conservatives tend to idealize 1920s or 1950s images of Modernism, while liberals-to-moderates prefer idealized

1930s and 1960s images. The twentieth-century version encompasses the spectrum of beliefs and politics from big-government liberalism to business conservatism, communism to capitalism, secularism to conventional religion.

The triumph of the Modern world is often celebrated as our liberation from authoritarian political and religious controls. Its great strength is simply in being the dominant culture of the whole planet in our time, able to set agendas, define the terms of discourse, and dominate the mass media. Its great success has been an impressive set of cultural inventions for solving problems that human beings have faced for most of history. It has found ways to:

- diminish toil
- harness the elements
- reduce plagues and illnesses
- create plenty and then distribute it
- house and feed an exploding population
- create effective and productive organizations
- come to terms with increasing social complexity
- build more universal standards of morality and social practices

Modern culture's ambitious agenda was inherited intact from the ancient and early modern worlds. It has solved these problems, often brilliantly. It has gone from village fairs to global market economies, from peasant agriculture to industrial societies, from tiny villages to an urbanized world, from human- and animal-powered handicrafts to a hundred powerful new technologies, from feudalism to nation-states, and from medieval guilds to large-scale corporations. It has brought us noble principles in the realm of political philosophy, which we are now slowly turning into actual political practice: greater equality among persons, personal freedom, justice, civil rights (for example, freedom of speech, religion, and assembly, and fair trials), representative and deliberative democracy, equality before the law. It then uses the principle of universalism to apply those principles to real people and situations. The struggles for civil rights and for women's rights were classic examples of actually living out Modern principles.

FOUR KINDS OF MODERNS

Our surveys show that there are four subgroups within Modern culture. They differ from one another in values and in social class.

At the top of the social heap are the *business conservatives,* 8 percent of Americans, or 11 million adults. These upper-middle to upper-class people are free market conservatives who believe in the "American Way," with a materialist focus on status and success and a heavy dose of the work ethic. They adhere to the Wall Street and Chamber of Commerce ethic of growthmanship. Though they are often interested in psychological health and growth, most oppose ecological sustainability as bad for business. Theirs is what writer Richard Eder calls "the comfortable America of a rising stock market and a falling awareness of whatever lives outside its concerns."[8] With 59 percent in the top income quartile, these people are the beneficiaries of Modernism and capitalism as it now is. They want to keep it that way.

Conventional Moderns are 12 percent of the population, or 23 million adults. They are more likely than other Moderns to dislike the values and lifestyles of both the Traditionals and the Cultural Creatives, and seem to be strong upholders of the ideology of Modernism. They are more likely to be found on the disdainful Modern side of the culture wars. They tend to reject idealistic values, are rather cynical about society, and disgruntled about politics. They stand pat and keep their heads down, focusing their energies on their own personal and family situations, and they refuse to look at many public issues. Theirs is the fashionable cynicism and discouragement found in so much of official Modern culture. Less oriented to making a lot of money and to the trappings of success and status display than other affluent Moderns, *conventional Moderns* regard *business conservatives* as rather crass. But they are quite affluent themselves, with 61 percent in the top income quartile.

The *striving center* are 13 percent of the population, or 25 million adults. They are at the middle of the income distribution or just below it. Most are serious strivers for success and intense believers in most values; they yearn for inclusion and success in life, for some spiritual and psychological meaning, but they also lean to conservative religion. They are generally white-collar workers like clerks and postal workers and bookkeepers, as well as lower-level professionals like practical nurses, public school teachers, and administrative assistants. Lower-level managers and bureaucrats are in this group, as well as a lot of small business owners.

Upward mobility is their creed. Many are African Americans, or are Asians or Hispanics, or are first-generation immigrants. They are working hard to achieve the American dream for themselves and their children, but because their occupations and educations are below the national average, most of them will probably not be able to crack the code of success.

These cultural and religious conservatives have many of the same person-centered values as Cultural Creatives. Many have values conflicts because they act as "boundary spanners" who go back and forth between subcultures. Many seem to be in transition between subcultures. Both the Traditionals and the Cultural Creatives may recruit from this population. A large proportion are actually falling behind in incomes, and if life gets tougher, the center may not hold. In that case, will they remain believers in the culture of winning? Or will they abandon Modernism for either Traditionalism or the Cultural Creatives?

Finally, the *alienated Moderns* reject the values and worldviews of all the other groups—Moderns, Traditionals, and Cultural Creatives. Basically, they disagree with any positive statement of values. At 15 percent of the population, they are 29 million adults. An outsize proportion of them are the "angry white males" of media cliché, but many are women, too. They are in the lower middle class, and about half of them are blue-collar workers. They are very likely to be "sliders" who have lost better-paying jobs or have poor job prospects. In recent decades, American life has not been working for them. They are by no means the worst off in socioeconomic terms, however. Their alienation seems to come more from dashed life prospects than from poverty. They seem to suffer from loss of an inner compass that gives their lives meaning and structure, and from social disintegration. Militia groups find their recruits among them.

THE UPSIDE OF MODERNISM

From the vastly different perspective of the twenty-first century, we may look back at preindustrial rural life through the glorious haze of Merchant-Ivory films and romantic novels and see a simple pastoral time. But this is sentimental nonsense. Before the industrial revolution, every country in the world was overwhelmingly rural, and rural life meant harsh poverty, illiteracy, frequent illness, and malnutrition for the vast majority of people. Life expectancies were in the range of thirty to forty years. Unless we understand the life of the medieval peasant—the mud, disease, hunger, resignation, fear, superstition, and early death—we cannot fathom what Modernism was reacting against. The creators of early Modernism seem to have been constantly afraid of slipping back into the brutality and ignorance of peasant life. Behind the bravado of city dwellers was the fear that a reversal of fortune would throw them back to the countryside. Townspeople took great pains to show how very different they were from the masses of country bumpkins, as if by some sympathetic magic they could ward off the terrible fate of once again becoming one themselves.

As whole industries were created and hundreds of millions of people moved from farms to cities, getting ahead and taking care of one's family became achievable goals. Most immigrants to the United States believed in these values as an ultimate good. It's only in the last thirty years that people have begun to seriously question the wisdom of going all out for material success. All signs are that those who are raising these questions already enjoy middle-class levels of life and the perspective of higher education.

The Value of Individual Freedom

Imagine a medieval world in which every aspect of your life is dictated by where you were born, the social class you were born into, who your family is, and what ethnic or racial group you belong to. At birth, your fate is settled. What work you can do, whom you can marry, where you can live, and where you can be buried—all are predetermined. Think what it would be like to live under such constraints. Then ask yourself what it would be like never to travel more than fifty miles from your birthplace. At each point, do not assume that you are the one out of a hundred who is a noble or part of the landed gentry or merchant class.

If you find this picture distinctly unappealing, you're not alone. Modern civilization is built on the story of breaking out of the prison of definition by race, ethnicity, gender, sexuality, region of origin, religion, occupation, education. It's hard for any of us who live in the modern world to even think of returning to that kind of limitation in our individual freedom. After all, we're the ones who invented individualism.

For those of us in the middle and upper classes, the prison-break story is true. Modernity finally liberated us from the traditional constraints, and many of us have been able to go wherever our dreams and talents led us. In the Western democracies, we are no longer compelled to believe in certain religious doctrines, obey priests and elders, or even belong to a church. We can speak out freely on virtually any issue that concerns us. If we are articulate and convincing enough, people will pay attention to what we say. We can travel almost anywhere we choose (if we can afford it). We can read or watch almost anything we wish, we can marry whoever will have us, and many of us can escape our social class origin. In this story, we can all look for new ways of making money, we can abandon family and community responsibilities if we choose, or we can take on great projects for social and planetary change.

But for those who are poor and poorly educated, the story is different. And it has been different for most women through most of modern history. The cornucopia of options that modernity provided has not been available to everyone equally, regardless of the prison-break story. But the story has been so compelling, and the dream of *more* has been so enticing, that most Westerners have ignored the disquieting side effects of Modern culture until recently.

THE DOWNSIDE OF MODERNISM

Today, almost all of Modernism's great solutions seem to bring terrible problems in their wake. Many victories in the practical and political realms have come at the expense of the people who still believe in traditional ways of life. The third world is in despair not only because its own cultures have failed to solve some ancient problems but because Western solutions put their ways of life—even their lives—at risk. Moderns, too, are suffering. Globalization of markets has changed the nature of work, with increased worldwide competition leading to wage-cutting and downsizing in the West. The quality of life is declining for Americans who are not in the top-paid 25 to 30 percent of the workforce—they must work harder and longer just to maintain a 1970s standard of living. And families in the bottom 40 percent of the income distribution have been slipping behind for twenty years, even when both partners work.

Breaking Bonds

Before the creation of an industrial economy, society lacked the financial means to build and maintain roads, bridges, ports, schools, hospitals, and all the other aspects of a modern infrastructure that we blithely take for granted. Anyone who wanted to launch a new factory could not find workers. Kings and lords couldn't raise armies that would stay through the harvest season. Eventually modernizing elites broke people out of their traditional roles and communities by creating new opportunities, but in doing so they changed far more than the economy. Those who left their communities for the pull of new opportunities often fatally weakened traditional bonds of friendship, religion, class origin, community, and locality.

Once the leave-taking from traditional ways began in earnest, all the king's horses and all the king's men couldn't put them together again. People would occasionally go home to visit their families and old friends, but their children grew up in a different world. Feeling nostalgia was not the same as living the old life, and the looser bonds of the cities, with opportunities winking so invitingly, were too attractive to resist. Perhaps the children forgot what had been nurturing about those bonds in the first place. Or maybe they couldn't imagine how to hold on to both at the same time—the old connections as well as town and city opportunities.

Today's modern achievers, too, often have to tear up their roots in order to succeed. By migrating to another city or state or another country, millions of business travelers are constantly leaving home. One woman executive who travels almost weekly told a *New York Times* reporter, "There are some things that require constant attention. Children, especially. And friendship. That has to constantly be worked on. I no longer make friends, because I'm constantly jerked in and out of my life. Travel's a pain. There's no way around it. . . . Whatever I do, my life feels all turned around, as if I can't focus on what really matters to me."[9]

Where once we were embedded in our communities for life, we now suffer the loss of roots on an epidemic scale. Moderns complain that their relatives and friends are scattered across the continent or across the planet. But at the same time, they want to be sophisticated and up-to-the-minute, not provincial and traditional, which they consider quaint and backward.

Self-Interest Elevated to a Moral Principle

To be a Modern today means to live on a kind of roller coaster whose route depends on your opportunities for success: you may be expansive and ambitious in good times, but you're likely to contract into an anxious ball of self-interest when times are hard. Many Moderns believe that living responsibly means "taking care of number one" (or at least yourself and your loved ones). It's a conviction amply reinforced by the growing disappearance of our social safety nets. Studies of participation in civic life and volunteering for good causes show that over the past generation, Moderns have cut their contributions in half, while Traditionals and Cultural Creatives have maintained much *higher* levels of involvement.

Self-interest seems justified, to those who are winners. Here's writer Nicholas Lemann's satirical winners' credo from his article on "government of, by and for the comfortable":[10]

We, the relatively unbothered and well off, hold these truths to be self-evident:

That Big Government, Big Deficits and Big Tobacco are bad,

but that big bathrooms and 4-by-4's are not;

that American overseas involvement should be restricted to trade agreements,

mutual funds and the visiting of certain beachfront resorts;

that markets can take care of themselves as long as they take care of us;

that an individual's sex life is nobody's business, though highly entertaining;

and that the only rights that really matter are those which indulge the Self.

Moderns who achieve financial success in the upper middle to upper classes, like those satirized in Lemann's piece, tend to enjoy getting and spending. Their lives are centered on acquiring ever more "stuff," buying prestigious services that save them time, displaying their status, looking out for their kids' future, investing in the stock market (most of them for the first time), and then making more money. Overspending is the addiction of many Moderns, from the poorest to the most affluent.

The success of the top 10 percent frustrates the rest of the Moderns because they aren't reaching those heights—though they're convinced they *should*. From the middle class on down to the lower class, Moderns ask themselves why they aren't making it in today's world, when the media shows them so many who are. Most have suffered from income declines over the last quarter century, as both husband and wife must work just to keep even. In 1999 people were working about eight more weeks per year than they were in 1969, for about the same income. About 40 percent of the workforce is worse off than in 1970, and an additional 35 percent are not sustaining their earlier income. That means about 75 percent of the workforce is working harder for longer hours. The psychological and physical stress of workers and their families is reaching a critical point, according to a 1999 conference of psychologists and health analysts.[11] One occupational health expert recalled, "Not so long ago we talked calmly about work overload. And then we started to hear the expression 'time poverty.' Now . . . we're hearing expressions like 'time famine.'"[12]

The Market Takeover

In the 1700s, when the market economy affected only a tiny portion of people's lives, free market ideologues were regarded as "harmless cranks."[13] After 1800 Moderns were delighted when the free market economy became an engine of progress, generating wealth and plenty, taxes and jobs. By the twentieth century, for both good and ill, businesses had taken over the greater part of household, church, and neighborhood work: raising and preparing food, making houses and clothes, caring for and educating children, entertaining ourselves, constructing the meaning of our lives, and passing on traditions.

Ruben Nelson, an adviser to Canadian executives and government officials, spoke to us about what he sees as the soul-destroying effects of the market economy. "Our economic theory tells us that the *heart* of our lives, our soul, our substance—and I use those terms advisedly—is caught up in goods and services." And we Moderns believe this deeply, he said. We evaluate everything by how well it delivers goods and services. As a result, we squeeze out the larger meanings and "present what's left over as the guts of life." When Adam Smith artic-ulated free market economic principles, Nelson continued, he lived in a society that knew better than to allow it to take over all aspects of life. That made all the difference. "If there is a deep social agreement, and you know better, then you can afford to have this kind of fringe doctrine [i.e., the market economy] around the edge, and you don't let it into the heart of your life. One of the rea-sons that it worked then, and was in a sense benign in [Adam Smith's] time and didn't look dangerous, and is absolutely soul-destroying today, is that we've had two hundred years to chip away at and to bring more of our lives under the mar-ket economy."

He concluded with a mixture of sorrow and amazement: "So now most peo-ple are in some measure what the marketplace tells them to be. We even coun-sel our kids in terms of career training, that they in fact should *be* their career. Rather than saying to them, 'For God's sake, be a person, and then be sensitive to what it is you are called to on this earth, and have a vocation.' But we don't do that. What we do is career-counsel and teach people to manipulate their lives externally. And [we say that] if you have a good career path, then you're going to live well."[14]

a fable of two millennia

The ancient Greeks spoke of *enantiodromia,* "a thing turning into its opposite." And that is what happened to the Western world between A.D. 1000 and 2000.

The church in a medieval town had a high steeple, with a bell that would be rung five times a day to mark the canonical times of prayer (around dawn, midmorning, midday, midafternoon, and around sunset).[15] Days were arbitrarily divided up into twelve "hours" in summer and winter alike, which gave the hours an accordionlike quality of expansion or contraction depending on the length of the day. In the more northerly countries, short of the Arctic Circle, "hours" could be as short as forty minutes in winter, and over ninety minutes in summer. But exact time measurement was not their object; it was reminding souls of their obligations to God.

This was an oral culture, one without reading or writing. Traditions had to be brought forth verbally from memory for the benefit of the next generation, then be memorized from someone's recitation. It was a world designed for recounting over and over again what was real, emphasizing cyclical recurrence, which helped to jog people's memories. If something was forgotten, it would be gone forever. Only the churches of the richest towns could afford a Bible, which had to be painstakingly hand-copied on scarce parchment. This was an auditory world, where the unseen held sway over the seen, where sound was believed to show the insides of things and where the Word was taken inside a person, to be learned by heart.

A medieval villager spent his or her entire life within a fifty-mile radius and never was away from the all-pervading sound of the churchbells. The bells regulated all of life. Today's Islamic world still holds to that medieval pattern with its prayers five times a day, called by muezzins chanting from the minarets. The sound penetrates everywhere. The Koran is famously a recitation, to be heard rather than read silently. Islamic cultures are still God-centered, and the power of the Word is preeminent.

One of the modern world's stunning departures from tradition is that it is visual and print-oriented, preoccupied by the surface appearances of things. "Seeing is believing" in this culture, while the oral and auditory culture of a thousand years ago was preoccupied with "things unseen"—but heard. Any visiting anthropologist from Mars could tell you what Western anthropologists won't say about modernity: You can tell what people really worship by what preoccupies them most. How do you know what that is? Look at what they measure out with great precision and keep with them constantly. The modern world worships a two-faced god: time-and-money.

Not only does modernity measure time down to billionths of a second, it puts clock faces in every public and private place. People carry small time-measuring machines strapped to their arms, so they have their practical god with them constantly. Time is money, after all. Time and money are conflated, and Moderns are preoccupied with both. The Modern can go anywhere on the globe but can never escape the two-faced god.

Worship of time and money is what would make the modern world completely unintelligible to a peasant of the medieval world. The peasant used coins only once or twice a year and was never precise about time, but was embedded in church and prayer all through the day, every day, and was obsessed by religion. The modern worker today is deeply engaged by religion only once or twice a year and is very unclear about doctrine, but is obsessed by time and money all through the day, every day.

The god of time-and-money is firmly in control, and for centuries the priests of all its competitor religions have been noisily naming it as the false god Mammon. The temples of time and money are banks, and the chief priests are bankers, guardians of the mysteries of what money actually "is" and of how it is created. Its theologians are economists, and like theologians everywhere, they are intensely rational, even useful, within their own logical premises. Time-and-money worship pervades modern societies the way prayers and sacred rituals pervade premodern societies. Its ritual forms are supervised by accountants, through "keeping records," "balancing the books," and other esoterica. Its discipline is clock time, and we are all monks in its monastery.

THE TRADITIONALS

Traditionalism is a culture of memory. Traditionals remember a vanished America and long for its restoration. They place their hopes in the recovery of small-town, religious America, a hazy nostalgic image corresponding to the years from 1890 to 1930. This mythic world was cleaner, more principled, and less conflicted than the one that impinges on us every day today. At that time "men were men," and authority was self-reliant, fixed on the task, and impatient with complexity. Its values are evoked in Jimmy Stewart and John Wayne movies, Fourth of July speeches, and Veterans' Day parades. Often this imagined world never really was.

In smaller cities and towns today, these images are kept alive in stable friendship networks and in communities that still work. A lot more mutual aid is available to Traditionals than to the more mobile Moderns and Cultural Creatives. Even in larger cities, many Traditionals build strong relationships and take care of one another through their religious congregations. Turning away from a daunting modern world they don't like or understand, they turn toward one another to create bulwarks of religious, racial, or ethnic unity against outsiders. Their organizations and congregations give them a sense of strength, safety, and coherence while rejecting or scapegoating those who are judged to be "alien" or "other."

Traditionals hate many of the so-called freedoms of Modernism, like the loosening up of women's roles and the sexual expressiveness and the crazy-quilt inclusiveness for all religions and ethnic origins. Novelist Allegra Goodman's description of the Orthodox Jewish atmosphere of "Kaaterskill Falls" evokes the Traditionals' contentment within a world that is "always safe and always binding."[16]

And they remember, or think they do, a time when society had a steady moral compass. A retired factory worker attending a gathering of the all-male evangelical Promise Keepers in 1997 told a reporter, "What I really want to see is all our leaders—the White House—get on their knees and pray for our country. This country was supposedly founded on the Bible," he said. "It's kind of gotten away from it, I feel." Another man at the same gathering, a shipping clerk from Illinois, agreed. "I want to see our nation restored, see us get back to God," he said. "If everybody got back to God, I'm sure crime would fall, racial prejudice would cease, the conflict between the sexes would cease, and abortion would be done away with, just name it. I just feel these things can happen."[17]

A good indicator of the gulf between Moderns and Traditionals is the different meanings they attach to words. To call someone *pious* is a compliment to Traditionals; to Moderns, it's an insult. Another example is *love,* in certain contexts. When *The New York Times* headlines "In Sickness and in Health: Building Loving Relationships When One Partner Has HIV," its large Modern readership will undoubtedly approve. But when Wesley Pruden, the conservative editor-in-chief of the right-wing *Washington Times* was asked to comment on the story, he was equally certain that his readers would find the story uninteresting and offensive. "I know our readers," he assured an interviewer, "and they don't want those kinds of stories."[18]

The strengths and weaknesses of Traditionalism are two sides of the same coin. Its political strength lies in its enunciation of shared beliefs, principles, and values that can claim a divine sanction, its use of simple images that appeal to less educated people, and its nostalgic appeal to tradition. Its weaknesses are an ethnic and racial politics that, with nostalgia and scapegoating, lends itself to authoritarianism, and its use of a biblical moral framework for every new event, which can make the complex realities of today's world even harder to deal with.

AMERICA'S FIRST COUNTERCULTURE

Traditionals were the first counterculture to defect from Modernism. They were already "leaning back" before the American Revolution.[19] Their yearning for a simpler, more moral past time appeared as early as the Great Awakening, in the revivalist movements under Jonathan Edwards in colonial Massachusetts. After the Civil War, the counterculture of Traditionalism took root as poor southern whites resisted Reconstruction with Jim Crow codes and the Ku Klux Klan.

Led by rural and small-town Protestant fundamentalist movements for personal salvation, the new subculture was fed by various protest movements as well. The first protests came from farmers, ranchers, and small-town businesses against the dominance of bankers and merchants in cities. The next targets were giant corporations, such as the railroads. Later waves of protest were set off by failures of family farms and outrage about boom-and-bust agricultural cycles that benefited big business and ruined many farmers. Defections from Modernism intensified as the nineteenth century came to a close. Many people in America's small towns and countryside hated what was going on in the big industrial cities and saw themselves as the ones who could and would uphold "traditional American ways."

Diverging Paths of the Three Subcultures

Leaning Forward

Standing Pat

CULTURAL CREATIVES' PATH

Leaning Backward

TRADITIONALS' PATH

MODERNS' PATH

The planet's new counterculture, founded c.1970

America's first counterculture, founded c.1870

The modern mainstream, still running after 500 years

Traditionals' Life Stance: Leaning Backward	Moderns' Life Stance: Standing Pat	Cultural Creatives' Life Stance: Leaning Forward
Rejecting the system. Reacting against Modern secular worldview.	Accepting the system. Doing the best they can with the Modern worldview.	Going beyond the system. Inwardly departing from the Modern materialist worldview.

But although the new Traditionalism presented itself as an alternative to "city ways," its people were in fact Moderns who were defecting. They were actually members of a counterculture whose *origins and life assumptions were root and branch part of the worldview of early Modernism.*

As their children found better opportunities in the cities and often embraced modern values, Traditionals were left behind in the small towns. The ones who lived in the cities were often left behind in the upward scramble toward affluence. Traditionals have been our repeated losers at the game of Modernism—not representatives of some premodern tradition that predates it. Most are people of less education and less skill at urban ways of life, and many are the elderly who remember a vanished world. Today's social conservatives, backed by wealthy conservative foundations and influential in national politics, are very different in social class from—and much more ideological than—the Traditional constituencies to which they appeal.

UNDERSTANDING THE SPLIT

A strong general principle underlies the split between the Moderns and the Traditionals. It's the principle of feedback, which regulates all living systems, including whole societies. You can see how it works in the diagrams on pages 85 and 86.

On the Straight and Narrow. The first diagram shows the Traditionals' usual stance in the culture war: trying to keep people on the straight and narrow. As soon as anyone gets too far out, approaching the boundary of what is conventional, the Traditionals will give them some pretty negative feedback that says, "Get back!" Negative feedback enforces conformity. Traditionals are trying to make the majority of society conform to their own ideas, and Moderns don't like it.

The Split Between the Old and New Story. The next diagram shows the split between the Moderns and the Traditionals. Positive feedback is the kind of change that feeds on itself, promoting innovation. It amplifies deviations from the old path, and sometimes it can lead a whole population away from the old ways into a new subculture. But here's the kicker: Exactly contrary to the claims of the Traditionals, *it was not the Moderns who departed from what was conventional—it was the Traditionals themselves.*

Culture Wars. The third diagram shows positive and negative feedback working together, which is how culture wars get started. Moderns and Traditionals blamed each other for all that was going wrong in life. Moderns contended that Traditionals were old-fashioned, inefficient, bigoted country bumpkins. Traditionals countered that Moderns were immoral in their big-city ways, deviating from biblical doctrines, accepting foreigners in their midst, and exploiting the good people of the small towns and countryside.

The Traditionals innovated by inventing fundamentalism, which hadn't existed anywhere in the world before the early nineteenth century.[20] After the Civil War, they invented the Ku Klux Klan and Jim Crow, as well as the temperance movement that gave rise to Prohibition. But the most important thing they invented, in the twentieth century, was the myth of virtuous small-town America. And they did all this in the name of preserving traditional ways, denying that they were creating anything new. This claim seemed plausible, because in the meantime Modern culture was inventing big cities, heavy industry, railroads, skyscrapers, big banks, and the limited liability, joint stock corporation. Traditionals needed to reject all of the above, because it was oppressing their way of life. Worst of all, the new ways were beguiling and stealing away many of their young people with the tantalizing promise of financial success.

When people of any culture oppose change, their negative feedback takes the form of all sorts of unofficial actions, from gossip to name-calling to shunning to blacklisting to firing people, and beyond that to mob violence, cross burnings, and police beatings.

But Traditionals are not the only ones who use negative feedback. Cultural Creatives in the environmental movement and the women's movement create new standards about what constitutes an offense against the public interest. They have effectively used the power of public opinion and official government action to enforce these standards. The fragile alliance of Modern business conservatives and Traditionals often opposes such new forms of negative feedback, wanting to keep only familiar, established ones. This opposition appeals to Traditionals—and favors corporations and the wealthy.

UNITING FOR THE CULTURE WAR

America's ethnic nationalists may have been the first to raise the battle cry against Modernism by identifying it with foreigners and claiming "ethnic purity" for themselves against the hated Other. Like today's ethnic nationalists in the former Yugoslavia and former Soviet Union, America's Traditionals have

On the straight and narrow

The approved path of cultures
that strongly maintain their
established pattern.

Keeping to the old story

The old path remains as
part of the culture stays in the
established pattern.

Finding
the new story

The new subculture
may adapt better to a
changing world.

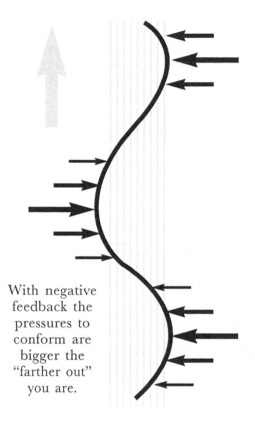

With negative
feedback the
pressures to
conform are
bigger the
"farther out"
you are.

**Negative feedback counters
deviations from the approved
path, and deviations may get smaller.**

**Positive feedback amplifies
deviations. It may create a new path,
a new story: a subculture.**

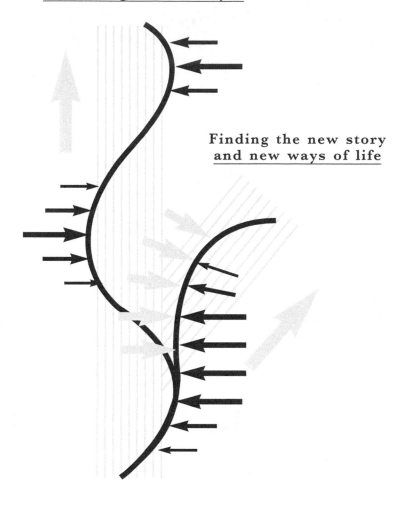

**Holding to the old story
and "the good old ways"**

**Finding the new story
and new ways of life**

Culture wars can be created as negative and positive feedback occur at the same time. The culture splits into contending subcultures. Those who stay with the old ways usually blame the other subculture because the old ways do not work as well as they used to. Those who try new ways may adapt better to changing times, but they often get a lot of pressure (negative feedback) for their departure from the old ways.

America's first split, all through the nineteenth century, was between urban-industrial Modernism and rural–small town Traditionalism.

The second split was when the Cultural Creatives made their inner departure from Modernism starting about 1970.

always been defined by their antiforeigner nativism. Before the Civil War, people of English stock denounced the immigration of Irish and Germans. After that, English, Irish, and German stock united against African Americans, Mexicans, Asians, and Central Europeans. (In the Deep South, ethnic nationalism also meant the revival of the Ku Klux Klan.) After 1900, people of Western European origins united against African Americans, Jews, and Southern and Eastern Europeans. Today people of European stock unite against Latin Americans, Asians—and still against African Americans.

Oddly enough, some of the incoming people whom fundamentalists hated most agreed with their complaints against secular Modernism: for example, traditional Catholic immigrants from Central and Southern Europe carried a conservatism of the kind persisting in the antidemocratic right in Europe today. In more recent years, however, Traditional urban Catholics and fundamentalist Traditionals have attempted to heal old wounds. As they focus on a common hatred of a common enemy, the culture wars grow more intense.

THE CULTURAL CREATIVES

Between the extreme positions of the culture wars lies a third way. It is not simply a neutral center but a distinctive expression. Rather than defending an old way of life, Cultural Creatives are bridging an old way of life and a new one. They seem to be unraveling the threads of old garments and weaving new fabric, cutting original designs and sewing together a new one. Many (though not all) want to carry forward what is valuable from the past and integrate it with what's needed for the future. Sometimes they want to integrate with what writer Michael Lewis calls "the new new thing"—Web portals and multimedia companies—or with technological and scientific discoveries that offer ecologically sound solutions, like the hypercar and the international carpet recycling program we saw in Chapter One.

Often the integration involves spanning differences between diverse groups of people, or bridging disciplines, or both. For example, in New York's Beth Israel Medical Center and Memorial Sloan-Kettering Cancer Center, Cultural Creatives are creating wellness centers that include both Western medicine and acupuncture, massage and yoga, psychotherapy and meditation. Cultural Creatives are also bringing 2,500-year-old meditation techniques into prisons and corporate America.

One of the most interesting such integrations is the project of an Episcopal priest named Lauren Artress.[21] Since 1989 she has been bringing an ancient

traditionalism is a recent reaction
to modernism worldwide

If you lived in an archaic traditional society, you might have spoken reverently of the inheritances from your ancestors, but you wouldn't have used terms like *tradition* or *traditional*. Your society as it existed was all you knew. Worldwide, Traditionalism today is about idealizing a nearly forgotten past. Its political leaders attempt to recapture legendary glories, and its religious leaders maintain congregations against a flood of competing new beliefs and loyalties. Cultural conservatives in Europe, Asia, and Africa claim to have roots thousands of years old, in a tribe, in an ancient religion, in an aristocratic lifestyle, or in a fundamentalist outlook. But the past they invoke is largely imaginary. Their Traditionalist politics is as recent as that of Americans: a reaction to Modernism. And they are just as selective about what they use from the past. In a real sense, Traditionalism is always neotraditionalism.

Modernism's ways of life and worldviews are just as legitimate as Traditionalist ones. This creates serious suffering for Traditionals, for Modernism can destroy naïve faith. In order to be vastly superior or "all there is," Traditionals need their own revealed truths— which is precisely what Modernism refutes. According to the Fundamentalism Project, led by Martin Marty at the University of Chicago, American fundamentalism came from such reactions. Islamic and Hindu fundamentalisms are analogous reactions to colonialism, imperialism, and multinationals.

During the last two centuries, Modern colonialism, markets, and technologies have overwhelmed traditional people around the world, upending old ways of life and imposing secularized values, religions, and symbols. Thousands of small cultures have been shattered and obliterated. In reaction, the reinvention of Traditions has intensified.

Neotraditionalisms have usually been developed in the modern era by farmers, owners of small business, and clerics. Sometimes they work closely with military groups or landed aristocracies that need a political base to come back to power. Traditionals also include conquered peoples, such as tribes or peasant groups, or cultures that have lost civil wars, like America's southerners and South Africa's Boers. Many Traditionals are people who feel wounded by Modernism—in their economic well-being, their social status, or their self-image—and feel a resulting moral outrage.

Traditional leaders reinvent their unique traditions by rearranging pieces of the past, often stating for the very first time principles that the ancestors or forefathers "must have" stood for. They are trying to protect their people from many of the changes that Modernism brings—and often to mobilize them against distant governments. By invoking tradition, they can say, "Things were morally better then." Naturally, these leaders are a lot more interested in finding what works for their own situation than in accurately reconstructing the past. Cultural conservatives invariably say that their society has taken a wrong turn in history and must restore a moral way of life from the past. They just can't agree on what that golden age was, or when, and they invariably idealize it.

In the face of a modern world they don't like or understand, neotraditional cultures everywhere gain strength and coherence by re-creating a shattered sense of community. Even in urban areas, they give aid and comfort to their own people who are often damaged by modern markets and modern wars. But their creation of an identity also requires them to reject and scapegoat whoever is different. This necessity carries them beyond prejudice to ethnic nationalism. The dark shadow of Traditionalism everywhere includes political murders, genocides, hate groups, and the far-right fringe.

path of prayer—the labyrinth found in medieval Christian cathedrals—to hospitals and prisons and schools and even cemeteries, from Shelbyville, Tennessee, to Morristown, New Jersey. One enthusiast calls walking the labyrinth "prayer in motion." Reverend Artress says that it is also a form of emotional and community healing: "When you walk into the labyrinth, the mind quiets, and then you begin to see through what's happening inside. You become transparent to yourself. You can see that you're scared or that you lack courage. People can see for the first time that their anger is in the way. You can see your judgments against people and against yourself."[22]

PERSONAL BRIDGES

Sometimes the integration is much more personal. Margery Anderson Clive and her husband, Mark Clive, live in Dallas where they both have multifaceted careers as artists and activists. After singing in the Houston Grand Opera, Margery moved to Birmingham to create an expressive art therapy program at the University of Alabama. When Mark had a job offer in the Dallas/Fort Worth area, they moved again and founded a nonprofit service where artists and art therapists provide creative support for physical and emotional healing. We met Margery when the artists' program was in its twelfth year, after she had worked with fifteen thousand people. She was putting the finishing touches on a one-woman musical production based on the life of Marian Anderson. She wrote the script, sang the music, and narrated the story of the great contralto's life.

It was overwhelming, hearing about all these accomplishments. Sitting across from this beautiful, serene fifty-year-old woman, it was easy to think of her as an acrobat, somersaulting effortlessly through the air from one flying trapeze to the next. We asked the obvious question: How did she do it? How did she find the confidence to leap from city to city and career to career with no visible means of support?

"I've been a survivor my whole life," she told us frankly. "I've been raised with rocks and stones and all kinds of stuff, and I'm still here. I come off very mild to a lot of people, but underneath, the more I'm presented with a challenge, the more I'm determined to get through it."

When we asked what kept her going through the hard times, she spoke about her parents' experience as African Americans. "My father and mother grew up in Birmingham under tremendous difficulties," she said. "They were very, very bright people who could not really get the kind of education they needed or acknowledgment for who they were. They had to fight and struggle to get out of Birmingham. And so I had that history. I remember Governor Wallace, civil rights, the German shepherds, and the fire hoses. I remember traveling from New Jersey every summer to Birmingham and not having any place to stop to use the washrooms, and wondering if we were going to get through certain states."

Her father taught her about singleness of purpose, she said, and her mother would make her do something over and over again until her work was excellent. Learning these lessons, and recognizing that her parents and grandparents lived what they taught, kept her "going and growing . . . able to keep at it with dignity, humility, and grace." She was dedicated to continuing her parents' spirit and finding her own unique way to express it. This kind of personal integration was a theme we heard often from Cultural Creatives, though rarely with this impressive array of accomplishments.

Another Cultural Creative from a traditional background is Eugene Cash, a psychotherapist and teacher of Buddhism, who described the love he received from his Orthodox Jewish parents in Pittsburgh. "Their pleasure in me and my brothers was always there, even after we left the family home. Wherever we were, they came to see us and support us. I remember living in a commune in the country and my mom coming with kosher chickens for everyone. And when I was performing radical street theater in the 1960s, my parents would be enthusiastic members of the audience. 'You shouldn't say bad things about our country,' they'd tell me afterward. But then: 'You were wonderful. A marvelous play. Good work, son. Good work.'" Eugene smiled at the memory. The continuity is something he feels deeply, as he extends his heritage of love not only to his daughter but to his meditation students, integrating his traditional heritage with his daily life.

A number of Cultural Creatives who come from traditional backgrounds told us that even when the choices they made were markedly different from those of their families—protesting the war in Vietnam, for example—this did not mean a lack of continuity. What continued, they said, was the belief that they should play a role in their community and give generously of themselves. Today Paul Milne is a labor organizer with the AFL-CIO and an adviser to Greenpeace. "About eighty percent of my family is affiliated with fundamentalist Christian churches, including a quarter of those with Christian Coalition churches," he told us. "These are like G. W. Armstrong's Worldwide Church of God, where you tithe, double tithe, triple tithe."

When we asked why he became so different, he looked surprised. He wasn't different, he told us. "I would say, in fact, that who and what I am comes right out of the same cultural milieu as my family. It's right from that root. It's not because I'm so different, but because I'm so much the same, that I've made other sets of choices." Becoming a conscientious objector during the war in Vietnam, joining the civil rights movement, and later becoming a labor organizer was a form of public service that "came right out of that Methodist Plains upbringing," he told us. And then he grinned. "My grandmother thought I would be an evangelist, and she turned out to be right."

Digging through the Pickle Barrel

As we'll see repeatedly, Cultural Creatives look for ways to connect what has been broken apart. Beck, a pop singer in his twenties, speaks about this in a way that many young Cultural Creatives could agree with. He is tired, he says, of sorting through the fragments of an era that offers too much information with no meaning. "I'm picking up the pieces and I'm putting them up for sale," he sang a few years ago. He's even sick of his own parodies, he said, and "dead ends that won't come to life anymore." He's making new music now, reflective and beautiful, that sounds old-fashioned to some critics.

"People write that I dig through the pickle barrel of the past," he told a reporter. "But I think of the music of the last hundred years as contemporary," as a continuity that has great value. Part of what has happened for him, he explains, is that he's tired of buying into postmodern superiority and disdain for everything that is different. In his own life, he's looking for a way to connect the end and the beginning, to try to grow beyond the differences and come up with something new.[23]

Cultural Creatives are sick of the fragmentation of Modernism, and they find the Modern-versus-Traditional culture wars to be just another instance of splitting apart what needs to be healed. (The strong exception is the issue of women's rights, where the Cultural Creatives side adamantly with Moderns.) Many describe the culture war as a deliberate ideological distraction from the serious issues that American society needs to come to grips with: that the planet is in peril with the fastest extinction of species in millions of years; that nuclear weapons are still incredibly dangerous; that pesticides and pollutants are contaminating our food, air, and water; that women and children everywhere are endangered by domestic violence; that poor people still have terrible life chances; that discrimination against minorities is still extensive; that medical costs are spiraling out of control and many people lack health insurance; that mainstream medicine is not responding to holistic health issues; that the official culture is still ignoring or mocking spirituality; and that politicians are fiddling with a hundred irrelevancies while Rome burns.

THE SECOND COUNTERCULTURE

The Cultural Creatives have emerged to a large extent because these failures of Modernism are so blatant that they call into question the official story that we are supposed to live by. Catholic priest and historian Thomas Berry writes, "It's all a question of story. We are in trouble just now because we do not have a good story. We are in between stories. The old story, the account of how the world came to be and how we fit into it, is no longer effective. Yet we have not learned the new story." The old explanation is no longer effective for many of us, but for the time that we believed it, it provided a meaningful context in which life could function.[24]

Earlier in this chapter, we saw two divergent paths away from Modern culture. The first counterculture was that of the Traditionals who have been "leaning back" in reaction to late Modern culture for over a century. The second counterculture is that of the Cultural Creatives. Their life stance is "leaning forward" to embrace new values and worldviews, rather than "leaning back" to the past or "standing pat" in the present. They are in the process of splitting off from Modernism, as the Traditionals have.

Leaning forward means stepping outside the old story and discovering a new one. It's not something you can do alone or quickly. Cultural Creatives are looking for ways, not so much to tell a new story—no one can *tell* a story deep and true enough to be useful now—but to evoke a new story, to discover a new way of living for a new time.

One of the new storytellers is an astute nursing administrator from the Midwest. She describes the difficulty of departing from the worldview she learned as a child: "Looking back at those years of trying to pull out of my old stance in life, it's as if my hands were bound behind me and my feet tied together. Somehow I was managing to move forward in little awkward hops. I'm amazed that I was so persistent, that I could keep going tied and bound like that. From where I sit now, I see that it's the culture itself that wraps us in so tight. It's the culture that keeps our eyes screwed shut. Not just in terms of what we should and shouldn't do—the things we learn as we grow up. It's more than that. It's what we should and shouldn't question, should and shouldn't long for, should and shouldn't imagine."

She pins the Cultural Creatives' dilemma exactly: Taking up a new world-view *is* a matter of culture. A worldview is to humans as water is to fish. It's the water we swim in. But only when something, or many things, disrupt our world-view does it become visible. That is the point where Cultural Creatives begin to look for a new story, to create a Third America. Like the Traditionals, they diverge from Modernism, but unlike both Traditionals and Moderns, they are not triumphalist. They're not given to grand statements like "God is on our side, and ours alone," and they don't believe that "winning is the only thing." They are looking for a new way.

A NEW CULTURE

As Cultural Creatives from all walks of life depart from Modernism, they are stepping firmly on the ground. Sarah van Gelder, the outspoken editor of *Yes!* magazine, wrote to us that she hoped we didn't trivialize the Cultural Creatives' concerns by saying, "Don't just do something, change your mind." She's really tired of the dichotomy that pits inner change against changing the culture. "The New Age stereotype is that it's all about changing ourselves internally and the world will take care of itself. The political activists' stereotype is that we ignore our inner selves to save the world. Neither works! . . . The Cultural Creatives are about leaving that dichotomy behind and *integrating* the evolution of the self and the work on the whole."

The promise of the Cultural Creatives is the promise of developing an integral culture that can bring together the traditional and the modern, the planetary and the local, and inner and outer change. The strength of the Cultural Creatives is that they are the part of the population most likely to carry forward a positive vision of the future. They have already begun imagining and developing alternatives to the urgent problems that confront our world. Over the past four decades, as we'll see, they have been predominantly the activists and moral publics of the new social and consciousness movements. Thus they have experience in thinking about, planning, and working through a variety of social solutions.

The weakness of the Cultural Creatives is that they don't yet have a basis for supporting each other and working together. Lacking social support, social isolation becomes a great problem for them. Until they develop a substantial sense of community, their fledgling movements, businesses, and institutions cannot grow, and potential political leaders cannot create a common cause with them.

As Cultural Creatives depart from the mainstream, the first question many people ask is, "Can they make it?" Others wonder, "Can they get away with it?"—implying that social and economic pressures are great enough to doom their efforts. In a time of major social change like today, the bad news is that all sorts of deviance appears, from the merely obnoxious to the criminal. But the good news is that there is space to innovate. When people learn how to see things differently, and help each other to live differently, great changes are possible. Despite the fears of social conservatives, Americans have always preferred to leave room for such changes.

BEYOND THE CULTURE WAR

So what position do the Cultural Creatives take in the culture war? They refuse to choose sides. They head off in a third direction that's neither left nor right, neither modern nor traditional. They have been deeply involved in most of the new social movements that have appeared since the 1960s and in a host of other cultural inventions as well. Oppositional political movements have influenced them less than cultural movements that try to educate our desires and change our minds about reality. They want to see the big, inclusive picture, and they want to work with the whole system, with all the players. They regard themselves as synthesizers and healers, not just on the personal level but on the planetary level, too. They keep cutting across social class and racial lines, across ideological lines of liberal and conservative, and across national boundaries, rejecting militarism and exploitation, seeking long-term ecological sanity.

Cultural Creatives are interested in experimenting with what might be called women's nonhierarchical models, including feeling *and* action, the personal *and* the political, in a search for humane ways of social transformation.[25] These are, of course, ideals. Their search, like any other, will cover the gamut of human wisdom and folly, honor and criminality. Their ideals are not a lived reality for all Cultural Creatives. But they are in there pitching, trying to create change that moves the culture far beyond the culture war to a new way of life.

part two

a creation
story

EVERY CHILD WANTS to know where he or she came from, and every culture has creation stories to answer those questions, giving sense and meaning to the lives of its people. Cultural Creatives think they know their creation story. Indeed, all of us who lived through the early years of the new social and consciousness movements think that we know that story perfectly well. We've seen the events and the famous people on television dozens of times.

We know that in 1955 a Montgomery seamstress was pulled off a city bus for refusing to surrender her seat to a white bus rider, igniting one of the greatest mass movements in American history. In 1962 a biologist and popular science writer pointed out that pesticides and pollution were potentially the death of nature, and a stodgy conservation movement was soon transformed into a planetary environmental movement. In 1962 a journalist described "the problem that has no name" and set off an intimate earthquake in homes across America, as women began to actively pull apart the social values that had crippled them. In 1964 Big Sur Hot Springs changed its name to Esalen and hosted seminars on human potential, spirituality, sensory awareness, yoga, and alternative forms of health and healing, accompanied by soaks in soon-to-be famous hot tubs.

And we remember the tens of thousands of marchers and demonstrators with their chants and their sit-ins, and the body bags being unloaded from military planes, and the screaming Vietnamese women and children—we know it all, don't we? All too well.

Because the images and the events are so indelibly etched in our collective memory, we think that we know what happened, and that it's over now, and that we've all pretty much gone on with our lives.

But we're wrong. As a nation, we don't know what happened. We know the first part of the story, but we think that the decades of great dreams went away, because we no longer see dramatic events on television. We don't know what happened next: how those early movements and the ones that followed have shaped the lives of the people who are Cultural Creatives today. And so the Cultural Creatives themselves don't know where they came from. And like any culture that lacks a history, they imagine themselves to be outsiders, strangers, out-of-place pieces in a puzzle that seems to fit together just fine without them.

We had a direct confrontation with this fact one night in late October 1999. We had promised a close friend that we would meet with her niece, who had "a question that won't go away." Our friend was sure that we would be able to help. We weren't so sure, but we agreed to listen.

AN OUTSIDER

We're sitting in our living room after dinner. Jan, a compact, intense woman in her early thirties, is curled up on our sofa. "I suppose I could start anywhere," she says. "This isn't a story that has a beginning, a middle, or an end. It's just been going on for years." She looks a little embarrassed. "I suppose it's just a psychological problem. Mine, my family's—I don't know. I'll just tell you about what happened last month. That ought to be enough."

Fine, we say. Tell us.

"It was my mother's sixtieth birthday, and her dearest wish was that we all spend the weekend as a family with her somewhere other than Cleveland, our family home. My father was willing to foot the bill for my brothers and sister and me to fly in from various parts of the country and spend a weekend some-where. We wrangled for weeks. My brothers and sister insisted on a big golf course, elegant meals, top-notch service, and a huge swimming pool. It had to be someplace that would be warm in April and in the continental United States. They all agreed. I was the problem."

"What did you want?"

"Well, I'm the weirdo in the family. I wanted yoga, organic food, simple sur-roundings, and, hopefully, easy access to hiking trails or the ocean. Because I knew it wasn't going to be easy, you know? So we tried to find a place that had all those things."

"Is there such a place?"

She laughed and shook her head. "We compromised. We found a spa in southern California with a big golf course, a swimming pool, and a view of the ocean. But even after we got there . . ." She sighed. "It wasn't one or two things. At every turn, I felt like the odd one. The one who didn't drink. The one who sneezed at all the perfume and cologne they wore. And when I complained, they were incensed. I was the only one who wanted to swim in the ocean instead of sit by the pool. Each time it seemed like what they were doing was the norm, a norm that fit the spa perfectly. I was the marble rattling around out of place."

The cumulative effect, she said, was overwhelming. "It sounds so petty, but all the differences kept piling up, until I felt invisible. We might as well be from different planets. Nothing I care about makes sense to them, and so there was nothing for me to talk about. The men talked about the family business, and my sister and mother talked about shopping. I didn't say much of anything, even though there's a lot I wished I could tell them. My passion for yoga. The Creation Spirituality courses I'm taking at Holy Names College. The way I live, the kind of friends I have, the kind of marriage I want. They didn't want to hear it, and frankly, I've given up."

She reflected for a few minutes, then said, "I have to admit, though, that a lot of what they love turns me off. I'd like to think it's just about lifestyles, but down deep it really hurts. What I respect, what I build my life around, is something they make jokes about. And what they value, quite honestly, is something I have no respect for. My brothers measure everything in dollars. So long as the resort was really expensive, it must be elegant. My mom and my sister adore shopping. Shoes! My mother's in rapture in a shoe store."

She went on, a little amused at how this must sound to strangers, the aggravating details of a family vacation, but at the same time, she seemed perplexed. "My family was so happy on the golf course, and gossiping around the pool, but I felt like I was in some kind of plastic prison. I finally took my dad's rental car and spent all of Sunday at the ocean. Sitting on the cliffs watching the white pelicans soar over the Pacific, I felt like I was finally crawling back inside my own skin, breathing the fresh air, at home."

She looked at us dubiously. We murmured sympathetically, hoping she'd tell the rest of her story. She went on.

When the weekend was finally over, she returned home ready to scream and rant to her friends about how awful it had all been. But how could she? Her father had been so generous, paying for all of them. And her mother had been so happy that everyone was together. How could she be such a brat at thirty, so ungrateful and difficult? She felt guilty, and furious, and frustrated. Because it wasn't just this special occasion in California, she explained. It was every time the whole family came together for big weddings and Thanksgiving and other ritual occasions.

WHERE DID YOU COME FROM?

After she returned, Jan asked her friends for advice. Her dilemma, they agreed, was really about maintaining her own integrity without throwing the family relationship away. They gave Jan a lot of advice about what was wrong with her family and what she needed to do to take care of herself. But what helped most was when her friend Eve, sincerely puzzled, asked, "Where did you come from, Jan? How could somebody like you come from a family like this?"

Jan looked at us. "That's really my question. Why don't I belong to this family? I've been in therapy, and this is something my therapist can't answer either. Nothing about this family of mine seems to fit me."

At this point, we understood why Jan was sitting in our living room. Her question was one that Cultural Creatives had answered for us, in great detail, over the past dozen years. We began to lay out the answer to Jan's question, as we understood it. It wasn't a psychological explanation of what had happened in her family when she was young, or what ethnic group she came from. It was about pieces that fall into place later, when a person is more mature and part of a new subculture that's just beginning to take form. You can indeed feel like a stranger in your own family. The shapes of these missing pieces are so particular and personal—your priorities, the way you make sense of the world, the kind of life you lead—that it's hard to imagine that they have anything to do with culture. But they do.

We began to describe Cultural Creatives to Jan, especially their values and the choices they are making. "Sounds a lot like me," she said, her eyes filling with tears. "I never dreamed there could be so many people like me. But what about my family? Why are they so damned—arrogant? So damned sure that the way they do things is the *only* way?"

They sound like Moderns, we told her, so that makes them members of the dominant culture. But your situation is not just about the personalities of your relatives (although they *could* be a lot more considerate). If you belong to a dominant culture—any dominant culture, not just Modernism—you think that your way is the norm, the standard, the obvious way to do things, the truth. And as for those who are different—well, they're the outsiders, the ones who need to get with the program or be left behind. It's not exactly personal, we explained. In fact, your family is probably just as mystified as you are by the scratchy, constant skirmishes. They probably wonder: What is Jan's problem? Why can't she be like the rest of us, so we can all relax and have a good time?

Jan sat quite still, not saying anything, letting the pieces of the jigsaw puzzle move themselves around. Finally she said, "Okay. I can see the culture clash. It's starting to make some sense. But you still haven't answered my original question. Where did *I* come from? How did I get to be the way I am from a family who's so different?"

HIDDEN IN PLAIN SIGHT

The answer is like Edgar Allan Poe's purloined letter, so familiar that everyone walks right past it. We walked right past it, until Cultural Creatives told us, again and again, that we had to look for what was hidden in plain sight. Practically everyone we interviewed for this book told us that they had been involved in the new social movements and the consciousness movements that began in the 1960s and continue today. Not just one or two, they said, more like three or six of them. Almost everyone said that their own convictions and life priorities had been strongly affected, even shaped, by engagement with these movements. At first we were afraid that we had interviewed a biased sample, some special group of activists who were not like the rest of the Cultural Creatives. But when we checked back in the survey data, we saw that there was no mistake.

When we told this to Jan, she looked irritated. "So what? What does that have to do with me? I'm no activist. When those movements were big, I was in diapers. That stuff is history."

A whiff of disdain floated in the room. Tell me something useful—please!

"Okay, hold on a minute. It wasn't just activists who were changed by these movements. It was the immense ring of supporters around them—many times more numerous than the activists themselves. And when you start adding up the social movements—civil rights, women's, antiwar, gay rights, ecology—and the consciousness movements—humanistic psychology, new spirituality, holistic health—you get a giant overlap of people in those support circles. So it's not just activists and it's not just one or two movements we're talking about. It's millions of people in many movements over the space of almost two generations."

"Oh." She perked up. "So let me follow this through a bit. My women's group in college, my passion for yoga, going to the gay pride parade last month (even if I just watched from the sidelines), the kind of transpersonal therapy I like—that's all part of it?"

"That's right."

"And I'm a real nut about nature—hiking, biking, river rafting, and just getting out in the big spaces as much as I possibly can. And oh, my vision quest in the High Desert Sierras! Like all that, you mean?"

"That's it."

Jan uncrossed her arms and sighed. We talked for another hour or so, and she began to put her own pieces into place. Sometimes, she said, she had learned new things. More often, what she already cared about was supported or elaborated by the groups she joined or the books she read or the late-night discussions she carried on with friends. It was a lot to think about, this question of how she grew to be who she is now.

Toward the end of the evening, Jan remembered something that made her brighten. It was about her father. He had gone to college in Chicago, she told us, and smoked dope and was fascinated by the Beat poets. When he went to law school, he volunteered for civil rights defense work. "If it weren't for him, I probably wouldn't have started out with my sense of justice and race consciousness," she reflected. "If he hadn't come home to run the family business, maybe he would have been more like the person that I've become." She sat quietly for a few minutes. "Maybe," she said softly, "I'm not as much an outsider as I thought."

Our explanation to Jan that evening covered just the smallest part of where she, and the other Cultural Creatives, have "come from." In Part Two, we take up her question—Where did I come from?—on behalf of this new subculture. To answer it, we will take a closer look at the new social movements and the consciousness movements. Once we realize that these movements were not a jumble of seemingly endless demonstrations and high dramas, we'll have a powerful new key to understanding the changes taking place beneath the surface of our collective life. The new movements were, and are, a massive social learning process, not simply for activists but for most Americans and especially for the Cultural Creatives. Once we uncover the fundamental patterns of the new subculture's creation, we can better understand where they, and perhaps our greater civilization, are heading.

Only against a wide-screen background can we begin to make sense of the headlines and TV images, the mass of seemingly unrelated events that describe the approximately twenty kinds of cultural movements that have given rise to the Cultural Creatives. It is not the individual events that we need to bring into focus but something much more basic: the culture-making itself. To discern the shape of these social change processes, we need to step back about fifty years. It takes that much time to catch sight of a whole civilization changing.

We'll understand that the Cultural Creatives are not an incoherent mess of bleeding hearts and do-gooders and me-firsters, but a slowly growing convergence of once-discrete movements into a great current of cultural change. At the very least, it is a change of mind for a quarter of the American population. And it could turn out to be a change of mind for the culture at large, the making of a new American integration.

chapter four

challenging
the codes

t o tell the creation story of the Cultural Creatives, we first turn to the social movements that nurtured them. And what a nurturing it was, with the most surprising nursemaids— tens of thousands of loud, sassy women striding arm in arm down New York's Fifth Avenue and exuberant college students hoisting their speakers atop cars to shout free speech messages into bullhorns. They were students and professors, poets and office workers, draft dodgers and Vietnam veterans, parents pushing baby carriages, priests and nuns and rabbis and school-teachers. Chanting "Hell no, We won't go!" they marched through the streets to sit in at draft boards and military installations. Earnest and listening hard, they gathered in circles and struggled to speak aloud what they had never told anybody. Sober and scared, they blockaded rail-road tracks in front of nuclear weapons plants, where thousands of them were arrested. Some were trying, as Denise Levertov wrote, to imagine peace, to oust the intense, familiar pictures of war and disaster.[1] Others were chaining themselves to trees and lying down in front of bull-dozers in old growth forests. Still others were protesting the poisoning of workers in grimy industrial towns and children in metropolitan areas. And every one of the movements, it seemed, believed that its efforts could change the world.

Cultural Creatives aren't simply the core activists of the new social movements who have grown up. After all, those activists numbered in the tens of thousands, while Cultural Creatives are tens of millions. It was rather that *the social movements fed the longings and hopes of a vast population.* It started with protest movements but turned into something much more. Unfolding at precisely the same time were the new consciousness movements for spirituality, new forms of psychology, and holistic healing and health. In Chapter Six, we'll see how significant these consciousness movements were to the emergence of the Cultural Creatives. But their influence was not widely felt for decades. The new social movements, on the other hand, catapulted all of us into flamboyant and volatile cultural classrooms that were in your face every day. By the end of the millennium, despite repeated backlash attempts, all of American society had gone through a profound period of social learning.

In the next four chapters, we will take a perspective that is now available for the first time. It is a long view across four decades and a wide view across the twenty or more kinds of social movements. It is a satellite perspective through survey research on about 100,000 Americans, a close-up of hundreds of focus groups, and an in-depth account of dozens of personal interviews. This is more data than has ever been collected before. Our interest here is not in the details of how the individual movements worked and what they advocate—there is already a large literature on that topic. Our focus is on how the new movements were part of a dramatic evolution of American society, in a spiral of changes that had an immense impact on what most Americans will and won't accept in their lives. The movements shaped a whole new worldview and set of values that became central to what the Cultural Creatives now believe. The people who became the Cultural Creatives were among the most influential in shaping the later course of the movements themselves. In short, we'll discover how the newest American subculture was born and how it is beginning to spread itself through our wider society.

Huge Clouds of Sympathetic Supporters

Political commentators have repeatedly underestimated the size of the new social movements. It's a natural error, in a world where the political and business news focuses on what is most dramatic and substantial: megamergers, war and peace, disasters and national and international traumas. The social movements don't appear to have much significance. Few activists are seen at any given moment. If we see only the publicly visible parts of a movement, it's easy to think that it's small. But a real social movement consists of all the people who support it and believe in it. The total population of all the new movements is immense. In the United States alone, at least twenty new social movements have emerged in the last forty years.

To understand the true size of a social movement, think of a target with three concentric circles. The center is the hundreds of visible leaders, demonstrators, and little organizations. Around the center is a circle of many thousands of active supporters. And around those two active circles is the circle of the sympathetic millions who are touched by the events, and may simply read the arguments, and as a result make different choices in some part of their lives. Across all the recent movements, there have been hundreds of national organizations, tens of thousands of local organizations, hundreds of thousands of activists, millions of loyal members who gave money and read everything, and tens of millions of sympathizers in moral publics who broadly agreed with the movement positions. The size of this population catches everyone by surprise. The whole population constitutes a moral public and surrounds each of the movements like a huge sympathetic cloud that encompasses visible activists and the less visible followers who paid attention to the messages of the movements, including the audience who watched and listened but were largely invisible to the media and even to many expert observers.

It's no surprise that most politicians, historians, and media observers mistake what's going on. Most center-left political parties around the world today began as social movements in the nineteenth or early twentieth century. So did most of the defeated fascist parties. Many commentators are prisoners of early-twentieth-century images of what it takes to be a significant actor on the political stage. They remember marchers for women's suffrage and Prohibition, unions and Wobblies organizing workers and demonstrating in the streets, Klansmen in robes burning crosses and lynching blacks, and progressives, socialists, communists, and fascists turning political movements into political parties that ran whole governments. Political and media analysts usually suppose that if a social movement is to be considered important, it must be a radical, well-organized political party like the Bolshevik and Nazi parties; or consist of political terrorists like the Palestinian Hamas and ultraright militias; or operate with focused and effective opposition like the early union movement, wringing concessions out of sweatshop owners and later big business, and changing laws.

Like Marlon Brando in *On the Waterfront,* expert observers want to know "who's a contender." They assume we're all spectators seated around the ring, caring only about who's going to win the next election. If a public figure is the next political contender, the pundits presume, we're interested; if not, forget it.

They're irritated by upstart social movements that don't know how to grab power, that keep asking the "wrong" kinds of questions: questions about deep ecology, gender roles, holistic health, personal growth psychology, the spiritual side of life, psychedelics—the consciousness movements that politicians think are too radical, too far outside the box for the political arena. Nevertheless, the new movements have outflanked the old political parties on a host of critical issues.[2]

THE NEW SOCIAL MOVEMENTS HAVE CHANGED OUR MINDS

A subculture whose members, taken together, number in the millions is impressive. But as a society, we're not adept at tracking subcultures. Because media eyes are trained on the big political battlefields, we've overlooked what is happening in the culture itself. In fact, virtually every facet of the American worldview and every one of its values has been affected by what the new social movements (and the consciousness movements) have taught us over the last forty years. To take a few examples, where the numbers are in the *hundreds* of millions:

- When Rachel Carson's *Silent Spring* appeared in 1962, the environment was a serious concern for no more than 20 percent of Americans. Today, at least 85 percent of Americans are concerned about it.
- In the Eisenhower era, people simply accepted nuclear weapons. By 1982, some 82 percent of the population wanted to get rid of them.
- Before the 1960s, the position of women in society was undeniably second-class. It was simply conventional belief in the 1950s that "it is much better for everyone involved if the man is the achiever outside the home and the woman takes care of the home and family." By the 1970s, there was doubt: in 1977, 65 percent of Americans agreed with that statement, while 34 percent disagreed. Conventional roles were still clearly alive and well. But by 1994, there was a complete flip in public attitudes: 34 percent agreed and 63 percent disagreed. Now there is no real doubt, even though the far right is trying to roll back women's gains. Or take the statement, "Most men are better suited emotionally for politics than are most women." The American public went from 49 percent disagreement in 1974 to 74 percent disagreement in 1994.

Many social problems that were tolerated or simply accepted before the 1960s are completely unacceptable today. If you are under the age of forty, you

How many of these are acceptable to you today?

- ❑ White supremacy, using systematic violence and discrimination against Native Americans, Asians, Hispanics, and African Americans.
- ❑ Discrimination against women in the legal system and the workplace, and abuse common at home.
- ❑ Corporate actions that cause large-scale environmental destruction and harm people's health.
- ❑ Justifying the pollution and poisoning of the global environment outside the United States—air, oceans, farmlands, forests—for economic growth and corporate profits.
- ❑ Ignoring massive global extinctions of plant and animal species, now occurring on a greater scale than in most of geological history.
- ❑ Creating a hair-trigger risk of nuclear war, in which "mutually assured destruction" is the main strategy: ignoring that it would kill billions of people or even all life on Earth (in a nuclear winter).
- ❑ Building nuclear power plants, based on false industry assurances that power will be "too cheap to measure" and completely safe, with no mention of cost and difficulty of decommissioning plants or storing wastes.
- ❑ Millions of deaths from heart disease and cancer, caused by poor diet or smoking.
- ❑ Commitments to wars like the one in Vietnam by foreign policy elites, with no real input from the people.
- ❑ The McCarthy-era suppression of civil liberties in the name of anti-Communism.
- ❑ Lack of free speech on college campuses, and treating the students as teens, not adults.
- ❑ Impersonal and mechanical health care, based on a purely physical concept of healing.
- ❑ Expecting people to stay in stultifying, dead-end, or harmful jobs in the name of security or loyalty.
- ❑ Expecting people to stay in stultifying, dead, or harmful marriages in the name of security or loyalty.
- ❑ Expecting people to stay in churches and religions that are stultifying, dead, and lacking in spirit.
- ❑ Treating the psyche as steeped in sin, or as nothing but a sewer of unconscious drives, rather than full of human potential.
- ❑ Permanent unemployment, ill health, and even starvation among a billion poor people worldwide.
- ❑ Gay and lesbian bashing.
- ❑ Mistreatment of animals in research laboratories.
- ❑ Drunkenness, old age, ethnicity, race, or gender as the butt of comedians' jokes.

may have no idea of how drastically our everyday lives have changed, and how much our notions of what is just have changed since the 1960s. Look over the old social codes listed in the box on page 111. All of these have been challenged by the social movements, often with considerable success. No matter how old you are, you may be surprised by what was seen as normal as recently as the 1950s and 1960s. That will give you a sense of how influential the new social movements have been in shaping your own values and views.

The top two-thirds of the list names issues that the new social movements have already won in the courts of public opinion. Large majorities of Americans and Europeans no longer shrug their shoulders and look away from these abuses. While they don't necessarily agree with the exact diagnoses that the new social movements have put forth, they clearly reject the old ways of behaving. The bottom third of the list gets much less agreement and consensus, but again the growing trend is toward public rejection of the old ways. More and more people are likely to say, "No, that's not right."

Practically every item in the list has a moral dimension. Shockingly, half a century ago, you could regard yourself as highly moral yet not be concerned with anything on this list. And what's more, your community would have shared your unconcern. Today most of us would say that only a moral monster could ignore all these items. Obviously, we've learned something.

For some of these items, the moral dimension is immediately evident, like white supremacy and legal discrimination. For others, like global destruction of the environment and massive extinctions of other species, we may have first thought of our own survival, then later come to recognize the profoundly moral implications. Our children are especially aware of them. Finally, consider some of the less obvious issues, like impersonal and mechanical health care, or stultifying jobs, marriages, and religious groups. Many Moderns and Traditionals may not see these as problems. Cultural Creatives, however, see soul-destroying treatment and relationships that are truly harmful as immoral. Many of the changes introduced by the consciousness movements address these "less obvious" issues.

With this great public mind-change as a backdrop, let us turn now to the foundational events that prepared the way for the first generation of Cultural Creatives.

THE DECADE OF GREAT DREAMS

Within a decade of Rosa Parks's arrest in 1955 for failing to give up her seat on a Montgomery bus to a white man, the civil rights movement overturned legal segregation and secured voting rights for black citizens across the South. Beginning with the sit-ins of 1960, black and white college students poured into the struggle, bringing a new level of mass activism and civil disobedience and launching what became known as "the decade of great dreams."[3]

This struggle was more than a civil rights movement. Historian Vincent Harding, at the Iliff School of Theology in Denver, urges us to remember the music of that time. It was not, he notes dryly, a music of civil rights. "Think of those haunting anthems with their deep spiritual roots, their calls for justice and optimism and bold words," he says. "They reminded demonstrators who they were and why they were risking their lives. It was again and again about 'freedom, freedom, freedom.'" Black people and their white supporters did not lay their lives on the line for *civil rights,* he insists.

Harding recalls his own experiences in the early 1960s, when he took time out from his doctoral studies at the University of Chicago to move with his wife, Rosemarie, to Atlanta. They set up a movement house there, counseling and meeting with hundreds of young people and with Martin Luther King, Jr., Fannie Lou Hamer, and others. "You could feel almost a *palpable* love of democracy for its own self," he said. People were obsessed with democracy, on fire with the wider meaning of what they were doing. It was about so much more than voting. It was about participating in the creation of something new and better, something more whole than what had been there before. And so the movement was first and foremost and in the end a freedom movement.[4]

Columbia University historian Eric Foner, recollecting how the anti-Communist 1950s came close to "reducing freedom to a sterile propaganda slogan," acknowledges the great debt the United States owes to this movement: "With their freedom rides, freedom schools, freedom songs, freedom marches, and the insistent cry 'freedom now,' black Americans and their white allies reappropriated the central term of Cold War discourse and rediscovered its radical potential."[5]

This longing for freedom, framed in terms of Americans' highest aspirations, was the beginning of a great cultural change process. Carried forward by new social movements that grew in the 1960s, the call for freedom came from the free speech movement in the universities, the women's movement, and the gay liberation movement; it came from the longing for self-actualization in humanistic psychology and the longing for liberation in the new spirituality. The peace and environmental movements followed the lead of the freedom movement.

Coexisting with the longing for freedom were the fears that preoccupied millions of people and that were formed by the Great Depression, the Holocaust, World War II, and for African Americans, the lynchings across the South. These were silent fears, fears you tried to keep hidden from your children. They were stirred mightily by the generation that changed the direction of our national life.

In the accompanying box, we list twenty kinds of movements associated with that change in direction, with the desire for freedom. All of them have strongly influenced the development of the Cultural Creative subculture. And those who became Cultural Creatives were immensely influential in shaping the later movements. Each movement contains anywhere from dozens to hundreds of organizations and groups. The first ones listed are the social and political movements, like the antiwar movement and the environmental movement. The last ones listed are those that address issues of consciousness and health. And in between are the movements that are a mix of political, social, and consciousness issues, like the women's movement. We also list, for comparison, five kinds of new conservative and backlash movements that have appeared since the 1960s. These are movements with values that the Cultural Creatives reject, like opposition to abortion and the ERA and support for militia organizations.

THE YEARNING

The emergence of the Cultural Creatives is rooted in the provocative education that our society began to receive in the 1960s. As thousands of young Americans became active agents of social change, they forced our nation to confront the most basic moral questions and set in motion changes that we are living out today. These "teachers" were mostly young, earnest, and furiously intent on telling the truths they were discovering. And the students who were most affected by this massive social learning process were, and still are, the ones listening and absorbing and eventually changing their values. They were the people who would become Cultural Creatives.

The social movements have inspired a new agenda. The range of issues that dominate public life—not only what's currently being debated in Washington, but what we talk about in our living rooms, in coffee shops and churches and synagogues, and in the state capitols and corporate boardrooms—is in the process of a profound redefinition. This change is occurring beyond the United States as well. As Vincent Harding reminds us, the songs of the black freedom

Twenty Kinds* of New Movements That Influenced Cultural Creatives

PRIMARILY SOCIAL AND POLITICAL ISSUES

- Advocacy for the poor, plus jobs and social justice movements

- Ethnic advocacy movements (Hispanic, Native American, etc.)

- Movements that support international NGOs (peace, third world development, environment)

- Civil rights movement (turned into freedom movement)

- Antinuclear movement (opposing nuclear weapons and nuclear power plants)

- Anti–Vietnam War movement (turned into broader peace movement)

- Environmental movement (forest conservation, regulation of industry, less pollution)

- Ecology movement (slow economic growth, change way of life, save the planet)

- Movements against violence and oppression (Amnesty International, Save the Children, sanctuary movement for Central American refugees)

A MIX OF POLITICAL, SOCIAL, AND CONSCIOUSNESS ISSUES

- Student movement (morphed into SDS and the New Left but also into psychedelics)

- Women's movements (political, feminist consciousness, and spirituality wings)

- Gay and lesbian liberation movements (both political and lifestyle wings)

PRIMARILY CONSCIOUSNESS AND CULTURAL ISSUES

- Human potential movement (humanistic psychology, bodywork)

- Holistic health and alternative health care movements

- Organic foods and vegetarian movements

- Psychedelic movement

- Spiritual psychology

- New Age movement

- New religions and Eastern spirituality

Five Kinds of New Conservative and Backlash Movements

All of these movements seem to have repelled the Cultural Creatives. Most are old-style movements that are primarily defined in positive or negative relationship to political authorities.

- Conservative movement (radical right, antitax, right-wing Republican, etc.)

- Religious Right (politicizing conservative religions: anti-abortion, anti-ERA, etc.)

- Anti-environmental movement (corporate-based "Astroturf" groups, Wise Use, etc.)

- Militia movement and neo-Nazi/Ku Klux Klan–related racist movements

- Libertarian movement

---

* We talk about "kinds" of cultural movements, even though the similarities and differences among hundreds of movement groups are likely to be in the eye of the beholder. Within each category of movement, there are dozens to hundreds of organizations. Not all who were involved in them became Cultural Creatives. We also list conservative movements because their backlash also shaped the new cultural movements and the emergence of Cultural Creatives.

movement—the cries and melodies of enslaved Africans in America—have spread worldwide. They were sung as the Berlin Wall was being razed, and in Eastern Europe and South Africa; the words of those songs were written on banners in Tiananmen Square. The inspiration came not from a contest for legal rights but "from the common hope which empowers people everywhere," Harding observes, "the deep yearning for a democratic experience which searches for the best possibilities—rather than the worst tendencies—within us all."[6]

This deep yearning is the sine qua non of a lived democracy, as opposed to one that is merely proclaimed in legal documents. Václav Havel, the brilliant dissident who became president of the Czech Republic, is very clear on this difference. Democracy depends on citizens feeling responsible for something more than their own little corner of safety, he says. It requires citizens with backbones. It must have citizens who insist on participating in their society, who hold and act on democracy from the deepest level, the level where religion itself is held. In a lived democracy, ideals that are written into a nation's constitution can actually catch fire to inspire and guide the life of its people.[7]

To understand how the Cultural Creatives learned to question the givens, challenge the social codes, and reframe the key issues that disempowered many parts of our society, we will look at two of the early social movements: the freedom movement and the women's movement. For all their drama, these movements were also submerged networks for cultural change. And they were intensive schools for advanced study in the moral, political, social, economic, legal, and educational issues of fundamental social change. Only after many decades of gestation is this clear. But those movements have prepared remarkably well for the emergence of some 50 million graduates who are intent on living in their daily lives much of what those movements hoped to teach.

THE BLACK FREEDOM MOVEMENT

To get a clear picture of Jim Crow, the segregated social code that prevailed in the South before the 1960s, it helps to see it through the eyes of a stranger, someone not yet inured to its "normalcy." Diane Nash was just such an outsider when she arrived in Nashville in 1959 to attend Fisk University. A native of Chicago, a shy and rather timid young woman, she was appalled by customs that her new friends barely noticed. On a date at the Tennessee State Fair, she encountered, for the first time in her life, signs for segregated rest rooms. WHITE ONLY, one sign announced, and the other, COLORED. She felt humiliated, as if she had been suddenly slapped hard across the face. But her date's bland acceptance of this blatant, legal discrimination shocked her even more. Other shocks soon followed. While shopping with friends in a large department store, she found that she could not enter the lunchroom. And then something clicked: the black people she had noticed calmly eating their lunches on the sidewalks of downtown Nashville, she realized, were sitting there because no nearby restaurants would allow them to enter.

As the sights and the shocks continued, Diane went through what journalist David Halberstam called a "remarkable transformation from scared young black student to black student samurai."[8] Within a year, she had become the chairman of the Nashville chapter of SNCC, the activists who led the sit-ins and later played a key role in the freedom rides that helped to eradicate legal segregation from the South.

Shocks are necessary, Anne Braden observes, if any growth is to come. There has to be turmoil of some kind, not violence, but inner, personal turmoil in the individual and shocks to the larger social body. As one of the relatively unsung group of white southerners who, at great risk, joined the freedom movement and "transgressed" the social and legal codes of segregation, Anne had her own shocks. Sitting with a group of students in Denver in 1997, she described her own shock the first time she was taken to jail. "So they took us into what they called 'protective custody,' took us to jail. And they were mumbling about how these outsiders were coming into Mississippi and didn't understand about Mississippi. . . . And I couldn't stand it any longer, and I said, 'Well, I don't really think I'm an outsider. I was a child in Jackson, and I have lived in Mississippi for a number of years, and I'm ashamed of this state today.' And one of the cops got absolutely furious. You know, it's the whole traitor thing. He turned around like he was going to hit me, but he didn't because this other cop stopped him.

"That was a very revealing moment for me because all of my life the police had been on my side. I didn't think of it that way, but I didn't bother about police, and they didn't bother you, in the world where I grew up. Except maybe if you were speeding, they might stop you, but if you talked to them real nice, they wouldn't give you a ticket. All of a sudden I realized I was on the other side. He said, 'You're not a real southern woman.' I said, 'No. I'm not your kind of a southern woman.'"[9]

In fact, Jim Crow, a term that probably grew out of a blackface minstrel show around 1830, did not begin in the South at all. It developed in the northern states before the Civil War, and it was a substitute for slavery—a varied, uneven, widespread system of discrimination, segregation, and repression in legal and extralegal codes, like those that eventually developed in the South after Reconstruction. It was in the South that legal segregation remained, so that is where the modern freedom movement began.[10]

All societies live by social codes. They tell us who we are and how to behave in our social roles as parents and children, workers and neighbors, citizens and churchgoers. Because we grow up with them from birth, they seem as natural as the rising and setting of the sun and the change of the seasons—unless we go to a land that has different codes. When northerners were shocked by the South, and southerners by the North, it was often the social codes they found most shocking.[11]

CHALLENGING THE JIM CROW CODE

Since Reconstruction, the freedom movement had been trying to change the social codes of Jim Crow and the legal codes of segregation. After the historic wrong of slavery was ended, new wrongs were imposed: legal segregation, disenfranchisement through poll taxes, literacy tests, intimidation, inadequate schools, discrimination by banks and employers, the constant indignities that came from exclusion from public facilities, and low-wage menial jobs. In parts of the rural South, a lynch law allowed the Ku Klux Klan, the White Citizens Councils, and individual whites to get away with murder and violence against blacks with no fear of investigation by the police.

In the 1950s, ninety years of Jim Crow had left African Americans in bad shape legally and financially. Everywhere in the South they were subject to Jim Crow laws, and everywhere in the North, the laws of the land were not enforced when they were harmed. They needed jobs, loans, and education if ever they were going to escape poverty.

In mainstream America, a disaffected group was supposed to solve its problems by ethnic pressure-group politics: trading favors, making deals, and delivering the vote. Established leaders bargained on behalf of "their people," while "their people" suffered in silence and worked hard so that eventually their children would be better off. To the political establishment, this process was the only game in town. If an ethnic group couldn't solve its problems this way, it was just too bad.

The one glaring exception to this ethnic-pressure-group game was "the Negroes." Respectable Negro leaders found themselves with very few bargaining chips. With their people at the bottom of the heap, they had few, if any, favors to trade. With voting laws against them, they couldn't deliver votes to politicians. They had no patronage to dispense, no campaign workers to get out the vote, and few campaign contributions to offer. Furthermore, the white population, in both the North and the South, was mostly indifferent to black problems. A large minority were actively hostile, while only a rare few were actively sympathetic.

Blacks had to find some way to flush out the accumulated sludge of racism and political foot-dragging that had been in place since Reconstruction. Under Thurgood Marshall, the NAACP Legal Fund tried to do it by nibbling away at the inner contradictions of segregation laws, for the entire decade after World War II. Its great triumph was the 1954 Supreme Court decision that ruled that the separate-but-equal doctrine in schools violated the Fourteenth Amendment. Within a year, however, the Court allowed southern states to delay desegregation. And segregationists in the South fought back with a campaign of massive resistance. The legal strategy had worked just fine, but as practical politics, it was already failing by 1955.

A Stroke of Genius

The second way the black community fought Jim Crow was so far from the usual pressure-group methods that black elders and deal makers at first did not recognize its genius. The freedom movement was, in effect, a children's revolution—a new kind of social movement with students and young ministers at the forefront. Its strategies were original and highly creative.

The new movement carried a message that few whites had fathomed: Jim Crow was devastating not just to African Americans but to all Americans. It was eating away at the core of our nation's values. The genius of the freedom movement was to invoke the nation's promises and ideals, laid out for all to see, in the Declaration of Independence, the Emancipation Proclamation, the Fourteenth Amendment, and the U.S. Constitution. The moral, rhetorical, and political brilliance of Martin Luther King, Jr., as the spokesman of the movement, was his ability to expose the old frames and to reframe segregation as an *American* problem. From the Montgomery bus boycott onward, King repeatedly connected African Americans' demands for freedom with the history of America's dreams for itself. As he worked to undo the cultural hypnosis of the old frames, he placed the meaning of protest in a new context. He reminded black people and the rest of the nation that the protests were motivated by a love of country and the highest moral values. This reframing appeared even in King's earliest speeches. He started his public career on that high note on the first evening of the Montgomery bus boycott.

Unraveling the Old Lies

King was twenty-six years old when he was hastily elected to head the black ministers organizing the boycott. The bus boycott had been successful for one day, and now the black community was gathering at the Holt Street Baptist Church. King, who usually spent a full day preparing a sermon, had scribbled down only a few notes. Pushing through the thousands of people gathered outside the church, he made his way to the pulpit.

"We are here," he told the enormous crowd packed into the balconies and aisles and standing in the street, listening on loudspeakers, "because first and foremost, we are American citizens, and we are determined to apply our citizenship to the fullness of its means." And then he went on to name the truth of what the people were feeling and to unravel the old lies about what black protest meant. "We are here this evening because we're tired now. Now let us say that we are not here advocating violence. We have overcome that." We are a Christian people, he said. The only weapon we have in our hands is the weapon of protest. And to be able to protest, he told the crowd, "is the glory of America, with all its faults. This is the glory of our democracy. If we were incarcerated behind the iron curtains of a Communistic nation, we couldn't do this. . . . But the great glory of American democracy is the right to protest for right."

Again and again he told the shouting, approving congregation, "We are not wrong." We are going to work to gain justice on the buses in this city, he said, and "if we are wrong, the Supreme Court of this nation is wrong. If we are wrong, God Almighty is wrong!" Tying their protest and their suffering to two high truths, he repeated: "If we are wrong, Jesus of Nazareth was merely a utopian dreamer and never came down to earth! If we are wrong, justice is a lie." And if anyone still harbored any doubts about the rightness of citizens and good Christians taking action, he delivered a soaring, rapturous, angry conclusion straight from the prophet Amos: "And we are determined here in Montgomery—to work and fight until justice runs down like water, and righteousness like a mighty stream!"[12]

The Power of Reframing

What King did in this speech was essential to the coming cultural mind-change and it set the pattern of protest movements for generations to come. The standard American interpretation of "the race problem" had been that it was just a matter of white prejudice: something individual, psychological, unchangeable. As far as most white Americans were concerned, prejudice "has nothing to do with me." This interpretation managed not to notice the economic, political, and other benefits of segregation to whites. And those benefits were most certainly there, because Jim Crow was not just psychological. It was part of the social order, a cultural code so pervasive that it shaped every institution and relationship it touched.

What preserved this code was a set of eyeglasses that virtually every American was given at birth. The frames for these eyeglasses were different for whites and blacks. The frames for whites organized facts and events in a way that made segregation look entirely natural. Looking through their cultural eyeglasses, whites saw who was entitled to be strong politically and who was weak, whose birthright gave access to good jobs and whose lot would be poverty, who had to be deferential and who not, and finally, regardless of actual appearance, who looked clean and good and who looked dirty and suspect until proven otherwise. Southern blacks, for their part, had their own set of frames. Theirs said, "Never question or protest injustice and poverty and disrespect. It will cost you and your family dearly." Their frames were held in place by deep and abiding fear of the brutal retaliation and loss of work that would almost certainly follow any protest.

When activists reframe a significant cultural context, they're like the child who shouts that the emperor is wearing no clothes. They expose a whole belief system for what it is—*a belief system,* not the natural order of things, not reality. Pretty soon everyone who is paying attention figures out that some group of people has constructed this belief system. Soon a question arises: Who's benefiting from keeping this view of reality in place? Then people who never before doubted the status quo, who took it as God-given and utterly legitimate, start to ask their own questions. They notice that they've been wearing distorting eyeglasses. Once they do so, they can choose to take them off and see reality in a new way. They can change their mind, their perspective, and their understanding about themselves. They also become free to take action in ways that they never considered before.

THE POWER OF NONVIOLENCE

Another piece of reframing also became a signature of the freedom movement: the tactics and logic of nonviolence. When Gandhi's independence movement expelled the British from India, it expected violence and decided to meet it with as much love as they could muster. By taking on suffering with dignity and showing empathy for their opponents, they intended to convert bystanders and even the opponents themselves.

The Reverend James Lawson was one of the freedom movement's leading teachers of nonviolence. A black minister from the urban North, he had served time in a federal prison as a conscientious objector to the Korean War and spent three years in India as a Methodist missionary. By the time he began to teach black students around Nashville in 1958, he could do the job well. But to the consternation of his angry young students, his instruction was focused on the power of love. He explained later that this focus was quite calculated. He did not want to set off his students' powerful emotions. Through role-playing and quiet, intelligent teaching, he taught the young activists to inoculate themselves against the shaming words and humiliating actions of whites.

Weaving together the heart of Gandhian philosophy with Christianity, he told them that true power lay in the rightness of their protest. "No matter how frightening the task and how dangerous the resistance, it will work to your advantage," he said. Others will see what you suffer, and they won't be able to sit on the sidelines. They will take your place. And what is more, as you act on your conscience, you will no longer be a handful of unknown students mounting a foolish challenge against an entrenched power structure. By your actions, you will be transformed. You will become, he said, "heroes, men and women who have been abused and arrested for seeking the most elemental of human rights."[13] And he was correct.

While nonviolence was Christian and moral, it was also something else of great importance: a tool that could strip away the mask of southern civility and reveal its violent underbelly to the whole nation. It was a way of making a moral statement in the course of breaking unjust laws.

The impact of television's coverage of the freedom movement is hard to overestimate. For the first time, a social movement had a powerful medium to amplify its protests, bringing millions of eyewitnesses and carrying its issues to all Americans. An immense public witnessed the sit-ins and marches and freedom rides on television. They saw police and state militia enforcing laws and, at the same time, committing moral crimes with their violence. Such images wedged open categories that had been nailed shut so long that nobody could remember how or why. They stayed with people and made them think.

The emotional drama and immediacy of television was far greater than that of newspaper coverage. It put enormous new pressures on the president and Congress to respond more strongly and honestly than they had to pressure-group politics. All the social movements that followed tried to emulate this success.

WALKING YOUR TALK

Finally, the freedom movement passed on one more social invention to the culture makers who would follow: "walking your talk." It meant that you didn't claim to be what you weren't actually living. A strong expression of the real meaning of this phrase comes from the Reverend C. T. Vivian, one of the freedom movement's most articulate speakers. With the fiery intensity that had marked his sermons throughout the 1960s, he told a rapt audience at the Iliff School of Theology in 1996 how the movement had catapulted him far beyond the safety of his church pulpit.

"Here I was preaching, both in Nashville and Chattanooga. Here you're preaching to people and trying to get them to hold on and understand and talking about love and truth and justice, and you are watching them suffer. . . . And you as the minister were not involved in that suffering directly. Yet you would be telling people, 'Be good. Be good.'

"Now, you're doing all that talking, but you're not involved in helping them overcome that condition—except for the talk. At what point do you grab hold and face the cause of their suffering, and then organize them in ways that stop their suffering? And in what ways do you then be worthy of the fact that you are loved, that they are loving you and supporting you and taking care of you . . . and you're doing nothing more than *talking*? If you are serious about your relationship, you've got to do a lot more than that."

C. T. Vivian and the other activists of the time had a conviction: You do not ask someone else to do what you aren't willing to do yourself. But they did the things they feared the most—they went to jail, faced fire hoses and men with clubs, took responsibility for their friends and fellow protesters. It swept them into the deepest fear they had ever known—but then it lifted them beyond that fear into a strength and steadfastness they had never expected.

Becoming Free

John Lewis is one of the outstanding examples of this kind of transformation. A founder of SNCC, he is now an influential congressman from Georgia. When he first left home in rural Alabama in the late 1950s, a serious boy headed for a Baptist college, one of the things he feared most was prison. Only bad people from bad families went there, his family had taught him. It was the most shameful of all things to be sent to jail. He also knew that terrible things could and often did happen there. A young black man might disappear and never be heard from again.

But when Lewis was arrested at a sit-in in 1960 for the first but certainly not the last time, his overwhelming fear disappeared. What made the difference was months of careful, loving teaching of nonviolence from Jim Lawson and the close bonds of companionship in that training. As a result, actually going to jail carried John Lewis across a formidable psychological and cultural divide. He went from feeling small and weak and afraid of the white power structure to being free. Years later, when he looked at the photographs of himself coming out of that first sit-in with police on either side, he said, "I had never had that much dignity before. It was exhilarating—it was something I had earned, the sense of the independence that comes to a free person."[14] What Lewis learned that day carried him into far more dangerous territory in the years that followed. He became the hero that Lawson had predicted.

Such heroism by activists had a huge impact on observers. Paul Begala, formerly an adviser in the Clinton White House, described what John Lewis meant to him, when he was interviewed along with a number of other men by the editors of *Esquire*. The editors wanted to know whether young men still had heroes.

"The world I was born into was designed for me: white, bright, and suburban," Begala explained, "so it shouldn't shock anyone that my faith in America is strong." But his hero, he said, was someone whose belief in America is hard to understand—John Lewis. "I was four years old when John Lewis walked into those club-wielding state troopers in Selma. [His] blood is on the Edmund Pettus Bridge in Selma, Alabama. His blood is in the bus station in Montgomery. John Lewis's blood consecrated lunch counters and back roads and dirty jail cells all across the American South." And yet Lewis still has faith in America, "in a system that was designed to keep him poor and powerless." That fact is astonishing and inspiring to Begala. "I live and work in a place and at a time when courage is defined as enduring a subpoena with dignity. So it is humbling to be in the presence of a man who faced down Bull Connor and his attack dogs, armed with nothing more than his courage, his conscience, and his convictions. If that ain't a hero, I don't know what is."[15]

John Lewis and other young people in the freedom movement definitely walked their talk. And those who joined them, the students who organized and demonstrated, learned that they could count on people whose actions matched their words. A trickle of participation turned into an avalanche. Youths in great numbers all over the country decided that they wanted to surpass their parents' generation in actually living out their values, and that this made their life more worthwhile.

"Walking your talk," the freedom movement's phrase, became central to the New Left and Free Speech movements that followed. Once again, it drew people from just nodding their heads or delivering blustering speeches into acting on their values and making them real. One way or another, it was used in every new social movement that followed. In the all-night meetings and councils of the freedom and peace movements, and the consciousness-raising groups of the women's movement, this specific insight about social action evolved into an even more basic conviction about living authentically. What you believe in your heart has to match what you do in your life, they said. And this also made them reject the cynicism and alienation they saw around them, in modern business, politics, and the media.

WOMEN CHALLENGE THE CODES

It was 1962, three years before white men deputized by the state of Alabama lashed out with clubs and clouds of tear gas at an orderly march of older, rural blacks on the Edmund Pettus Bridge, and before President Lyndon Johnson responded to that event and others with a strong voting rights act to Congress. Another social movement was about to begin. It had an exceedingly quiet start, almost as quiet as the slow, brave approach to that bridge in Selma on what came to be known as "Bloody Sunday." But where the freedom movement's march was covered by network television and the wire services, the new movement began with barely a ripple. And this was to be expected, because it was addressing what Betty Friedan memorably called "the problem that has no name."

It takes a kind of genius to name a problem that has no name, because if you do it honestly and if the timing is right, millions of people who have been stupified or hypnotized by that problem will wake up. Martin Luther King had that kind of genius when he named the problem of segregation an American problem, and when he reframed the black role as one of a courageous, necessary, moral activism. Betty Friedan showed that kind of genius when she named the set of social values that crippled women and stole their freedom to use their full capacities. And when she called the suburban home a "comfortable concentration camp" for women, she reframed the belief that talented, educated, bright women could possibly fulfill their "femininity" in suburban kitchens.[16]

To get a sense of the earthquake that *The Feminine Mystique* created across North America, and eventually in Europe and South America as well, it is best to sit down with a woman who read the book in those early years. Anne Kerr Linden was thirty years old, with two school-age daughters and an unusual husband who encouraged her to return to school for a master's degree. "It was a difficult, painful time," she told us. "Virtually everyone in my neighborhood in West Vancouver was very disapproving of my going back to school, and disgusted that I was planning to work afterward. The women told me that I was emasculating my husband. Both the men and the women were certain that my children would be ruined in some way or other. And I was rather shy and certainly not looking to be a pioneer of any sort."

One day as Anne was sitting on the beach, a neighbor woman hurried over to her, carrying a small brown paper bag. "I've been looking for you," she said with evident relief. "Here, take this. My husband won't allow me to have it in the house." Anne opened the bag to find *The Feminine Mystique.* It became a map for the path she was already walking, she told us, a path that until that moment had no name.

Like the freedom movement, the women's movement of the modern era was initially marked by a civil rights concern with discrimination. In 1966 the National Organization for Women (NOW) was formed, with Betty Friedan as president. Explicitly political, it was dedicated to gaining full equality for women in public life, including employment, education, and political participation. It was the first and oldest branch of the movement, soon to be called "equal rights feminism."

THE POLITICAL TAR BABY

When you've got a national problem in public life, you go political with it, right? Those who start a political movement are usually convinced that politics alone will make the critical difference. But as we've just seen in the early civil rights movement, the old ways of solving problems may be inadequate. When the NAACP under Thurgood Marshall struggled to end school segregation, it gained great legal victories. But at a deeper, more practical level, the old culture was rolling those victories back.

So it was with the highly visible political arm of the women's movement. Just like Bre'r Rabbit with Tar Baby, the harder they hit, the more they got stuck. "Large P politics"—the politics of elections, government regulation, and the passage of laws in Washington, the state capitols, and big-city government—is an intricate game. It virtually dictates what issues its political players can take up and what they can say in open public debates. Political activists routinely have to juggle a whole array of necessities: who to make deals with, how to balance multiple constituencies to look powerful, how to lobby with legislatures in the style of pressure-group politics, how to look good in the press, how to reframe and spin news releases, how to appeal to contributors, and finally, how to deliver voter blocs.

No wonder the burnout rate for the political arm of the women's movement was so high. Tar Baby forced the activists to stay with conventional political strategies, because that's what could win agreement from all the factions. But there was no room for cultural innovation. One of the most important insights that feminists learned was this: When you are trying to change the old culture, you must not accept the solutions supplied by that culture. You have to discover or invent your own.

BREAKING THE SPELLS

"In concealed workshops, Spinsters unsnarl, unknot, untie, unweave," feminist Mary Daly wrote. "We knit, knot, interlace, entwine, whirl and twirl," mending a consciousness that has been split against itself, that has focused only on externals. Feminists, said Daly, "spin out the Self's own integrity, [to] break the spell of the fathers' clocks."[17]

Most social movements have two arms: the political and the cultural. The cultural arm is often much bigger, and here, as Daly suggests, people have time to explore new values, ways of life, and interpretations of events, to craft and weave new philosophies, to write new friendship and personal stories. Contrary to the convictions of the political arm, the cultural arm is at least as important, and sometimes far more so, in its effects on the culture. The news media, government and industry, and academia tend to reinforce the political arm's view of its own importance. But the spell-breaking power of the cultural arms takes place in submerged networks.

In the women's movement, a second, "younger branch" of women emerged that set about "unsnarling, unknotting, untying, and unweaving" millennia of cultural hypnosis.[18] Away from fame and public visibility, they puzzled out the culture's assumptions and reframed them in ways that made new kinds of sense. Culture is made in reframing old problems and familiar ideas into whole new forms, new poetry, and new images; and in developing a new sense of identity for those who join the movement for cultural change.

The cultural arm of the women's movement began with small groups of friends from the freedom movement and the New Left who had grown tired of their usual assignments: kitchen work, mimeographing, typing, and cleaning. "The Movement is supposed to be for human liberation," Marge Piercy complained in the late 1960s. "How come the condition of women inside it is not better than outside?"[19] Their tentative objections were met by male reactions ranging from lofty contempt to fury. Thereupon they stalked out of the kitchens and left behind the office work at SDS, SNCC, and a host of other groups dominated by men.

By 1967 small consciousness-raising groups were sprouting up across the country. Women read about these groups in movement periodicals and newspaper and magazine articles.[20] Some merely heard rumors at third hand. With almost no information but a willingness to experiment, they met in one another's living rooms and the ever-important church basements, in YWCAs and dormitories. They told one another things they'd never said and sometimes never thought before. And they did something that was even more important—they listened to one another. In the words of theologian Nelle Morton, they were "hearing each other into speech."[21] Decades later, women were still clear on their aching need for mutual listening. There is an immense difference, one writer explained, "between having permission to speak and enjoying the hope that someone might actually listen to you."[22]

THE TRUTH ABOUT TAR BABY

These women encountered another kind of Tar Baby, one much stickier and harder to get free of than the political one: the social codes, the religious texts, the literature and art and history that for millennia had been written down and interpreted from a male point of view. The result was that many women felt that they did not know what it meant to be a woman. And without that understanding, it was almost impossible to know themselves. Historian Gerda Lerner, reviewing a thousand years of women's critiques of biblical texts, describes how over and over again women repeated the thoughts of earlier generations whose work was not preserved. "Endlessly," she writes, "generation after generation of Penelopes rewove the unraveled fabric only to unravel it again." After fifteen hundred years of reweaving, women finally saw that "their condition was societally determined."[23] But the next step—joining with other women to remedy the wrongs—was much harder to accomplish.

What made it so devilishly hard was the lying: lying about the facts of their own lives and lying about their feelings. The polite term for it is *cultural conditioning*. It means being convinced, by the time you are an adolescent, that honesty is too risky, too "stupid, selfish, rude, or mean" to be worth the trouble. This is what Lyn Mikel Brown and Carol Gilligan reported in their study of a hundred adolescent girls' development.[24] It's also what Carolyn Heilbrun described in her study of the lives of women writers. Until well into the twentieth century, she wrote, it was impossible for women to admit in their autobiographies "the claim of achievement, the admission of ambition, the recognition that accomplishment was neither luck nor the result of the efforts or generosity of others." As a result, until recently, women have "had no models on which to form their lives, nor could they themselves become mentors since they did not tell the truth about their lives."[25]

Women's frank explorations of truth came when they recognized what their cultural conditioning had cost them. The toll, they said, was immense: betrayal of oneself, disconnection from genuine intimacy with others, and a lack of accountability to the larger community and the planet.

The first step was to "dive into the wreck," as poet Adrienne Rich put it. Just as young African Americans in the freedom movement had invented ways to tear off the polite cultural frames around racism, feminists had to plumb below the culture's myths of civility, romance, and power. But where the freedom movement's deconstructing and reframing were directed externally, the women's work was much more intimate.

When women said "the personal is political," this is what they meant. They believed that if they did not tell the truth about their lives, they had nothing to trust and nothing to base their actions on. The personal was not just political—it was foundational. What they advocated had to spring from, or at least be consistent with, what they knew most intimately and directly from their own experience.

The people who became the Cultural Creatives were strongly affected by this perspective. They learned that directly experienced truth brought a radical new way of slipping free from the heavy-handed authority of centuries. It was a basis for breaking out of political and medical and church doctrines, of Big Daddy in all his forms. It extended the powerful insights of the freedom movement's "walking your talk" to a deeply personal meaning of authenticity. It was women who opened this door most decisively because they had to. Learning from their own experience was, in many cases, the only thing they could trust.

Fertile Darkness

But if liberation is simply a matter of turning to one's own truth, then why hadn't women always done this? Why hadn't they seen beyond the dominant cultural codes that told them they had little to contribute to civilization, that they were passive and inferior to men? Why hadn't African Americans, and gays and lesbians done the same? Why haven't all of us seen beneath the cultural lies of racism, and nuclear arms as a "deterrent," and our disastrous shortsightedness about our planetary future, and a host of other blind assumptions?

One reason is that challenging existing social codes takes a kind of brilliance, a laser beam slicing through the old frames of reference to a new clarity about what is possible. Another reason is that when you stop doing and sit still until your mind chatter slows down, sooner or later you experience nothingness. On the way there, all of the sad, angry, blaming opinions of yourself that you've kept at bay with busyness fling themselves into your mind.

The "dark core," Virginia Woolf named it. It is the place underneath the masks: the void, the creative womb, the matrix. The "dark core" is what we fear, and what will free us. It's the mystic's dark night of the soul—and the fertile openness that brings us to our true self. It means finding the ground of being in ourselves rather than striving to fit society's images. But again, as with social codes, it's so easy to get caught in the old story about who we are, and why we are this way, and why we can never be different. To be willing to dive down deep, into the wreck or the void—fertile or otherwise—takes immense courage.

It also takes a sense that what we discover will be important, a trust that the undoing and being undone will yield some richness, some benefit, not just for ourselves but for others. An extraordinarily important contribution of early consciousness-raising groups was to provide this sense. Today many supportive environments lead to this kind of exploration, especially within consciousness movements: humanistic and transpersonal psychology, the various meditative practices in Buddhism, mystical Christianity, and Judaism, the caregiving in groups for HIV men and women, hospice programs, wisdom circles modeled on Native American teachings, and many others.[26]

These "awakenings," as Carol Christ calls them, did not happen—probably could not have happened—by women going off into solitude.[27] They arose in the context of community, in relationship to other women: "inspiring the behavior" in each other to act outside the culture's categories, "breaking the silence" and "taking back the night," as they found links to each other and looked for remedies for the larger society.

WHERE DID EVERYBODY GO?

The women's movement publicly emerged in August 1970, when the older equal rights feminists and the younger women's liberation groups came together in their first mass mobilization. Tens of thousands of women went "on strike" for equality in the largest protest for women in U.S. history. In Chicago there were sit-ins at restaurants that barred women. In downtown Minneapolis guerrilla theater performances portrayed key figures in the abortion drama. And in New York City thousands of women marched down Fifth Avenue carrying signs that read "Eve was framed" and "End human sacrifice! Don't get married!"[28]

The size of the mobilization meant that the women's movement would now have to be taken seriously. And it was, both as a political movement and as a much less visible cultural movement. Together, the two parts set off depth charges through Western culture. But by the end of the 1980s, most of the activism seemed to have disappeared. Marches and consciousness-raising groups were no more. A lot of activists wondered, "Where did everybody go?" In Wendy Wasserstein's play *The Heidi Chronicles,* Heidi Holland asks this question as the play moves her through the prehistoric unenlightened days to the consciousness-raising groups of the 1970s and into the era of "super-women" and alienation. "It's just that I feel stranded," Heidi tells her high school alumnae association. "And I thought the whole point was that we wouldn't feel stranded. I thought the point was we were all in this together."

It wasn't only feminists who asked these questions, and it wasn't only activists. The huge population of sympathizers and supporters who had changed their minds and their lives as a result of the women's movement were wondering the same thing. In a 1988 interview after the play opened, Wasserstein reflected sadly, "If we were all in this together, why does it feel so separate now? . . . What happened to these movements? What happened to a generation together?" And what happened "to the 'we' that wanted to make a better world," she asked, the "we" who wanted to make sure "that not only can you pursue your potential, but that others can too? [To] think about others, as well as about 'me'?"[29]

Here is what happened:

- They focused on local rather than national issues.
- The news media drastically cut back its coverage of the movement.
- The cultural arm continued as always, largely invisible to outsiders.
- Parts of the political arm entered the mainstream.

THEY WENT LOCAL

Many of the sympathetic, interested women who had been profoundly affected by the movement were disheartened by the attempted rollbacks of the Reagan years. The media told them that 1960s activists had gone directly from the barricades to Wall Street. But that's not really what happened. In *Beyond the Barricades: The Sixties Generation Grows Up,* sociologist Richard Flacks showed that 1960s activists did not go the way of a yuppie sellout. They continued to believe the same things as they had earlier, and they were still involved in political action in the 1970s. But now they were engaged in grassroots groups closer to home and therefore were less visible to the national media.[30]

What Flacks found was generally true for many new-social-movement activists in the 1980s and 1990s as well. After a period of national visibility, they continued primarily with local action. The environmental movement, for example, was started less as a national movement than as thousands of local community actions, operating in tandem with more visible national organizations. And when national organizations didn't seem to be serving them, the activists returned to local work.

THE NEWS MEDIA CUT COVERAGE

The news media had much less interest in covering the new social movements in the 1980s than in the early days of the freedom movement and the anti–Vietnam War protests. Perhaps the media were suspicious of movement desires to manipulate coverage, as some thought, or perhaps the media were serving the conservative interests of advertisers. Certainly they did not seem interested in the substance of what demonstrators had to say. The documentary *Fear and Favor in the Newsroom* exposes the degree of advertiser-driven bias in media coverage of issues raised by local movements.[31]

Marilyn Ginsberg, a psychotherapist who has participated in several movements, recalled that "a large contingent of my women friends flew up from L.A. to the San Francisco Bay Area to join a march of fifty thousand women for peace and nobody covered it. And in the spring of 1999, I went to another march for better medical treatment of breast cancer, and the same thing happened. This time it was in L.A. And again, amazingly, nobody covered it, not even the *L.A. Times*. I've grown to distrust the media, because I can't help wondering how much is happening that never makes it into the news."

Protests are no longer regarded as interesting. If a protest is no bigger than or markedly different from the last one, it is declared to be "not news." The publisher of one respected national newspaper told us that his decisions were not biased by advertisers. Rather, "if you're sitting in the seat of judgment on these questions," he said, "the decision is based on how many readers you think care about the issue and whether there's something *new*. Because the protests were repeated so often with the same message, our coverage went down."

Much of television news has a tabloid quality. Driven by a race for audience ratings, it has become another form of entertainment. This reinforces its inclination to avoid substantial issues. Sociologist and media observer Todd Gitlin argues that the decline of movement coverage reflects traditional assumptions in the news media: "News concerns the event, not the underlying condition; the person, not the group; conflict, not consensus; the fact that 'advances the story,' not the one that explains it."[32]

This tendency has worsened in recent years. The news industry believes that if news is to hold the interest of the audience, who want to be entertained, it should resemble a sports event or soap opera. "What's news," by that criterion, is bad news—conflict, drama, shady deals, objectionable behavior—and horse race politics, and the personalities and ambitions of politicians. Politics thus becomes a spectator sport, not something citizens need to be concerned about.[33] The strategic moves of politicians are the cynical frame through which public issues are viewed. A movement's idealism must be discounted because it doesn't fit the story line. When there's a protest, it's more important to cover what a politician said about it, and what strategy he's using, than to cover what the protest is about. The movement behind the protest, and its concerns, gets no coverage at all. As journalist and former editor James Fallows argues in *Breaking the News,* the net effect of punditry, avoidance of issues, cynicism, and "infotainment" is that news coverage diminishes citizens' involvement in the workings of democracy.

In short, the news business seriously misleads the public, and the movements themselves, about what's going on. But the problem is not just the bias we know about—it's the hole in the news that we don't know about. Most of us assume that the news media are out there covering what's going on. Apparently it's not so.

THE CULTURAL ARMS ARE LESS VISIBLE

As we mentioned earlier, the cultural arms of the movements were not nearly as visible as their political parts. Charlene Spretnak, a founder and chronicler of the women's spirituality movement, describes the cultural arm as "a rich array of cultural responses stemming from a strong impulse to create positive alternatives." This meant "a flowering of women's expression in poetry, music, literature, and spirituality. For some it also meant developing a women's culture, composed of businesses and services run by and for women and their children; thousands of such enterprises were in place by 1973. It became clear by the following year that the women's culture would not be spiritually barren."[34]

Feminist spirituality was one example of this flowering. Many women found it more enlivening and meaningful than purely political activism. Some newly spiritual women brought their awareness into their political action, especially in dramatic confrontations with the churches. Others left the political scene, slowed down, and found ways to live in closer connection to the natural world. They met with friends to create rituals honoring the seasons and births and deaths and other passages, to meditate, and generally to celebrate what they regarded as the larger community of life.

The cultural arms of other movements developed differently, of course. But in every case, the submerged networks offered personal support and a place for nurturing fresh ideas and creative expressions that were inestimably important to the spread of the movements. Rarely were these networks known to the wider public.

SOME PARTS WENT MAINSTREAM

The final reason why the movements seemed to disappear was that many of their activities became so popular, they entered the mainstream. For example, in Toronto, WRECS, a free counseling and education service for women, began in the 1960s with six volunteers. It was so effective and popular that by the mid-1970s, foundations supported the service and paid for several full-time staff members. By the 1980s, the service was sponsored by the provincial government. Another example is the freedom movement's success in integrating many schools and registering voters in the South, until finally local and state governments took over the movement's work in this area.

For the peace movement, the results were even more obvious. In the 1980s the Vietnam War was long over, the draft had ended, and a number of draft resisters had accepted amnesty. So obvious was the danger of nuclear war that most of the major powers officially limited nuclear arms and worked for disarmament—much to the dismay of the cold war establishment. And the environmental movement became so successful that Washington lawyers took over the task of getting industry to clean up its pollution and reduce its destruction of natural areas. The leading edge of environmentalism moved on to local and planetary ecological issues, including global warming and extinction of species.

THE GIFTS

What is the legacy, after all, of the new social movements? The short answer is that they have changed our national mind. Our ideals and values are no longer so compromised by the racism, sexism, and other denials of a half century ago. We still have a very long way to go, but it is critically important that we have begun. Vincent Harding, who in his seventies is an honored elder of the freedom movement, considers himself also a part of any movement that furthers democracy by challenging unjust codes. Such movements bequeath a great gift that is almost always unwelcome, he says. A nation needs a "kind of wisdom and maturity to recognize the possibility that those who challenge our status quo may be offering us all a gift. The central idea is not hard to grasp . . . there are times in our experience when we are living lives which contradict and deny the best truths that we claim for ourselves. Therefore we are crippling ourselves, damaging our spirits, but have grown accustomed to the process."[35] Any movement that helps us wake up from that self-deception gives us a gift.

If we look again at the movements since the 1960s with this in mind, we can better understand the nature of their legacy. The chart gives an overview of the movements in terms of their primary emphasis: politics, culture, or consciousness. The key feature for our present interest is the middle column, which shows movements that challenged the social codes of mainstream culture. These have been the most successful, in two senses: they developed moral publics that numbered in the tens of millions; and they changed the hearts and minds of Americans so significantly that the old social codes are no longer acceptable to most of us. This is not to say that the movements have won all their objectives, or prevailed over their opponents in Washington, D.C., and elsewhere, or that the pundits and political elites approve of them. By "success," we mean that they succeeded in changing the culture.

Look down the center column, and you'll recognize the very movements that challenged and delegitimated the old social codes: the freedom movement, the peace movement, the ecology movement, the student movement, and so on. And notice something else: the successes have come predominately through the cultural arms of *both* the new social movements and the consciousness movements. Some (like the antiwar movement) started as political movements and broadened out to challenge codes and emphasize reframing, while others started with purely inner aims (like the human potential movement) and broadened out to challenge codes and try to change the culture. In a third alternative, a movement (like gay and lesbian liberation) actually began by challenging codes, then broadened to develop political and consciousness arms.

Overall, movements that exclusively tried to influence politics (like the jobs and social justice movement) seem to have been much less successful in affecting American life. The consciousness movements, which kept their exclusive focus on spiritual or psychological change, may have been equally limited, but we will look more closely at this last point in Chapter Six.

What is missing from the chart, simply because the graphics cannot show it, is the extensive interchange that now goes on among the movements. This con-

Movements Important to Cultural Creatives

Political Movements Challenge Establishment	Cultural Arms Challenge Codes	Consciousness Movements Change Individuals or Culture
Take direct action in political or economic arenas, only for changing actions/policies "out there" in the world	Take direct action to change many areas of social life, beyond "normal politics"; educate moral publics	Change own psyche, culture, world-view, way of life. Both direct personal action and change "in here"; private and apolitical

Broadening Political Movements into Cultural Movements,
Challenging First the Establishment, then Cultural Codes

Civil rights movement ⟶ Black freedom movement

Antinuclear movement and ⟶ Broader peace movement
anti–Vietnam War

Environmental movement ⟶ Ecology movement (slow economic
(regulation, less pollution)   growth, change lifestyles, save the planet)

Cultural Change Movements That Start by Challenging the Codes, Then Split or Differentiate
(Some parts also blend political with cultural; others also blend cultural and consciousness movements)

SDS and New Left ⟵ Student movement ⟶ Psychedelic movement

Feminist politics and social critiques ⟵ Women's movement ⟶ Feminist consciousness and spirituality

Gay rights and AIDS activism ⟵ Gay/lesbian lib ⟶ Camp, gay pride, drag scene

Movements That Start with Personal Change,
Then Broaden into Challenging Social and Cultural Codes

Psychological sophistication of most ⟵ Human potential movement,
movements, much of society   alternative psychotherapies

Alternative health care ⟵ Holistic health

Natural/organic foods ⟵ Vegetarianism

Political-Economic Movements Single-Issue Politics Only	Movements that don't challenge codes are less successful: they have less influence on the culture and create smaller moral publics	Personal Change Focus Only
Advocacy for the poor, and jobs and social justice		Psychedelic and hippie
Ethnic advocacy (Hispanic, Native American, etc.)		Spiritual psychology
Sanctuary for Central American refugees		New religions and Eastern spirituality

Note: This diagram does not show the large amount of interchange among different kinds of social movements (vertically) within each column, especially in the cultural arms of movements.

vergence is developing into a great current of change for our larger culture. The Cultural Creatives are involved in this change in two ways: they learn from the new movements, and they support many of the movements. There is, in other words, a spiraling effect of influence between the movements and the Cultural Creatives, as we'll see in more detail in Chapter Seven.

As a society, we all have gained from the new social movements, but the Cultural Creatives are probably the greatest beneficiaries. Our research shows that they are the part of the population who have been listening, learning, and—as our teachers used to say in grade school—"applying" what they learned. Activists may ask in dismay, "Where did everybody go?" but when we present our research on Cultural Creatives, people ask in astonishment, "Where did everybody come from?" The new social movements, larger and more influential than anyone imagined, had their greatest influence on the people who have become Cultural Creatives. And as we shall see, the Cultural Creatives in turn have helped to shape and further develop these movements as well as the consciousness movements.

We turn now to the most successful of all the movements, one that has made sympathizers of Moderns and Traditionals as well as Cultural Creatives: the environmental movement. It has been immensely important to the Cultural Creatives in particular, in calling forth their most energetic efforts and inventive responses to the urgent problems that affect our planet and our future.

chapter five

turning green

the natural world has been one of our great sources of learning, not only for what it is in itself but for the way we love it ("we" meaning the great majority of people on the planet who care about preserving and sustaining the Earth). Just as the black freedom movement and women's movement helped to shift our cultural priorities, so too has our concern for what was long called simply "the environment." This chapter is about how concern for the natural world has come about and how a massive subterranean river of cultural change is now surfacing. As it turns out, the Cultural Creatives are leading the way. "The environment" means much more than merely "our surroundings." Alice Walker says it simply and directly:[1]

> We have a beautiful
> mother
> Her hills
> are buffaloes
> Her buffaloes
> hills.
>
> We have a beautiful
> mother
> Her oceans
> Are wombs
> Her wombs
> oceans.

We have a beautiful
mother
Her teeth
the white stones
at the edge
of the water
the summer grasses
her plentiful hair.

We have a beautiful
mother
Her green lap
immense
Her brown embrace
eternal
Her blue body
everything we know.

The environmental movement is the most successful of all the new social movements. It has succeeded in changing the central beliefs and desires of the population—not just in the United States or even the West but in the entire world. In opinion surveys, 70 to 90 percent of people in most countries worldwide are deeply concerned about the environment. One twenty-four-nation study covering both the developed and the developing world found "virtually world-wide citizen awareness that our planet is indeed in poor health, and great concern for its future well-being." People in poorer nations are just as concerned about environmental issues as people in richer nations, if not more so. The worse the national environment, the greater the concern.[2]

The level of concern in the United States is about average, at 85 percent. In a 1999 survey for the EPA, American LIVES found that 79 percent of Americans agree with the strongest possible position favoring changing our way of life to aid ecological sustainability. So do 96 percent of Cultural Creatives. A team of anthropologists recently found that the sacredness of nature has so completely become a part of our central belief system in the West that it plays the same kind of role as a religious ideal. We'll give more details about this later in the chapter.

In half a century, most people in the West have done an about-face in their beliefs about the natural world. We have stopped regarding it as a storehouse to plunder, or a resource to provide us with work and wealth, and we've begun to accept it as our home. Most of us now identify our own grandchildren's future with the future of the natural world. We see, as biologist David Suzuki puts it, that "we are one brief generation in the long march of time; the future is not ours to erase."[3] This perspective represents a stupendous change in our collective consciousness. It shifts our focus from self-centered convenience to an awareness of our interdependence with nature.

A cultural change this big must have many origins. One cause, in the West, is our greater education and affluence. Releasing us from a daily fight for survival, our advantages allow us to take in new information. Another cause is the work of the environmental and ecology movements. And finally, a profound shift in awareness grows out of our urgent concerns for the dangers confronting the Earth—and therefore ourselves. No matter how self-serving we may be, we all basically recognize the truth of the Indian proverb: The frog does not drink up the pond in which he lives.[4]

At the beginning of the environmental movement, naturalist Aldo Leopold described his own deep feeling about the natural world. Once you change your mind about what the environment is for, he said, you change your mind about everything.[5] Fifty years later, this statement can serve as a succinct insight into the Cultural Creatives' worldview and values. They have changed their minds about what it is all *for,* and that changes everything. They are the strongest, most consistent of the three subcultures in their commitment to the Earth, in valuing the natural world for itself, and in regarding it as sacred. The Earth does not belong to us, they say. We belong to the Earth.

While worldwide concern is growing fast, the planetary environment is deteriorating even faster. There is overwhelming agreement that unless we move quickly as a whole planet, we will face an avalanche of disastrous consequences. Yet some of the biggest and most powerful institutions of the modern world are battling to safeguard their power and profits by opposing these changes. Right now, there seems to be a stand-off between the concerns of three-quarters of the world's population and the prerogatives of the corporations, governments, and the wealthy elites that benefit from things as they are.

Cultural Creatives are urging the environmental movement into a new phase. Having educated us through protests and information, some are moving beyond that now, to develop new kinds of businesses, technologies, and cooperative ventures. Others are creating sculptures, ritual theater pieces, dance performances, and novels and poetry. These new solutions and inventions may carry us forward to a new way of life, perhaps a new kind of civilization, across the planet.

But before we can look forward, we must look back to the many seedbeds that nurtured the Cultural Creatives. In this chapter, we'll focus on the birth and development of the environmental movement because it is one of the richest parts of the story. Insights and solutions worked out over a whole century in this movement are guiding the emerging culture today.

AN END TO THE GILDED AGE

The environmental movement is roughly a century old. Its beginning was one sign of the end of the Gilded Age, of exploitation by robber barons. But the word *environment* was not yet used. The key word was *conservation.* The most famous conservationist in this period was the naturalist John Muir. His writings on the Sierra Nevada wilderness inspired initiatives for national parks and forest preservation. The new life he wrote about, the beauty "unfolding, unrolling in glorious exuberant extravagance" that one meets in the mountains "hushed by solemn-sounding waterfalls and many small soothing voices" was deeply inviting to all who read about it. More than inviting, Muir's verbal pictures were indelible.[6] Generations afterward, environmental activists tell stories of how their work began when they read John Muir's descriptions of rejoicing in the natural world.

The conservation movement started as an attempt by wealthy nature lovers to protect natural beauty spots and ancient forests from depredations by loggers, miners, ranchers, and shortsighted developers. The Sierra Club and the Audubon Society are examples of such conservation clubs, started exclusively by rich, WASP men. Slowly, as they shifted from defense of beautiful areas to advocacy for nature in its own right, they became more democratic and diverse. But they met with intense opposition and hostility from financial, timber, mining, ranching, industrial, and agricultural interests. Teddy Roosevelt was one of these renegade disturbers of the status quo, often called "a traitor to his class" by wealthy Eastern Republicans.

THE ANCESTOR'S GIFT

William Kent was another renegade, a wealthy landowner who later became a California state legislator. His efforts were so consequential and so inspiring that, along with John Muir and a few others, Kent deserves to be called a venerable ancestor of the Cultural Creatives.

"It must have been about 1890," Kent penned in a neat hand in his private memoir, "when the necessity of saving the last portion of virgin redwoods in Marin County, California, was first urged upon my attention."[7] Kent had been active in Chicago and San Francisco government reform, and he must have seemed like a promising savior for the last of the big trees. All that remained of the forested valleys along San Francisco Bay were about three hundred acres of virgin redwoods and Douglas fir. They grew in a place called Redwood Canyon, which was protected by a high ridge too steep to be overcome by the lumbering methods of the time.

"I had never seen the canyon and had no idea of taking up the matter of saving woods," Kent noted briskly. In 1903, Lovell White, president of the Tamalpais Land and Water Company, which owned the canyon, asked Kent for help. But Kent was heavily in debt and told White flatly that he "could not afford to own any more white elephants." Besides, Kent demanded, why didn't the company preserve the woods itself? White replied that it was impossible. "Unless I would buy the woods," Kent wrote, "Mr. White informed me they would probably be cut down."

He thought about White's offer again and again over the next few days and finally rode over on horseback to have a look at the canyon. Dismounting and walking among the immense trees, he was seized by some irresistible attraction. "The beauty of the place got on my mind," he wrote, "and I could not forget the situation."

Kent bought the land for $45,000. According to his wife, Elizabeth, "it meant borrowing and adding to the debts which at that time were a heavy burden and anxiety. And when [I] demurred at his taking this additional responsibility, all discussion was silenced by his reply . . . : 'If we lost all the money we have and saved those trees, it would be worthwhile, wouldn't it?'"

Kent was clear that his purchase was "for preservation, and not for exploitation," but he had not decided who could best preserve it: "I had long been worrying about how to dispose of the land—whether I would give it to the State or the University or the Federal Government." The matter was brought to a crisis when the North Coast Water Company started condemnation proceedings on the land. They intended to create a reservoir in Redwood Canyon, destroying most of the virgin forest and selling the timber. Since domestic water supplies had legally higher use value than land held by individuals, the forest Kent had tried so hard to preserve was once more under a death sentence.

What followed was a whirlwind of wheeling and dealing through the highest levels of government. The chief inspector of the U.S. Forest Service, F. E. Olmsted, suggested that Kent use the Monument Act, which allowed the federal government to accept lands of historic or other great interest from private individuals. Kent immediately applied to Gifford Pinchot, head of the Forest Service, who in turn went directly to Theodore Roosevelt.

Meanwhile Kent was busy on other fronts as well. "I am frank to confess," he recorded in his journal, "that I did as much advertising as possible of the woods in order that the country might be stirred up and public opinion focused to prevent the depredation and ruin" that would result from the condemnation proceedings. He arranged with photographers to take countless pictures of the redwoods, invited college professors to write the history of the great trees, and asked his friend John Muir and other nature lovers to compose "word pictures." All of this he not only advertised but sent to the secretary of the interior and to President Roosevelt.

Finally, on Thursday, January 9, 1908, *The Marin Journal* blazed with the headline MARIN COUNTY HAS A NATIONAL PARK, and in just slightly smaller type: GENEROUS ACT AND QUICK WORK BY WM. KENT. WATER COMPANY BLOCKED FROM DESPOILING GIANT TREES.

But despite the headlines and the celebration that greeted Kent's gift, the owners of the water company were outraged. They told everyone who would listen that Kent had stolen the land from under them and was, moreover, depriving the good citizens of Marin County of a reservoir they most certainly would need sometime in the future. The good citizens themselves were divided. Some refused to believe that a big property owner like Kent could be acting altruistically. He had to have ulterior motives. Rumors spread like a summer brushfire across Marin's thirsty hills.

Kent's wife, Elizabeth, and his sons and daughters-in-law found themselves in the heat of a firestorm of daily gossip. His new daughter-in-law, Anne, who had recently arrived from the East Coast, was most perplexed, and when she could bear it no longer, she approached the elder Kent. "Dad, why are you going to all this trouble, even going in debt, when so many people are attacking your character? Why not back out?"

"Anne, my dear," Kent replied, "don't worry about those people. The children I'm buying these woods for are not even born yet."

Kent had one request of President Roosevelt: he wanted Redwood Canyon to be renamed to honor John Muir. Two weeks later, he received an enthusiastic letter from the president, thanking him but urging him to reconsider his request. "I have a very great admiration for John Muir," Roosevelt wrote, "but after all, my dear sir, this is your gift . . . and I should greatly like to name [it] the Kent Monument if you will permit it."

Kent would have none of it. He wrote back immediately, explaining that "so many millions of better people have died forgotten that to stencil one's name on a benefaction" seems to imply that immortality can be bought. Besides, he added, "I have five good, husky boys that I am trying to bring up to a knowledge of democracy and realizing the sense of rights of the 'other fellow.' . . . If these boys cannot keep the name of Kent alive, I am willing it should be forgotten."

Roosevelt's answer arrived the following week: "By George! You are right. It is enough to do the deed and not to desire, as you say, to 'stencil one's own name on the benefaction.' Good for you, and for the five boys who are to keep the name of Kent alive! I have four who I hope will do the same thing by the name of Roosevelt."

Today, about 2 million people visit awe-inspiring Muir Woods National Monument each year. One of the regular visitors is William Kent's granddaughter. Now in her seventies, with perfectly white hair braided on top of her head, Martye Kent goes down to walk through the woods from time to time. "I like to see the children and adults from all over the world craning their necks and laughing and trying to stretch their arms around the gifts that Grandpa provided for them, long before they were born," she told us.

THE SACRED GROVE

In our time, such marvelous gifts can still be given. About five hours north of Muir Woods is Humboldt County, the heart of the recent battles over logging the last of the old-growth forests. Here about 850 women have set out to save fourteen acres of redwoods in a forest they call the Sacred Grove.

Catherine Allport, the initiator of the project, told us how it began. She had been invited, along with seven other women, to a retreat at Whitethorn Monastery, near the Oregon border. To her delight, they spent the weekend walking through the rain forest along the Mattole River. They were guided along the Mattole, the headwaters home of the wild salmon, by one of the monks from the monastery. One afternoon, he brought the women to a small forest with thousand-year-old virgin-growth redwood trees. Someone asked if this place had a name. "Raven's Watch," the monk replied.

Catherine explained to us, "The raven in Native American mythology is the bird of death. As soon as I heard the name, I knew there was something wrong. Why would anyone call such a beautiful place Death Watch?"

She asked the monk, and he explained that coastal tribal people had named the forest. "They remember a time when the river that runs through here was sparkling and fresh. That's what *Mattole* means—'crystal clear.' The salmon were so abundant that during the spawning season the people could walk across the river on the salmons' backs. Each year the salmon returned, it was said, because Fog Woman spread out her cloak for them. It was woven from the mist that gathered in the tips of the trees, so it cooled the river so the salmon could live.

"The salmon made a covenant with the people. In exchange for protection of the forests and the streams, the fish promised to come back every year so the people would have food. But the humans have not kept their promise, and the King and Coho are dying. Groves like Raven's Watch are the barest remains of what was once a gigantic forest system. The salmon are an indicator species for the whole Northwest ecosystem. So you see," the monk concluded, "what we are witnessing here does seem to be a death watch."

What do you do upon hearing a story like this? Most of us would probably do what Catherine did: enjoy the tall trees and the good company, then drive home to our busy lives. Catherine had just returned to the States from months of photographing rain forests in Asia and Australia. She wanted to get her photojournalism career going again and catch up with her old friends. And that's exactly what she did. But about a month later, camping with a few friends, she found herself lying with her belly on the earth, weeping with grief. "I was overwhelmed with the sense of how much the Earth gives to us and how we just grab it and then use and destroy the giver," she told us. The next morning, as she was meditating, she had a new certainty: "I saw very clearly that we were to buy the Raven's Watch in the name of women, as an act of reconciliation and healing with the Earth. I called my friend Tracy Gary. She didn't hesitate for a moment. 'Yes, let's do it,' she said."

When we interviewed Catherine in 1997, the project was three years old. She and Tracy and a few others had contacted more than a thousand women, and most of them had donated funds and agreed to donate more. "We are technically a land trust," Catherine explained, "which means that we've written conservation easements into our agreements for buying the land. So now the old-growth areas, the river, and the whole riparian zone are protected in perpetuity." And as they were setting up the land trust and applying for their nonprofit status, the women did one more thing: "We changed the name of this beautiful land from Death Watch to Sacred Grove."

USING THE ANCESTOR'S GIFT

William Kent's bequest was one of the symbolic events that launched the conservation movement, which in turn created many national parks and forests. In a real sense, his altruism laid the basis for the efforts of Catherine Allport and

Tracy Gary and hundreds of other women to save a redwood grove. In a further development of what we might call the ancestor's gift, the women's story moves beyond what William Kent accomplished and reveals some of the ways in which Cultural Creatives are changing our culture today.

Facing the Losses. In contrast to those who set up the first forest preserves, those who act now to preserve natural areas have to face the great loss that has taken place. When we asked Catherine what it was like to donate so much of her time to preserving a little redwood grove, she said at first that she felt inspired and healed. But then she mentioned that in parts of the forest, hulks of redwoods lay among ragged stumps left by loggers. Doesn't this upset you? we asked.

"I feel like I'm developing a relationship with the land," she answered quietly, "getting to know it better and love it more. It's true that there are places that are very scarred. For a long time I didn't like to walk there. It was too painful. But when a few of us were up there in July and it seemed like the land was so joyful to see us, as if it had gussied up for us, I decided to walk into some of the areas I'd been avoiding. And I saw that the forest is healing itself. It is different now than even two years ago because we've been able to protect it. It would take something very extreme to dissolve the protections we've created."

Financing and Other Small Acts. William Kent took out a loan merely on his signature, but the women banded together to create a women's foundation and a land trust. They collectively agreed to negotiate and pay off the loan, each contributing from $10 to $500 per quarter. Rather than a grand act by a heroic man, it is a collection of small acts by the many. Both then and now, however, preservation requires a long-term commitment. Kent supported Muir Woods with roads, maintenance, and insurance for about twenty years beyond his original donation; the women are fund-raising to continue to pay off their loan over an eight-year period.

Naming and Blessing. Rather than rename Death Watch after a famous man (or woman), the women found a name that reflected the forest's own special quality: Sacred Grove. The name explicitly recognizes this natural spot as blessed. It's a recognition shared with most Americans. Surveys for many years have shown that when Americans are asked to think of something sacred, they are more likely to think of redwood groves than churches. The mainstream worldview has evolved toward protecting nature as a holy task.

Many Cultural Creatives unembarrassedly speak of meditating and entering nonordinary states of consciousness. Annie Dillard describes it for everyone who ever sat by a stream and felt the blessings of renewal: "My God, I look at the creek. It is the answer to [Thomas] Merton's prayer, 'Give us time!' It never stops. . . . You wait for it, empty-handed, and you are filled." The Earth is, she says, the one great giver. "It is, by definition, Christmas, the incarnation. This old rock planet gets the present for a present on its birthday every day."[8]

A Cultural Shift. Today a new kind of values commitment is part of the whole culture. This culturewide consciousness didn't exist in the West until the Romantics of the 1800s. Previously, what had been valued in landscapes was productive fields and meadows, not the threatening sense of disorder that came from untamed nature. Before the 1800s, people avoided mountains and wild areas. Neither Americans nor Europeans really valued nature. But in the 1800s visionaries like Emerson, Thoreau, and Muir told them about pure mountain days and new life unfolding everywhere. Artists like the Hudson River School, and those who first painted scenes like the Grand Canyon, showed both Europeans and Americans the magnificence of their own landscapes. Only then did people begin to seek out the wild beauty.

In the twentieth century, a growing army of poets and nature writers elaborated this expression, and hundreds of millions of tourists and watchers of nature films echoed the experience. Scarcely a child today can grow up without exposure to thousands of beautiful images by nature photographers and filmmakers. Natural areas as symbols of belief, and the planet Gaia as a new reality in our hearts, are foundational themes of the emerging culture.

Becoming the New Ancestors. The women who are buying the Sacred Grove, unlike Kent, are linked with other groups across the country and around the world who are also saving forests, lakes, and wilderness lands. Their *collective* sense of the future is that they, like Kent and others before them, are acting for the sake of the generations who will live after them.

This relationship through time extends the caring of a relatively few early visionaries into the future. As the women of the Sacred Grove and thousands of other groups accept collective responsibility to the future, they are, in effect, becoming the new ancestors.

Buddhist activist Joanna Macy makes this explicit in a poem for the millennium: "O you who come after," she calls, "you attune us to measures of time where healing can happen. . . . You reveal courage within us we had not suspected, love we had not owned." By remembering our relationship to future children with no faces and no names, she writes, the people of our time can discover their direction and connection to the life that links us all together.[9] This arc of connection extends across species as well as through time, embracing the whole ecosystem of pooled ancestors and future offspring. It is the web of life, the delicate living system that Cultural Creatives are so intent on preserving.

The New Cathedrals. Through their time and energy and money, the women who formed the Sacred Grove are setting aside sacred space, in the way that towns and villages built cathedrals in the Middle Ages. It is a need common to people throughout the world: to make a place in their midst for the ineffable mystery. Goddess worshippers in prebiblical times created *asherah,* altars in laurel groves throughout the Middle East; Celts prayed in the forests of Old Europe; and Buddhists, Hindus, and Muslims erected massive temple complexes throughout Asia. So too does today's worldwide ecology movement preserve natural beauty spots and endangered species.

Although many of today's preservation efforts come from individuals and communities, without explicit reference to the larger culture, they nevertheless reflect an emerging collective understanding. Catherine Allport was quite clear that saving a redwood grove is not about getting a task done. "Everyone who visits the Sacred Grove comes away with a kind of energy," she told us. "We take the trees home with us, and we discover that they feed us from afar. I can tap into those trees from here, in the Bay Area—the connection is that solid and real. Every woman who has been there takes the forest into herself in a personal way and builds a relationship with it."

Unlike many tasks in our urban-industrial culture, preserving this grove leaves the women feeling more connected, joined with one another in a deeper purpose. Work that makes sacred values manifest is the kind of change that is changing American culture.

In contrast to the headlines that proclaimed the new Muir Woods National Monument, the creation of the Sacred Grove and its thousands of counterparts is mostly invisible to the public eye. In all areas of life and all across the country, Cultural Creatives are responding to pressing problems, yet because their responses are not news, they believe that "it's just us and a few of our friends." This belief doesn't stop them from acting, but it probably slows them down. Still, if they knew how many others are also working to create a good future for "the children who are not yet born," would it make a difference? How many more ideas might they introduce, and how many more solutions could they help to create?

AGAINST THE DEATH OF NATURE

Between 1910 and 1960, the emerging environmental movement was fed by four separate streams:

- The conservation movement, built around the love of unspoiled natural areas and wilderness
- The land preservation movement, which tried to slow down soil erosion and the destruction of forests and farms by shortsighted farmers, ranchers, miners, and timber companies
- The occupational health and safety movement, which grew out of unions trying to protect their workers against being poisoned by industries that cared more about profits
- In an expansion of the public health movement, citizen protests against industrial pollution and waste dumps

These four streams had no common focus. For the most part, they started as local confrontations between intensely self-interested parties. Yet after engaging with the issues for a while, local activists often came to see the larger environmental issues at stake. At times their self-interest would broaden to something more like altruism. Like upstart springs, thousands of local community actions appeared unexpectedly in response to the ever-growing destruction of the natural world. Other actions responded to the parallel degradation of the quality of life all over the modern world. But because they could not see the overall picture, and because of the power of business interests, most of these movements were not notably successful. Each one was a holding action at best. Moreover, because governments had not yet begun to collect data in any systematic way, the movements lacked sufficient basis for legal action. At the same time, all levels of government came under intense pressure from businesses and conservative groups to look away from the damage in order to protect jobs and property rights.

SILENT SPRING

In 1962 Rachel Carson's *Silent Spring* put the word *environment* on everyone's lips. A gifted nature writer, Carson evoked a wide and passionate public response against the silencing of "robins, catbirds, doves, jays, wrens, and scores of other bird voices." Like her contemporaries, Martin Luther King, Jr., and Betty Friedan, Carson reframed an issue in an electrifying way. Environmentalism wasn't just about keeping pollution out of people's backyards or preventing ugly clear-cuts in a few forests; it was about averting the death of nature. It was grappling with a threat to the lives of one's own children and grandchildren. Even the most hardened cynics had to pay attention.

Science could be purchased and therefore corrupted, Carson showed, because scientific and technical knowledge had been divorced from any larger public good or public input. The rise of pesticides pointed to "an era dominated by industry, in which the right to make money, at whatever cost to others, is seldom challenged." And she revealed how hazardous technologies like pesticides could pollute both human and natural environments.[10]

The response Carson received was scathing. Book reviewers, scientists, consultants, "pesticide experts," and especially the chemical industry issued vituperative blasts of disinformation. This woman, they said, was biased, "hysterically overemphatic," and certainly incapable of mastering a scientific and technical subject like pesticides. A *Newsweek* senior editor warned that "thanks to a woman named Rachel Carson, a big fuss has been stirred up to scare the American public out of its wits."[11] Some even made McCarthy-style innuendoes that she was a Communist.

But thousands of critical facts soon broke through the denial and outright lying. Huge numbers of Americans could see for themselves that the air and water, fields and forests, mountains and seas were increasingly degraded. Scientific measurements newly available to activists propelled the debate far beyond exchanges of heated opinion and broadsides. Industries that had delayed cleanups by demanding proof of pollution claims were suddenly handed that proof—and more. Activists won many of the lawsuits and the fights over regulation, and the cleanups slowly got under way.

REFRAMING THE GROWTH PARADIGM

Earth Day in June 1970 marked a turning point in the environmental movement. For the first time, the diverse streams agreed that the real issues were not just regulating discharges from industries, protecting waterways, or stopping tree-cutting, but rather involved a planetary problem. By 1972 the theme of the now rapidly growing environmental movement was *survival*—the survival of children and grandchildren, survival of life on the planet. This theme was stated in two landmark publications: the Club of Rome's *The Limits to Growth,* and *The Ecologist* magazine's *Blueprint for Survival.*

Led by systems theorist Donella Meadows, the "limits to growth" group used computer models to argue that the planet as a whole cannot continue to bear unlimited population growth, economic growth, and pollution. The most likely outcome of "business as usual," they argued, would be an overshoot of the carrying capacity of the Earth, a drastic population collapse, and the collapse of much of the natural ecology.

This argument was not just an academic or futurist exercise. It was a direct affront to Modernism's main project—the unending growth of prosperity—and a direct threat to the giant organizations of both capitalism and socialism. Like Rachel Carson's book, the Meadows group's report drew sustained attacks from virtually every defender of the old paradigm: industrial hirelings, academics, economists, bankers, media pundits, and government officials (especially in Europe). Numerous experts claimed that the report was fatally flawed—and then the official public policy world turned away with relief and forgot about it. Unfortunately for the planet, as the Worldwatch Institute has been showing since 1984, the report was essentially correct. The carrying capacity of the Earth is indeed limited—though we don't know what those limits are.

What is clear, however, is that the risk of an eventual collapse from degradation of the environment coupled with population pressure is real and growing, just as Meadows and her colleagues argued. The scientific and satellite measurements are incontrovertible: "business as usual" *will* kill us. And although the policy establishment waited about fifteen years before facing it, practically everyone else was paying close attention to the possibility of overshoot and planetary collapse. By the 1990s, *Limits to Growth* had sold 9 million copies in twenty-nine languages. In 1992 a second volume, *Beyond the Limits,* revisited the argument, showing how the critics had been mistaken. Able to draw on better data, they now say that with its all-out commitment to growth, humanity is walking on thin ice and may soon be past the point of preventing the ice from breaking. The policy establishment, for its part, pretends that the argument never happened.

Blueprint for Survival was the first document to state outright that the urban-industrial way of life, indeed the whole commitment of modern civilization, cannot be sustained. Initially, its impact was greatest in Europe, where it became a critical platform document for many of Europe's Green parties. But the theme of this book, and of *Limits to Growth,* has become a central tenet for many American Cultural Creatives: the idea that unlimited growth cannot continue and that a new, ecologically sound way of life must be discovered for our civilization.

A New Relationship

The first photographs of the Earth from space made a greater impact on the popular imagination than all the scientific evidence put together. Except for industries that make a living from exploiting "natural resources," most Americans began to see that the Earth itself is alive and is, in itself, inestimably valuable.

Poet Susan Griffin is one of countless artists who have explored and celebrated this relationship. In "This Earth, What She Is to Me," Griffin writes: "As I go into her, she pierces my heart. As I penetrate further, she unveils me. When I have reached her center, I am weeping openly. I have known her all my life, yet she reveals stories to me, and these stories are revelations and I am transformed. Each time I go to her I am born like this. Her renewal washes over me endlessly, her wounds caress me; I become aware of all that has come between us, of the noise between us, the blindness."[12]

Stars, winds, birds, grasses, our bodies, and every human concern—most educated people were coming to have a sense not just of "environment" but of a new space, a new time. No longer a relationship of user to used, or even steward to resources, our new relationship with the Earth was intimate and mysterious. Nature's purposes, its justification, its beauty did not depend on our understanding or even our appreciation. Its variety and possibilities, we began to see, were precious in themselves. And our awareness of all this was sharpened by our growing realization of the peril that threatened the natural world.

OBSTACLES AND SEDUCTIONS

In the midst of its growing popularity, the new environmental movement encountered three stumbling blocks. One was the conservative backlash that rose up in the 1980s against all the new social movements. One was a Tar Baby that looked like the right direction at the time: the idea that the only important part of the movement was the political deal-making. And the third was the seductive old paradigm, which dictates what makes sense and what is unthinkable. Encountering all three of these obstacles comes with the territory of making cultural change.

The environmental movement may have begun respectably middle class and polite, but "Sue the bastards!" soon became the refrain from the activists in the field. The environmental organizations urged the passage of legislation on a national scale so that big-business polluters couldn't simply move to a neighboring state with fewer regulations, and so that their ability to buy state legislators wouldn't matter so much. Environmental protection had to get legal teeth, and it took a cadre of Washington lawyers drafting national laws and regulations to make this happen. With the new laws, polluters could be stopped, and lawsuits could force other big players, corporate and political, to the bargaining table.

At this point, what appeared to be the most powerful and publicly visible part of the movement started to go off course. Mark Dowie in *Losing Ground* puts it this way: for the big national environmental organizations, "the main event, almost always, takes place in the national capital."[13] With their new, strong financial base in direct mail, these organizations believed that they could simply pull away from the messiness of citizen participation and go back to their older pattern of negotiations among elite power brokers. In Dowie's words, "They see regional grassroots activity, which receives little or no national media attention, as at best helpful, at worst an embarrassing sideshow to the main event."[14]

It was Tar Baby all over again. We saw it with Thurgood Marshall and civil rights lawsuits, and with the heavily constrained political activists of the women's movement, and we see it again here. To change the culture, you cannot depend on the terms and solutions the old culture provides. If you do, sooner or later Tar Baby gets you all tangled up. Leaving the heavy lifting to the political side of the movements, the cultural side started drying up, and the submerged networks began to lose touch with one another.

National organizations like the Sierra Club and Audubon Society recruited people who could become power brokers themselves and who had connections to big money. Polite negotiation was the rule, as big law firms with deep conservative roots had veto power over what happened. The vetoes were often exercised through the foundations that were major funders of the environmental organizations. Being respectable and moderate was important, because the organizations wanted to be national power players. "Leave it to us," they said. And for twenty years, people did.

To develop a movement, people need to be engaged, to develop relationships, to explore their passionate concerns, to build shared meanings. But elitism by national organizations can kill a social movement, because it cuts off meaningful participation. Citizens became passive recipients of dozens or hundreds of imploring fund-raising letters. They would respond generously by writing a check to the national organizations—and get more pleas for money in return. The direct mail solicitations were poisoning the well. There were no ways for citizens to get involved, no discussions, no contacts with their fellow environmentalists. When behavioral psychologists want to extinguish a habit in a rat or pigeon, they do something very similar. First they provide a come-on, like the smell of food, an initial reward, and then they make sure nothing happens. The habit goes on sporadically for a little while, then disappears. It's called the extinction response. (Appropriate, wouldn't you say?) After a while, environmentally concerned people learned that no matter how many checks they wrote, nothing much was going to happen.

THE OLD PARADIGM

We cannot solve the problems we have created with the same thinking that created them.

ALBERT EINSTEIN

The same lesson that the black freedom movement and the women's movement had to learn faced the environmentalists as well. When power players frame the issue being negotiated, the entire game is played within the old paradigm. When you're trying to change the old culture, as environmentalists were, you can't play within the old culture's mind-set.

The negotiations in Washington were framed entirely within the conservative economics of resource utilization, rather than the liberal politics of government regulation on behalf of the public interest. Neither economics nor the law, which had developed at the height of the Modern era, could wrap its professional mind-set around ideas like ecology and the death of nature. That business should change to preserve the long-term survival of the species was unthinkable.

Even the most successful deal-making led to short-term success and long-term failure.[15] Over about thirty years, hundreds of environmental regulations and resolutions were passed, but all too often the money to enforce them wasn't appropriated. And as soon as political winds shifted, conservatives in Congress rolled back the protections.

Throughout the 1990s, mainstream public opinion in favor of the environment was at an all-time high—yet the movement in Washington was ineffectual.

National opinion had shifted massively toward ever more action—yet national organizations were lapsing into irrelevancy and impotency.[16] On almost a daily basis, scientific evidence of the need for action continued to pour in. In great frustration, the environmental movement turned itself around, away from the big organizations and back to its local roots. In effect, it was a new start. This time a radical new stream was added.

THE ECOLOGY MOVEMENT

Today the broad environmental consensus is becoming an ecology movement. The Cultural Creatives at the leading edge are taking the movement deeper and farther than the original environmentalists ever dreamed. Exasperated with James Carville's refrain, "It's the economy, stupid!" they say it's the stupid economy that's killing us. The original environmental movement, content with technological fixes and making economic growth cleaner, sat comfortably within the Modern paradigm. But the ecology movement tends to be Cultural Creatives who are going well beyond that.

The change in focus has come primarily from new and vastly better information: new measurements that support and extend the "whole systems" models of what growth means for the planet. As new scientific knowledge becomes available, and as experts now look at the problems (rather than just defending various industries), measures over time from critical sites improve. We have aerial and satellite photos for comparison over two decades, and studies from the new sciences of ecology and climatology, and a new biochemistry of life. We have better theories of the oceans and the atmosphere. All of these sources are telling the same story: Nature is dying faster than ever. *Beyond the Limits,* in 1992,[17] extended the Meadows group's earlier systems models into the next century. It concluded that significant reductions in material consumption, in the use of materials and energy, and in population were unquestionably needed. Collapse, they said, is not inevitable, but the world was already well into overshoot of some of its limits.

Unfortunately, as industry and governments go all out for economic growth, the faster the better, environmental degradation has accelerated. Worldwide, business conservatives have succeeded in putting roadblocks in the way of many pro-environment actions. Only some of our air and water pollution has been reversed, while the extinction rate of species worldwide is faster than at any time since the extinction of the dinosaurs. Global warming is no longer speculation but scientists' strong consensus. All of these factors have contributed to the momentous growth of the ecology movement. Today the environmental and ecology movements together are like the Amazon River at flood stage, with a dozen interconnected currents flowing together to influence everything they touch.

THE AMERICAN CONSENSUS

On any given day, a typical opinion poll will show that about 85 percent of Americans call themselves "environmentalists" or pro-environment, with small variations depending on the wording of the question. This support is much stronger than just knee-jerk sentimentality. A team of anthropologists headed by Willett Kempton at the University of Delaware recently completed a study of environmental values in American culture. They found that Americans see nature as sacred in a way closely related to religious ideals; that we are very concerned about our responsibility to leave a decent environment to our descendants; and that we see intrinsic value in the biosphere. The only difference between activists and the general population is that the activists are more consistent across all the issues. Kempton's team concluded that Americans' values and beliefs about the environment are foundational and have sacred overtones.[18] That is, they now guide Americans' perceptions and life choices. Our own work supports and extends these results.

In a 1998–99 study for the Environmental Protection Agency (EPA) and the President's Council for Sustainable Development (PCSD), American LIVES queried nine focus groups and conducted a national survey to ask, "What would it take to get Americans to adopt ecological sustainability in their everyday lives?"

The term *ecological sustainability* is a mouthful, and most Americans don't like it. It's a "techie" term, they say. But they do care a lot about the issue when it is rephrased as: What will it take to get Americans to stop damaging the environment and restore it so that we can continue to live in a good way for a long time? That question was posed to two kinds of focus groups. One kind was identified as pro-environment. (The EPA wanted to hear from people it thought of as its constituency. But when we sat them down in the room, they turned out to have nothing in common besides their attitudes to the environment.) The other kind was Cultural Creatives. (As usual, they had a lot in common.)

One striking finding of the research was that everyone was concerned about the kind of world their children or grandchildren would live in. They all spoke about how much the environment has deteriorated over the past thirty years, and they could easily see what that meant for the future. These focus group results were backed up by the results from the 2,181 responses to the national survey.

We asked people in the focus groups whether they would willingly change their lives toward being more sustainable for the future by, for example, installing more home insulation, doing more recycling, and driving less. This is where the two kinds of groups differed. Pro-environment people, who tended mostly to be Moderns, said things like "I see what you mean, and if it didn't cost me too much time or money and I had a decent payback, I'd probably do it. But you'd have to tell me precisely what you want me to do." By contrast, the Cultural Creatives said things like "I'm already doing some of that, and of course I'd do more. I'm sure glad you raised it, because I'm really upset that big business and big government aren't showing more leadership on this. We've got to get our communities mobilized so that more people will do it!" Many of the Cultural Creatives are clearly community oriented rather than individualistic and self-concerned, and many seem to be the opinion leaders on these issues in their neighborhoods, churches, and other local groups.

For our survey, we developed a set of measures for the very strong ecological sustainability position that the ecology movement favors. The respondents were a representative national sample, and their responses tell us about the country as a whole as well as the Cultural Creatives. The results show that 79 percent of Americans support the strong position. Cultural Creatives, as you might expect, are a large majority of the strongest supporters, despite the fact that they are only a quarter of the population. Essentially we found that Cultural Creatives are by far the strongest opinion leaders for ecology positions. But they do not really differ from an already-powerful Americans consensus. They are simply much stronger and more consistent on environmental issues than most people.

In the accompanying box, the first four items are themes and key survey results. Each itemized theme combines large groups of survey questions that were very closely related. The fifth theme sums up the first four, to give an overall measure of support for ecological sustainability.[19]

The data in response to Theme 1 flatly reject the position long held by business conservatives. In a dozen statements that probed all aspects of this issue, Americans overwhelmingly said that growth and the economy should be compatible, if only we use technology well, do business differently, and change our lifestyles. When 90 percent of Americans agree on anything, it's effectively unanimous.

thematic measures from the epa/pcsd survey

1. Economic growth and protecting the environment are fully compatible: 90 percent of the whole U.S. population agrees, and 96 percent of Cultural Creatives agree.

2. The environmental crisis justifies change in our way of life: 77 percent of U.S. agrees, and 95 percent of Cultural Creatives agree.

3. The planet is a living system and we need to protect it (the Gaia position): 49 percent of U.S. agrees, and 65 percent of Cultural Creatives agree.

4. Actions for greater social justice are justified, especially for poor children: 54 percent of U.S. agrees, and 62 percent of Cultural Creatives agree.

5. Ecological sustainability summary measure (combines measures 1 through 4): 79 percent of U.S. agrees, and 96 percent of Cultural Creatives agree.

The data in response to Theme 2 reflect a surprisingly strong consensus that a serious environmental crisis threatens all life and harms life prospects for our children. Obviously this perception of danger is the reason people are quite willing to change their way of life and want business and government to protect the environment. At 77 percent agreement, this result is a national mandate for action. But the survey results, like the focus group results, suggest that most people are unclear about what to do next and want some leadership from both business and government.

The data in response to Theme 3 signal a change from a worldview that wants to exploit the planet for its natural resources to a view that says the planet is alive and must be protected. Although it's not yet a majority opinion except among the Cultural Creatives, the results are surprising, because this changing worldview has dramatic long-term implications. It is closely related to the common American view that nature is sacred.

The data in response to Theme 4 were also a surprise. The more people believe the first three themes, the more they favor actions by government that promote social justice, caring for the rights and the employment prospects of the poor, and supporting the needs of poor children. Contrary to decades of assertions from all points of the political spectrum, a majority of Americans, and especially Cultural Creatives, see no incompatibility between ecology and social justice. This means that poor urban communities, concerned with both environmental justice and jobs, can make common cause with the larger, more

Consensus on the Ecology Movement Position

Percent who agree with value/belief

● Cultural Creatives ▪ Rest of U.S.*

	0%	10	20	30	40	50	60	70	80	90	100

We should change how we live now so future generations can enjoy a good quality of life. ▪ at ~80, ● at ~90

We should follow the Native American motto "Do things so they will still be good seven generations from now." ▪ at ~85, ● at ~92

We will destroy our environment if we continue living the way we do. ▪ at ~65, ● at ~92

Human survival depends on finding better ways to balance economic growth with environmental protection. ▪ at ~68, ● at ~88

Humans are part of nature, not its ruler. ▪ at ~66, ● at ~88

We have a moral duty to protect and preserve all God's creatures. ▪ at ~80, ● at ~88

The Earth is headed for an environmental crisis unless we change. ▪ at ~60, ● at ~86

I'm concerned my children will live in a much worse world than I do. ▪ at ~63, ● at ~86

To protect the environment, we need big changes in the way we live. ▪ at ~65, ● at ~86

Humans can only afford to preserve species that are useful to us. (disagree) ▪ at ~63, ● at ~84

Nature has value far beyond the practical uses we can make of it. ▪ at ~65, ● at ~82

Business and government don't pay enough attention to our longer-term future. ▪ at ~62, ● at ~84

I agree with the people who see the whole Earth as a giant living organism. ▪ at ~45, ● at ~76

*Note: This table contrasts Cultural Creatives to everybody else. "Rest of U.S." is not U.S. total but the Moderns plus the Traditionals. Cultural Creatives are so numerous that when they are included in the total U.S., they raise the percentages and it's harder to see that they are much stronger than the other subcultures on these issues. (Source: 1999 EPA survey) middle-class environmental movement. In fact, they share a common constituency and common goals.

Theme 5, which sums up the other data, shows a strong pro-sustainability position. At 79 percent agreement, American beliefs closely match the ecology movement's position. As usual, the Cultural Creatives are virtually in unanimous agreement on this theme, at 96 percent.

The "Consensus on the Ecology Movement Position" table shows some of the actual survey statements that went into the themes we've been discussing. They show how strongly ecological sustainability has become a mainstream belief. What is surprising is that Americans still agree with these statements even when very strongly worded. Mainstream America is far, far ahead of its politicians and completely at odds with the foot-dragging and opposition from much of the business and financial community. Cultural Creatives differ from mainstream America only in being more consistent and well informed in their beliefs.

SEEKING A NEW KIND OF CULTURE

Cultural Creatives who take the ideological stance of Ecologists[20] say that the Western world is going through a full-blown crisis of culture and of character. A lot, they say, needs to change.

Ecologist theorists say a slow-growth version of our present-day economy just won't work, because our present industrial culture is irrevocably committed to more growth than the planet can stand. Many of them see the financial community as a key problem because it demands that our economy grow exponentially: seeking to accumulate ever more wealth, pushing for more and more transactions and sales, pressing stock prices ever higher, demanding ever more money to cover compound interest payments. The global financial system pretends that it is not limited by the natural world. But in fact nature is cyclical and can scarcely grow at all, the Ecologists point out. If we take ever more materials out and put ever more waste into nature, it will die, and that is precisely what's happening now. Most Americans agree with the Ecologists' position. But one giant dissenter has so far been almost impervious to any of the new social movements.

THE WALL STREET PRESSURE COOKER

Most people, including most Cultural Creatives, have difficulty grasping the intense pressure that financial markets put on business managers to commit to unending growth, or why financiers impose that pressure. Are they just in denial about the dangers to the planet? Well, sometimes. But the real reason lies in the power of financial numbers and the compound interest calculations of bankers and financiers. It's a whole worldview, one that's been gaining in power since the rise of Modernism. Kings and governments once felt free to tell bankers that they simply couldn't have what they wanted. But since World War II, the international financial community has continued to grow in power, to the point where in any given week, more money sloshes around the globe than any government has control over in a year. Worldwide, politicians are now at the mercy of financial markets, and so are corporate executives. Financiers get what they want, and this is dangerous to life on Earth.

Compound interest is the most obvious form of Modernism's commitment to exponential growth. Exponential growth is an upward curve that keeps accelerating without limits—and it is often viewed in terms of how fast its "doubling times" are. The doubling sequence of 2, 4, 8, 16, 32, 64, 128, 256, 512, 1,024, 2,048, and so on, goes up to astounding and unreal numbers in just a hundred steps or so. You can tell that dollars doubling like this have become unreal, because they can start to exceed the number of atoms in the universe in a few more steps. If the global economy keeps on demanding fast doubling times and using up nature to achieve them, then the death of nature is near. If it accepts doubling times on the order of decades or centuries, we can put off disaster for a while. But on a finite planet, unending exponential growth is physically impossible and it is biologically impossible in terms of the survival of species—including us. This is something that financiers would just as soon forget.

Suppose a corporation wants to be a good corporate citizen. It is willing to slow down the growth in profits and think about the longer-term future. But the stock market analysts are not happy, and the financiers get the CEO fired. Or a corporate raider comes in. If a whole country acted in this way, the currency speculators would drive down its currency. Then the financial analysts with the "sharp pencils" take over. Jobs are cut, assets and natural resources are sold off, social programs are left to die, community philanthropy dries up, and day care at workplaces goes away. The employees left in the company are traumatized, anxious, and guilty. Ecological destruction has become just one more excuse for getting "lean and mean." But the profits! Wall Street goes wild with applause. It's a way for modern capitalism to preserve itself against serious change.

Today, most Cultural Creatives show no signs of knowing how to address this problem. But some excellent new approaches do work for some problems, and they may soon become visible to many Cultural Creatives. Here is one approach that is particularly engaging.

A New Design Assignment

William McDonough is dean of architecture at the University of Virginia. He is used to giving unusual design assignments to his students, to break them out of their old, blinding technological frames. In his first lecture, he throws out two challenges. The first: "Let's do a retroactive design assignment of the first industrial revolution. Could you design a system for me that produces billions of pounds of finely hazardous toxic material and puts it in your soil, your air, and your water every year? Could you design a system . . . that measures your prosperity by how much natural capital you can dig up, cut down, bury, burn, and otherwise destroy?" He goes on, ending this first assignment with the question Is this system ethical? Then he gives them a second design assignment: "Design a system that doesn't produce any hazardous toxic material or put it in your soil, your air, and your water. Measure prosperity by how much natural capital you can put into constant closed systems that are healthy and propitious." And build a system, he says, whose legacy will not create "intergenerational remote tyranny." Wouldn't this be interesting? he asks invitingly. Wouldn't you like to reimagine the world?

In fact, Bill McDonough is already engaged in creating what he and others call "the next industrial revolution." Like Amory Lovins at the Rocky Mountain Institute and Ray Anderson at Interface, McDonough has had some inspiring successes. One of them came from what would seem like a small assignment: Design a line of upholstery fabrics that can go back to the soil safely. McDonough and his colleagues went on a worldwide search, using not just research skills but considerable persuasion as well. Starting first with wool from New Zealand, they found additional fibers in the Philippines and then headed for Europe to look for the dyes, finishes, polishes, and fire retardants that were "clean," meaning no mutagens, no carcinogens, no heavy metals, no persistent toxins, no bioaccumulative substances, no endocrine disrupters. Who wants to work with us? McDonough asked. Sixty chemical companies refused.

The team went to the chairman of Ciba Geigy and explained the protocols and far-reaching impact that this work could have on his business. The chairman agreed and personally helped to look at more than eight thousand chemicals in the textile industry. They had to eliminate 7,962. "We were left with thirty-eight chemicals," McDonough told his students. "We did the entire fabric line with thirty-eight chemicals. It's completely safe. You can eat it." The fabric line has won medals, he said, and it is doing quite well in the marketplace. But what he finds really astonishing are two telling details. One, the local garden club uses the waste for mulch. And two, when the Swiss inspectors came to the factory to inspect the water coming out of the process, they couldn't find the things that were normally in the drinking water. They thought their equipment was broken. So they tested the equipment on the incoming water and discovered that the fabrics were further filtering the water. McDonough told his students, "When it turns out that the effluent from the textile mill is cleaner than the water going in, you realize that you just hit what I call the next industrial revolution."[21]

Like Bill McDonough, most Ecologists want a completely new kind of economy based on something other than industrialism. They want technologies that are good enough for humanity's survival: "appropriate technology," or small-scale, local technology that does not use much energy or materials, or that doesn't pollute and that recycles everything. Developing such technology is not about just challenging the location of a nuclear power plant, freeway, or chemical plant, or getting better regulation and pollution controls. It is about creating a benign industrial base, using technology in new ways. Many Ecologists would love to find new technologies that would put the big energy companies, big auto companies, and big resource extraction companies (timber, agribusiness, mining, chemicals) out of business altogether. They're on a search for alternatives to practically every technology and practically every kind of business that will not, to use Bill McDonough's phrase, "create intergenerational remote tyrannies for our children's children's children."

A WONDERFUL COMPLEXITY

Cultural Creatives are not necessarily better at tuning in to ecological needs than anyone else, but they want to be. In their personal lives and in the social ventures they are creating, they are eagerly—sometimes awkwardly and haltingly—making room to learn wholly new ways of working. And they are taking time, or trying to, to listen to how their consciousness and their conscience responds.

Amory Lovins, cofounder of the Rocky Mountain Institute, spent several years designing a large bank building in Amsterdam. He created a biological, whole-systems building, he says, using an integrative, engaging process. If there is an emblematic story about Cultural Creatives taking time, this might be it.

For the half-million-square-foot building, the bank's board of directors told Lovins, "we want an organic building, full of light, air, water, Ecologist plants, nice sounds, happy people. And it shall not cost one guilder more per square meter [than any other design would]." Lovins and his team took several years to design this building because they created it as a living system. Evolution never designs one part in isolation, Lovins explains, "because, as we're starting to learn in engineering, if you do that, you pessimize the system." Meaning, you get the least out of the components instead of the most. The team in Amsterdam was intent on getting multiple benefits from each expenditure. And that took time.

The full design team included designers and artists and construction people and those who would work in the building and those who would run it and the landscape architects. Their agreement, according to Lovins, was this: "If anybody didn't understand something, they had to stop the process until it was all satisfactorily explained. You had to explain the landscape design to the mechanical engineer and the air-handling design to the landscaper." This extraordinary guideline led, he said, "to quite a magical level of integration where the expansion joints in the walls are brass and colored stone works of art, and where light bounces down the atria off these colored metal patches that the artist put there, so as the sun moves around during the day, you get different colors of light at the bottom." And for humidity control and acoustic masking, a bronze flowing-form water sculpture runs down the banisters.

In the completed building, where people in suits now dabble their fingers along the banister handrails, the bank reported large increases in productivity. This was no surprise to Lovins, who has eight case studies showing the success of workplaces where people can see better and feel comfortable and hear themselves think. And the bottom line on the integrated design process? The building ended up using one-tenth of the energy and costing not one guilder more to build than one with conventional design constraints. Moreover, the designers evolved a way of working that mirrored what they ended up building: a dynamic, organic environment that was a lot more lively, creative, and humane than the static, mechanical work context that many Moderns take for granted. People, Lovins observes, are really complicated organisms, and part of the fun of working with this in mind is finding out "how that complexity can be turned into something quite wonderful."[22]

NEITHER LEFT NOR RIGHT—IN FRONT!

Political observers find the ecological movement perplexing. It takes only a mild interest in power politics, be it in elections or as pressure groups. It is much more concerned with redesigning every aspect of our culture to be ecologically sound:

how our cities and towns can be laid out; how our transportation system could work; how new technology can be used in products, businesses, and industrial processes; how business can be organized; how we measure the value of a company or the cost of a government project; how we live in our homes; how we can get our clubs and associations involved in a new way of life; how we live in community, or fail to; and how we participate in civic culture, or not. Without making these technological and cultural changes, Ecologists argue, even being in charge of the political machine would be pointless.

Most Ecologists are neither liberals nor conservatives, Traditionals nor Moderns. To political observers, they seem to be a strange mixture of all—and none. As they urge caution in the use of technology and work to preserve old forests and ancient natural sites, old buildings, old values, and older ways of life, they sound rather traditional. (The former editor of *The Ecologist,* Edward Goldsmith, can sound like a mossy-back Tory when he argues for preserving "vernacular culture," the small villages and farm life of early modern culture. But it's because he believes they have a low enough impact on their environs for long-term sustainability.) Most leading-edge Ecologists, however, want an egalitarian and participatory society, so they reject both the Religious Right and business conservatives as too regressive and authoritarian. At the same time, most also reject both liberalism and Marxism as too growth-oriented and too in love with material goods. They are not some "radical middle." They are off the left-right spectrum. The German Green Party sums up their position with the slogan "We're neither left nor right—we're in front."

Interestingly, the Ecologists often recognize their interdependence with other new social movements. One reason is that those who want to redesign practically every aspect of our culture will need a lot of help. Another reason is that many Ecologists were, and still are, engaged in the women's movement, the peace movement, and other movements. So they're looking for a larger community that will share their personal interests and commitment. This sense of inclusiveness and overlapping interests is evident on almost any day at any meeting. If you meet with the activists at Rainforest Action Network in San Francisco (known as the "pit bulls" of ecoaction), for example, you'll hear more than just a planetary perspective from the twentysomethings around the table. You'll also hear about feminism, gay liberation, social justice, organic foods, spirituality, and people of the third world. All these issues are in the air they breathe. They're taking their creativity and going for that new design assignment—reimagining a whole new culture.

In fact, Ecologists are at the leading edge of a revolutionary change in worldview. It's the Gaia position from the EPA survey: "The planet is a living system and we need to protect it." Sixty-one percent of Cultural Creatives agree, and 47 percent of all Americans agree. This position turns topsy-turvy the human-centered view that merely wants to exploit the Earth for our needs—the ten-thousand-year-old view that appeared with the agricultural revolution and intensified with the industrial revolution. The emerging Ecologist worldview is "biocentric" or "ecocentric," with similarities to the worldview of indigenous peoples, like those in the rain forest. Rather than seeing the planet as a pyramid with humans on top, it sees the Earth as a web of life, and humans as just one strand in the web: what we do to the Earth, we do to ourselves; we belong to Nature, not nature to us; we have obligations to Mother Nature, not just for us. For Her.

chapter six

waking
up

The breeze at dawn has secrets to tell you.

You must ask for what you really want.

People are going back and forth across the doorsill

The door is round and open.

Don't go back to sleep.

Don't go back to sleep.

where the two worlds touch.

Don't go back to sleep.

JELALUDDIN RUMI[1]

Poets and mystics have been telling us for centuries: Wake up. Wake to your true self. Wake to your own connections to what is around you right now. Gaze into someone's eyes, and discover who looks back. Penetrate the mysteries where the worlds touch. Don't go back to sleep. The qualities of consciousness that are involved in waking up are beyond counting. They are what lies beneath the surface of our lives, beyond the taken-for-granted, the actions on automatic pilot, the hurry-up-I-want-it-yesterday mind-set that doesn't care how it's done or who's doing it. Though not easily put into words, waking up is recognizable. James Joyce described it as epiphany. Aldous Huxley talked about cleansing the doors of perception. The poet Mary Oliver calls for it constantly, whether she's talking about goldfinches or peonies or whelks lying cracked and broken on the beach.

Waking up can be immediately physical, a quiet deep contact between yourself and everything. It can come as the fruit of long practice, leaving you melted and grateful. Or it can be felt as grace, or simplicity, or a brilliant clarity of intelligence. Waking up can be filled with pain. An icepick between the shoulder blades. A tearing apart in the soft tissues of the heart. You see how you have harmed someone, or betrayed yourself, or failed to speak out against injustice. You recognize poverty, loneliness, grief that you have resolutely walked past for years, or a lifetime.

Regardless of the content of your experience, when you begin to wake up, you recognize something as genuine. You don't wake up to what is false, but always to what is true at a level you never knew before. Or to what you knew but have forgotten. What comes then is what psychologist Mihaly Csikszentmihalyi calls "flow" and Zen calls "suchness" and spiritual teachers of all sorts have called "freedom." The brittle shell of the old self dissolves—if only for a moment or an hour—and you are no longer who you thought you were. And whether it is a fullness, a freshness, an unswerving "hereness," or any of a thousand other states of being, what matters is that you have arrived, finally, at the radiant center of your own life.

INVITING CONSCIOUSNESS IN

In every age, people engaged in disciplines from prayer to martial arts to healing have sought ways to invite consciousness in. Practices of concentration, meditation, and contemplation have been known for millennia, and so have the gifts of sacred plants and holy places and special practices like fire walking and the dervishes' turning. But there has never been a time like ours for the great art and craft of waking up.

While our ancestors knew of only one true way, we have a cornucopia of spiritual and psychological and physical possibilities. More is known today about the diverse practices and insights of all the cultures and religions of the world than at any time in history. Every day now doors are flung open and we are invited to come and see, to taste, and to know what it means to be human. This cultural process of waking up goes far beyond the standard modern repertoire of waking and sleeping, or getting drunk and then sober. And it takes us beyond the traditionally fierce protectiveness that gave rise to so many religious wars and inquisitions. It has a sense of ice floes breaking up, of deserts being watered, of new ways of knowing and being unfolding within us and around us.

This cultural awakening is the concern of a great heterogeneous mélange of movements, organizations, and trends. They include the human potential movement; psychedelic explorations; the so-called new spirituality, which is extensively based on quite ancient Buddhism, Hinduism, Taoism, Native American traditions, Celtic practices, and mystical Judaism and Sufism and Christianity, as well as Wicca (which is very old or very new, or both); body-work, yoga, and the various martial arts; healing practices, including acupuncture, therapeutic touch, and laying on of hands; and a wide spectrum of prayer and meditation. We call them "consciousness movements" because of their common intention to throw open the windows and doors of the musty old mind-sets we live in, shake the dust out of the covers we wrap around our bodies, and in a thousand old and new ways, guide whoever is willing to show up and pay attention to a fresh experience of being human.

INTRODUCING THE CONSCIOUSNESS MOVEMENTS

The consciousness movements can trace their origins to European religious and social movements over the past fifteen hundred years and to the American Transcendentalists and others in the nineteenth and early twentieth centuries. Ralph Waldo Emerson, Emily Dickinson, Margaret Fuller, and Henry Thoreau are well-known names, as are psychologist William James and naturalist John Muir. But also important were the Canadian physician Richard Bucke, who wrote *Cosmic Consciousness,* and Mary Baker Eddy, the founder of Christian Science.

The more immediate beginning of the consciousness movements, however, took place relatively recently. The context was a generation that had sacrificed and struggled throughout the Great Depression and then during World War II. Many of its members lost friends and family. They entered the 1950s committed to getting some material prosperity and security for themselves and their children. As writer and educator Elizabeth Lesser recalls this generation, they "formed their inner identities in a time of scarcity and fear. . . . Their love of order and hygiene, their sacrificial attitude toward their own emotional needs, their prudent ways with money and their respect for material things were a direct response to what they had lacked."[2]

During the late 1950s, much of this generation of mainstream white America struggled to digest some grisly realities. The rights of African Americans had been trampled on. Our vaunted freedoms—held up like a banner through World War II and the beginnings of the cold war with McCarthyism, and the bomb, and the Eisenhower era—had acquired some pretty muddy stains. And to compound it all, a Catholic had just been elected president.

Then in 1962 it must have seemed like all hell broke loose. Numerous fingers were pointing out unspoken fears, and loud voices were complaining about smelly things hidden under the collective living-room rug. The ones who were pointing the fingers and exposing the hidden assumptions were, of course, the children of that anxious and prudent generation. The feisty, earnest, determined offspring wanted to leave behind the order and hygiene and structure and enter into new ways of thinking and knowing and—especially—experiencing. And like their parents' generation, they had a profound sense of purpose. It wasn't defeating some far-off enemy like Hitler or Tojo—they were sure of that. Their purpose, rather, was directed much closer to home.

But what precisely that purpose was and how it was going to be fulfilled—these were questions that anguished the generation for decades. Two great streams of change developed out of their desire for change. One was the new social movements, and the other was the consciousness movements.

Just as the new social movements were critically important in shaping the worldview and values of the Cultural Creatives, so too were the consciousness movements. But where the social movements' influence was spread broadly through the emerging subculture, the consciousness movements had a concentrated effect on the Core Cultural Creatives. About half of the subculture, 24 million people, are its opinion leaders and strongest voices. They differ from the remaining Green Cultural Creatives who are interested much more in social and environmental issues than in inner development. Core Cultural Creatives are profoundly concerned with *both*. In this chapter, we'll get a picture of how this influential Core group has developed, and how it is leading a groundswell of interest in consciousness throughout the wider society.

ALARM CLOCKS RINGING

It was as if alarm clocks set for about 1962 started ringing wake-up calls across the country and nobody could turn them off. In an astonishingly compressed period, events that had been building quietly through the Cold War 1950s began to surface as whole choruses of questioners attacked ideas and ways of life that had seemed unassailable. The new social movements tore into America's complacency about its perfect freedom and democracy. At the same time, the consciousness movements turned their gaze inward, challenging intimate assumptions about everything from personal identity to reality itself. The alarms resounded across the entire culture, disturbing everyone's sleep.

Clearly, the 1960s were not just a jumble of exotic gurus and hot tubs and strange religions mixed with demonstrators marching in the streets. As we've seen already, the events of that time gave birth to significant cultural innovations. But where the new social movements' responses were urgent and out there and in your face all the time as much as possible, the consciousness movements' responses were quieter and more subtle. It was quite possible to be exhilarated by one or another development in the consciousness movements and still be quite vague on what you were a part *of*. Something thrilling was going on, it seemed, and if you looked, you could find the rhetoric and theory in Huston Smith's *The Religions of Man,* Fritz Perls's *In and Out the Garbage Pail,* Will Schutz's *Joy,* and books by Alan Watts, Krishnamurti, and later by Carlos Castaneda and Mary Daly and Ram Dass, to mention only a few. And it could be found in special places: Esalen in California, the Findhorn Community in Scotland, the Farm in Tennessee, and later the Omega Institute in upstate New York and the Open Center in New York City.

Gathering in ashrams and zendos and church basements and living rooms across the country, the first generation of enthusiasts seemed to feel that nothing could be more important than what they intended to do: To understand themselves. To learn how to be grounded, centered, so secure in their own truth that they could not be thrown off by another person or by the culture itself. To embody compassion. To be truly free.

The premise of the consciousness movements was that the achievements attributed uniquely to saints, poets, and great thinkers are in fact our common inheritance. If there were freedom from the restrictions and ignorance of the past, and support for the unfolding of this potential, anyone willing to put in the time and effort could discover the deepest truths of being human. The sense of a birthright was profound. But how to get access to it, whom to trust, and where to find the teachers—this was a great puzzle. It wasn't nearly so straightforward as, say, showing up for a march on Fifth Avenue or meeting your friends at the SNCC office in downtown Atlanta.

Other questions arose as well, rarely spoken but present nevertheless, like: How long is this going to take? Jennifer Welwood, a psychotherapist in her forties, recalls going into an ashram at fifteen. "I thought, giving myself some extra time, that for sure I'd be enlightened by seventeen," she says, laughing. They wanted to know: Isn't there an easier way? How much unimaginable grief, joy, bliss, and despair await me? When I get to where I think I'm going, will I know myself? And the constant worry was: How do I tell the difference between the good stuff and the bad, the sages and the hucksters? Caroline Alioto, who is now a lama in the Tibetan Kagyu lineage, remembers joining "Vietnam Summer" when she was a teenager. "I ended that summer by recognizing that the war was inside me, inside all of us, as much as it was in the soldiers going into Vietnam. I decided that I needed to root the aggression out of my own heart first, before I could work for peace. But it took many years of searching before I could find a teacher that I trusted to show me the way."

WAKING UP OVER TWO GENERATIONS

In the long view, the first generation of the consciousness movement was focused on what might be called *personal waking up.* Its questions were individual. Often painfully honest and intimate, they appeared from the outside to be astoundingly egocentric. Spiritual teachers from Asian countries were disturbed to find that the traditional essentials of ethics and spiritual community were simply not interesting to their Western students.

This focus on the self was the keynote of the first two decades of the consciousness movement, in the new psychotherapies and the bodywork and the spiritual approaches. The young seekers and explorers had a definite predilection for burning their bridges with the past, declaring their personal independence, and setting off in search of their own unique way. In part, this was because they were literally leaving home. They wanted to push away from the context that had once given their lives meaning and support, even if they secretly felt unsteady about their own resources and vision. But it wasn't only that. They felt a real need to cut away the old cultural bonds to make way for new developments.

By the 1980s and 1990s, the second generation of the consciousness movement was growing into what might be called a *cultural waking up.* As seasoned practitioners became concerned with the very questions that had previously seemed irrelevant or daunting to them, they broadened the personal into a strong concern for the social and planetary good. Women, especially, became avidly concerned with ethics and ethical guidelines for teachers and practitioners, and with the condition of women and children worldwide. Those who had become parents wanted communities that included their children, and they began to feel a longing for elders. Some joined or created neighborhood associations and local action groups. In private musings at first and later in their own groups and newsletters, they pushed the premise of the first generation one step further. If the achievements of saints, poets, and thinkers are our common inheritance, they asked, then how can we make this inheritance available to everybody? Are there ways to make waking up easier, more accessible, more normal?

In a sense, the second generation was articulating the traditional Eastern perspective in a new way. The purpose of inner work, in the East, had never been only for the benefit of the individual. All that effort could not be just for yourself. Especially in the spiritual approaches, the path was not intended to get you high or to catapult you out of the aggravations of your daily life or to lower your blood pressure. The path was for awakening from the sleep of unconsciousness—not for yourself alone, as the Buddhist vows put it, but for all beings.

It is one thing, however, to voice your deepest intention, and another to get up off your cushion or walk out of your expressive arts group or healing center and actually join in addressing the problems and concerns of the world. This has been the work of the second generation of the consciousness movements: to see and feel and bring awareness to their own lives and to help to heal our world.

Let's examine the chaotic experimental beginnings of the first generation to find out how they brought the issues of consciousness into their own lives. Then we'll follow the second generation and see how they are bringing new cultural forms into American life.

THE FIRST GENERATION

As activists were going off to demonstrate against the bomb, hippies were going off to drop acid. While some college kids were sitting in at southern lunch counters, others were sitting Zen. And while some small groups of women were creating consciousness-raising groups, others were learning healing and massage therapy. Throughout the 1960s and 1970s, the consciousness explorers and the social activists seemed like polar opposites. And although there was some sniping, for the most part they couldn't be bothered with each other. Each movement saw itself as the apotheosis of all that was necessary in life. Why would you waste your time looking elsewhere?

One of the most down-to-earth accounts of this period can be found in Joan Tollifson's memoir, *Bare-Bones Meditation*. As a political and disability rights activist in the 1970s, she describes what it was like to consider leaving her radical left group: "I still believed, in some part of myself, that they were the only real solution to the problems of the world, that by leaving them, I had stopped participating in the survival of the earth, that I was a self-serving coward."[3]

What made leaving especially hard was the fact that Joan was going to take up meditation. She wanted to "sit down, shut up, and listen," she said. And eventually she did make the move, becoming an ardent Zen student. But not before she had a dream that, in retrospect, characterizes the chasm between the new social movements and the consciousness movements: "I dreamed that I was in a big political march or parade. I was marching with a contingent of Hare Krishna people in saffron robes beating on tambourines and chanting. We passed by all my comrades from the left, and they were shocked and horrified to see me marching with the spiritual contingent. I felt ashamed, as if I were doing something terrible. But there I was. There was no going back."[4]

Despite the surface differences, however, a lot of people were waking up at the same time. For those in the consciousness movements, the most inviting wake-up calls were coming from a small hot springs resort perched on the lip of the Pacific Ocean.

ESALEN

How do you describe the beginnings of a movement that is rooted beneath the surface of people's lives? The most visible, earliest beginning was Esalen Institute. Started by Michael Murphy and Richard Price in 1962, it became the launch pad for a truly remarkable assortment of teachers and practitioners and speakers and writers in what would become the consciousness movement.

Esalen began with an ambitious plan for exploring human consciousness.[5] The early seminars came complete with reading lists and involved a couple of dozen people seated on wooden chairs, listening to verbal explorations of Great Ideas ("The Vision of Sri Aurobindo," "The Evolution of Human Experience"). There were discussions about opening up new resources in the human soul, poetry readings, and concerts of folk and chamber music from time to time. Political scientist Walter Truett Anderson recalls, "It was thrilling, in a cerebral way, and it was safe."[6]

Within a year, Esalen underwent a distinct shift from the purely intellectual toward the experiential. A weekend prayer and meditation retreat would be sandwiched between two seminars on psychedelics (during which, Walt Anderson recalls, some of the participants were "inspired by the subject matter to bring their own supplies"). It offered samplings of encounter groups, gestalt therapy, and bodywork. In the years that followed, these personal development offerings became so strongly identified with Esalen that many people believed that these approaches had been birthed in California. In fact, they were all rooted in early-twentieth-century European philosophy and psychology.[7]

Esalen's contribution was different. Because it was the first center of its kind in America and because it was so eclectic, it provided a crucible for the consciousness movements. And because it was a business, it introduced elements and teachers of those movements to a growing public. And finally, because the founders and longtime staff of counselors and teachers were wholeheartedly invested not just in the business but in the exhilarating adventure of it all, Esalen endured.

This last contribution turned out to be immensely important. In a movement where the real work was largely invisible, it mattered a lot that would-be consciousness explorers had a place to go. If they wanted to plunge into the further reaches of human nature, they could drive down the gorgeous (and appropriately precarious) Route 1 to this bubbling sourcepoint of the consciousness movement.

Esalen was not as grand and noble as its founders had envisioned. It was, after all, a small, groping, idealistic, unclear nexus of just about everything that could and would develop in the consciousness movements in the last four decades of the twentieth century. It was visionary and naïve, alluring and off-putting, often brilliant and rolling with momentum as well as a hotbed of roiling personal ambition and competitiveness. It was so easy to dismiss, and yet it was the place where the issues of consciousness became visible in American life. As with so much that would come later, Esalen's chaotic experimental beginnings were the signs of truly new cultural forms being birthed.

Findhorn, a spiritual center in northern Scotland, was started in the same year as Esalen, in 1962. In our depth interviews, many Cultural Creatives described their experiences with one or both of these early centers with gratitude. These centers, they said, were havens of healing and support, ships that helped to carry them through some of the darkest nights of their journeys. Both Esalen and Findhorn, they said, provided precious resources that were altogether lacking in the larger culture.

The story that follows took place at Esalen in the 1970s. It describes the experience of a young woman who arrived not knowing quite what to expect and who came face to face with a wholly different level of consciousness from any she had known before.

In 1975, anticipating the cement-colored skies of a Canadian January, I did something almost unimaginably adventurous for a professor at a staid university. It grew out of a sorrow that I was trying mightily to ignore. On the outside, my life was going beautifully. At the relatively young age of thirty-two, I had acquired a professorship, a book contract with a major publishing house, and an elegant downtown apartment. But on the inside, I felt like pressed cardboard. I had been separated from my husband and stepchildren for a year, living alone, and nothing I did seemed to matter much.

One day I attended a lecture at a nearby institute and something peculiar happened. The constant heaviness in my heart lifted for a few moments, and a sense of peace wafted in like a quick spring rain. I was amazed. What happened? I hadn't the faintest idea, but I knew I had to get more of this. At the end of the talk, the speaker told us that he was leading a program at Esalen for "therapists and healers." I was a research psychologist, by no stretch of the imagination a healer or even interested in healing anybody but myself. I signed up anyway.

A few months later, I was in the airport on my way to California, feeling quite contentedly anonymous. No one knew that I was headed for the notorious institute by the Pacific with all those people indulging themselves. The customs official checking the destination on my travel papers looked up brightly. "Esalen? I saw a movie all about that place. Hot tubs, right?" I cringed.

The first week was an extra, tacked on to the month I had originally planned. "Almost all of you are professionals," the woman organizing the retreat announced briskly on the phone. "Your minds will be so full of what you know that you won't be able to take in anything new. We recommend this extra week to open your minds." The whole trip seemed so crazy to me, I thought I might as well go along with the extra week. It was to be a "Zen *sesshin*," fourteen hours a day of sitting facing a wall, alternating with slow walking in a circle, she explained. Since we wouldn't be used to sitting in the Zen posture for that long, we could stand up occasionally, as we needed, and try to stay in meditation. And there would also be a one-hour lecture by the Zen master, during which you could ask questions. I mentally shrugged. Whatever.

On the first day of the retreat, about twenty-five of us were seated on large round cushions and flat mats around a spacious living room, on the edge of one of Esalen's famous cliffs. It was a glorious room, full of sunlight reflected from the Pacific and the sounds of the surf smashing against the rocks. But judging from the noisy jumping up and sitting down of the participants, most of us were already in misery. I knew for sure that I was. My knees were aching, and my mind was filled with angry hornets dive-bombing urgent messages: GET UP, GET OUT, GO HOME!

Finally it was time for the Zen master's talk. I could rest back against the wall and listen to something other than my obsessive mind chatter. In a heavy Korean accent, he told us a story about a Zen master named Un-mun and a student. Un-mun was working in the fields, spreading manure. The student bowed and asked, "What is enlightenment?" The master replied, "Dry shit on a stick." The student shook his head and wandered away. He traveled on until he came to Zen master Dong Sahn's temple. Dong Sahn was weighing grain. Again the student bowed and asked, "What is enlightenment?" The master replied, "Three pounds of flax."

The Zen master faced us, grinning. "So I ask you, which answer is better?" Several people in the room tried to answer, and he adroitly engaged them in "dharma combat," sparring back and forth. "You must find the mind that is before thinking," he shouted. "If you are thinking, you have good and bad, enlightened and unenlightened. But open your mind, and everything is just as it is." He looked around. A few people shifted. He didn't say anything for a while. Then, in a voice filled with delight, he boomed, "Deep in the mountains, the great temple bell is struck. The truth is just like this."

I was hanging on by my fingernails. I understood the individual words, of course, but my mind felt like it was slamming into a brick wall. At the same time, the whole thing was kind of fun. Everyone was laughing at the way he was catching us in our own earnest, determined mind-sets. Then someone raised a question that set off a few knowing smirks.

"Soen Sa Nim," he asked, using the Zen master's Korean title, "I heard a rumor that you were invited to teach Werner Erhard's staff." Erhard, the founder of est trainings, was one of the many blending psychology, Buddhism, and his own particular version of getting ahead in the marketplace. Yes, the Zen master acknowledged, he had been teaching the American guru and his assistants.

There was an excited murmur in the room. "So what's he really like?" someone else wanted to know. "Is he as enlightened as he claims?" We were all grinning by now, feeling ever so slightly superior from our morning of doing the real thing, enduring our aching joints to sit with a *real* Zen master.

"Werner Erhard is the Buddha," the Zen master replied coolly.

Consternation. I peered around at the others. They looked irritated, confused. How can Werner Erhard be the Buddha? He's so slick, so self-promoting. Can it be true? He's the Buddha? Maybe the Zen master's been bought. After all, Erhard is probably paying him a bundle. . . .

"And so," the Zen master announced gleefully, "is dried shit on a stick!"

ZAP! This was my first, but not nearly my last, Zen hit. The pile of opinions I have been carrying clattered to the floor. I felt a shock of clarity, like the snap of cold air before a snowfall. "Let go of your opinions, your situation, your condition," the Zen master shouted again. "Then your mind is clear like space. And *enlightened* and *unenlightened* are empty words."

He looked immensely pleased. As for me, I was more awake than I could ever remember. By the end of those five weeks at Esalen, I was ready to strike out on a new life path that would carry me back to my husband and stepchildren, out of the university, and eventually to start a Zen center and a talk radio show on consciousness in my hometown.

PSYCHOLOGY AND ITS DISCONTENTS

Before the 1960s, twentieth-century psychology had two streams. The first one flowed from the university, where it followed the course set by physics (among themselves, psychologists willingly acknowledged their "physics envy"). But the goal of measurement ended up biasing the entire field, dictating simple laboratory models for both experimental psychology and behaviorism. So much that was human had to be excluded: thinking, feeling, creativity, friendship, and love, not to mention mystical states of awareness, spontaneous healing, and altruism. The later appearance of cognitive psychology, based on computer analogies, hardly solved the problem.

The second stream in psychology flowed from hospitals and clinics, as physicians attempted to relieve the suffering of their disturbed patients. But this medical model offered another rather amputated picture of a human being. The healthy, well-functioning individual, the resilient and genuinely responsive family, the loving relationship that could mature and include conflict and differences—all were missing from the meticulous analyses of psychopathology. Spiritual life was dismissed as an unfortunate regression to the infant's longing for oneness.

In the 1960s, a third stream in psychology burst like a fresh spring into the established landscape. In a series of revolutions, group therapy came onto the scene, along with models and whole schools of technique designed to evoke what Aldous Huxley termed "the human potentiality." Abraham Maslow, with his insistence that "optimum development is a proper subject for scientific study," threw open the gates to what would eventually be a flood of interest in health and well-being.[8]

The more psychology and spirituality were influenced by this third stream, the more they started to touch and even blend into disciplines that had once seemed off-limits: the new science, including biology, cosmology, and quantum physics; alternative medicine, healing, and all manner of health care; art and art therapy and art as healing; dance therapy, intuitive movement, and various combinations of bodywork and psychology; and spirituality and religion, including pastoral counseling and transpersonal psychology.

This blooming, buzzing variety of blends and mixes made psychology and spirituality vastly more interesting to the general public. By the 1990s, a new, more user-friendly kind of psychology with some spiritual aspects was trickling—and sometimes pouring—into virtually every social movement and into a host of other developments in American culture as well. At the same time, conventional religious denominations set about rediscovering their own spiritual roots and their need for better psychological counseling, for ministers and congregations alike.

New concerns for consciousness thus wound up permeating every aspect of the emerging new culture. The actual practice of the new spiritualities and psychologies outran anyone's ability to understand their implications. The consciousness movement was so diverse, so huge, and everybody was either standing on the inside looking out, or standing on the outside looking in, aghast at all the hullabaloo. As much as they tried to be honest, even the most articulate commentators tended to idealize or exaggerate or denigrate what was developing. Not until the 1990s did the deeper, quieter notes of the growing awareness begin to find a balanced expression and more evenhanded commentators.

ON THE PATH FOR TWENTY-FIVE YEARS

John Davis is a slim, rather shy professor of psychology whose capacity for expressing the simple, direct truth of his experience can catch you by surprise. You wouldn't expect someone so unassuming to be so open. Just as you probably wouldn't expect an intellectual from one of the nation's prestigious experimental psychology programs to be leading wilderness programs or teaching in a spiritual school. But John is weaving together his love for nature, psychology, and a spiritual path. This kind of interweaving is typical of the Core Cultural Creatives, as they develop ways to integrate what they value into their daily lives. As we listen to some excerpts from John's story, we can hear how this kind of texturing emerges gradually in a conscious life, and how many threads there are to be pulled through.[9]

John had moved with his wife and infant son to Boulder, Colorado, to study for his doctorate in cognitive psychology. A few years later, he found himself in the midst of two different worlds of consciousness. On the one hand, he was enjoying the intellectual challenge of his cutting-edge research on the nature of thinking and conceptualizing. On the other, he was plunging into the new world of the consciousness movements of the 1970s: "I had . . . begun to discover an entirely different dimension of my life through encounter groups, meditation, hypnosis, biofeedback, and other consciousness-raising techniques. Rock climbing gave me a new sense of confidence and power in my physical body and, along with massage and yoga, woke me up to the deeper potentials for body-centered growth."

His comment about all of this activity could almost be a mantram for the fledgling Cultural Creatives of that time: "Boulder was a hotbed for the human potential movement, and I was trying out as much as I could." But collecting experiences, as almost everyone discovered, was disheartening after a while. "My mind was pretty adept at shielding me from anything that would truly alter my world and my sense of self," John explains. "I was accumulating experiences without changing very much."

A NEW SORT OF WORK

After several years of trying one or another training, John Davis met the teacher that he would stay with for twenty-five years. Hameed Ali had what John called "an undaunted quality," which was a quality of presence: "the most steady, unobstructed presence I had ever encountered, before or since. Some part of me responded to him."

It wasn't easy. The "new sort of growth work" began with three months of intensive psychological delving, bringing up repressed rage and pain along with many childhood experiences. At the end of the process, John had opened up a great deal, but he still felt his familiar sense of disappointment. Some core of his life was unchanged, and he was tempted to move on to the next thing.

"I was a tough nut to crack," he admits. His intellectual defenses were very strong, as his mind constantly tried to figure out what was going on. His description of this process is precise. "I was busy trying to look good and trying to impress my teachers, while at the same time I was constantly fitting these experiences into my preexisting categories, keeping myself at an ever-so-slight distance from them. And when that didn't work, I would go to sleep, both literally and figuratively."

In the end, he didn't go back to sleep, and he didn't leave either. He signed up for a small group with his teacher that met every other weekend. At the same time, he began a continual practice of sensing, looking, and listening designed to help him awaken—to examine and understand his experience so he would not fall back into unconsciousness. It took five years before he found himself trusting the process that was opening up his restricted emotional life. Then the spiritual work began.

"At first, it seemed to me that Hameed must have been making it all up because, in my own experience, I had so little reference to what he was describing. As I continued to explore, however, I began to see and feel what he was talking about." Although the ideas were new, the experiences felt very familiar. At times, John had a sense of discovering something within himself that had been hidden away. At other times, he felt that he was developing new capacities. Again and again he was grateful when something that he thought was complete, that he already understood, opened into an even greater context. "It was as if the journey were a set of inside-out Chinese boxes. I had started in the smallest and most restrictive, and every time I stepped into a newer, larger one, I felt a great sense of relief and freedom. Instead of finding smaller and smaller boxes inside, I was finding bigger and bigger boxes outside, each more radiant and refined than the one before."

One of the surprises was that he didn't have to "get rid of my ego." The work was simply to understand himself and allow the ego to unfold. "I began to realize that the emotional and psychological work was really the doorway—necessary, but only a beginning." In time, he discovered more and more subtle states of unconditional peace, strength, self-worth, love, and intimacy with life itself. But these were intricately interwoven with defenses, personal issues, pain, and fear. More and more John was surprised to find himself loving the process itself of uncovering the truth. He found that he was interested not just in the experiences but in the background, the medium of what he was feeling. "The important question was, so what? How was I holding on to (or rejecting) my experience? Was it touching me? How was I letting it into my life and living it?"

Eventually, it was this last question that was most important. The work, he says, "has been about a quality of my everyday life, not only about remarkable experiences. The remarkable times are richer, clearer, and easier to describe, but they are only the peak experiences. Most of the landscape of my life feels more ordinary, yet precious and rich. As I reflect back over twenty-four years . . . I notice that I feel more at home in my life and the world. Most of the time, there is a curiosity about my experience and a confidence that I have what I need to live my life to its fullest."

This, after all, is what the journey is for.

THE SECOND GENERATION

In the first two decades, despite the glamour and dazzle and media publicity, the consciousness movements were important only to thousands of people. But then it was tens and hundreds of thousands. As the ranks of beginners kept growing, hundreds of thousands stayed with the process and went deeper. By the 1980s, the movements' numbers had swelled to a million or so, and by the 1990s, tens of millions were involved. Each decade, the gradually increasing numbers of experienced practitioners were virtually swamped by the incoming waves of beginners.

A rapidly growing movement is like a fast-growing sport, as golf and tennis once were, or today's stupendous acceleration of Internet users. At any given moment, the pros are a small percentage of the total, the good players are probably under 20 percent, and the eager beginners are a walloping 80 percent. Looking at the whole picture over the big-growth years, your first impression may be that the average level of skill isn't going up. But that's because the numbers of duffers and newbies are ballooning far more quickly than the gradually increasing longtime players.

It takes a long time to learn well the substance of what the consciousness movements have to teach. You can pick up a new idea or technique or change your favorite hobby in a few weeks or months, but it takes decades to change yourself. John Davis's story is one good example. And it takes a long time to become a skilled therapist or bodyworker or yoga teacher or healer, one who knows not simply the technique but how to use it consciously and appropriately.

When you put a movement's rapid growth together with this relatively long learning cycle, it can be easy to focus only on the excesses of pop psychology and pop spirituality that media critics love to hate. But to take the surface for the substance of the consciousness movements would be an error. The key to understanding what is going on is to distinguish the great swell of new people searching for a taste of something authentic from the longtime practitioners who have been slowly learning to live authentic lives. Both groups have grown over the last four decades, but the beginners' numbers are still ballooning, making them by far the most visible part of the movement.

To get a sense of this dizzying rate of growth—which shows no signs of leveling off anytime soon—let's take one easy-to-track indicator: the businesses that serve the consciousness movement. These businesses provide products and services for personal growth, alternative health care, natural products, and organic food. The market for the books and videotapes is voluminous. The development of acupuncture and yoga is galloping. The new health food supermarkets are massive. Where the growth rate for the U.S. economy as a whole is 2 to 4 percent a year, many of the industries that serve the consciousness movement are growing at 10 to 20 percent a year. The size of the population they serve, and the money involved, is doubling every few years. The expected earnings for the industry as a whole in the year 2000 are about $75 billion.[10] (We'll look at this powerful trend in more detail in Part Three.)

HEARTWOOD

The consciousness movement as a whole is increasing not only in size but in depth. If the beginners are like the fast-growing greenwood close to the surface of a tree, the longtime practitioners are the heartwood at the center. The proportion of greenwood to heartwood has probably stayed about constant at 80 to 20. As the greenwood has grown, the heartwood has been growing, too. By the 1980s, it was substantial enough to change the tenor of the consciousness movement. The greater maturity was evident in thoughtful, sometimes startlingly honest critiques and overviews in magazines like *Tricycle, Yoga Journal,* and *Inquiring Mind* and in books like Elizabeth Lesser's *The New American Spirituality,* Roger Walsh and Frances Vaughan's *Paths Beyond Ego,* and Jack Kornfield's *After the Ecstasy, the Laundry,* to name just a few of the many examples.

The experienced practitioners themselves are displaying a long-overdue sense of humor, a willingness to reflect on and criticize their own path, and an interest in collaborating with and learning from others. The first generation's individualism has been tempered by decades of experience. At this point, the experienced are no longer interested in big-name celebrities. The celebrities have been immensely helpful as popularizers, opening the doors and welcoming the beginners. But after a while, the practitioners settle down to cultivate the truth in their own lives. Sage Kimble, a counselor from Albuquerque, told us, "At a certain point, it was time for me to let go of the teachers, stop looking for new tools, and dig down deep inside myself." And Gay Luce, a longtime spiritual practitioner, pinned it down. "At some point you no longer want comfort or inspiration," she said. "You just want the truth."

More and more the longtimers are bringing their spiritual, psychological, and holistic health practices into their personal and community life, learning to walk their talk. As they've birthed and raised their children and cared for their friends and their aging parents, they've begun to extend what they've learned. As they've consciousnessly faced personal grief, serious illness, and death, they've taken back some of the power of professionals to minister over birth and death. They are blending their concerns for consciousness with larger social concerns. And probably most interesting for our larger society, they are actively looking for multipliers for their efforts to create new kinds of schools, centers, institutes, service programs, and community groups.

A HOLE IN THE CULTURE

Cultural Creatives and others who are deeply interested in a conscious evolution face a situation that is rather like the one that generation after generation of women writers and artists faced. No one had passed on the history of women's own accounts of what they had created and thought over the centuries, so to each new generation of women, it was as if none of that important work had ever been done. Generations of women had to weave and reweave their understanding over and over again. Cultural Creatives today must also constantly invent and reinvent the basic supports for the way they want to live. It takes up a lot of time and energy, and precisely because many of the issues are new, there is a great deal of confusion and conflict.

Lacking a tradition of monasteries, ashrams, churches, mystery schools, pilgrimages, and libraries that have supported consciousness movements throughout history, Cultural Creatives took recourse in making analogies from the past.

"Well, it's sort of like that problem we solved before. . . ." And sometimes the analogies worked somewhat. Histories of science show that even the brightest scientific minds meet every new phenomenon with analogies to what they already know and make up new categories that are just small advances beyond their old perceptions. So it is with all of us: our new cultural forms are usually adaptations of older ones.

In the 1970s, when new forms of psychotherapy, spirituality, and healing were springing up everywhere, it was exhilarating for people to get an inspiration and try it out, to sit down in somebody's living room or a church basement or a grade school on a Saturday morning and throw a course or program together as quickly as possible so they could offer it to the public. "We're getting our act together and taking it on the road," the new explorers told one another, laughing and teasing. But they weren't kidding.

It was all slapdash and improvised—and, after several years, exhausting. The first generation had no way to get organized, no standards of good practice, and no place to meet over the long term. They had no steady source of income, no long-term, reliable staff people, and no good way to get the word out. Each time they built something promising and gained momentum, it fell apart and had to be rebuilt.

It was as if there were a hole in the culture, and the energy kept running out. No one knew, or even thought about, how to create cultural institutions to support the work that was so important to them. The first generation practitioners were very psychological, very individualistic (even the spiritual ones), and hardly any could manage their way out of a paper bag.

Some people initially imagined that America needed ashrams and zendos, like India and Japan, or simply new churches with different names and furniture. Others wanted seminars in a new kind of college. Many thought that healings could simply take place in renamed medical offices. Some of these solutions worked reasonably well, but others hardly at all. For the most part, using the old way with new labels didn't work. And sometimes the old ways were stunningly inappropriate: failing to question the guru or the great teacher led to abuses; neglecting to charge money or charging whatever the teacher wanted both failed; and the church model of the preacher and the congregation clearly wasn't going anywhere. There really was a hole in the culture—the old ways didn't work, and the new ones hadn't yet been invented.

What happened next—the social inventions, the development of "conscious commerce," the gatherings of elders and circles and initiations, the evocation of a new mythos—can all be seen as Cultural Creatives' efforts to address the sense of what is missing in the culture. But this does not mean, as some media observers claim, a flood of New Age solutions.

RUNNING AWAY FROM THE NEW AGE

Nobody wants to be called New Age anymore. Not David Spangler, the midwestern teacher and philosopher who was probably the first of the 1960s generation to use the term. Not the Cultural Creatives. And not even the trade association called NAPRA, which once stood for New Age Publishers and Retailers Alliance but in 1998 renamed itself New Alternatives for Publishers, Retailers, and Artists. The media's zest for attacking New Age concepts and systems has made just about everyone shun the term. Lance Morrow's May 1996 *Time* magazine essay, to take one of countless examples, pronounced New Age offerings as "meretricious junk, an idealism gone clueless and narcissistic."[11]

But this does not mean that the general category of spiritual and psychological popular culture has gone away. It just has new names, and a very large and interested public. Trend-setters and businesspeople within the broad consciousness movement now use terms like *natural products and services, natural or holistic health, wellness, alternative health care, complementary medicine, personal growth, self-actualization, new consciousness, perennial philosophy, wisdom literature, spiritual psychology, self-help, New Thought,* and so on.

The strongest continuing use of the term *New Age* is as a catchall category in book, magazine, and music publishing and retailing. Booksellers acknowledge that a lot of "New Age"–related material has splintered off into many themes that belong in other parts of the bookstore. And concepts that were innovative in the first generation of the consciousness movement are now permeating the wider culture. Amy Hertz, a HarperSanFrancisco editor, observed, "Something's definitely happening in this country. Open up any women's magazine—and they're all kind of closet New Age magazines—and you'll find a topic that HarperSanFrancisco has a book on."[12]

What's going on? Where does the disdained and disclaimed "New Age" fit in with the consciousness movement? Is it all fool's gold, all folly and romanticizing and magical thinking? The answer, as we see it, is no. There is an order beneath the chaos that makes sense when you think about the tremendous growth of the consciousness movement. The "chaos" is about experimental beginnings, with the unpredictability and high error rate that always accompanies genuine innovation.

With the enthusiasm and naïveté of beginners eager to improve themselves, wanting it all now, there's bound to be what Tibetan Buddhist teacher Chogyam Trungpa Rinpoche named "spiritual materialism": it means, he said, "deceiving ourselves into thinking we are developing spiritually when instead we are strengthening our egocentricity through spiritual techniques."[13] Is there anyone with an ego who doesn't know this all too well? One midwesterner who has studied Sufism for twenty years described it to us this way: "At first, it's the childish hope that buying something will make the ineffable more accessible. I'd buy the incense and the meditation cushions and the spiritual *tchotchkes* to—oh, I don't know. To be part of the whole thing. To join up. To comfort myself."

Elisabeth Lesser says that with her 1960s feminism and antiwar activism and her 1970s work as cofounder of the Omega Institute in upstate New York, she would qualify "for the New Age Hall of Fame." She writes: "I have watched people arrive at Omega looking for a way to drop their illusions about themselves and the world, and then leave with even more baggage: a Hindu name, a foreign mantra, and an ancient set of rules governing everything from diet to sex. What begins as a genuine spiritual search soon becomes a way of dressing up and hiding out behind esoteric explanations." It is a shame, she concludes, "when the possibility of spiritual transformation is traded for spiritual materialism."[14]

But spiritual materialism, like chaos and glitz, comes with the territory. The territory is the boundary between one cultural era and another, and the people in the rapidly growing consciousness movement are bound to be caught in some of the "New Age" hype as well as in the creative experimentation. Some media observers will probably continue to mistake the 24 million Core Cultural Creatives for the fewer than 5 million Cultural Creatives who might actually qualify as New Agers or the equal number of New Agers who are Moderns.

The key point about the New Age is that it is a transitional phenomenon, something that will fade as the newcomers find their way into a deeper understanding of what is required in a spiritual life, and as the new culture becomes normal in society. In reality, much of the characterization of the New Age is put forward by those who oppose idealistic and spiritual change in the culture, in an attempt to stereotype it and reduce its popularity. This resistance is one of the many cultural conflicts that accompany fundamental change.

Using the term *New Age* as name-calling is simply beside the point. The vast majority of people concerned with consciousness issues are not New Agers at all. But most are Core Cultural Creatives, and because they are the opinion

Values and Beliefs in Consciousness Movements

● Core Cultural Creatives
▪ Rest of U.S.*

Percent who agree/disagree or say it's important

0% 10 20 30 40 50 60 70 80 90 100

Nature of the spiritual or sacred

Human capacities probably include some sort of psychic powers: telepathy, knowing the future, communicating with spirits, etc.
. . . . *agree*

All that talk about psychic powers, telepathy, and knowing the future is bunk.
. . . . *disagree*

I have been born again in Jesus Christ.
. . . . *disagree*

I believe the literal truth of the Bible, including the world's creation in six days.
. . . . *disagree*

I reject the whole idea of reincarnation.
. . . . *disagree*

I lived before this life and may be born again.
. . . . *agree*

The divine nature completely permeates throughout the world. . . . . *agree*

How important to your life is: finding more time to be alone in meditation and spiritual pursuits? . . . . *important*

I have had a transformational experience that causes me to see the world differently than before. . . . . *agree*

Sacredness of nature/love of the Earth

Americans should have more respect and reverence for nature. . . . . *agree*

I agree with those Ecologists who see Earth as a giant living organism. . . . . *agree*

How important to your life is: living in harmony with the Earth? . . . . *important*

Redwood groves are sacred. . . . . *agree*

Churches and prayer are what is sacred, not a bunch of trees. . . . . *disagree*

How important to your life is: finding more time to be in nature? . . . . *important*

Values and Beliefs in Consciousness Movements

● Core Cultural Creatives ▨ Rest of U.S.*

Percent who agree with value/belief

0% 10 20 30 40 50 60 70 80 90 100

Self-Actualization

How important to your life is:

the belief that every person has a unique gift to offer

developing more self-awareness—that is, not sleepwalking through life

discovering new things about yourself

needing to express your own creativity

putting more time and effort into your psychological development

Altruism

How important to your life is:

the caring quality of your relationships with people

helping other people

finding your purpose in life, rather than making money

having your work make a contribution to society

involvement in volunteer work

Religious Affiliation

None (evidently secular)

Roman Catholic or Greek Orthodox

Mainline Protestant

Conservative Protestant

Non-Christian (Jewish, Muslim, Hindu, Buddhist, etc.)

Make own synthesis from several traditions

No answer

---

*Note: This chart contrasts Core Cultural Creatives to everybody else. "Rest of U.S." is not U.S. total, but Moderns plus Traditionals. Cultural Creatives are so numerous that when included in the total U.S., they raise the percentages and it's harder to see they are much stronger than the others on these issues. (Source: 1995 Integral Culture Survey and 1999 EPA survey)

leaders and the strongest voices of the emerging culture, their great interest in consciousness is likely to have powerful momentum in the new century.

THE CORE CULTURAL CREATIVES

What's striking about the Core Cultural Creatives is the way consciousness issues and social concerns come together for them. Our survey data show that the stronger Cultural Creatives are on spiritual and psychological issues, the stronger they are on social and environmental concerns, activism, and volunteering, as well. This means that, in the second generation of the consciousness movement, the Core group contains most of the strong activists in the social and consciousness movements.

To find out more about what this influential Core group says about consciousness, let's look at the charts on pages 190 and 191. The questions to which they responded are shown in four kinds of issues important to the Core group: what they consider to be spiritual or sacred; love of the Earth; self-actualization; and altruism.[15]

Notice that on the question of the spiritual or sacred, the Core group tends to be open to various ways of perceiving and experiencing the sacred in life. They say that they believe in the reality of both psychic and spiritual events. They tend to believe that the Divine is both here in the world and transcendent (that is, they're pan*en*theistic, taking the "both/and" position on the immanence and transcendence of God). While only a minority are meditators or likely to believe in reincarnation, they'll stay open to the possibilities. But they tend to reject fundamentalist statements, like those affirming the literal truth of the Bible.

As you can see, the Core group regards nature as sacred. Self-actualization is part of their values, and so is altruism. They are part of neither secular Modernism nor Traditional fundamentalism. Overall, a sense of the spiritual is central to them. But while most of them belong to conventional religious denominations, they are conducting their search for the sacred along innovative lines.

Strikingly, about 89 percent of the Core group say that it is very important to develop more awareness, to "not sleepwalk through life," compared with 61 percent in the general population. About 95 percent say that the caring quality of their relationships is important to them, while 77 percent say that finding their purpose in life is more important than making money. These figures are 25 and 36 percent higher, respectively, than in the general population.

Finally, most of the Core group tend toward a kind of theological liberalism, with relatively few (compared with the overall population) Catholics and conservative Protestants and about the expected number of mainline Protestants and non-Christians. More of them are secular than in the general population, and more make their own synthesis from several traditions. Even those in the Core group who belong to conservative denominations agree on the sacredness of nature and the importance of many consciousness issues, including self-actualization.

By contrast, the 26 million people we call the Green Cultural Creatives have the same kind of strong values on social and environmental issues as the Core group, but when it comes to consciousness issues, the Greens are about the same as most other Americans. That is, like average Americans, Greens are not very interested in inner experience. But about 30 million Moderns are broadly interested in this kind of experience from time to time, and they too are part of the consciousness movement. This group of Moderns are more materialistic and less environmentally oriented than most Cultural Creatives. From our survey and focus group data, we expect that in the next decade more and more of the Green Cultural Creatives, and probably more of the Moderns on the less active fringe of the consciousness movement, will follow the Core group's lead.

As Core Cultural Creatives bring consciousness into their daily lives, they inevitably address our larger culture's lack of support for inner work and spiritual concerns. We turn now to health and healing, where Cultural Creatives are addressing the hole in our culture in three characteristic ways: as individuals, as creators of new stories, and as builders of what might be called "person-centered" institutions.

HEALING IN THE SECOND GENERATION

In her introduction to *Anatomy of the Spirit,* the medical intuitive Caroline Myss tells about something that happened just after she graduated from college. She had arrived in Alaska for a summer job and was visiting a Native American woman in her eighties. They spoke for some time before the elder woman mentioned casually that the next day she would be going to a ceremony for a man who was "preparing to leave the earth." It would be a potlatch ceremony, she explained, in which the man would give the tribe all of his belongings, and then he would leave.

"How does this man know he is going to die? Is he sick?" Myss asked.

"Oh," the elder replied, "he went to the medicine man. The medicine man looked at his energy. His energy told the medicine man what was happening to him."

"How does the medicine man know these things?"

The older woman seemed shocked at Myss's ignorance. "Tell me," she asked, "how is it that you do not know such things? How can you live without knowing what your spirit is doing and what your spirit is saying to you?"[16]

How indeed? How can we live today without knowing the state of our soul? How can we suppose that our body is separate from our spirit, or that we exist apart from the great web of being? The first generation of the consciousness movement almost always asked these questions, and they were almost always answered in terms of the needs of the individual. Even in healing circles and prayer groups, the focus was primarily on one person or a group of people. At times, a group prayed or meditated for a country or for the Earth. But not until the second generation were there efforts to come up with cultural solutions.

To get a sense of this change from personal to cultural, let's turn to a case study in what's generally called "healing and holistic medicine." We'll see how consciousness is coming into a field that has a long and vigorous history of resisting it.

STIFF WHITE COATS

Even a glimpse at Western medicine today reveals that it is in the midst of a baffling time, with cost expansion, shrinking training hours for doctors and nurses, demands for increased speed, and diminishing resources for the poor and elderly. Most doctors and nurses are working with, or anticipate working with, HMOs, which many people regard as public enemy number one. For all these reasons, many doctors now ask, is it worth it?[17]

Though most doctors took off their stiff white coats decades ago in a literal sense, many still seem to be wearing them in a symbolic sense. A shell of reserve, compounded by intense time, resource, and money pressures, is making automatons out of people who hoped to be healers. A great deal of research shows that many if not most patients are sick of modern medicine's impersonal approach and that it is bad for everyone's health—patients and nurses and doctors alike. In 1998 the New England Medical Center's Health Outcomes Institute studied more than six thousand patients and their doctors. On almost every measure, it found that the doctor-patient relationship was critical to the patient's health and well-being. One of the surprising results was that the doctors' knowledge of their patients' home life, health beliefs, and personal values had a significant influence on improvements in their patients' health. A study by researchers at the University of California, Davis, School of Medicine, also done in 1998, reported very similar results.[18]

When caregivers don't have the time or energy to give more than physical care, the patients are not the only ones who suffer. Doctors face high levels of emotional exhaustion and work stress, and they feel harried by the HMOs on the one hand and malpractice litigation on the other. A stunning one-third of doctors today say that they would choose a different profession if they could start over.[19]

THE NEW HEALERS

In its core meaning, *to heal* means "to make whole." At the most universal level, *to heal* means "to wake up to our true nature." At the level of the individual, it means to recognize as one wholeness the body, mind, emotion, and spirit. At the level of community, it means to recognize interdependence and to repair what has been broken apart. And at the level of the Earth, to heal—the Hebrew word is *tikkun*—means to call home those who have been in exile, to redeem and bring peace to our world.

The most visible healers in America today are those whose explicit vocation has been the healing of the body. Physicians like Deepak Chopra, Larry Dossey, Rachel Naomi Remen, Christiane Northrup, Bernie Siegel, and Andrew Weil, and medical researchers like Joan Borysenko and Caroline Myss, are probably better known than most of the spiritual teachers and psychotherapists in the consciousness movement. Maybe it's because, for those who live in a profoundly materialist culture, the body is our great touchstone of the real. Those who can heal the body or keep death at bay are bound to be sources of great authority, potentially able to quiet our confusion and relieve our anxiety.

The doctors, medical researchers, and other healers who are part of the consciousness movement depart more or less radically from the contemporary medical model. All of them have taken off their stiff white coats, symbolically as well as literally, in an effort to link the scattered parts of ourselves and our society. Some build bridges across areas of research that have been separated. Others weave connections between people in different professions. And all welcome into the examining room realities that modern Western medicine has exiled: mind and emotions and also spirit, mystery, and miracles. Physician and author Larry Dossey says that we are entering the time of the practice of "Era III Medicine" when therapies will combine spiritual and physical, holistic and conventional Western approaches to physical and emotional healing.[20]

Rachel Remen, medical director of the Commonweal Cancer Help Program in Bolinas, California, elaborates on this idea. Health, she says, is not the manipulation of the body, nor even the mind and emotions, to attain some optimal functioning. "Health is a means. Health enables us to serve purpose in our life, but it is not *the* purpose of life." The real questions of health, she says, are not about the mechanisms of healing but what gives meaning and purpose to our lives. Speaking not only as a physician but as a longtime patient with decades of Crohn's disease and numerous major surgeries, she says that the process of illness, with its limitation and suffering and its shocking isolation, "awakens in us the seeker, which is so much more than the scientist. We begin to sort values, what matters and what doesn't. We become open to looking at the meaning of life, not just the meaning of pain, of one's own pain, but even the meaning of life itself."[21]

This perspective—that nothing can be left out, that no part of us is dispensable or unwelcome—places healing at the heart of the consciousness movement. From this context, let's look at three different ways of bringing healing into the culture.

NINETY-FIVE PERCENT COMPASSION AND COMMON SENSE

Before Mariquita West retired in 1998, she was a popular instructor in psychiatry at Stanford Medical Center. The young medical residents said she was a breath of fresh air, honest and open with them at a time when those qualities seemed in short supply. Her colleagues in social work and psychology, the nurses and other psychiatrists at Stanford, and the ones who mattered most to her—her patients—agreed. We'd heard that she was interested in alternative medicine and had studied hypnosis and Gestalt therapy and various spiritual approaches, integrating some of what she learned into her clinical practice. We wondered how this open, person-centered approach fit in with teaching at one of the nation's high-powered medical centers.

When we met with Mariquita in the fall of 1996 in San Francisco, our first question was about her vision for medicine. Did she want to change the way medicine is practiced? She laughed and shook her head and looked a little embarrassed. She said that she's like former president George Bush: "pretty passive when it comes to the vision thing." And then she went on to tell us about her very personal way of practicing medicine and building bridges.

"I was in school until I was almost thirty, so I grew up steeped in the tradition of professionalism," she said. In that tradition people were learning how to do the particular thing that would earn them money and prestige in life. Wanting money and prestige is not limited to doctors, of course—it is found all through our affluent contemporary society: "There's a jockeying for some kind of elevated position. Fairly early on, I had some sense of the downside of that approach—the anxiety of always having to guard your important position, and the fact that even within your profession, there is such a great hierarchy that you're constantly preoccupied with what your position is relative to everybody else's." In her work with her patients, she said, she never adopted as professional a position as some of her peers did. This gave her healing a much more human impact.

How does someone go against the dominant model of a modern physician, especially within a high-tech medical establishment? "I think I was brought up to feel that love was the most important thing," Mariquita told us, "and even when I was a painfully shy medical student, I knew that as soon as I started being a doctor in my own way, I could do something very valuable: to be interested in people, to listen to them, to care about them. It was as simple as that. All this other stuff that we learned in medical school was important also, but it was only about five percent. That's what I've taught my students. It's ninety-five percent compassion and common sense, and then five percent expertise. You're going to spend years trying to get that five percent, but it's the other that's most important. I think that's been a very helpful teaching."

Many of Mariquita's colleagues admire her ability to jujitsu the fierce competitiveness that takes place inside academia. Toward the end of the interview, we asked her how she managed this. "I think I've been what I would call a bridge person," she explained. "I've held a secure position in the conventional medical world at the same time as I've explored some of the fresher, newer approaches to healing, and I've been able to integrate the two in my work and teaching." She says it's fun, that making connections heals the fractures in her own life. It had better be fun, she told us, because if you don't enjoy what you're doing, nobody else will want to do it with you.

Ordinary Miracles

The kinds of bridges that Mariquita West has built with her hundreds of students and patients and colleagues span gaps in status, role, values, and worldviews. Many Cultural Creatives build the same kind of bridges. It's the culture making of people who stand with one foot in the middle of the mainstream and the other in alternative currents that are not yet accepted.

Another form of bridge building is the kind that creates new groups and organizations in the culture. When it comes to healing, many of the most successful bridges are started by those who have been through the isolation of illness or loss or addiction themselves. The shock of their own suffering wakes them up to the suffering of others. If they were helped, they want to extend that help to others. If they weren't able to find resources or friends, their wish to help others may be even greater. Our next story is one of conscious healing and the creative response that followed.

We met Maureen Redl at a friend's birthday party in September 1999, where a number of the guests were nurses and doctors and therapists. In the midst of a lively conversation about the merits of alternative medicine, someone described in hushed tones a miraculous healing that he had witnessed. A gray-haired woman with alert blue eyes jumped in. "The miracle about healing is how *ordinary* it is," she said in a no-nonsense tone. "We act like somebody has to be some kind of saint or mystic to be healed. But it's the most natural thing in the world." She paused for a moment, but no one spoke. "And that doesn't make it any less miraculous," she announced.

We were among the users of hushed tones ourselves and were eager to hear more about the ordinariness of healing. A few weeks later, we were sitting in Maureen's living room in Mill Valley, California, drinking tea and looking over green hills softened by fog. After some small talk, Maureen told us that in 1989 she had been diagnosed with metastatic ovarian cancer, a virulent form of the disease with "bad statistics." She had heard about Rachel Remen (the physician we quoted earlier) and arranged to see her, expecting some straightforward medical counseling. But what happened in those sessions with Rachel changed Maureen's mind about what was happening to her and what she was going to do about it. This is what she told us:

"Sometime during the session, Rachel asked, 'How is it for you to lose your health?'

"I was taken aback. 'I haven't lost my health,' I retorted.

"'Well, Maureen,' Rachel said in that slow, gentle voice of hers, 'you're sitting in front of me perfectly bald, on very high levels of chemotherapy, not at all able to do the things you used to do. What do you think is going on?'"

Maureen paused to sip her tea and look out at the fog, which seemed to be lifting. She wanted us to understand, she said, that she felt strongly that she wasn't going to die of the cancer. It was simply something she'd have to go through for a while. She didn't mention this to Rachel. Instead she said calmly, "I expect that cancer's going to be an important teacher for me."

Rachel was quiet and then folded her hands under her chin. "It may or may not be a teacher for you," she replied slowly, "but you should know that it's a teacher with its own agenda."

"What's that?"

"Its agenda is to kill you."

Maureen stopped talking and looked out the window for a while. Then she gazed directly at us. "For the first time since I got the diagnosis, I began to fathom what I was up against."

Over the course of the next year, Maureen had to make a decision that was extraordinarily difficult for her. "After some time of working with Rachel, I began to see that I had to be one hundred percent responsive to what was trying to heal in me. The way I became aware of that was often to stay up all night and wander through the house, write poetry or drum or draw. At the time I was living with a man who was my good friend and companion. The place where he had been living had burned down some months earlier, and it seemed obvious that he would join me in my rather spacious home.

"Now I felt that I had to ask him to leave. Taking that step was the hardest thing I've ever had to do in my life. On the surface, it looked like the most mundane act. Many women would have been able to do this without anguish.

"But it seemed absolutely impossible for me to ask for this. Slowly, over several months of working with Rachel, I began to understand my fear. Something devastating had happened earlier in my life that convinced me that if I asked for what I needed, someone would be badly injured or would die. After that, I had done my best to become incredibly independent, so independent that I didn't even know what I needed. That made it a lot easier not to ask for anything!

"When I recognized my absolute need to respond to the cancer and to be totally available to the healing process in myself, I just could not find a way to do that and respond to someone else's ordinary needs. It wasn't about my friend. It was about what I had to do. It was my task in my own life.

"It took me weeks to prepare. I had to write out what I would say. I can still feel it in my gut now, like I was kicking the loyal old family dog into the midst of a Minnesota blizzard. When I finally sat down with him and began to tell him that he was going to have to leave, when I got the first sentence out, an amazing thing happened. All of a sudden, it was easy. I felt like a mother bird, pushing the last little fledgling out of the nest, knowing very well it could fly.

The rest of the conversation flowed. And months later, when I told him how difficult it had been for me, he actually cried. 'I had no idea,' he said. 'It wasn't a big deal to me at all.'"

This was the turning point. "In challenging serious illness," Maureen told us, "something very central often has to die. It can look very mundane from the surface, but in the depth of ourselves we'll do almost anything to not go through that loss of the old self. But if we can find the courage to let it happen, we can eventually move to a new place in consciousness—whether we return to health or go on to our dying time."

SACRED SPACES FOR STORY

By 1999, ten years after Maureen Redl's recovery from cancer, she had created circles of people with what she calls "life-challenging illnesses" in both the United States and Europe. Under the umbrella of a nonprofit group called Voices of Healing, these circles gather to share "true adventure stories that begin when a diagnosis threatens to destroy you and everything you love about life." In what Maureen calls "the sacred space of a story circle," the journey of body and soul, heart and mind can unfold. In time, people learn to listen to the personal meanings of their illness, to feel the anger and fear and despair, and to know that they'll be held through that. They allow the images and energies and wisdom of the soul to come to consciousness. In this way, she said, the integrity of each person's life can surface.

As we heard about the circles, which Maureen organizes as a volunteer in addition to her work as a psychotherapist, we thought of the early women's consciousness-raising groups. The story circles, too, are places for "hearing each other into speech." As people begin to trust themselves to speak and reframe the meaning of illness and death, they seem to be reaping the fruits of almost two generations of earlier activists and explorers. It is a richer, more integrative process than was possible in the first generation of the social change movements because a sense of sacredness is explicitly included.

Maureen hopes that an evolution can occur through groups like these: "Whether healing is physical or at the level of transforming consciousness, I am so sure it is available to all of us. And as people in large numbers share their stories of healing and recovery, we're going to trust the naturalness and ordinariness of it much more easily. By hearing these true stories, we hope that a collective group wisdom will develop and evolve. As we listen to the uniqueness of each person's story, what we hear, in the end, is what is universal."[22]

This is the promise and the possibility of building bridges through the creation of consciousness in groups and organizations: to arrive at what is universal through what is personal and particular. It is a very deep kind of culture making. The exploration is in its early stages now, but clearly it has begun.

FOR THE CHILDREN

After you hear inspiring stories for a while, especially stories in which you recognize yourself, a strange kind of sadness can affect you. If you let it touch you and ask yourself what is wrong, you may discover the kind of weariness that some of the Core Cultural Creatives described to us. Or it may feel like impatience, a sense of the urgency of what is needed now. Not that the inspiring stories aren't hopeful, but for some people they are not nearly enough. It's time to get going, they say, to get moving at a level that works over the long term. This is the stance of the change agent, and it is the perspective we turn to now.

In 1992 theologian and activist Thomas Berry, well into his seventies, led a yearly retreat for nuns and students and environmental activists. On the first evening of the retreat, he looked especially tired. At the end of his lecture, he asked for questions. A young man stood up. "Why do you insist on working so hard, Thomas? Why don't you take a rest?"

There was a murmur of approval in the audience. "I do what I do for the children," Berry replied. "I want to bring a healing to what my generation has brought to the planet. The pathos is, we thought we were doing good. The fact is, we have irreparably damaged the Earth.

"The second way I think about what I'm doing is this. There is a widespread movement for change taking shape. I hope it is a healing movement. I hope that I am assisting in establishing a constituency." He paused and repeated, "Constituency." Scattered *yeses* and *okays* were heard through the audience. "We need," he continued, "a constituency now. The industrial age is over. It will go on for a few decades more. Petroleum will slowly disappear. My generation won't see the consequences, but the children will. The planet is what is basically at stake in our time. So I do what I do for the children."[23]

LOOKING FOR MULTIPLIERS

When you meet someone who has given his life to healing the Earth, it is profoundly moving. But what can ordinary people do to foster change? One answer is that they can create institutions that will endure over the long term, where many people with many different talents and skills can develop things greater than any single person's efforts can accomplish.

What kind of healing you feel called to do, and on what scale, is a very individual matter. But as the second generation of the consciousness movement matures, they are looking for ways to create programs, projects, and solutions that will last longer than a few brief seasons. They are tired, they say, of having to build again and again from the ground up. They are seeking to create new institutions, or change old ones, rather than simply rolling over the usual structures again and again.

Core Cultural Creatives told us that they wanted to make their actions effective for the greatest number of people. They wanted, they said, to maximize their resources for the greatest good. The word they kept using was *multipliers*. It reminded us of Thomas Berry's word, *constituency*. We need enough people who care and will get involved, they told us, and we need leverage on our actions.

One of the most interesting efforts in the field of healing is the nonprofit health and environmental research institute where Rachel Remen works, Commonweal. Founded in the 1970s, it has had nearly thirty years to become what we consider a key example of a Cultural Creative institution, combining consciousness issues with environmental activism and social justice. One sure sign of Cultural Creatives at work is bridging and integration, which is Commonweal's signature.

The institute works with doctors and other health professionals to address the disheartenment among doctors that we talked about earlier. It offers contemplative and reflective retreat-weekends for physicians who work with patients with life-threatening illnesses. Workshops teach doctors to use a range of mental, emotional, and spiritual resources in support of physical healing. The sessions are heartfelt, transformative, and meaningful, the participants say in letters, e-mails, phone calls, and program evaluations. Most telling is the fact that many "alumni" of these programs go on to teach with the Commonweal staff in what they call "tradecraft workshops," training other physicians and health professionals in the United States, Canada, and New Zealand. The majority of alumni hold "leadership positions in clinical teaching, academia, or health service organizations around the country," according to the institute's literature. In other words, they have clout. If you train opinion leaders and professional leaders in integrative medicine, and if your program is good, you're going to get the multipliers that all change agents look for.

How do the institute's multipliers work? Half the workshop participants go on to offer training for others. Local alumni meet in monthly training seminars where they explore topics like suffering, listening, dignity, mystery, hope, joy, fear, gratitude, and grace. Each physician brings a story from his or her personal life on the selected topic or a story or poem, and some even prepare exercises so the group can explore the topic in greater depth. And finally, alumni and staff teach first- and second-year medical students. Forty-five students (one-third of the first-year class) at the University of California, San Francisco, School of Medicine learned holistic medicine in 1999, including a module titled "Death As Mystery."

It's hard to convey the scope and impact of an integrative healing program in a few words. Michael Lerner, who has been with Commonweal for more than one hundred programs and almost as many retreats, writes about the depth and continuity that have kept him committed over the long term: "Why do we keep doing these programs? Why do people keep coming from all over the United States to attend them? Why is there a year-long waiting list for the Cancer Help Program? . . . I believe that a lot of what the [program] offers comes from the close relationship participants experience with a staff that has been largely stable for over a decade, and that has learned together how to create and sustain a healing community in a very deep and unusual way. The point is that what makes the experience powerful is not . . . a technique, but rather a relationship—in this case the relationship with a healing community."[24]

GOING THE DISTANCE

As it matures, much of the consciousness movement is learning something important: when you're trying to change a culture, persistence pays off. As Rocky Balboa said when he was training for his big fight, you gotta be able to go the distance. In the consciousness movement, the people who can persevere for ten, twenty, and thirty years are the ones who can have a dramatic impact on the culture—because that is the true time horizon of effective action. Those who need fast results and instant gratification had better go into some other line of work. As a number of Core Cultural Creatives told us, you have to enjoy the people and the process, and you need the maturity to work in a longer time frame.

At this point, the consciousness movement is still emerging. We've seen how the ideas of the hundred-year-old environmental movement have been accepted by nearly the whole of American culture. Ecologically sustainable ways of life have not yet been implemented, but they are part of our central belief system and are what nearly everyone wants. But the consciousness movement—full of contradictions, shallow and deep, bubbling with new developments—is still in the phase of accelerating growth.

Today, as Core Cultural Creatives are creating a phenomenal demand for resources to feed their growing interest in consciousness, they also need something more basic: institutions that can support their values, so they do not have to create support structures for themselves over and over again. They need not only healers and practitioners of holistic medicine but colleges to train those practitioners; not only classes and courses, but teachers, and schools for the teachers, and centers where they can take the classes. Sometimes it will not be healers or teachers that are needed but gathering places in which circles of people with common interests can explore new ways of knowing and sharing their gifts and experiences, experimenting over time.

Where will the funds come from? And how will the people who want to meet one another make contact? Cultural Creatives need to be able to find one another through magazines and Web portals and television channels that provide fair and honest mirrors and access points. And they need classes and institutes that will train new media people, and businesses that will support new programming. What is needed, in short, is a scaffolding for a new kind of culture.

chapter seven

a great current
of change

imagine a hundred rivers from the North American continent flowing together into the Atlantic Ocean. Heated by the sun, they create a new Gulf Stream that reaches all the way to Europe. The current is almost invisible at the surface, because unlike a river, it has no clearly visible boundaries. But within itself, it supports a different kind of life than the wider ocean.

We believe that something like this is happening now in the life of our larger culture. Influences of different kinds are converging and creating a general movement for change. In this chapter, we will look at three kinds of convergences. The first is a change in the social movements of the last forty years: they are becoming more similar in their approaches and worldviews and are working together on some big issues, and they are moving toward the consciousness movements. The second kind of convergence is the emergence of a constituency that all the movements have in common: the Cultural Creatives. And the third is the development of a new kind of movement that contains the convergence within itself right from the beginning. Just as the Gulf Stream's warmth moderates Europe's weather and shapes the global climate, so the confluence of these several influences may already be contributing to a climatic change in our civilization.

CONVERGING MOVEMENTS

One of the earliest observers to spot a convergence of the social movements and the consciousness movements was a draft resister named Mark Satin. In 1978 after twelve years in Canada, Satin wrote: "One fierce winter's day in Montreal, over a cup of steaming cocoa and *The New York Times,* it dawned on me that the ideas and energies from the various 'fringe' movements—feminist, ecological, spiritual, human potential, and the rest—were beginning to come together in a new way . . . in a way that was beginning to generate a coherent new politics. But I looked in vain for the people or groups that were expressing that new politics (instead of merely bits and pieces of it)."[1]

Satin didn't find what he was looking for, but he wrote about it in a pamphlet that he typeset himself and sold from his home in Canada. A second edition, published by a friend, sold ten thousand copies in less than a year. After Satin accepted amnesty in 1978, he was invited to speak at a gathering in the States. He had just returned, and he was awake all night before the talk with excitement and fear. A friend walked with him for hours before the talk, as he wondered whether anyone would want to hear what he had to say. The speech got a standing ovation, and Satin wept. His vision of what was possible, of what in fact was already moving through the culture, had evidently struck a nerve. He called it "an entire third force in American politics" and said it represented "what this country at its best has really been about: personal responsibility, self-reliance, freedom of choice, belief in ethical values and ideals, and an all-encompassing love for what some of us choose to call God."

Two decades later, we know that Satin's hopes for a new political platform did not materialize. But over those long years in Toronto and Montreal and Vancouver Island, he caught sight of and began to plan for the general movement for change that is taking form now. Today the movements he was observing—"not only those in the national spotlight but also those on the fringes of society where the real beginnings, the real rediscoveries often take place"—are no longer pushed off to the edges of our awareness. They are front and center, standing in our midst, and our public embrace has already opened to many of them.

Living in Canada for so long, "trying not to wish I was back in the United States—in other words, wishing I was back in the States," Satin paid close attention to what was happening to all the social movements in this country. He read everything he could find, not only newspapers and books but movement periodicals, posters, newsletters, and letters from his friends in the various movements. He saw something that few activists of the time recognized: that each of the new movements was a fragment of a greater whole. A quarter of a century later, the convergence Mark Satin spotted is showing up everywhere.

There were other visionaries as well. George Leonard's *The Transformation* came out in 1972, beating just about everybody to the punch with his observation that a civilizationwide shift in social organization was coming.[2] By the early 1980s, several other observers added their predictions: Marilyn Ferguson's *The Aquarian Conspiracy,* Alvin Toffler's *The Third Wave,* Fritjof Capra's *The Turning Point,* Hazel Henderson's *The Politics of the Solar Age,* and Theodore Roszak's *Person/Planet.* Like Satin, these authors drew on anecdotal accounts and extended them into the future. But none foresaw how long it would take for that shift in consciousness to impact our larger culture. Indeed, throughout the 1980s and 1990s, many activists, artists, and other concerned people asked, with Wendy Wasserstein, "Where did everybody go?"

THE BATTLE IN SEATTLE

The 1999 Seattle meetings of the World Trade Organization (WTO) were scheduled to be another bureaucratic yawner, one of those international meetings among trade representatives to which you couldn't drive reporters with bullwhips and chains. It was to be something for page twenty-seven, across from the obituaries. Instead it was the 1960s redux, with clouds of tear gas hanging in the air and the demonstrators chanting, "The whole world is watching! The whole world is watching!" as police in riot gear scuffled with black-clad anarchists right in front of the TV cameras. In some ways, the battle in Seattle felt just like the 1960s protests of the black freedom movement and the antiwar movement. But the protesters had deftly used the Internet to get organized, and they managed to carry protest to the next octave by combining it with zany celebrations to draw media attention. The convergence of interests and organizations caught almost everyone by surprise.

Dressed as sea turtles and monarch butterflies, death's heads and victims of violence, fifty thousand activists showed up from around the world. Ecologists and feminists, Teamsters and steelworkers in union jackets, witches and nuns, consumer and health advocates, native people, human rights activists, and people against multinationals and globalization came prepared to engage in the great ritual drama—parading and shouting slogans, linking arms to block streets and buildings, getting arrested and going limp, and finally being dragged off to jail. But the police wouldn't play the forty-year-old game. Unprovoked, they shot pepper spray into the faces of sitting demonstrators and beat them with clubs, fired tear gas and rubber bullets into peaceful crowds. Often they didn't arrest anyone, not even the looters of electronics stores or the window-smashers at Starbucks. Their only task, it seemed, was to move all those people away so that trade delegates could get to the meetings of the WTO to negotiate some new trade accords.

In five days of protests, with mutual acrimony on all sides, the trade talks collapsed. Even without the protests, the trade reps from third world countries might well have staged a walkout to collapse the talks. In the end, everybody got mad and went home. The hundreds of protesting organizations withdrawing from Seattle celebrated their victory, claiming a strong role in disrupting the WTO talks and forcing new issues onto the future global trade agenda.

One striking feature of the demonstrations was that most of the protesters seemed to know just what to do. They fell into a kind of peaceful order in the marches and demonstrations, regardless of what movement or organization they represented or what country they were from. Except for a few dozen anarchists who managed to provoke violence, the thousands were following a culture of nonviolent civil disobedience that had been developed originally by Gandhi. According to accounts on the Internet, the DAN (Direct Action Network), which provided infrastructure for the protest, had been working for months coordinating logistics, housing, nonviolence training, legal backup, and the opening day "People's Convergence" at the WTO. They also worked with the police in those months, promising that the protest would be nonviolent.

What Really Went On in Seattle?

Contrary to the spin put out by angry trade reps and lobbyists, the protesters actually did know what they were about, and they did agree—if not on what they were for, then on who and what they were against. Though they represented a wide variety of specialized interests, they shared common values and a similar view of the role of megacorporations and globalization.

The demonstrations had a simple, agreed-upon purpose—to show everyone the bad points of the WTO accords and disrupt the process—but there was no central command structure or headquarters running things. The coordination among groups was extensive, including agreements on strategies, logistics, and information, both before and during the protests. Between the Internet, faxes, and cell phones, much more technology was used than in any previous demonstrations. When DAN's communication system was shut down by the authorities, another group immediately bought radiophones and became the tactical communications squad for the rest of the day.

The ability to maintain control and focus in the face of the police violence depended, too, on a strong consensus process within hundreds of small "affinity groups." The groups had trained in nonviolent tactics together, and they worked closely on their own particular piece of the demonstration. Overall, the demonstrations formed a creative self-organizing system that showed a lot of collective intelligence, and that made it much harder to stop or disrupt.

In a column in *Business Week,* just after the failed meetings, economic commentator Robert Kuttner wrote: "Global trade politics will never be the same after Seattle. For the first time, the issue is squarely joined: Shall human rights take their place alongside property rights in the global economic system?" Through institutions like the WTO and the International Monetary Fund, he said, "the world's investors want to resurrect the capitalism of the robber baron era—a global charter for property rights but not human rights."[3]

The protesters were not opposed to trade as such. They were opposed to rule *of* the corporations (designing the rules), *by* the corporations (controlling the decisions), and *for* the benefit of the corporations. They objected to the WTO's processes, which they saw as antidemocratic: secret meetings of an elite club representing developed nations and the megacorporations, and many governments' cozy relations with those corporations. They objected, too, to the meetings' outcomes, which would mean exploitation of workers and children in the third world, eroding blue-collar wages in the West, destruction of health and the environment, extinction of species, bioengineered products (which threaten most of the above), threats of big corporations to small countries and native peoples, and human rights violations. All the protesting groups feared a race to the bottom, where nations would be forced to compete to weaken environmental and social safeguards.

A NEW LENS

At the end of the week, the most far-reaching result of the protest was the fact that an enormous range of social movements and NGOs came together and made common cause, based on a shared worldview and values. Richard Flacks, a sociologist at the University of California, Santa Barbara, who helped form the radical 1960s anti–Vietnam War group Students for a Democratic Society, told the *San Jose Mercury-News:* "This was historic, cutting-edge. . . . The linking of groups that have rarely been in coalition before—like labor and the environment—is a real breakthrough in social movements in American history." Flacks went on to say that the WTO protesters are "nudging the public to look at the global economy through a new lens," much as the women's movement forced a reconsideration of beauty pageants, and as neighbors of nuclear power plants sounded the alarm on the trade-offs between atomic energy and public safety."[4]

When Flacks talks about "a new lens," he's referring to the classic actions of reframing and challenging codes that we've seen in previous chapters. He's pointing to the growing political convergence worldwide among groups like those protesting the WTO meetings. It's still early in the political process, so these political coalitions are still uneasy. But as we've seen, the cultural arms of these movements have been growing more similar for a good twenty years. It's the political convergence that is the latecomer to the great current of change moving through Western culture.

SOCIAL AND CONSCIOUSNESS MOVEMENTS FLOWING TOGETHER

The first "convergence of movements" graph shows how the social and consciousness movements have been flowing together into a great current of cultural change. It's as if all the rivers of North America were social movements flowing together, and all the rivers of South America were consciousness movements flowing together, and those merged rivers were then joining at the Gulf Stream.

The next graph gives an "X-ray view" of the first, showing how the cultural arms of the movements have been converging outside of the public view. At the same time, the more public arms of the movements—the social action arms and the consciousness movements' public aspects—have seemed quite distinct.

The old political movement pattern that was evident in the 1960s was built around opposition and conflict. Some observers still talk about *protest* movements as if what defines a movement is what it's against. In almost every social movement, you knew who you were by what you were opposed to, or what you hated, and you knew who your friends and allies were, too.

Gradually, the basis of collective identity has shifted from protest to a positive agenda and a vision of the future. It took a decade or two for the antiwar movement to redefine itself as a peace movement, and for the women's movement to outgrow blaming, even hating, men and decide what it was for. One of the pivotal influences in this change was the consciousness movements. Spirituality and psychology brought in new ways of thinking: activists' ideas

Convergence of Movements
Important to Cultural Creatives

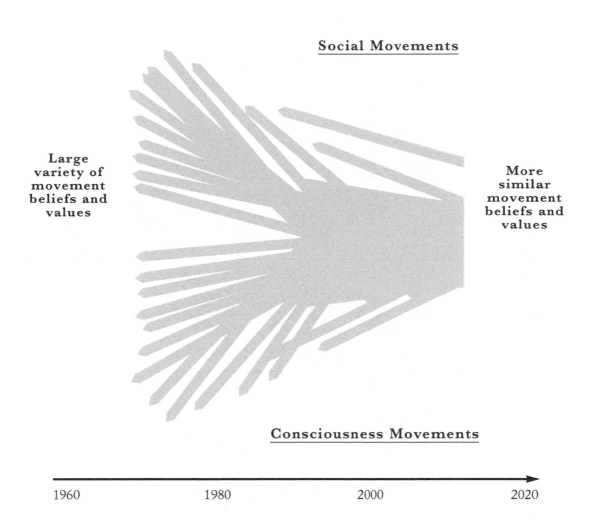

Social Movements

Large
variety of
movement
beliefs and
values

More
similar
movement
beliefs and
values

Consciousness Movements

1960   1980   2000   2020

Social Movements Challenge the Establishment. Direct action in conventional political or economic arenas is focused on changing actions and policies "out there" in the world.

Consciousness Movements Change Lives and Culture. They change the individual psyche, the culture, worldview, way of life, through both direct personal action and change "in here." Change tends to be private and apolitical.

Convergence of Movements
Important to Cultural Creatives:
An "X-Ray View"

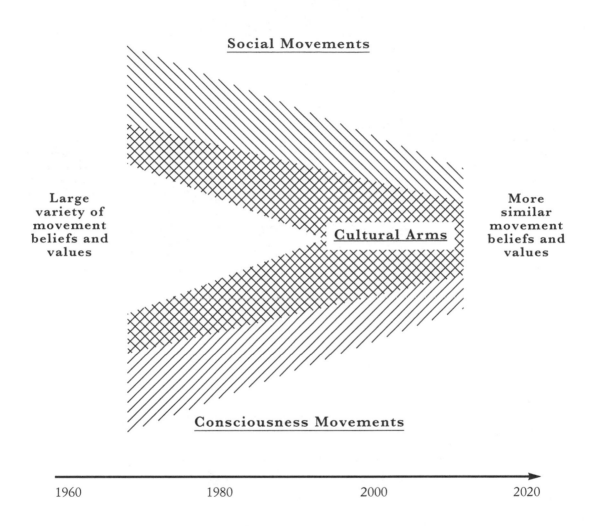

Social Movements

Large variety of movement beliefs and values

Cultural Arms

More similar movement beliefs and values

Consciousness Movements

1960　　　　1980　　　　2000　　　　2020

Social Movements Challenge the Establishment. Direct action in conventional political or economic arenas is focused on changing actions and policies "out there" in the world.

Cultural Arms of Movements Challenge Codes. Direct action changes many areas of social life, going beyond "normal politics" to try to educate moral publics, change the rules, change worldviews and paradigms.

Consciousness Movements Change Lives and Culture. They change the individual psyche, the culture, worldview, way of life, through both direct personal action and change "in here." Change tends to be private and apolitical.

about process and purpose began to change, and relationship and community became much more important. A significant part of this change came from women.

To take one recent example from the WTO demonstrations in Seattle: When the author and Wicca leader Starhawk was arrested with other protesters, her concerns for relationship, community, and social change were evident. In an open letter on the Internet, Starhawk described her experience in jail: "We sang songs, told stories, shared meditations and learned to ground and call on the elements. About fifty of us held an impromptu ritual while waiting in a holding cell for arraignment and later danced the spiral dance. We practiced 'the art of changing consciousness at will'—and it worked. The guards, the threats, the violence and the concrete could not keep out the love, commitment and true joy we shared. The women I was with in jail were mostly young, but amazingly strong, caring, thoughtful, intelligent and politically aware. There were also a sprinkling of older women whose courage and humor were an inspiration to us."

Reflecting on how she felt, Starhawk brings in a clear connection to the personal, spiritual, and communal aspects of the protest: "I was hungry, sick, exhausted and in pain a lot of the time—but I was never for a moment unhappy to be where I was. Instead, I experienced a depth of almost radiant happiness like a pure current in a roiling river that I could tap into whenever my spirit started to flag. . . . I'd close my eyes and see the ancestors marching with us in great rivers, turning the tide. And I could feel a depth of strength in myself that I didn't know I had. It was the most powerful initiation I've ever experienced."[5]

Consider the power of this convergence of consciousness and social action in the context of the information age. Starhawk's letter from prison links into a long tradition of moral witness, where letters took months and even years to reach their destination. The young German pastor Dietrich Bonhoeffer sent his censored letters to his parents and friends as he faced trial by the Nazis from 1942 to 1945. His letters did not reach the public until 1970, years after he had been executed. Martin Luther King, Jr.'s 1963 letter from Birmingham city jail was addressed to eight white clergymen who criticized the protest demonstrations in that city as "unwise and untimely." A month later, King's letter reached his supporters and eventually a wider public. Starhawk's open letter, on the other hand, sends political conscience into cyberspace, where it can slip like lightning into public awareness, uncensored and direct. Spreading independently of authorities and news editors, personal witness from the front lines can reach millions of citizens within hours.

The convergence of movements in the information age is driven most powerfully by the nature of the problems themselves. When you look deeply and honestly at a real problem today, you see that it is part of a webwork of unsolved problems reaching far and wide into a massive system. At this point in history, that system is the whole planet.

Troops massacre civilians in out-of-the-way places like East Timor, Kosovo, and Chechnya, and suddenly the whole world is up in arms. The Europeans won't let Turkey into the European Union unless it stops killing and oppressing its Kurds. A generation ago the world would barely have noticed, and only a few NGOs would have complained. Today, pressures are put on the national governments, and sometimes they are effective.

What's happening? The issues are more encompassing and interconnected than they ever were. We have more and better information, and every practical problem is connected to several others. After World War II, there were about two hundred NGOs dealing with human rights issues. Today there are more than ten thousand. Each organization has kept its primary focus: for example, on refugees, hunger, children, women, gays, indigenous peoples, disabled people, elders. But each group is learning to work with others and to leverage their efforts. This makes the NGOs very successful in getting public attention when there's an outrage. At long last, the moral conscience of the world is slowly being awakened for people who are not one's own tribe or nation.

The peace and human rights movements exemplify the living web of connections that is being created today. Both evolved from about three hundred years of Quaker and Mennonite traditions. The modern peace movement began with demonstrators urging "Ban the bomb" in Europe and the United States. By the early 1960s, the cry became "Hell no, we won't go!" against the war in Vietnam. As the two movements merged, they focused on nuclear disarmament, especially after the United States lost the Vietnam War. Then they moved into joint work on ending land mines and chemical-biological warfare. Concern for human rights led the movement to focus on the mistreatment of political prisoners in the Eastern bloc countries and spread to prisoners and the disappeared in third world dictatorships. This concern widened again to include refugees and people disabled by land mines.

As the international NGOs proliferated, they learned the new story of interdependence again and again. As soon as they took hold of one human rights problem, they'd see it ramify wildly. After a few such sequences, no single movement can imagine itself as the best or only answer. The sex trade in children across Asia is one of the many intricate, urgent examples of this.

When close to a million women and children are held in virtual slavery in Indian brothels, human rights groups, women's groups, and peace groups discover that to be effective they need one another. The first heroic response is to try to rescue the women and children and regulate the acts of criminal gangs. The issue seems clearly to be a matter of women's rights. But paper legalities fall far short. The causes of the devastation lie in women's poverty, their meager economic foothold, high illiteracy rates, debt bondage, terrible working conditions, and both traditional and legal discrimination. As fieldworkers track the tragedy farther, they find that it has roots in rural areas, where deforestation and ecological destruction are driving people deeper into poverty. Whether the families flee to the cities or remain in the countryside, some of them are selling their girls into bondage and sometimes boys as well. At this point, development workers and Ecologists get involved in trying to solve the underlying problems, and the various movements and NGOs overlap some more.

Across Asia and Africa, AIDS has become the huge time bomb of the sex industry, because it is through prostitution that AIDS gains its widest spread. The epidemic is out of control in dozens of countries where almost no one is willing to act on it or even talk about it The public health issues and human rights issues are completely entwined. One Nepali physician, Dr. Aruna Uprety, describes another complication of the story. Recruiters for Indian brothels come to Nepal, pretending to offer young girls jobs or marriage contracts. Their desperately poor rural families face the choice of paying a large dowry for their daughter sometime in the future, or receiving money immediately. The families who accept the money may suspect that they are selling their daughters into prostitution but are often in despair. "The problems are getting worse because the age of the girls they are selling is going down. They are taking girls younger and younger. Because of AIDS, they need fresh meat. Now it goes down to six years old. More and more children are missing, boys too."[6]

INTERWEAVING IS EVERYWHERE

While we can cheer that the movements are reaching out to one another for the first time, this is no time for congratulations. The urgent need for solutions calls forth a futher interweaving as the movements look for ever-more compelling rationales for their work. As they do so, they become more similar—not in their programs but in their language, their diagnoses of the problems, and their assumptions about the underlying causes. The evidence of convergence is almost everywhere:

- The women's movement links to human rights groups worldwide, but it also morphs into spiritual, psychological, and family-oriented forms of the human potential movement, and to the ecology movement through ecofeminism.

- The human potential movement connects to the new spiritualities and alternative health care, and to the women's movement. It has also taken on organizational psychology issues about quality of life in the workplace.

- The holistic health movement has links to psychological development, but it also has dropped its purely personal stance to oppose some of the positions of the medical establishment. It is making vitally important connections to organic and natural foods, and it opposes the role of biotechnology firms doing gene manipulation in agriculture and medicine.

- The black freedom movement took up the issues of jobs and social justice, and then the issues of environmental justice, starting with the conditions of the inner cities and working out into the countryside and other countries. It also has its own links to the women's and international human rights movements.

- The environmental movement turned into the ecology movement that started to take on the industrial growth machine of the modern world. It joined with the union movement by insisting that the exploitation of workers is linked to exploitation of the environment in the way corporations operate in many third world countries. And the ecology movement overlaps with each of the movements listed above.

A General Movement in Western Culture

Our sense of a general movement in the culture is supported by one of the senior sociologists who follows social movements. Ralph H. Turner argues that over the past generation a large general movement has unfolded in Western Europe that encompasses all of the new social movements' concerns. It includes the moral publics of these movements from stances that are both moral and practical. Turner believes that the conviction underlying all the new movements is that "a sense of personal worth, of meaning in life, is a fundamental human right that must be protected by our social institutions."[7] He explains how this conviction plays out in each case. The Ecologists, in particular, stress the need for humans to take their place in the natural order, "rather than as a race apart from and above nature." The peace and antinuclear movements and the assorted "slow growth" movements also embrace this view. The women's movement actively concerns itself with opportunities for self-fulfillment and human dignity, not only for women but for all people. Add to this the student movement's early articulation of personal worth and meaning, Turner concludes, and you have an impressive general movement for change in the culture.

CULTURAL CREATIVES AT THE CENTER

Perhaps it goes without saying, but let us state it clearly. Our research indicates that the people at the center of the general movement for change are the Cultural Creatives. They are the shared constituency of the social and consciousness movements. Almost everyone we interviewed told us that they had been active in several movements and were vitally interested in the issues and literature of several more. We heard this so often that we began to realize that it was the norm. Over the years, Cultural Creatives have carried what they learned from one movement to the next. Much as traditional women once shared recipes and patterns, and traditional men shared techniques for farming and fishing, Cultural Creatives have shared what they believe, what they feel, what they have read and are thinking about, and most of all, their moral concerns.

For each person, this has meant a lot of commitment and a lot of reading, thinking, and interacting with others who are concerned about the same issues. And it's meant rethinking old positions and opinions and reinterpreting the conventional wisdom of parents, teachers, and the society at large. Though someone could conceivably be intensely involved in several of these movements and not change his or her values and lifestyle, it's not likely.

Our survey data support these impressions. We looked at the sympathizers and supporters—the moral publics—of five of the major movements:
- The ecology movement (as distinguished from conventional environmentalism)
- Feminism
- Alternative health care (used in the previous year)
- Self-actualization psychology
- Spirituality with a psychological (as opposed to traditional religious) focus

As you can see in the "Moral Publics" chart on page 219, Cultural Creatives are about twice as likely as anyone else to be involved in these large movements.[8] And their engagement isn't limited to these five alone. For example, in a 1999 survey for the Environmental Protection Agency, we found 67 percent of Cultural Creatives are in the moral publics of the jobs and social justice movement, and so are 60 percent of those who support ecological sustainability. So the social justice movement shares the same tendency to overlap all the others, and again, Cultural Creatives are at the core.

CULTURAL GLUE

One more key piece of evidence points to convergence. Where the movements were once quite separate, today their moral publics—that immense population whose life priorities have changed because of the movement—are overlapping.[9] Each of the five movements we examined shares from 40 to 80 percent of its support (both sympathizers and activists) in common with each of the others. Wherever the movements share a common population, that population contains proportionately far more Cultural Creatives than you'd expect. Cultural Creatives stand at the intersection of these movements. In effect, they provide the cultural glue that holds the movements together.

Let's look at how this works. In the "Values and Beliefs" graph on page 220, you can see the pattern of connection. Measure by measure, more Cultural Creatives agree with each value than either the Moderns or Traditionals. Notice that ecology issues are important to almost everyone, while consciousness issues are significant primarily to Cultural Creatives. Contemporary consciousness movements are newer and have not penetrated as far into the culture. Cultural Creatives are also twice as likely as other Americans to say they want to get involved in creating social change.

What does all this mean? Are the Cultural Creatives shaping the movements, or are the movements shaping the Cultural Creatives? It's both. What we are seeing is not a cart-and-horse, straight-line causality, but a whole system changing, with positive feedback loops that reflect thousands of mutually reinforcing causal connections. All of the movements have been drawing most heavily from the Cultural Creatives as the shared pool of people who form their moral publics. And over forty years, the Cultural Creatives' multiple involvements have been shaping the movements' values and perspectives.

If the new movements had had no basis for coming together, it's hard to imagine how the Cultural Creatives could have emerged as such a definite subculture. And if there had been no Cultural Creatives, there would not have been such a convergence of trends and tactics across the movements. Think of the 1960s and 1970s. The peace advocates had no relationship to the Greens, who

Moral Publics of New Social Movements: Number of Moral Publics to Which Subcultures Belong

Cultural Creatives		Moderns		Traditionals	
29%	71%	64%	36%	67%	33%
0–2	3–5	0–2	3–5	0–2	3–5

stayed separate from feminists, who had no connections to alternative health care or spirituality or varieties of humanistic or transformational psychology. We would still see separate enclaves of advocates today, each one regarding itself as special and uniquely equipped to solve one specific important problem of tomorrow's world. The level of conflict between the movements would likely be high, with each new movement contributing to the further fragmentation of late modernism.

A NEW KIND OF MOVEMENT

So far we've seen two kinds of convergence pointing to a general movement for change in the culture: the movements are becoming more similar and are working together on some big issues, and the Cultural Creatives are the common constituency of those movements. There is one more factor that is significant now. It is the development of a new kind of movement where the participants take convergence for granted because they carry that convergence within themselves.

To get a sense of what this looks like, we turn to the emerging "environmental health" movement, as described by health researcher Michael Lerner.[10]

The name *environmental health* has a double meaning. It refers to the impact of the environment on the health of human beings, and it refers to the

Values and Beliefs in Converging Movements

● Cultural Creatives ▨ Rest of U.S.*

Percent who agree with value/belief

New Social Movements

Environmental/Ecology

0% 10 20 30 40 50 60 70 80 90 100

Supports ecological sustainability

Believes environmental crisis justifies changing way of life

Believes nature is sacred

Likes what is foreign and exotic

Wants voluntary simplicity

Believes planet is a living system and we need to protect it

Women's Movement

Is concerned about violence against women and children

Believes relationships are important

Supports feminism in the workplace

Supports general feminism

Social Justice/Activism

Wants more justice, especially for kids

Wants to help create a better society

Consciousness Movements

Alternative Health Care

Used it in previous year (1994)

Human Potential/Spiritual Psychology

Believes in helping others/altruism

Promotes self-actualization

Wants more time for creativity

Supports spiritual psychology

*Note: This chart contrasts Cultural Creatives to everybody else. "Rest of U.S." is not U.S. total, but Moderns plus Traditionals. Cultural Creatives are so numerous that when included in the total U.S., they raise the percentages and it's harder to see they are much stronger than the others on these issues. (Source: 1995 Integral Culture Survey and 1999 EPA survey)

impact of humans on the health of the environment. But the interconnecting concerns shaping this movement reach even wider, revealing once again that the problems are simply too massive for any narrow solutions to work. Consider the basic facts that are creating the environmental health movement:

- We live in a sea of 75,000 man-made chemicals, most of them untested for their effects on human health. Some are partially responsible for the epidemic levels of cancer in our time, and some are disrupting fetal development and affecting intelligence, fertility, and health.
- Holes in the ozone layer are resulting in rapid rises in malignant melanoma and weakened immune systems in humans, and they are having devastating effects on other species.
- Climate change is disrupting weather patterns that affect all species, including humans, with bigger storms, floods, droughts, changing infectious disease patterns, melting polar icecaps, and rising ocean levels.
- Disrupted ecosystems in the Americas, Europe, Asia, and Africa are unleashing new infectious diseases at the same time that human immune systems are weakened by toxic chemicals and ozone depletion.

Where can you stand to get a view ample enough and true enough to take all this in? There are dozens of standpoints, each one providing a glimpse as through a facet of a diamond, giving a clear but different perspective on the whole. One standpoint is the deep spiritual awareness of the oneness of all life. Whether you call it "InterBeing," as the Vietnamese monk Thich Nhat Hanh does, or "the great Web of Life," as many Native Americans do, or "Gaia," it is a view of the interdependent wholeness of the Earth.

Another standpoint is that of the host of social and consciousness movements that are shaping the new cultural worldview. The perspective here can be strictly environmentalist or it may derive from alternative health movements; it may come from labor unions and others concerned with occupational health; or from women's groups, civil rights groups, or spiritual groups, to name only some of the possibilities.

A different perspective is that of people concerned with social justice. They see how the greatest burdens of illness from environmental destruction are almost always carried by poor people and by third world countries, by farm workers, by those who live near toxic waste dumps, and by people who cannot afford to buy organic fruits and vegetables or obtain clean water.

Another perspective is that of conscious businesspeople and politicians concerned (or needing to appear concerned) with ecological and health disasters.

They'll want to seize on good business opportunities or win elections with a commitment to health.

Finally, the most basic, most common ground in taking in the dangers is that of ordinary people who recognize that what is happening will hurt them, and their family and friends, and their children's children. This perspective may be the most powerful of all.

Bridging the Gap. At the present time, all these perspectives have not come together as a unified force. But the potential for new social action is impressive. Michael Lerner asks, "What will happen when ordinary people, whose lives are often mortally wounded by the destruction of the biosphere, come to understand that their wounds are so often intimately related to the wounds of the earth?"[11] What will happen, that is, when the usual gap between the personal and the planetary collapses? When the personal, intimate reality of my own breast cancer, my brother's melanoma, my daughter's learning disability, and my friend's immune system disorder are linked to the infertility of the fish, to shifts in gender orientation in birds, and to the disappearance of frogs and songbirds?

The patterns that underlie these changes, Lerner says, "may be telling us a story that is also our story . . . the story that all life on earth is truly, breathtakingly, concretely connected *right now,* and that what we do to the mice of the field and the birds of the forest, we also ultimately do to ourselves and our families *right now.*" And he concludes, "I do not believe we can hide from this story much longer. It is among the great stories of our time."[12]

What makes it so hard for most journalists to write about the interconnected links? Why doesn't the public insist on having those linkages discussed? There are two reasons. One is the fact that we have no guiding stories that give us a basis for expecting those separate threads to be part of a pattern. Moderns and Traditionals don't see themselves as members of an interdependent planetary community, and don't see their problems as interconnected either. But without this understanding, how can we ask the critically important questions? How can we find the stories that will guide us in the time ahead? Modern culture's story is not true enough, and Traditional culture's tale cannot address the massive interlinked problems that now face our world. The emerging environmental health movement may be one seedbed of the new stories.

The second reason the linkages are not discussed is the corporate interests. In reporting the news, big media have become critically dependent upon handouts from corporations and their PR firms rather than doing their own investigative work. For example, journalists usually cannot distinguish between the hype of a biotechnology corporation and a legitimate research finding. As one critic put it, the media have announced a hundred of the last ten medical breakthroughs. That certain industries are big advertisers influences the creation of false favorable stories and the omission of true negative stories. The independent magazine of the news media *Brill's Content* reported numerous cases through 1998 and 1999 where aggressive corporations squelched news stories that were not to their liking.

A critical aspect of telling the new stories is calling things by their true names. This is the goal of one small part of the emerging environmental health movement that calls itself Breast Cancer Action.

AN ARMY OF ONE-BREASTED WOMEN

Before the African American writer and activist Audre Lorde died of breast cancer in 1992, she envisioned an "army of one-breasted women" descending on Congress to demand more research on the causes and treatment of breast cancer. In less than a decade, this army seems to have formed. But instead of descending only on the American Congress, they are spreading out across the continent and to Australia and Europe as well. They look less like battalions of soldiers than like fingers of a many-armed Hindu goddess, opening doors that were locked long ago and finding their way into once-forbidden rooms.

The San Francisco Bay area group called Breast Cancer Action (BCA) is one of those fingers. It started in the summer of 1990 when a woman named Elenore Pred got tired of trying to find accurate, understandable information on the disease she would die from within a few years, metastatic breast cancer. Instead of giving up, she got angry and organized a grassroots campaign of survivors and their supporters. By 2000, the organization had grown to five thousand members and was linked to three hundred other grassroots groups in the United States alone.

BCA epitomizes how the environmental health movement is taking form. Within BCA the fear level is intense. Everyone involved has had cancer herself or knows somebody who has it. In the past twenty years, more American women have died from breast cancer than all Americans killed in World Wars I and II, the Korean War, and Vietnam.[13] If women face breast cancer alone, their sense of helplessness and worry is utterly debilitating; but if they join together, they become a force to contend with. Directly challenging the code that says cancer makes you a victim, they are becoming instead protesters and marchers; group leaders and storytellers and speakers to community groups;

advocates for health care and environmental issues to the legislature; media watchers; and researchers. Each October, they hold a town meeting on the occasion of what they call "National Cancer Industry Month." This is a strong reframe, to say the least, of what is otherwise known as National Breast Cancer Awareness Month.

October is the time when women everywhere hear the messages "Get a mammogram" and "Early detection is your best protection." Members of BCA, along with breast cancer activists in Canada and the United States, reject that good-girl frame. (Did you do what you're supposed to? Then you'll be okay.) They say that focusing on personal responsibility for early detection pulls everyone's attention away from the research evidence that breast cancer has both lifestyle and environmental causes, while research into the environmental links gets shockingly little funding or attention. They're asking: What about the environmental connection to breast cancer? What can we do about it?

To focus on these questions, BCA has followed the money trail through the corporate links to what they call "Cancer, Inc." It is impossible to track down what causes the disease, they say, without recognizing the stakeholders, naming them, and educating the public about it all. The beginning of wisdom, they insist, is to call things by their real names.[14]

One trail they've followed a long way is that of AstraZeneca, a British-based multinational that manufactures the cancer drug tamoxifen as well as fungicides and herbicides, including the carcinogen acetochlor. Its Ohio chemical plant is the third-largest source of potential cancer-causing pollution in the United States, releasing 53,000 pounds of recognized carcinogens into the air in 1996. The company created Breast Cancer Awareness Month in 1985. At that time it was owned by a multibillion-dollar producer of pesticides, paper, and plastics. That company was sued by state and federal agencies in 1990 for allegedly dumping DDT and PCBs into Los Angeles and Long Beach harbors.

AstraZeneca is still the primary sponsor of Breast Cancer Awareness Month. Is it any wonder, the women activists ask, that in the glossy promos for the event, cancer-causing chemicals are not mentioned? And then they point to the next turn of the spiral for AstraZeneca: the acquisition of the Salick chain of cancer treatment centers in 1997. Dr. Samuel Epstein, a professor of occupational and environmental medicine at the University of Illinois School of Public Health, calls this acquisition "a conflict of interest unparalleled in the history of American medicine." He explains: "You've got a company that's a spinoff of one of the world's biggest manufacturers of carcinogenic chemicals, they've got control of breast cancer treatment, they've got control of the chemoprevention [studies], and now they have control of cancer treatment in eleven centers—which are clearly going to be prescribing the drugs they manufacture."[15]

Several other companies interlink the manufacture of breast cancer drugs and pesticides. The breast cancer activists are following these trails as well and adding other odd and alarming bedfellows to their research efforts. To name just a few:

- There is a new "public-private partnership" between the University of California at Berkeley and one of the world's largest chemical companies, Novartis, which also makes both carcinogens and breast cancer drugs. In exchange for donating $50 million, the company representatives will sit on college committees and get to negotiate for patent rights on discoveries made at UC's College of Natural Resources.

- Funders for the Department of Health Policy and Management at Harvard's School of Public Health include a number of large chemical and drug manufacturers. Is there any connection, the women ask, to the fact that the 1997 "Harvard Report on Cancer Prevention" focused on individual responsibility for cancer prevention, insisted that most environmental links to cancer are behavioral (like smoking), and failed to note any corporate or governmental responsibility for the incidence of cancer?

- The women are poring through medical research studies, asking a number of fundamental questions: What gets studied in the field of breast cancer? Who pays for the research, directly or indirectly? Who benefits from these studies? An offshoot question is: When medical and scientific critics write reviews, who pays for their research? To take one recent example, *The New England Journal of Medicine* ran a book review that dismissed Sandra Steingraber's *Living Downstream: An Ecologist Looks at Cancer and the Environment*. The reviewer, identified only as Jerry H. Berke, an M.D., M.P.H., said that Steingraber was obsessed with environmental pollution as the cause of cancer. Berke, it turned out, was a senior officer at W. R. Grace, the chemical manufacturer that was forced by the EPA to help pay for a $69 million cleanup of contaminated wells in Woburn, Massachusetts. (This was the setting for the book and movie *A Civil Action*.)[16] The parallel to the chemical companies' attacks and dismissals of Rachel Carson's *Silent Spring* impressed many who read and wrote about this event.

Spirituality in the Fast Lane. Barbara Brenner, executive director of BCA, was diagnosed with breast cancer in 1994. She got involved after writing a letter to the *San Francisco Chronicle* complaining about one of its lead articles,

"We Don't Need More Money for Breast Cancer Research." She told us, "It made sense to me to join a group that's fundamentally political. My mother took me on civil rights marches in Baltimore when I was ten years old. I was in the antiwar movement. BCA was talking about what I thought the real issues are. So now it's my job *and* my passion."

There are hundreds of breast cancer groups, she told us, most with a focus that is not political but more spiritual and psychological. We thought of Maureen Redl's story groups and Rachel Remen's work with doctors at Commonweal (discussed in Chapter 6). Were many of the political activists in BCA also on a spiritual path? we asked. It was a naïve question, which we realized as soon as Barbara paused in her rapid-fire response. "Look," she said finally, "there's nothing like a life-threatening illness to get you right down to what matters. Among women with breast cancer, many are on an explicitly spiritual path. Others, like myself, are not. But all of us are determined to find the most honest answer we can to how to use this experience. It is a thoroughly radicalizing experience to live with breast cancer. It takes all of us to the root of the most important questions in our lives. And each of us follows those questions in our own best way."

Audre Lorde would certainly have agreed that the root questions have to be asked, loud and clear. "What I most regretted," she wrote, "were my silences. Of what had I ever been afraid? . . . I was going to die, if not sooner then later, whether or not I had ever spoken myself. My silences had not protected me. Your silence will not protect you . . . it is not difference which immobilizes us, but silence. And there are so many silences to be broken."[17]

WHY DON'T WE SEE IT?

As we look at the different patterns of convergence, one theme recurs: the theme of interdependence. Each time we follow one of the confluences— among the movements, the presence of the Cultural Creatives themselves, and the new kinds of movements with their inherent convergence—we see the braided problems and the need for interweaving solutions. It's not hard to take the next step: the problems and their solutions arise because we are living in a webwork of connections. Pick a wildflower, you disturb a star, Blake said. Poets and mystics have always known this, but now we are all living it. Spirituality in the fast lane, some call it.

We know this—and we don't. As individuals, we know that we are part of a living system and that what we do to part of that system affects all of us sooner or later. But as a society we don't know this. As yet we have no guiding story that places us in a context of relationship to our planet. And our institutions and our usual way of thinking have substantial blind spots that prevent us from seeing the interconnections. To name a few:

Business As Usual. Modern bureaucracy demands business as usual. The organization chart may be reorganized to be lean and mean, new technologies may be put in place, and the individual actors may come and go—managers, politicians, political programs, and individual firms—but the logic of a machine-based system may not be questioned. The three Bigs—big government, big business, and big media—have difficulty dealing with issues that cannot be isolated from other issues and solved with the tools at hand.[18]

This blind spot is not just a matter of bureaucratic policy. The hired experts, including in-house scientists and public relations specialists and lawyers, have become successful by narrow and precise focusing. Rarely are they interested or able to look at wide-ranging systemic effects or the interdependent parts of a system. They've learned to be very good at cutting each issue into thin salami slices. To do otherwise is, as the many expressions go, to open Pandora's box, stir up a hornet's nest, open up a can of worms—in short, to wade into a swamp of sticky, interconnected, and politically explosive problems. Why would anyone want to do that?

The film *The Insider* tells the true-life story of a three-way confrontation between the staff of CBS News's *60 Minutes,* whistleblower Jeffrey Wigand, and the tobacco company Brown and Williamson. The tobacco company threatened a very disruptive and costly lawsuit if *60 Minutes* aired an interview with Dr. Wigand. He had been their former vice president of research, and he knew the inside story on how they'd hidden the addictiveness of tobacco and manipulated the speed at which a cigarette could deliver nicotine to give a bigger "hit."

At a point when CBS was about to be purchased, running the interview might have delayed or even killed the business deal. The movie shows the head of CBS News and the *60 Minutes* star Mike Wallace caving in to the CBS corporate executives in the name of "realism." They killed the interview. They did so despite their long insistence that the highest values of CBS News, and especially *60 Minutes,* were journalistic independence and integrity.

In the face of corporate pressure, the news executive explains in the film, the realist folds. The statement is true to life. To be a "realist" in legislative politics and in all kinds of business and government bureaucracies worldwide means to make deals and to "go along to get along." It means to act as if every big problem could be isolated from every other one, parceled off and dealt with neatly. It means not "dragging in larger values" but containing the problem, throwing boundaries around it, and handling it with small extensions of existing policy. A realist meets new problems with old formulas that reflect political deals and existing power arrangements. In totalitarian systems, everyone must become a realist or suffer dire consequences. The tougher the system, the more hard-bitten and cynical the realist.

When confronted by unprecedented new demands, most bureaucrats and practical politicians look for ways to avoid accommodating them: they contend that they don't have the authority to act, don't have the budget, don't have the legal basis, don't have the coalitions built, don't have the backup studies that justify action, don't have a consensus among contending parties, don't have agreement from the power blocs of industry and first world governments, and would face a torrent of criticism from their superiors if they met the demands.

People who call themselves realists say there simply are no other choices. Things are as they are for overwhelming reasons, and there is nothing anyone can do about it. In fact, the history of the West since the Marshall Plan after World War II has been a series of collapses of this position. Changes that were called "impossible" were made anyway, in spite of all the entrenched objections: the nuclear arms race was ended, environmental regulations and laws were passed, workplaces were made safer and healthier, and the full rainbow of human rights issues was addressed.

News Media Blind Spots. Think about what calls a matter to public attention. Isn't it drama or urgency of some kind? Something shocking or full of conflict that rings our fight-or-flight alarms? The news and especially "infotainment" media pretty well run on the urgent and the shocking, and so does most advertising and whatever else tries to capture our attention. The roving, impatient eyes of the media generally register discrete, unrelated dramas—as if, like a frog's eye, the only thing they can detect is something in motion. Moreover, journalists, like modern scientists and other specialists, are trained to narrow their focus. If today's demonstration was 49,000 and last month's demonstration was 50,000, then today's demonstration is "not news" unless it advances the story in some other way. Reporters are not trained to look for the larger significance, much less the big picture, because no editorial rules lead them in such a direction. The decision rules of journalism are fifty to one hundred years old, made at a time before any whole system was a valid focus.

Should a story come with an intellectual overview, using the big categories and abstractions, reporters generally distrust and dismiss it, using the classic newsroom expression *MEGO*, "my eyes glaze over." Regardless of the importance of the topic, it is likely to be ignored until it's too late, as with the failures of the savings and loan institutions. We need good ways to convey big abstractions in human, relevant, and symbolically meaningful terms.

Movement Blind Spots. Finally, like the three Bigs—government, corporations, and media—many of the politically based social movements themselves are still caught in narrow, specialized viewpoints. Many still operate as if they were mom-and-pop stores selling just to their own neighborhood: cultivating a constituency, honing issues they can call their own, and emphasizing how unique they are in their fund-raising letters and other publications. They do this in part because each organization tends to believe that it is in competition with all the others for a limited supply of volunteers, funds, and even media coverage. Activists, too, are Modernism's children, believing that they must become specialists.

Some activists seem content just to protest and stop there, without going on to do economic analyses or conduct a political negotiation. Yet Cultural Creatives say that protest is not enough, that new institutions need to be built to uproot problems before they start, and that they won't support groups unless they have positive agendas for the future.

Finally, a movement may overemphasize what it opposes because a number of activists still believe that political protest is what really counts in changing society. They are convinced that the real purpose of the movement lies in its media-bedecked and hard-won political accomplishments. They overlook the power of the great currents of change set in motion by the movement's cultural arm.

DEPARTING FOR THE NEW TERRITORY

We've seen how a general movement for change is growing now, cutting across dozens of social issues, and affecting hundreds of millions of people, not just Cultural Creatives. The various social movements themselves are converging on common themes and have an immense overlapping constituency. The constituency, and the leading edge of the movements, is largely the Cultural Creatives. To these two factors—the general movement and the Cultural

Creatives—add the new movements with convergence already built in, and you have a powerful momentum for cultural change. As we'll see, one more dynamic factor must be added to the mix: the transition period. When a force for change moves into an inherently unstable time, the potential leverage is very great indeed.

What's needed now are maps to the new territory. In Part Three, we'll see that these come in many forms: scenarios, history, scientific models, personal stories, ancient myths, and rites of passage. None are directions on precisely where to go. Rather, they are schemas for how to proceed when the road ahead leads through a dark wood and the future feels like uncertainty itself.

part three

maps for the
journey

Economic historian Karl Polanyi titled one of the best books on the emergence of the modern, urbanized, industrialized world *The Great Transformation*.[1] It is a good name for our time as well. The evidence says that we are entering a period that will require transformation—fundamental structural changes in how we live and work, how we think about ourselves, and how we conduct our politics, economics, and technologies. If we can go through those changes well, or well enough, humanity will be able to live on this planet without destroying the environment, and our children's children will have a future worth living.

Achieving this end will mean not just traveling *in* the great transition period but negotiating our way *through* it. This is the focus of Part Three of this book: the maps and models and metaphors we'll need to travel through the Between to a new and sustaining integration. In James Cowan's contemplation of maps, *A Mapmaker's Dream*, Fra Mauro, sixteenth-century cartographer to the court of Venice, describes the role of the mapmaker and the merchants, travelers, scholars, missionaries, and ambassadors who informed him of the larger world beyond his experience. "We sit on stools opposite one another," he writes, "a breeze from the Adriatic cooling our faces on hot summer days. We gaze at maps that our eyes chart in each other's hearts. Together cartographer and adventurer argue over distances and routes while silently acknowledging that these are really only diversions, since we are struggling to make sense of disparate knowledge. We are like oar and rowlock, trying to exact a measure of leverage from one another, even as we acknowledge that we are probably traveling toward the same destination."[2]

This is how it will be for us, too, as we contemplate the routes before us now. The Cultural Creatives sit across from us, twenty-first-century adventurers who have already departed from Modernism. But we will also call in other informants from near and far: historians and scientists, artists and merchants, and travelers who made a passage across the Between before any of us were born. We will not, of course, be uncritical of their opinions, and we'll analyze their observations with care. But because all of us now are "people of the parenthesis," as Jean Houston calls us, we must break free of our restricted worldview and make our way into the new territory.

chapter eight

into
the between

"We are living in the time of the parenthesis, the time between eras," John Naisbitt declared in 1984 in his best-selling *Megatrends*. We're not quite leaving behind the America of the past, he said—the centralized, industrialized, economically self-contained old world where we relied on institutions, built hierarchies, and looked for short-term solutions; and we're not quite embracing the future either. What we are doing is "the human thing: We are clinging to the known past in fear of the unknown future."[1]

It is still so, almost two decades later. More than ever, we are living in the Between, in the time between eras. The passage between eras may be quite long. The Between is not caused by the turn of the millennium, although that may give many of us permission to try something really new. The Between is the time between worldviews, values, and ways of life; a time between stories. This transition period, Naisbitt concluded, "is a great and yeasty time, filled with opportunity." But it is so, he added, only on two critical conditions: if we can "make uncertainty our friend," and "if we can only get a clear sense, a clear conception, a clear vision of the road ahead."[2]

Isn't this a contradiction? Why do we need to befriend uncertainty if we can clearly see the road ahead? Why not just head on out? The answer is that when the road before you leads through a dark wood, the entry point to the future is uncertainty itself. The sign on the threshold reads "This way is unknown." Taking the next step is guaranteed to make you feel feckless, confused, even like an idiot. It's precisely when you need to be on good, friendly terms with uncertainty.

If you refuse to enter the dark wood or the swamp or the messy unknown places ahead, you're going to stay right where you are. Or if you're determined to charge ahead, you are likely to leap on your horse, like Don Quixote, and ride off in all directions at once. Playwright Naomi Newman's wise old character Rifka would no doubt add: "And don't pretend you know where you are going. Because if you know where you are going, that means you've been there and you're going to end up exactly where you came from!"[3]

Getting a clear vision of the road ahead may be a matter of consciousness more than information. We are facing not just the "great and yeasty time, filled with opportunity" that Naisbitt anticipated but a breathtakingly dangerous tipping point for our civilization and our planet. Our need to discover a way through is the most urgent, most central question of our time. Art critic Suzi Gablik puts it succinctly: "The question is no longer how did we get here, and why? But, where can we possibly go, and how?"[4] The first answer, to where we can go, is toward a sustaining new culture. The second answer, how we will get there, is something we begin to explore now. We start, as the ancient navigators always did, by gathering up our maps for the journey ahead. Our maps will come from scenarios of the future and insights from the great sweep of history, and from scientific, cultural, and mythic models that lay out the nature of the dangers and opportunities that await us in the Between.

GAZING INTO THE BETWEEN

At the end of Modernism, we stand gazing into the Between. If we avert our eyes from it and focus instead on the absolute morality associated with fundamentalism and religious orthodoxies, we'll be pulled toward the force field of the Traditionals. We will believe that after a long moral slide, the end times of retribution and judgment are near, as their stories tell us. If we turn our eyes to secular Modernism, our attention will be caught by a different story, something like the "long boom" that futurist Peter Schwartz describes, a run of "a greatly expanding economy that will do much to solve seemingly intractable problems like poverty and to ease tensions throughout the world. And we'll do it without blowing the lid off the environment."[5] But if, like many Cultural Creatives, we espouse deep ecology, we will see that the fate of the planet is at a great divide, dependent on the choices we make.

As we try to get a clear view of the future, competing forces pull us this way and that. It's as if we're standing in the midst of Mars's multiple magnetic fields, clutching our compass and valiantly trying to find true north. The compass needle spins wildly. To determine where we need to go, we must know where we're starting from. What is this time? Is it a period of chaos—or a transition to growing up as a species? Death—or gestation to a new birth? It all depends on how we read the signs and how much we want—or can bear—to see. Cultural historian William Irwin Thompson may have named it best. We are living, he said, "at the edge of history."

THREE SCENARIOS

When you're contemplating a world beyond your experience and need to step out of your usual frame of mind, you can start with premises that interest you and build some scenarios. The point of constructing a scenario is not to be a fortune-teller but to be a deep-sea diver, plunging beneath the obvious appearances to see the possible alternatives and their implications.

Scenarios are useful only in bunches. The idea is to ask "what if" and survey a number of futures, each one distinct from others. Doing so will help you to get ready for unexpected outcomes. To consider the promise and dangers of the Between, we'll use three scenarios of our planetary future. We'll be particularly interested in the contribution of Cultural Creatives.

Scenario 1: Falling Apart

This scenario emphasizes the fragility of the planet, the great power of the global financial markets, and the strength of the multinational corporations. It supposes that the convergence of the social movements and consciousness movements (which we discussed in Chapter Seven) doesn't have much of an impact, and that the Cultural Creatives do not become conscious of their potential as a subculture.

In this unlucky and misguided world, Modern institutions cling to the twentieth century. The huge majority of people around the planet are left out of economic benefits, and their sense of deprivation is heightened by Western television. They start wars and revolutions. Globalization barrels through everyone's lives with the momentum of a freight train. When it finally hits a tight curve, it veers off the track. Meanwhile the proliferation of nuclear, chemical, and biological arms takes its toll. Ecological problems turn out to be every bit as bad as anticipated. Overpopulation results in huge die-offs from war and famine, and health crises from pollution and disease. For a while, first world countries may stay on top because of their superior armaments. In the long run, things fall apart; democracy and human rights are early casualties, and the disintegration of civilization is the end result.

Scenario 2: The Highly Adaptive World

The second scenario supposes that the great current of change makes a difference, and that the Cultural Creatives become conscious of one another and effective in the world. It supposes that people work together to anticipate coming problems, develop ecological sustainability, and head off the kind of conflicts typical of the twentieth century. Some Moderns become Cultural Creatives, and others are willing to work with Cultural Creatives and Traditionals to find new solutions. Traditionals work with Cultural Creatives in some collaborative projects, based on their shared moral values.

In this scenario, a movement toward greater efficiency in the use of technologies and businesses finds ways to change over to more sustainable production. The transition may be expensive, but it's rather smooth. Just as Internet users ballooned from a tiny minority in 1995 to nearly a third of U.S. adults by 2000, business moves fast in this scenario, once it sees where the future lies. Human rights and social justice spread around the planet, aided by better communications. Planetary integration develops, at the same time that people are interested in individual and cultural uniqueness. As a result, traditional wisdom is highly valued, as are the contributions of musicians, dancers, and expressive artists around the world.

Not all parts of the world change at the same time. Conflict among social classes, ethnic groups, regions, and religions are still a big problem, but the spread of new values makes the conflicts more manageable. It's a world with hope for the future. In this lucky world, the worst ecological problems turn out to be manageable.

Both of the above scenarios are "surprise free" futures. They correspond, respectively, to the worst and the rosiest pictures put forward by commentators in our time. It's unlikely, however, that we'll be either as unlucky and foolish as the first scenario, or as lucky and wise as the second. Which brings us to the third scenario.

Scenario 3: Muddling Our Way to Transformation

Suppose that the Cultural Creatives do get their act together, and the great current of change puts a lot of pressure on society to move to a new way of life. But all over the developed world, the institutions of modern finance and megacorporations buy a lot of support from governments and decide to resist change for all they are worth. Traditionals as well use all their resources to resist an ever-more-threatening set of cultural developments. It is a world of cultural conflict and uneven change.

In some sectors of society, Cultural Creatives are welcome and even lead the way to positive cultural changes. Some industries, especially those that see ecological sustainability and the information revolution as their greatest sources of profit, decide that the Cultural Creatives are their natural markets and become allied with them. And politicians come along who regard the Cultural Creatives as their natural constituency.

In these sectors, cultural and economic capability build, offering a lot of potential for the future. But these leading sectors don't necessarily win out. A number of other sectors of society are staunchly opposed to major cultural and political change: not only because of self-interest but because most people resist new paradigms and worldviews, even if it is not in their economic or political interest to do so. With all these oppositions, cultural conflicts worsen.

Meanwhile, ecological destruction continues, overpopulation takes its toll in many parts of the world, and military conflicts heat up between the haves and have-nots. The world is increasingly unstable, with a lot of opportunity for chaos. As a result, it may collectively "fall into a hole": another Great Depression, or a partial ecological calamity that triggers famines and megadeaths in some parts of the world, or a debilitating series of wars triggered by great inequalities and ethnic conflicts. Destruction of rain forests and/or climate changes could trigger new plagues. Whatever form the hole takes, the suffering and deaths could be devastating.

What happens next may be the most surprising aspect of this scenario: historian Arnold Toynbee called it "challenge and response." When a society gets itself into trouble, a creative minority (the Cultural Creatives in this scenario) develops very different beliefs and ways of life. Having fallen into a hole, our resources and cultural resilience are great enough to let us bounce right back—

or spring into a new place. The adaptive response might be worldwide, because global societies and the Cultural Creatives within them are already so closely linked through communications networks and through the NGOs.

In this scenario, the world draws upon a large population that knows how to reframe events and develop new cultural solutions. More people listen and take a chance on building a new future. At the same time, a number of old authorities are discredited, and some of the rich and powerful lose their status and power. In the process, we transform the structure of our societies. Cultures can be very innovative when they are up against the wall, especially if a large seed population within is making creative changes. Many cultures around the planet might clamber their way out of a partial disaster and wake up to their potential. It would be social learning the hard way, but at least it would be learning.

Making a guess, this scenario probably has about a fifty-fifty chance, because it supposes that humans are neither lucky and wise, nor unlucky and stupid. It's a middling, muddling way through, in which many different combinations of pluses and minuses could lead to a similar result. It says we all fall down, but then we get back up again. It says we learn from the past, but not as quickly as we might wish. Most of all, it says that our creative minority is now large enough that we've got a chance to respond well to the challenges of our time—if, instead of stumbling about with business as usual, then blaming one another and/or denying the dangers, we can meet the future consciously.

A Time of Danger, a Time of Promise

At the turn of the millennium, as we struggle with a flood of endings and upheavals, the story of the *Titanic* is being told and retold. The story seems to be resurfacing from the oceanic depths of our collective unconscious. Long after the film has been seen and seen again and the books read or leafed through, the part that keeps coming back in our dreams and reflections is the response of the ship's passengers. They, like us, could not comprehend the scale of what was happening. Like us, they threw up thick walls of denial against the fear. Even after they felt the dull thunder of the iceberg, business went on as usual. "The ship was large and reassuring; it had been their home for the better part of a week. Bankers still intent upon returning to their New York offices continued to plan upcoming business deals. Professors returning from sabbatical leaves still mulled over lesson plans."[6] Many on the upper decks preferred to stay with the ship rather than descend on the lifeboats into the icy waters. For passengers in steerage, there were no lifeboats. In the end, it didn't make much difference.

The sense of amorphous confusion among the passengers is familiar today. It can take hold of any one of us. Whether we expect the tragic fall from grace of the Traditionals, the progressive advance of the Moderns, or the great transition of the Cultural Creatives, many changes lie ahead of us, with many choices for us to make. And sorting out wishful thinking and catastrophic expectations from the facts is so devilishly difficult. The ambiguity—and our sense of helplessness to be sure about anything—can drug us into passivity. Like people who have eaten too much dinner, we feel logy, sleepy, needing to rest back in our chairs and watch a mildly entertaining TV movie. "The experts can't agree," we shrug, "so let them argue it out and get back to us." This is how an avoidable crisis becomes a full-blown catastrophe—when the ones who could and should be averting it sit back, mere spectators to the drama.

FOR GOOD AND ILL

The great events that face us now are not like the iceberg that destroyed the *Titanic,* although we too have been taken by surprise. The difference is that we have inadvertently set these events in motion ourselves, for both good and ill. On the good side are the miraculous advances in technology that we have so often celebrated, ranging from mass production of consumer goods to the invention of the automobile and the airplane; radio and television; computers and the Internet; antibiotics and scientific medicine; new metals and materials that have reshaped our everyday lives; greater productivity in agriculture; exploration of space and a whole new view of the cosmos. More people live middle-class lives than ever before in history. We have better education, good health, good nutrition, comfortable houses, personal safety, and a promise of a good future for our children. We do less physical toil at work, and we live nearly twice as long as people at the beginning of the modern era. These are good resources, and we need them for the times ahead.

On the bad side are some of the same technologies, expressed as side effects: car congestion, air pollution, and destruction of the countryside (sprawl); television as an advertising monster that makes our politics dependent on increasingly large campaign contributions; the massive destruction of the environment by logging, chemicals, overfishing, and air and water pollution; the return of many strains of bacteria that have become antibiotics resistant; the release of new bacteria and viruses as tropical forests are destroyed; the mass production of mass-destruction armaments that put the whole world at peril; rockets that can carry nuclear warheads that could plunge us into nuclear winter; and a worldwide population explosion that could put us far beyond the carrying capacity of the Earth. Management consultant Margaret Wheatley puts it this way: While we were trying, with our best efforts, to make the world work in a particular way, we couldn't see what lay beneath the surface of these iceberg events. We couldn't know that these problems would be among us now, larger and stranger than anything we imagined when we began.[7]

These developments, and others we don't even know of yet, carry grave dangers for our future. We know this, if not in detail, then certainly in the back of our minds, as we read the morning paper and try to fall asleep at night. So we fear the Between. The fact that old solutions no longer work does not make it easier for us to trust the ones we haven't discovered yet. No wonder so many of us feel paralyzed by the hard choices.

A FERTILE OPENNESS

The dangers of the Between shouldn't obscure its other notable characteristic—allure. The invitation of something not yet explored can call forth our most creative, inquisitive, desirous nature. Scientists, artists, mathematicians, and explorers of every sort know the delicious pleasure of lifting the veils that cover what they love. We know this experience as the fragrances of mystical and romantic poetry, where the lover longs to know the beloved completely, but these delights await all who pursue a mystery that they long to understand. Exploring might be writing poetry or skiing a virgin mountain; building a bridge or pulling apart a brand-new computer; carving a mask or navigating a river.

Or it could be peanuts. Someone once asked George Washington Carver how he discovered so many different uses for the peanut. "Whatever you love opens its secrets to you," the great inventor replied. Or patterns. What thrills developmental biologist Christine Nüsslein-Volhard most about her zebra fish studies is not the impressive applications of her work to medicine but the exquisite fun of puzzling out what the fish can tell her about development as a whole, "finding enough pieces and enough connections between them to recognize the whole picture."[8]

The curiosity to explore, or to follow a vision, is juicy and fertile. It is fed by love—longing to know more about what you love and not even thinking of parting from it until you've uncovered every secret. To be in this state is a melting, luxurious affair of the heart. It is also the Between, the aspect of the Between that is the entryway to all human endeavor that is vibrant and original. Demanding a surrender of stale-mindedness, it is the green growing tip of life that, nine hundred years ago, Hildegard of Bingen named *viriditas,* the joyous, wet greenness of God's creative presence in the world.[9]

NOT SPLITTING BIRTH FROM DEATH

How can the Between be at once a fertile openness and a death space? To fathom this, we have to give up our usual view that splits birth and death. No longer at ease in an old way of life, but not yet established in a new one, we are in the midst of a paradox. If we let it stretch us wide, we can grasp the mystery of our time: birth is the death of the past we have known; death is the birth of the future we have yet to enter.[10] And the Between, with all its danger and all its promise, is where we stand now.

The Western world is uncomfortable with the imagery of death and rebirth, unless it happened two thousand years ago. Our daily habits are formed around rosy images. The business press extols the astonishing promise of new biotechnology industries and all the new Internet commerce, with fortunes to be made in a matter of months. Each new prospectus promises a curve of sales and profits smoothly ramping up to delicious heights. All the while, successful entrepreneurs smile at us from magazines arrayed in every airport and supermarket.

Almost nobody talks about the giant shakeout that occurs about halfway up any arcing curve to success. Think of, say, the automobile industry, or computers, or agribusiness. For every hundred firms that are started, eighty or ninety die. Very often, an earlier industry must fail before a new one can be born. All the false starts, the disappointed scientists and engineers and venture capitalists, the bankrupt entrepreneurs, the confusion and uncertainty, the hype and hope will be left out of the history books—not just because history is written by the winners but because it's written as if there were only winners. Those who dream of success do not want to hear about the deaths that accompany the births.

As a result, we are left to face not just the rise or fall of an industry or two but a great transition of the kind that occurs once every 500 or 1,000 years. It leaves us, as we know all too well, without operating manuals for the time ahead. Any popular account of the industrial revolution describes the march of progress rolling inevitably forward from one triumph to the next. And the PR for today's megacorporations promises that our future too holds glittering possibilities, lots of room for creativity, and enough resources for (almost) all concerned. That's a variation on the rosy scenario we looked at earlier, a Modernist variation. Maybe that's what we'll have, but it's not likely.

If we are going into a period of fundamental change as momentous as the industrial revolution, then we had better take a much more careful reading of history. The process of industrialization was devastating for most of the workers involved. It reflected a carelessness about human life and a lack of concern about the destruction of the natural world. Almost no one would find that kind of unconsciousness acceptable today. We've had a lot of moral development, and democratic education of our population since then. This time around, we need to bring far more intelligence and care to social transformation.

FINDING A THIRD WAY

When you're faced with a paradox, the one response that is certain not to work is to choose sides. The creative response to today's Between is going to be one that bridges differences, that uproots the old statement of the problem with a new perspective. William Ury, an anthropologist who has become an expert negotiator, makes it his business to find new perspectives in conflicts around the world. He challenges the "necessity" of conflict, the pattern of challenge and response that has occupied nations and empires for the last several hundred years. In his recent book, *Getting to Peace,* he points out the effectiveness of developing the "third side": win-win-win solutions that go beyond contending parties to include the community as well. He offers several examples of such solutions, from Boston's reduction of murders among teens to South Africa's way of defusing conflict and going peacefully to majority rule.

Based on his research, Ury says that for the first 99 percent of human history, our ancestors followed such a pattern: "The myth is that human beings have been killing each other most of the time for as long as they have existed—that it's our basic nature and if you scratch the veneer of civilization, you get a Bosnia or Rwanda."[11] But we've been "maligning our ancestors," he says. "It's not that they weren't capable of violence, but they worked hard at preventing and resolving conflict—and found ways to do so."

Something quite fascinating is happening now, Ury says, that is making our global society resemble the preagricultural period in human history. We are shifting from fixed resources, like land, to an expandable resource—information. Pyramids of power and authority are flattening as self-organizing, cooperative networks develop. In our increasingly interdependent world, we have "the most promising opportunity in 10,000 years to create a co-culture of coexistence, cooperation, and constructive conflict." Though Ury expects conflict to increase because of interdependence, he is convinced that our increasing vulnerability to the consequences of conflict will spur us to find nonviolent solutions.

CHALLENGE AND RESPONSE

Life in the twentieth century followed a particular variation of the challenge-and-response pattern that Arnold Toynbee described for cultures throughout recorded history: a pattern of violent conflict. The scale and destructiveness of wars between nations in that century gobbled up more than their share of the resources and attention. There seemed to be no alternative to being caught in a win-lose game. It was either kill or be killed, defend your borders or be taken over or destroyed. This was especially true in the wake of the colonial empires that conquered tribal people for the last three centuries.

Many of the major public institutions of the Western world—industrial, governmental, and military—were built up for "spending our blood and treasure" on waging wars. Much of the developed world's identity was tied up in these battles of empires. Again and again, the West found itself in "crusades." We knew who we were because we were anti-Them, the hated and feared "other." This conflict pattern shaped the other big trends of the century. Much of technology was not autonomous but served the war machines. After the Great Depression, mobilization for war rebuilt the industrial base. Not until the fall of the Berlin Wall in 1989, when Americans and their allies had no other empires to fight, did mainstream public attention turn directly to the destruction of ecologies, families, and communities, problems that had been ignored or set aside.

At this point, the possibility of another kind of challenge and response pattern can be introduced. Instead of violent conflicts that throw a culture into mobilization for war, society can make wholly new patterns of responses. William Ury's "third side" is one of those responses: bringing the influence and concerns of the larger community into smaller-scale conflicts. Other challenges that the West is facing now include the slow buildup of population, economic, and ecological stresses on the planet as a whole, as well as within nations and cities. The response to this kind of challenge is where Toynbee saw the pivotal influence of a creative minority. In his massive *Study of History,*[12] he described how new solutions could be invented that would critically rearrange and elaborate new structures of the society. In the face of accumulated stresses, rather than disintegrating, the creative minority helps to invent a new culture.

In the twenty-first century, a new era of challenge and response is taking hold. The Cultural Creatives may be leading the way with responses directed toward healing and integration rather than battle. For these responses to contribute to the creation of a new culture, grassroots activism and social movements will have to evolve into new institutions. This is the normal American recipe for cultural change, and it may spread. The advantage of institutions is that they can mount a response to the problems that the culture is willing to perceive and to act upon. Furthermore, while new social movements are transitory, institutions can turn the energies of those movements into everyday action. A key question is whether Cultural Creatives can help to invent such institutions in response to the critical challenges that face us now.

MAPS FROM THE GREAT SWEEP OF HISTORY

One way to learn from the past, maybe the best way, is to survey the great historical fluctuations for the patterns you want to understand. Harvard sociologist and scholar Pitirim Sorokin specialized in such sweeping perspectives, and we can ride on his coattails for awhile to catch sight of when, and how, periods like the Between have appeared.

Sorokin was justly famous around World War II for carrying out the largest and most thorough empirical study of social change ever attempted. He looked at the last three thousand years of Western history and analyzed a staggering number and variety of historical trends in war, economics, philosophy, law, science, technology, art, and religion. Aspects of culture move roughly together over time, he found, and more materialistic eras alternate with more religious ones. The differences between such eras depended on what people considered to be real. Moderns believe today, and the Romans thought two millennia ago, that reality is essentially physical. Medieval Christianity, Brahman India, Taoism, and other ancient civilizations believed that reality is primarily religious, controlled by a God that is elsewhere. This underlying belief affected almost every other aspect of the dominant culture.

Most interesting for our purposes are Sorokin's observations about the periods between the great alternations of materialism and religious ideologies. Highly uncertain crossover times could produce either a flowering, as people made a creative synthesis of both views of reality, or a disintegration, as people thought of little but the sword and survival. In the transition period, a Dark Ages was as likely as a Renaissance.

Sorokin concluded that our overripe modern culture would come to an end in the twentieth century.[13] In a variation of the pessimistic scenario we looked at earlier, he expected not the destruction of civilization, but a messy disintegration where materialism would release its hold over our view of reality. The great Achilles heel of this era, Sorokin argued, was its refusal to admit its limits. He would have taken the Ecologists' "limits to growth" thesis as a further sign that the era is definitely on a downhill trend. The current disarray in our politics and other institutions is also typical of what he expected. But globalization, the worsening of social inequality, and threats to the livelihoods of huge numbers of people around the planet are happening on a much larger scale than he anticipated.

Sorokin was more pessimistic about the short-term course of Western history than events have justified. After sixty years, the middle and lower classes of the advanced countries are better off than when he wrote around 1940. The violent, chaotic falling-apart he described as typical of a declining materialistic culture has not begun—yet. But there are plenty of signs of just the kind of decadence in popular culture and the arts that he expected. Clearly he underestimated the role of technology, the preeminence of giant corporations and markets, and the successful spread of Modernity to the rest of the world. So far, it's a moderate transition, though many pessimists would argue that we've just postponed Sorokin's disaster.

Most important for us is Sorokin's finding that in periods of transition, what people take to be real is repeatedly turned upside down. On the time scale of centuries, this reversal seems to be under way now. The late-twentieth-century movement of science away from the hard-edged physicalistic world to a more indeterminate quantum physics is one sign of that change, and so is the programming of life with DNA and the genetic code, and the coming of the information age. The values and beliefs of the Cultural Creatives are exactly what Sorokin predicted if a new era of synthesis were to emerge between religious and secular periods. By Sorokin's reasoning, what should come next are creative awakenings in religion and the arts, and the development of more idealistic social institutions, frequently in response to great hardship.

Is it realistic to hope that our transition period will be a time of Renaissance rather than a Dark Ages? That we will be able to create a new synthesis, an integral culture? Sorokin's reading of culture says that it is, if the promising starts to a new era continue to grow. And if, as we saw in the three scenarios, we have wisdom and a lot of luck.

MAPPING BENEATH THE SURFACE OF THE BETWEEN

We said earlier that sometimes a crisis can give rise to a response so adaptive, so fresh and original and appropriate to the need, that a whole culture can bounce back or even spring up to a new level of functioning. But we didn't say how that happens, other than the fact that sometimes a creative minority provides the springboard. Still, it seems odd even to think that it could happen. You fall into a hole, and then somehow you bounce up or out?

We need to understand this process because we are certainly going to encounter a lot of holes in the Between. We'll look at one way of peering into this process, taken from the cutting edge of evolution theory.

EVOLUTIONARY CHANGE

In *The Choice: Evolution or Extinction?* and in *Evolution: The General Theory,* systems theorist Ervin Laszlo argues that successful evolutionary surges to a higher level are likely to come just after a big, nasty chasm.[14] Both the fossil record and the historical record show long periods of stability that suggest an environment in equilibrium. But then comes a punctuation mark, a sudden shift where the system leaps *from one level to another.* When systems theorists see such shifts, they recognize the presence of chaotic processes. Big, discontinuous-looking leaps are normal in living systems that have moved far from equilibrium. Any living system—human beings and their societies included—can and does make such leaps.

The figure "Human Evolution from Era to Era" shows what leaps might look like across three kinds of civilization: ancient agrarian empires, the modern urban-industrial world, and the new emerging culture. In stairsteps of change, the cultures become increasingly complex, flexible, creative, and efficient, and they make more effective use of information. At the same time, each culture is reluctant to change. It acts self-protectively to keep its long-established structures and patterns intact. As a result, at each level there is a kind of equilibrium. This doesn't mean that there's no change at all, but rather that the system self-corrects as long as it can. Like our business cycles, our cycles of fashion, and the alternations of liberal and conservative administrations in Washington, so in every era cycles oscillate and adjust within a stable way of life.

Human Evolution from Era to Era

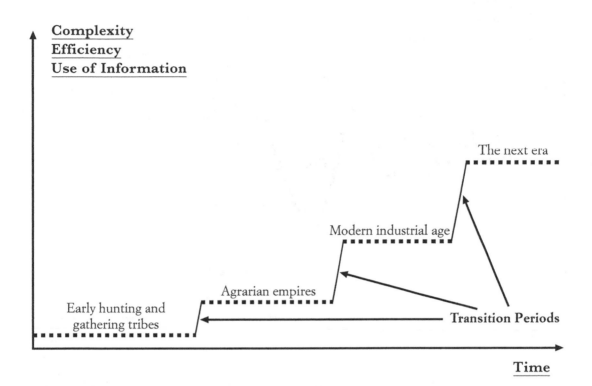

Transitions

But what about the transitions, those risers on the stairsteps of cultural change? How does a system that self-corrects ever grow and change? The next figure, "The Dynamics of a Single Era," shows Laszlo's close-up picture of how large-scale change happens. As a system wanders further and further from equilibrium, it begins to take on chaotic and unpredictable fluctuations. These aren't just random changes, and they're not cyclical either. They are literally chaotic—one consequence of which is a fascinating underlying dynamism that systems analysts call "hunting." The fluctuations seem to hunt for new possibilities, as if the whole system were searching for a new evolutionary level—not just any new level but a more successful way of life than it has had before.

Unconscious systems like cells and amoebas might make many thousands of tries, millions even, before they arrive at the next higher level. Once they find

The Dynamics of a Single Era

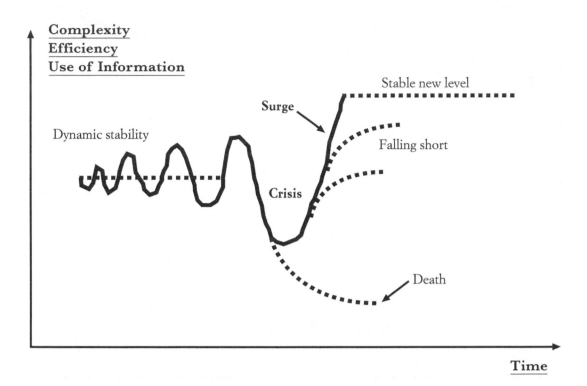

that level, the system preserves it. More conscious systems like human societies might be able to reach their new level with only a few dozen or a few hundred tries. In every kind of living system, evolutionary leaps are likely to be preceded by chaotic searches and stumblings into crises that cannot be resolved at the old level. The system, in effect, falls into a hole. As you can see in the diagram, there is a possibility that the system will die at the trough of the hole. It may also fall short of finding a stable new level or make incomplete transitions with partial failures. The evolution of a living system is really that uncertain. But what gives humans a considerable evolutionary advantage is that we can learn from our mistakes, or even plan ahead—if we can make sense of what is happening.

A PLANETARY RITE OF PASSAGE

In nearly every age before our own, relatively stable societies provided ways for their members to trust the profound transitions of human life. Dutch anthropologist Arnold van Gennep gave these rituals their most widely used name: rites of passage. Changes that could be cataclysmic for the individual and the community were woven into the fabric of life so that each change was meaningful and connected. Indigenous people created sacred procedures to carry their people through birth, puberty, marriage, becoming elders, and into death, and to bring their tribes through war and famine and other crises.

What if we had something like this today—procedures that could support us through the changes, guiding stories to help us stay the course, a few good maps to show the way? While cultural history offers some models and modern systems theory offers others, rites of passage are themselves a model, based on the biological processes that ancient people saw around them every day. The caterpillar transforming from a crawling worm to a butterfly was a new being, and so was the bear who disappeared into the death of winter to be reborn in the spring. Surrounded by natural changes, our ancestors understood change as the sacred order of things.

Our culture does not provide such rites today, yet we are immersed in them anyway. Richard Tarnas, a cultural historian who wrote *The Passion of the Western Mind,* argues that Western culture is in the midst of a collective rite of passage. The entire path of modern civilization, he says, is carrying humankind and the planet on this trajectory. We have gone through the stage of separation already and are now in the most critical stages of the death-rebirth mystery, catapulted here by "an encounter with mortality on a global scale—first with the nuclear crisis, followed by the ecological crisis." The encounter is no longer personal but planetary, Tarnas says, and it is carrying us into "a collective dark night of the soul."[15] What makes this passage so critical from the traditional perspective is that we are undergoing it with virtually no guidance. The wise elders who would be expected to guide our journey are caught up in the crisis themselves. This process is so epochal and so unprecedented that it is bigger than all of us.

Tarnas believes that our current rite of passage is a transition to a new worldview, a new vision of the universe and ourselves in it. What is being forged now, he speculates, is a highly autonomous human able to participate in a meaningful universe. Futurist Barbara Marx Hubbard has a similar but even more optimistic perspective. We are in a gestation process, she suggests, and if we can see ourselves from the point of view of our whole planetary body, we will recognize that "our crisis is a birth."[16] Many other thoughtful observers foresee a "global mind change," an era of awakening or emergence or transformation. They believe that the Western world—and in its wake, the Earth itself—is in the midst of a critical passage.

Rites of Passage As a Special Case of Laszlo's General Evolution Theory

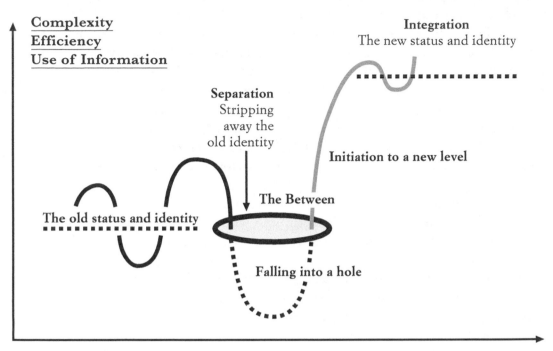

While the details of these views of the transition differ, the overall perspective maps directly onto the stages of a rite of passage: Separation, the Between, and Integration. If we are in an initiatory process—and the first two stages suggest that we well may be—then that process should carry us through to a more mature and more responsible human community. That is the logic of the process if it can run its course.

To get a sense of how the stages of a rite of passage can be an evolutionary step, look at the "Rites of Passage" figure above. First, at the stage of Separation, the system undergoes a greater and greater departure from the old institutional supports and social codes. On a global scale, we can expect major losses of wealth, property, population, efficiency, and organizational effectiveness, along with a breakup of old forms: perhaps nation-states, or multinational corporations, or giant cities, or our exploitative relationship to the ecology, or our exploitation of third-world poverty. At the same time, capabilities for a new way of life are being envisioned, designed, and developed.

At the next stage, the Between, the system experiences some kind of megacrisis or -crises. The planet, or significant parts of it, fall into a hole. In a traditional rite of passage, this is the liminal period where the neophyte's old identity and secure status dissolve. He becomes "nobody and nothing," betwixt and between. No longer who he was, he is not yet who he will become. If one is not prepared for this stage, it feels like a death. Even if one is prepared and open to the influx of spirit, it still feels like a death. In the collective rites of passage of our ancestors who turned from hunting and gathering to agriculture, or the Jews who wandered in the desert of Exodus, it is also a time of openness and not knowing. In our own time, this liminal stage may be a worldwide transition when, as T. S. Eliot put it, "In order to arrive at what you do not know/You must go by a way which is the way of ignorance."[17]

Laszlo's model as our map through the Between tells us that falling into a hole is neither an automatic disaster nor an automatic springboard to a new level of integration. Rather, it's a critical opportunity where we can search for a more adaptive and successful human society. As we've seen, conscious systems "hunt" and find their stable new levels much more quickly than unconscious systems. The question is, what aspects of our social system support an evolutionary surge to a new level, rather than falling short or falling apart?

For this process to be successful, many capabilities will probably have to be built up, ones that would not be diminished too badly by the crisis phase. These capacities would probably include our collective memory, wisdom, and technological know-how; our compassion, generosity, imagination, intelligence, willingness to learn, perseverance, and courage. A rite of passage should enhance these adaptive aspects of our collective self.

The appearance of the Cultural Creatives and their new worldview might be part of this growing capability, if they become self-aware as a subculture. Another source of support might be a negative capability, what lawyers term "releasing the dead hand" of the past. At the end of the Middle Ages, the northern and western European countries cleared away the power of the Church and the feudal nobles and moved into the urban-industrial era. Eastern Europe didn't do so and was left behind.

Another element that is immensely important to making our way through the Between is implicit in the rite of passage and evolution models. It is our need to collectively envision a positive future. A vision of the future can inspire a culture to invest in and provide for a better, more viable world. No matter how many maps we pore over, how many models we study, it is the deep promise of a better life for our own children and all the children that will call forth the imagination and steadfastness necessary to build a new kind of future. And nothing reaches so deeply into our collective imagination as a story that tells the truths we need to hear.

A GUIDING STORY

In Daniel Quinn's novel *Ishmael,* the exasperated student objects at one point that letting go of the culture's version of reality is simply too hard. "People can't just *give up* a story," he complains. "That's what the kids tried to do in the sixties and seventies. They tried to stop living like Takers but there was no other way for them to live. They failed because you can't just stop being in a story, you have to have another story to be in."

His teacher, Ishmael, asks, "And if there is such a story, people should hear about it?"

"Yes, they should."

"Do you think they *want* to hear about it?"

"I don't know. I don't think you can start wanting something till you know it exists."[18]

As we know now, the "kids of the sixties and seventies" didn't fail. It simply has taken about forty years for their efforts to begin to integrate into our larger culture. But the story that they tried to leave behind them is part of the story that today all the Cultural Creatives and perhaps many others are actually leaving. In order to stop being *in* a story, you need another story, another framework; otherwise, the old story still holds you in its grip. And maybe, as the student says, most people don't long for another story until they find out that it exists. A vision of the future that is true at the soul level of a culture can inspire the creation of a new way of life.

One of the great examples of this power of vision comes from a story that is three thousand years old: the Exodus, one of the central narratives in the Western canon. Of all of the resources we have today—particular and global, mythic and scientific, centuries old and as fresh as last night's dream—this story is especially useful to us now because it's about a whole people who made a transition between stories. It describes in great detail how twelve fractious tribes of slaves literally walked out of an old story and created a new one. Exodus is a wake-up tale of a cultural shift, a liberation manual about how people enslaved for generations can break a suffocating story line.

Jews around the world retell the Exodus story in their springtime Passover rituals. Exodus was also a polestar for African slaves in the American South, reminding them that liberation was possible, that they must never lose heart. The great Underground Railroad guide Harriet Tubman used to sing the songs of the Israelites leaving Egypt as she led her own people through the swamps and woods to freedom. "I would have freed more people," she is reputed to have said, "if they'd known they were slaves."[19] And the Exodus is linked with the immigrations that most Americans made, either in this generation or in previous ones, crossing the great oceans the way the Israelites crossed the Red Sea and fleeing from pogroms, or potato famines, or death squads as the Hebrew slaves fled from Pharaoh's army.[20]

There are many ways to understand the Exodus metaphor.[21] In the next section, we retell the story from what we imagine would be the voice of the people themselves. Interspersed with that story are some thoughtful comments by Rabbi Shefa Gold. Shefa is a leader in the Jewish Renewal movement, one of the new breed of ministers and rabbis who are revitalizing religious practice in America today. When we met with her in the fall of 1997, she told us that when it comes to letting go of an old cultural story, Exodus is a map for the journey. The story tells what can happen when nothing familiar lies ahead and you long with all your heart simply to return to the old familiar slave pits.

A RETELLING OF THE EXODUS FROM THE PEOPLE'S VIEWPOINT

MAYBE IT'S NO ACCIDENT that this story begins when we were slaves in Egypt. After all, what else could have persuaded us, a people as numerous as the stars in the sky, to leave all that we knew for the wilderness? Even after the old pharaoh tried to kill our firstborns, even after a new one came who made our lives impossible by refusing to give us straw for our task of making bricks, we could not dream of leaving. Even though we grumbled every night about the cruelty of our masters, about our hard and narrow life, we could not imagine anything different. What we knew was this: By the Nile there was life; in the wilderness was death.

It was, finally, the plagues that did it. Only after the waters of the Nile turned to blood and the stench of dying fish became so great, we could not drink the water; only after frogs swarmed into ovens and kneading bowls and beds, and lice followed the frogs, and swarms of insects followed the lice; only after pestilence killed the Egyptians' horses and asses and camels and cattle and sheep, and fine dust inflamed the skin of all those that remained; only after thunder, hail, and fire shattered the trees of the fields and ruined the crops and struck down all who were out in the open places; and in the end, most awful of all, only after the Angel of Death struck down every firstborn in the land of Egypt, except our own, from the firstborn of Pharaoh to the firstborn of the slave girl—only then were we ready, finally, to leave.

God must have sent all those plagues as much for us as for Pharaoh. To get our attention. To shake our heads loose from the bondage that made us stupid and kept us ignorant of what we could be. To make our hearts ache for something we were afraid to name. To make us hunger for our own land and for a new way of life. Maybe it took every one of the nine plagues and the terrible last one with its screams in the night to strike terror in our hearts for our own children. The terror that tomorrow would bring if we were not willing to leave.

Moses' men came around to our villages again and again and told us that we were one people, not just twelve tribes—but most of us could not fathom what that meant. The messengers kept saying: "There's another place for us, a better way to be. Even if that will not move your hearts, be ready to leave to save the children." We were afraid, but because of the children, we faced our fear. Even so, it was hard. Who can abandon everything intimate without regret? Our homes. The soft mud of the Nile between our toes. Cucumbers and melons. Leeks and onions and garlic. Knowing what to do and how to do it.

The First Stage: Leaving Egypt

"First, there's leaving Egypt," Shefa told us. "Which means that you realize that you're caught. And then you hear a call. Something pushes you out, wakes you up, makes you realize what slavery is." She had been studying the Exodus story for a long time, she explained. She started in the year she took off from rabbinical school to explore the retreat process. Traveling to Buddhist centers and a Catholic monastery to learn how other traditions created time out of time for silence and deep reflection, she was searching for a model that would work for Jews.

"I kept coming to the Exodus," she told us, "as the process that we go through to get free." Soon she found herself with pens and big sheets of paper mapping out the three-thousand-year-old story, dividing it into several stages. It seems to us that Shefa's interpretation of the stages can be helpful here, as we search for how to be awake, flexible, and open in times every bit as challenging to our culture as it was to those reluctant nomads long ago.

Finally, Pharaoh couldn't wait to get rid of us. And finally we, too, were ready to leave for a promised land that none of us had ever seen. We fled, a stream of refugees blackening the land to the horizon. Suddenly Pharaoh's army was thunder-ing behind us. But we were just as stubborn in motion as we'd been in bondage, and our great mass surged on to the Red Sea. Then death was behind us and before us. It took great faith to continue. Whatever tales the priests told afterward, it was a miracle of escape.

The Second Stage: Crossing Over

"The second phase is the crossing, actually crossing the Red Sea," Shefa said. "The Egyptian army was behind the slaves, the sea was in front of them, and there was no place to go but into the sea. Nobody wanted to do it." A *midrash,* a rabbinical story, explains what happened at that point: the waters did not part until a man named Nachshon walked into the sea up to his nose. When Shefa told us the story, we giggled. There was something very funny about Nachshon and his nose. Was it noble and large? we wondered. Upturned? Shefa laughed and told us that it didn't matter what his nose looked like. What mattered was his faith, she said, "and also the knowing that there wasn't anything else to do." When the forces of the old life are behind you, and the sea is ahead of you, the waters aren't going to part unless somebody starts walking. As one Christian evangelical minister from Georgia put it, "The good Lord can't direct your steps if you aren't taking any."

The Third Stage: Wandering

"The third stage is wandering," Shefa said, "which is going into the unknown, going through a process of purification. The whole wandering stage is about all the deep complaints coming up and how there has to be a purification in order to continue on the journey." One of the stories of this stage is about a great thirst that plagues the wanderers. "Eventually, they come to some waters, and they're so relieved. 'Oh, finally, we have what we need.' And they taste the waters, and they are bitter. They can't drink them until Moses throws a piece of wood in the water and it turns it sweet."

Shefa reflected on this story. A transformation of bitterness has to happen at some point in your wandering, she said, whether you're an individual on a retreat or a nation in search of a new way of life. Without this step, your heart is hard and you cannot find the spirit to continue.

It all happened in the wilderness. Everything we needed to stop being slaves and become a people. Just as a boy is initiated into manhood, or a girl into womanhood, one must enter the nothing-place to learn the deepest secrets of a new way of life.

So it was with us. We needed to wander in the Sinai to arrive at our initiation as a people.

You probably heard a lot about how stiff-necked we were, how rebellious against Moses and the priests. Well, what did you expect? We needed to grow up, to give up the ways of slavery, and we hadn't a clue how to do it. We were alone in the wilderness, wandering with no support from the old ways. Open to grit on the slightest breeze, and loss, and God.

We complained every day. Some of us urged the others to return to our masters, to our bondage, to the known and imaginable. Better than to die in the wilderness, we grumbled. Better than to have to eat manna every single day, we wailed. Better than not knowing what tomorrow would bring.

But frankly, none of us would have gone back. We couldn't have made it alone. Journeying through the dangers of the Sinai, we needed to band together for safety and support. The cooks and the scouts and the ones who could hear the Still Small Voice; the mothers and children and the elders; the hunters and healers and the skilled carpenters—every one of us was needed in the wilderness. And it didn't take long before we learned this.

But how long did it take before we realized that there was no point in hurrying? A long time. It was definitely a long time before we figured out that what needed to happen was going to happen right where we were—or not at all. First, all of us who were slaves to Pharaoh in our hearts had to die. Because we were being initiated to a wholly new way of life. The hard old shells of who we thought we were and what we were convinced couldn't be done had to crumble into sand before the new way could take shape through us.

We admit it. We needed many signs and wonders. A bush burned and was not consumed. A great cloud hovered over a great mountain and did not move until forty days and nights of laws were recorded. You may know of these miracles. There were many others: learning to trust each other, even those from the eleven tribes that were not our own. Sharing our grandmothers' secret recipes and whispering to each other our sacred healing spells. Miriam—a woman prophet!—taught us dances, and we taught each other to sing new songs. We learned to make maps and walk in the wilderness at night. We comforted each other against the unknown and listened to each other's stories. And slowly, over what seemed a long time, we developed the qualities we needed to sustain us through that vast and dreadful desert.

The Final Stages

"The fourth stage is receiving revelation," Shefa told us. "It's the coming to Mount Sinai, traveling through the void and being empty enough to be able to be re-created." She said that she created a retreat for herself based on the stages of the Exodus, five days in a small hut surrounded by ponderosa pines in the Sangre de Cristo Mountains of New Mexico. And on the final day of her retreat, she realized that the last stage of the Exodus for her was not going into Canaan, the Promised Land. It was instead building a place in her own heart for a sacred connection that could never be lost.

It was the solution to a puzzle that she'd never been able to solve. "In the Book of Exodus, a good third of the book is about building a *mishkan,* and when you're reading the Torah, it's spoken of in mind-numbing detail. Part of the time I wanted to skip over it, it was so boring and so full of these details. There's the plan to build it. The measurements, colors, what kind of wood, skins, and on and on. But by the end of my retreat, I realized that my life's work was building a *mishkan,* building a place for God to dwell in my life."

Our initiation in the desert changed us from slaves to free people—the dream we were afraid even to speak in Egypt. And not only that: it transformed us from uncommitted people into a sacred community. There is an ancient word for all of this. What we were doing all that time in the wilderness was building a mishkan. *In English, this translates as* tabernacle. *And of course we did build a splendid ark of the covenant out of acacia wood overlaid with pure gold inside and out, and golden poles on either side to carry it. And around the ark we wove the tabernacle from fine-twisted linen in blue and purple and crimson yarns. All this and more was done. Another miracle: we gave all of these materials to the priests out of our own private hoards, for the good of our whole people.*

But while our carvers and goldsmiths and weavers and embroiderers were making the physical tabernacle in which the Presence of the Holy One would dwell, each of us was also building a dwelling place in our hearts. That is what mishkan *really means: a dwelling place for Presence. And while each of us was building a* mishkan *individually, to our joy and inexpressible satisfaction, our community itself was becoming a dwelling place for that Presence.*

Later some would say it was the feminine face of God, the Shekhinah, who abided in the mishkan *we carried with us everywhere we wandered. It was She, they said, who guided us as a cloud by day and a column of fire by night across that empty and waterless land. We cannot say for sure. What we do know is that not only Moses received revelations, but we ourselves standing as a people entered a new covenant with God. We received the new laws that we would live by. We were the ones who did this, not just the priests. When finally we emerged from the wilderness, every last one of us was free. We each had a new relationship with God, with our family, and with our people. The old collective memories and emotions disinte-grated and became sources of new life. And we became a whole people for the first time—a people with new vision and a new way of life.*

How long did it take us? Some say forty years, but that's priest-talk for "the fullness of time." Four and ten are magic numbers of completion, so four times ten means "long enough to grow into our maturity."

It Matters How You Build It

On the last day of her retreat, Shefa said, she understood that all these details about building were making a point. After all that you have left, and crossed over, and wandered through, after all of the letting go of the old bitterness that hardens you, you have to build something real in order to complete your journey to the new land. "It matters how you build it," she said, "and with what intentions, and what kind of generosity you can call forth in the building. This attention to detail was very important." And when you take the time to build the structure for a new life, she told us, you will have it always.

"I understood building the *mishkan* on all these different levels. In my own heart. And when I'm with another person, it's between us, the structure in a relationship that draws in the presence of God. And then there's the level of my community, and then the whole world. Suddenly all those years in rabbinical school of those numbing details about building the tabernacle made sense to me. I felt like I left that retreat with a clear mission for my life and that I knew what the Exodus was about. Before I had lived that day, I didn't know what my freedom was for. Now I knew that being free means being connected, being in relationship to God, and that that can flow into your community and all your relationships."

The winter is past,
The rain is over and gone.
The flowers appear on the earth;
The time of singing has come,
And the voice of the turtle is heard in our land;
The fig tree puts forth its green figs,
And the vines in blossom give forth their fragrance.

Song of Songs 2:12–13

When you're free to be in relationship to what you love, and you develop the vessels and structures to support that relationship, any place you go is the promised land. It's not only on retreat, Shefa assured us. It's all through your life. So every year in the springtime, people whose ancestors were slaves remember the Exodus and tell the story to their children. And all of us who have heard the story, or just heard about the story, can tell it, too. To help us remember that a whole people can leave a way of life that is destroying what they love and can find their way through to a new land. It isn't easy, and it is possible.

chapter nine

caterpillar, chrysalis, butterfly

a t the same time that rites of passage can describe the critical passage of a whole culture to a new way of life, they also—and much more commonly—are explicitly transformative procedures designed to carry an initiate through profound encounters with the darkest aspects of existence. They begin with a separation from the old way of life. The initiate is then taken into a threshold period and often a holding place, where the stripping away continues until the old identity is dissolved. This is the fertile void, the place of death and rebirth. A Caribou Eskimo shaman, telling about his own initiation as a young boy, recalled: "I died a number of times during those thirty days but I learned and found what can be found and learned only in the silence, away from the multitude, in the depths. I heard the voice of nature itself speak to me, and it spoke with the voice of a gentle motherly solicitude and affection. Or it sounded sometimes like children's voices, or sometimes like falling snow, and what it said was, 'Do not be afraid of the universe.'"[1]

The rite of passage is designed to take the initiate to this point of absolute, internal security. It is intended to open a knowing that cannot be taken away. The certainty of this knowing is what "grows" the neophyte and makes possible the third and final stage of the rite of passage: the return, bearing the gifts of wisdom and a deeper sense of responsibility to the people.

In virtually every age before our own, boys became men and girls became women, youths became warriors or shamans or healers and neophytes of every sort were guided through a time of falling apart in order to grow into a greater maturity. Our culture does not provide such initiations for our young people, and this means that our adults and elders are uninitiated, too. Still, despite the absence of formal rites of passage, initiations are happening anyway, all around us.

In this chapter, we'll follow the life stories of three Cultural Creatives, using the rites of passage as our guide. The absence of formal rites of passage today is evident in all three stories, especially the first two, which are adult passages. As we'll see, without an initiation, each person has to piece the elements together of his or her departure from Modernism, transition, and integration back into daily life.

We've chosen these particular stories not because they are typical but because they are exemplary. In an age that lacks structured initiations for changing cultures, it is useful to have some detailed examples of what the process looks like. Certainly not all Cultural Creatives go through changes as personally disruptive or as socially significant as the two adult passages we describe. But every Cultural Creative will recognize some, perhaps many, of the elements of these stories as part of their own experience.

Our hope is that these stories will serve as support for Cultural Creatives who are in the midst of making their own changes in their own way. Each person's path is unique, but true stories can be maps of some of the major landmarks and compass settings for the journey.

THE SHAPE OF CHANGE

The quintessential model of the individual's journey of transformation is the metamorphosis from caterpillar to chrysalis to butterfly. These changes trace the shape of a most mysterious development. A worm disappears into a translucent shell or a dusty pod, and nothing happens for months or a year. Then one day something occurs that is so odd, so unexpected, that only a child's voice can truly capture the wonder of it: a creature with wings emerges, rests helplessly until its wings dry, and then takes flight. Jungian analyst Marion Woodman gives us a child's-eye view of this event:

"I was three years old when I made the most important psychological discovery of my life. I discovered that a living creature, obeying its own inner laws, moves through cycles of growth, dies, and is reborn as a new creation.

"One day I was smoking my corncob bubble-pipe, helping my father in the garden. I always enjoyed helping him because he understood bugs, and flowers, and where the wind came from. I found a lump stuck to a branch, and Father explained that Catherine Caterpillar had made a chrysalis for herself. We would take it inside and pin it on the kitchen curtain. One day a butterfly would emerge from that lump.

"Well, I had seen magic in my father's garden, but this stretched even my imagination. However, we carefully stuck the big pins through the curtain, and every morning I grabbed my doll and pipe and ran downstairs to show them the butterfly. No butterfly! My father said I had to be patient. The chrysalis only looked dead. Remarkable changes were happening inside. A caterpillar's life was very different from a butterfly's, and they needed very different bodies. A caterpillar chewed solid leaves; a butterfly drank liquid nectar. A caterpillar was sexless, almost sightless, and landlocked; a butterfly laid eggs, could see and fly. Most of the caterpillar's organs would dissolve, and those fluids would help the tiny wings, eyes, muscles, and brain of the developing butterfly to grow. But that was very hard work, so hard that the creature could accomplish nothing else so long as it was going on. It had to stay in that protective shell.

"I waited for that sluggish glutton of a caterpillar to change into a delicate butterfly, but I secretly figured my father had made a mistake. Then one morning my doll and I were eating our shredded wheat when I sensed I was not alone in the kitchen. I stayed still. I felt a presence on the curtain. There it was, its wings still expanding, shimmering with translucent light—an angel who could fly. Its chrysalis was empty. That mystery on the kitchen curtain was my first encounter with death and rebirth."[2]

The butterfly with its empty chrysalis is a model for the traditional rite of passage. It is also an image everywhere present today, in the dreams and paintings and symbols of a civilization on the brink of a great divide. Does the pupa in its cocoon dream of lifting high on luminous wings, just as Cultural Creatives envision a fuller, more harmonious way of life? Dreaming is the first step to becoming. To dream of the time ahead is to welcome an inner fold of reality we long for but have not yet realized. It is an act not just of hope but of inspiration.

In the story that follows, we will hear how evolutionary biologist Elisabet Sahtouris first dreamed, then lived into questions rooted early in her life. Her story has clearly demarcated stages, like those in the ancient rites of passage. But it is also a modern passage, because Elisabet made the separation from her old life alone, found her way to the Between alone, and over a period of several years pieced together her return largely alone. This process is common today, as the subtle transitions of a real-life rite of passage wind tendrils through all the phases of Separation, Between, and Integration. The fruits come slowly, as the initiate finds her way back to the world, to a new community and a new kind of work.

A PLACE BETWEEN THE STARS AND THE PLANKTON

We arranged to meet Elisabet Sahtouris at her daughter's home in northern California, after one of her many trips to South and Central America. We'd been hearing for some time about an outspoken white-haired biologist who had "fallen in love with the Earth" while living on a Greek island. She now travels in Europe and the Americas, we learned, putting the technical language of systems theory and evolutionary biology into clear, simple prose in her books and public lectures. "Elisabet has the disconcerting ability to say what every expert knows but almost nobody will talk about," one futurist told us with evident approval. "And she insists on asking the prickly questions that most of us don't even want to contemplate."

When we finally sat down with Elisabet one spring evening in 1998, she began by telling us the story of butterfly metamorphosis. It's a story she tells often, she said, because it's such a good entry point to the evolutionary process we are in the midst of today. We thought of Marion Woodman's "mystery on the kitchen curtain" and wondered what a scientist's version would be.

"The biological story is that the caterpillar eats many times its weight per day, and then when it forms a chrysalis, it goes into the quiescent state," Elisabet told us, in what we discovered was her usual rapid-fire delivery. "At that point, precellular entities called imaginal discs start to form. They're not full-fledged cells yet, and when they first appear, the immune system actually wipes them out. So long as the discs are independent and separate, they are snuffed out as if they were foreign bodies. But as the metamorphosis goes on, more and more discs are created, and soon they start coming quicker and faster and clustering together and the immune system just breaks down. At that point, the body of the caterpillar begins to turn to a soupy nutrient fertilizer that nourishes the discs as they grow into full-fledged cells. These cells develop into the body of the butterfly." Elisabet paused, leaned back on the sofa, and smiled at us. "It's a real kind of chemical transmutation," she concluded. "A natural force."

In retrospect, Elisabet was giving us a map for tracing the changes in her own life. It was a transmutation seeded by her earliest stubborn refusals to parcel her questions, and her actions, into what she calls "little separate categories." From the time she was a small child growing up in New York State's Hudson Valley, she told us, "I've always asked big questions and crossed barriers." Her mother, a gardener and nature lover, let her run free in the woods along the riverbanks, an experience she considers invaluable for living in the world today. "Climbing trees you're usually stopped from climbing, crossing fences that say 'keep out,' and walking on thin ice [all] teach you to walk where angels fear to tread," she announced with conviction.

On her forays in the woods, she studied dead snakes and communed with woodpeckers in the high trees. By the time she was about ten, Elisabet knew that the natural world "is a wonderful world, friendly to children," and she had a powerful curiosity to explore it. At sixteen, she graduated from high school and felt equally sure of something else: it was time to leave home. She climbed onto a bus to New York City, enrolled herself in college on a full four-year scholarship, and was engaged to be married, all within a year.

By 1969 she was immersed in comparative research in evolution on a postdoctoral fellowship at the American Museum of Natural History. She was positioned nicely for a smooth ascent up the scientific career ladder, one might think, except that she had some questions that wouldn't go away. "My big questions—Who are we humans? Where do we come from? What are we doing here? Where are we headed?—remained unanswered. I got very discouraged with science for not answering those big problems. Nobody seemed to want to take the global view, or the universal view, about humanity as a species."

And there were other perplexities closer to home. "When I was in Manhattan, I saw people being evicted onto the streets, people who were homeless sleeping in the parks, and everyone breathing foul air," Elisabet told us. In one small but significant incident, she challenged the museum to account for what she saw as a gaping contradiction between its expensive, highly publicized pollution exhibit and "the black smoke it was belching across northern Manhattan, so filthy that women couldn't hang out their laundry." Shortly afterward her political activities intensified, and she left her budding academic career.

SEPARATION

By 1971 Elisabet had divorced and was raising her two children while working as a researcher in Boston. On the surface, it was the normal, busy urban life of a middle-class single mother. "Life revolved around work that made possible the acquisition and maintenance of all those nameless things—a virtual glut of them—that pile up and become so difficult to part with," she told us, "and with rebuilding an old house." Time spent with friends "induced mild guilt, while time spent—heaven forbid—in pure thought was, well . . . unthinkable."

But just as a quiet stream gathers twigs and leaves and then, one day, is dammed up, so Elisabet—not exactly a quiet stream—knew, on the day her youngest child graduated from high school, that she had had quite enough of her frenetic pace. At that point, an utterly alluring idea entered her mind: "I could give all this up and move to a Greek island." To the astonishment of her family, friends, and colleagues, that is precisely what she did.

Most difficult of all, she said, was undoing the "thing glut" of eight rooms and a basement full of furniture and appliances, a car, a color TV, closets full of food and clothing, countless books and files, a tent, a canoe, an immense type-writer, and her children's old toys and games and bicycles. Her description is one that any ordinary American can recognize: "I will never forget the swelter-ing hot summer day when I sat in the middle of the floor surrounded by half-packed boxes and piles of things, making endless difficult decisions about what should go where. Sell it? Put it in storage? Take it along? Give it away? Give it where? To whom? Would I ever finish the process?"

But her response to this familiar agonizing is not one that most of us would make. "It was so difficult and painful that I vowed then and there that I would never, ever go through this again. I'd never own a house again, never fill one up with things, never have to undo it—and I was dead serious." At the time of our interview some twenty years later, Elisabet told us that she had kept this vow faithfully. (She was, however, still struggling with one small thing: "Paper glut! It follows me everywhere, no matter how I try to hide from it.")

Elisabet's fervent vow to vacuum the "thing glut" out of her life is a char-acteristic of the first stage of the rite of passage—though most people don't stick to it for decades, as Elisabet did. Many Cultural Creatives go through this period of separating from their old lifestyle and values. They empty out their closets and give away piles and piles of "stuff"; they may leave a relationship, a profession, or work that no longer has meaning for them.

One former professor told us of dumping the contents of every one of her bookshelves, as well as her file cabinets bursting with journal articles carefully preserved over a decade, into dozens of cardboard cartons. She dragged the cartons into the hallway outside her office and, with immense satisfaction, scrib-bled in black marker "Help yourself, all and sundry. They're yours for the tak-ing!" A well-known artist took several months to give away her sculptures and paintings, art books, brushes and oils and canvases, keeping only a few small sculpting tools for herself. "It was an utter relief," she said, "to close my studio and drive away to the mountains."

Anthropologist Victor Turner describes how, in every age and in indigenous cultures today, initiates prepare for the Between by letting go of status, property, insignias, secular clothing, rank, and position in their community and family. They *have* nothing, he says, because they are preparing themselves to be "undifferentiated raw material," invisible to the world of politics and law and other culturally defined states. It is, Turner concludes, "the very prototype of sacred poverty," to prepare the neophyte to enter the unbounded, eternal realms.[3] It is not always this way, of course. Many rites of passage occur without anyone leaving home or work or family. On the surface, nothing changes. But at the most intimate level, initiation always means leaving the old identity behind.

IN THE BETWEEN

When Elisabet arrived in Greece, she told herself that she was just going to write a novel and return to the United States at the end of a year or two. In fact, she stayed thirteen years. At one level, she was learning to gather and cut fuel wood, wash clothes by hand, cook simply, and enjoy Greek social life with its music and fellowship. But she was also learning a more intricate lesson in what she called "undoing the Puritan ethic that, combined with materialism, had been a cruel slave-driver in my life" and exchanging it for "the fine Greek art of sitting and doing nothing." She squirmed through those lessons for a long time, she said, but eventually was able to spend long periods in silence or in thought "without the smallest pang of guilt."

In formal rites of passage, the time in the Between has a doubleness. It is a death space where the initiate's old sense of self is undone and dissolved. And it is also a rich and fertile openness where the old elements of self are transmuted into new patterns. Traditionally, the Between often took place in a hut that was considered both a tomb and a womb. The initiates were sometimes naked, at once like a corpse and a newborn. This coincidence of opposites coming together in a single wholeness marks the peculiar unity of the Between, which is "neither this nor that, and yet is both."[4]

So it was with Elisabet in Greece. On the one hand, she was "nobody and nothing" in the ever-so-gentle stripping-away process of living in a small fishing village. "I went through the whole experience of being stripped of identity with people who have no idea what a Ph.D. is, and you can't tell them anyway because you can't speak the language well enough to describe anything like that. It was a big rite of passage. I got my marbles by making good cookies. My new friends would come to my house and see my books, and say, 'What do you do with those?'"

At the same time, she was discovering what she called "living in the flow," as she let the Aegean and Greece itself pull her back into the natural world she had loved as a child. When a walking stick insect fell on her arm one day as she was meandering through the island's forest, tears sprang to her eyes for this long-lost friend from her childhood. When a speared cuttlefish looked her in the eye from a pier where it squirted its last store of ink before dying, she wept again, feeling her link with an evolutionary ancestor.

Toward the end of the second year, Elisabet married a Greek fisherman. She began to go to sea with him and his friends, helping on board and preparing meals. At first, she spent all her free time reading. But gradually she discovered that her busy mind could be lulled by the rocking waves: "Sometimes at night, the fishermen slept like cats dropped about the deck, while I could find no comfortable position on the hard planks. I would sit up then and contemplate my place halfway between the stars and the bioluminescent plankton in the sea, between the macrocosm and the microcosm."

At peace with the endless sea and sky, Elisabet found herself still wondering about "the same old questions." She wanted, she told us, to know who human beings are in relationship to the natural world, and she wanted a scientific explanation of nature that was a lot better than the one she had learned in graduate school. She began to write poetry during this time, and then several essays, and then she set herself the mind-boggling task of writing the story of the evolution of Earth and humanity in one little book. Only someone who had really lost her mind would take on an assignment like this, she assured us cheerily. The first version, called *Big Blue Marble,* was for five-year-olds. Eventually she wrote one for adults. She called it *Earthdance.* It described the evolution of the planet as an improvisational dance that humans entered recently as a new, still immature species.[5]

Her longing to bring together her scientific training and her love of the natural world led her to what she regarded as her most conscious spiritual practice: "I would look up at the star-studded night sky, extend my arms toward it, and ask very sincerely, 'Use me!' Somehow I believed there was a larger intelligence to hear my willingness to be of service with whatever talents I could bring to whatever it might want of me."

By 1987, ten years after Elisabet so precipitously left New York, she was traveling outside Greece for speaking engagements. She began to turn her attention back to America—not just the United States but Costa Rica, Mexico, and South America seemed to be calling her. After a few exploratory trips, she found that she was making an increasing commitment to working with native people. She saw them as the crucial link between the modern scientific worldview and the reality of the natural world she had reentered in Greece: "The conclusion I reached was that we humans will have to learn very quickly to organize ourselves by the principles of living systems within the larger living system of our planet or go extinct. It became obvious to me that native cultures know far more about this than Western industrial culture does."

As she lectured more and more widely on these conclusions, she reluctantly began to recognize that her time in Greece was coming to an end. Most of her final two years were spent in relative seclusion on a new island, Hydra. Sometimes she would walk all night in the moonlight pondering what lay ahead. But just as traditional rites of passage end with a careful and sometimes quite extended period of reintegration, so Elisabet's return took several years. In a recollection of this time, she wrote: "Reentry shock! It was much harder than I'd anticipated, much harder than had been the entry into Greek culture. I felt like the proverbial fish out of water—sometimes literally, in my hunger for the sea."[6]

At the end of our visit, we asked Elisabet if she would make the same decision today that she had made twenty years ago. Without hesitation, she replied with a radiant smile. "It turned out to be a brilliant inspiration, launching me into a total life transition that is now under way and ever more fascinating." Does this mean that the journey isn't over? "The part up to now is only the beginning," she declared in a tone that left us with no doubts whatsoever. "As I rounded the bend of my sixtieth birthday, my excitement with life grew even stronger. This is a time of such rapid transition that we can all lead many lifetimes within one." She told us that she had learned to shelve any task that didn't flow and to replace it with one that did. In 1998 she published two new books on the changing scientific story of evolution and was traveling and speaking almost constantly.[7]

As we were packing up our tape-recording equipment and saying good-bye, she added one final thought. "A larger intelligent system surrounds us and works for us—call it by any name you choose—if we acknowledge and let it guide us," she told us. "So I remain an open-minded seeker and a server at once. While I am not good at taking orders from humans, I accept the guidance of Spirit more than willingly, for life has never been better than under its auspices." And with that she summed up a life so full of transmuting changes that her story of the caterpillar's metamorphosis seems beautifully matched to her own hard-won fulfillment.

A WORK IN PROGRESS

All Cultural Creatives have changed their values. Many have changed their lifestyles as well. But integrating those changes into daily life is a substantial further step, a whole curving staircase of steps really. For everyone, it's a work in progress. When Elisabet Sahtouris assured us that her life transition wasn't over, she could have been speaking for all Cultural Creatives—those who have been in and out of the chrysalis for forty years and those who entered yesterday. At one point in our visit, just after she had described the process of the caterpillar immune system breaking down, Elisabet said reflectively, "You know, the Cultural Creatives are acting as the imaginal discs for the new culture that is evolving. They can be the transition to the butterfly."

She may be right. As Cultural Creatives make their way to a new integration in their own lives, they may be part of a collective rite of passage that is moving beyond Modernism toward a new kind of culture. As we saw in Part Two, a powerful current of change has been building in this direction for the last half of the twentieth century. At the same time, individuals are changing too, each one contributing in a unique way to the general movement for change. Without formal rituals, and without what any traditional person would consider halfway adequate preparation, millions of modern-day North Americans are separating themselves from the cultural values that once defined them and are stepping into the Between. Some, like Elisabet, are stepping away from a life that is no longer acceptable to them. Others are stepping away, too, but not without a nose-to-nose fight.

The story we turn to now is that of another scientist, a physicist who started out as one of the fighters. What began as an activist's tale deepened to a journey to consciousness, as Will Keepin followed the trajectory of a Core Cultural Creative all the way through to a new beginning.

TRUSTING IN THE UNKNOWN

Nobody was surprised when Will Keepin, the son of a nuclear physicist, decided to major in physics and mathematics in college. Growing up in Los

Alamos in the 1950s, Will was in love, like virtually everyone else, with "a sense of great promise, an almost palpable intoxication, about the power of science." In less than fifteen years, scientists had gone from the discovery of fission to the achievement of fusion to the invention of the H-bomb. "There was almost a sense," he recalled, "though it was never spoken, of being able to dispense with the need for God because man had somehow usurped that power for himself. And with that came a kind of hubris about the potential of science. It didn't seem like arrogance but simply reasonable speculations for the future."

Will rode that promise through college and into graduate school, delving into quantum theory and quantum mechanics and the new chaos theory. In 1981, with a shiny new doctorate in mathematical physics in hand, he headed for the International Institute for Applied Systems Analysis (IIASA), in Austria. The prestigious think tank had just put the final touches on what was regarded as the most authoritative study of global energy problems ever done.

The sheer magnitude of the energy project was stunning. A seven-year project involving more than 140 scientists from twenty countries, with a research budget exceeding $6.5 million, the IIASA study was intended to present some definitive answers to the world's energy problems. It claimed to be globally comprehensive, incorporating significant findings from macroeconomics to studies of oil reserves to advanced computer modeling. When the study was finally published in 1981 in the wake of two oil embargoes, its scenarios were trumpeted as benchmark forecasts for the Western world. Its impact on energy policy was to be momentous. The study concluded that world energy consumption would increase so dramatically over the next fifty years that fossil fuels and nuclear power would be urgently required. Simply to meet global demand, it asserted, a new nuclear power plant would have to be built every four to six days for the next fifty years.

DIVING IN

Will arrived eager to dive into the big energy model. But almost immediately he encountered problems with the analysis and the methods used to get the quantitative results. The more he probed, the worse it got. The published conclusions seemed to be "simply scientized guesswork," he told us. "Although the premises got massaged and played around with, the model essentially said whatever you told it to say. It was a bit like *The Wizard of Oz*. Some guy was pulling on levers and making a big show, but it was a show determined by the little guy behind the curtain."

Will was charging through a minefield. The IIASA energy model could not have been more politically and economically important to the nuclear power industry. Activists and regulators had been making life miserable for the industry, posing serious challenges about the cost and safety of nuclear power. Electric utilities, facing much higher costs than expected, were pulling back on their orders for nuclear plants. And the industry itself, worried that the future was going to pass it by, had been searching hard for a rationale that would call for a big recovery. The IIASA model filled all those needs. It was just what the industry had been hoping for.

"It was a major crisis for me," Will recalled, "because I quickly became persona non grata. I felt really lost and completely alone. Of the three hundred scientists at the institute, only three or four sympathized with my perspective, but most treated me like I was absolutely off the wall. How dare I criticize this well-established, scientifically reviewed piece of work? So there was this incredible pressure to conform, all in the name of scientific truth."

What kept him from caving in? "I went through incredible turmoil and self-doubt," Will replied frankly, "because the study's authors were leading scientists. But like them, I had a Ph.D. in mathematics and physics, and I *knew* certain things. I knew a fudge job when I saw it, and I trusted my calculations. I knew when things didn't add up. You would flunk your qualifying exams for the kind of stuff they were trying to pull. So I knew that it was wrong."

But being sure of what he knew did not make Will invulnerable to the dense force field of anxiety and disapproval that enveloped him at every turn. After several agonizing months, he reluctantly composed a letter of resignation and packed his bags. But just at this time, a British scientist named Brian Wynne arrived on the scene with a two-year contract to study the politics of science. Wynne had heard, through the scientific gossip underground, about problems with the energy model, but he hadn't found an insider who would talk. Until he met Will.

AN INSIDER

"We had a meeting, which was one of those great moments in life, because Brian knew exactly what I was talking about," Will told us, and he added candidly, "He saw me as someone who could spill the beans with some credibility and technical authority." Wynne hired Will a couple of months later. Within six weeks, Will had drafted a critique of the energy model. They circulated it through the institute's departmental mail, and predictably, "the place came unglued. There was a huge uproar. And then Brian said, 'What I'm going to do is focus my own two-year research program on the relationship between science and politics in this very institute. I want to study this institute's reaction to Will's critique of its work.'" And to the horror of the directorate, Will told us, that's exactly what Wynne did.

As Wynne began to map the sociology of the institute's reaction, Will set out to prove in detail what he had asserted in his preliminary report: that the vaunted energy study was largely wishful thinking and biased guesswork, and the mathematical basis was so fragile that even slight changes would change the conclusions substantially. The director of IIASA and the leaders of the energy project were extremely distressed, and almost everyone else was shaken and furious. "There was incredible denial," Will told us. "I started getting threats."

At stake were the long-term career choices of many of the engineers and physicists. If the big energy model was all that it claimed, it would justify the construction of hundreds, even thousands, of nuclear plants, with countless new jobs and continual refinement of nuclear technology. But if the model was fudged, the field would stagnate or even decline, and thousands would be looking for new careers. During the two years when he was virtually shunned by most of his fellow scientists, Will patiently worked his way into the guts of the energy model. At the same time, he was in turmoil. "I was absolutely intimidated," he told us, "and at times I was overwhelmed with doubt."

In 1984 Will became a research scholar at the Royal Swedish Academy of Sciences in Stockholm. He completed his work on the energy study there. That December, in the sober and restrained language of high science, Keepin and Wynne's critique was published in the prestigious science journal *Nature*.[8] It demonstrated that the IIASA models and scenarios that favored the nuclear power and fossil fuel energy producers were patently biased; that the original researchers had concealed the fact that the models were neither stable nor valid; and to top it off, that the validating procedures the researchers claimed to have followed were never actually used. In short, it was a scandal.

Almost as soon as the critique was published, Will started getting job offers. Far from becoming a pariah, as he had feared, institutes and universities in several countries wanted him to investigate other suspect science projects. For a while, he turned them all down. "I wanted to do something constructive and creative with my life," he explained. "I had exposed a depressing case of politics masquerading as science in its top journal. I had seen for myself the unhealthy interpenetration of politics and science at the highest levels. I wanted out." What he did not want, he told us emphatically, was to become "a mathematical hit man exposing fraudulent science."

But that's pretty much what he became. And while "mathematical hit man" is far too slighting a description, Will's work with environmentalists around the world undoubtedly had a powerful impact on the nuclear industry. As a fellow at Princeton and later a research scholar at the Rocky Mountain Institute and the Energy Foundation, his studies on global warming and renewable energy helped shape energy policy debates in the European Community, Australia, and the United States.

If this were the end of the story, it would make a fine whistleblower yarn: an honest young David confronts the twin Goliaths of big energy and big science for the good of humankind. It's a story we wouldn't be surprised to see on television, and maybe even Hollywood would turn it into a movie. But Will was following a different kind of path, one that started during his years of isolation at IIASA, when he entered the Between.

CATAPULTED INTO THE BETWEEN

Once you see the lie in the old culture's story, you have some choices. You can close your eyes, dive back under the comforter, and forget you ever saw it. You can, in other words, deauthorize yourself. Or you can keep on looking and keep your mouth shut, not telling anyone what you know, but not forgetting either. You can isolate yourself, or you can leave. But you can also do what Will Keepin did: keep your eyes open and start asking questions, refusing to be silenced until the old lies are exposed. If you make this choice, you almost certainly will find yourself catapulted out of the old nest and into the Between.

Being in the Between does not make you look different on the outside. Indeed, as he traced the lines of argument and evidence for the energy scenarios and models, Will was working more meticulously than ever. On the inside, however, something else is happening: a not-knowing that can feel like an open receptivity or an agonizing emptiness—or both. In any case, the old certainties are gone.

The Between is the unknown territory. It is the gap between what once was trustworthy and what, in some long-off future time, may be so again. In the mythologies of world cultures, it's the kingdom beneath the waves or above the sky, the territory that must be negotiated if any true change is to occur. It is the time, as mythologist Joseph Campbell puts it, when one's "spiritual center of gravity" must be transferred from an old life horizon to a new one.[9]

"There was a point when I really started my spiritual work," Will told us. He had written his letter of resignation to IIASA and had begun reading a book by Krishnamurti, *Think on These Things.* As a scientist, he was drawn by the renowned thinker's assertion that "truth is a pathless land. . . . You cannot approach it by any religion, any sect" but rather must go into your own inner source of authority. "It was a kind of epistemology of self-inquiry," Will explained, "that was consistent with the scientific worldview where you test things out for yourself. That, I could accept." And he read Emerson's essay "On Self-Reliance," which helped him speak his own truth when hundreds of fellow scientists were "saying I was wrong and [putting] pressure on me to go along with the big lie."

Silent Allies. These authors and others were Will's earliest supporters. In the absence of a community or wise elders, they guided him toward his own inner authority. Books can do that. They offer a logic outside the one that your own local subculture is constantly repeating. When you cannot make sense of what is happening, books can provide a map or a password. Writer Annie Dillard remembers surviving the suffocating school environments of her childhood by thinking of phrases from poems that she memorized "behind enemy lines." They said: "There is a world. There is another world."[10]

Books are accessible, silent allies. Whenever you have time, you can drop into their world and, as more than one person confided to us, they won't give you away. Native American activist Choqösh Auh-Ho-Ho describes a book she smuggled into her convent school at fifteen, Huston Smith's *The Religions of Man,* as her "survival route": "On my knees on that cold, hard marble floor with my back as straight as it could be, I'd drape my school sweater over my shoulders like a curtain, hiding this little red book. I'd read . . . 'There is an essence, wonderful, perfect. . . . All life comes from this essence, and I rejoice in its power!' "[11]

Many Cultural Creatives told us that when their lives started to change definitively, just about the first thing they did was to go to a bookstore or library and come out with an armload of books. They were hungry for a new perspective, something they could use to give words to their inexplicable experiences. Many were also trying to shore up their sense of self-worth in the face of criticism and hostility. Will Keepin, too, relied on the hidden companionship of his books. "When I recognized that there was something deeply wrong [at IIASA] and started exploring spiritual works," he told us, "I felt I had to do it in secret and couldn't talk to anyone about it."

A Strong Nest. Another source of support was a spiritual community on the northern edge of Scotland called Findhorn. Started in 1962, the community was known for its amazing garden where plants thrived in sandy gravel, exposed to the harsh, dry winds blowing off the North Sea. But by the early 1980s when Will began his visits, Findhorn had grown into an international community of several hundred members who worked in craft studios, the performing arts, and a publishing business. It offered symposia on ecological issues and on psychology and spirituality with an overarching concern of service for the Earth. For a young scientist just arriving from the embattled institutional politics of IIASA, the experience was, in his words, "paradigm breaking." Both IIASA and Findhorn had their enthusiastic supporters, but for Will the difference was pivotal. At Findhorn, he said, his most querulous questions were welcome. Over the years, he returned often, not only for what he called "worldview-shattering experiences" but for the shared ideals of a spiritual community.

Will's departure from IIASA and his eventual separation from the discipline that he had found so beautiful and elegant took almost the full decade of the 1980s to complete. In hindsight, it is fascinating to see how carefully Will constructed a whole sequence of containers that could hold him through the tumultuous processes of the Between—though he did not consciously plan to do this. Nevertheless, the activities he chose during that period, the communities he found and the books that he delved into, look today like grasses and threads selected by a wise father bird to make a strong nest for his fledgling. The books, including Fritjof Capra's *Tao of Physics* and E. F. Schumacher's *Small Is Beautiful,* provided maps and alternative logics for what were out-of-context experiences for most physicists.

After Findhorn, Will found other communities. At a Zen center in Vienna, he began learning meditation and other tools for concentrating and stilling his mind so he could be relaxed and focused enough for sustained self-inquiry. When he realized that he was "very shut down and unaware in ways that I didn't want to be," he entered depth-level psychotherapy and a three-year training program with Stanislav Grof and enrolled for further graduate work at the California Institute of Integral Studies. Soon he was doing psychotherapy and spiritual work simultaneously, and "it just completely blew my whole worldview wide open."

This is the point in the story when readers who have not made their own journey through the Between will quite sensibly grumble, "And this is supposed to be a good thing?" Indeed, many of Will's colleagues and friends worried aloud and often that he had "totally blown his career and for *what*?"

"I guess the point," Will told us, "is that just going through those times, rather than fending them off, somehow ends up bringing the deepest gifts. It's the fending off," he said forcibly, "that keeps you stuck and kills your soul." And what carried him through, he told us, what continues to sustain him today, is the disciplined inner work that is central to his life.

A Change of Heart in the Culture

You can be pulled into the Between by a life-threatening illness or a loss. You can be pushed, as Will Keepin was, by an institution or community that breaks faith with its principles. Or you can enter on your own, longing for something far deeper than what you have been living. What matters is allowing the process to unfold in its own time. When we spoke with Will in December 1997, about ten years after he had formally left his work as a nuclear physicist and completed his courses in psychology and spiritual work, he had a new vocation as a social change activist. "The work I'm doing now," he told us, "is *all* based on faith." He emphasized the word *all*. The crises he went through "led to a whole new gift that I never would have guessed. It developed a quality of trusting in the unknown."

At first he noticed that he was shifting the way he worked as a consultant on scientific studies. When he sat on policy committees on solar energy, he told us, he didn't take his familiar, fiercely adversarial position. Still an advocate for ecologically sane policies, he began to extend his awareness to the concerns of all parties to a conflict. "At one level you hold a particular position," he explained, "but at a deeper level you want a win-win resolution for everyone."

Like Elisabet Sahtouris, Will also returned to an active, engaged life in the world, and also like Elisabet, he found that the integration took its own good time. In 1996 he and two colleagues founded what is now called the Shavano Institute, to train a new kind of social change agent. The next real push in social change, Will is convinced, will focus not just on ecological issues or social symptoms but on underlying cultural values. "What we need now is a cultural transformation," he says, "and what will be crucial are leaders who can facilitate a change of heart in the culture. The ones who can do that will be those who have transformed their own hearts. The real leaders of the next century," he concluded, "will be those who have done their deep spiritual work as well as their work in the world and are able to combine the two."

Will's insight precisely matches the powerful convergence we have observed between the consciousness movements and the new social movements of the last forty years. When consciousness informs a sense of social justice, the cultural effects are profound. The great current of change moving through the larger culture is one that has been mirrored in the particular unfolding of Will Keepin's life. And evidently, for Will at least, it is an ongoing creative development.

The story we turn to now is about a very rare experience in our time: a young woman's guided rite of passage. In this story, the guides were not the traditional elders but parents determined to reverse the effects of modern culture. How they did this and worked with their extended family and friends to create a year-long adventure seems to us to be an example of culture making at its most creative.

PREVENTING OPHELIA

America today is a girl-destroying place. Everywhere girls are encouraged to sacrifice their true selves. Their parents may fight to protect them, but their parents have limited power. Many girls lose contact with their true selves, and when they do, they become extraordinarily vulnerable to a culture that is all too happy to use them for its purposes.

MARY PIPHER, *Reviving Ophelia*[12]

On a quiet Sunday afternoon in August, we sat down with Laure Katz and her parents, Iris Gold and Steve Katz. It was a little more than a year ago that Laure completed her initiation, and the family was quite interested in talking with us about it. They wanted to reflect on what happened and hear each other's comments as well. Sitting in soft chairs in their sun-filled kitchen, we drank tea, watched the gulls circling the lagoon beyond their window, and settled back to hear what happened.

Iris began. "When Laure was about ten, I read a report that came out of Harvard that girls in the third and fourth grades who were up there raising their hands, speaking out, and being ahead of the boys had decided by the time they got to the ninth and tenth grades that it wasn't cool to be smart. They were just sitting in the back of the class, being quiet and trying to be pretty. Then when Laure was around twelve, I read *Reviving Ophelia* and got very upset by it. I showed it to Steve and Laure, and we really felt very strongly that we were not going to allow Laure to become an Ophelia, if we could prevent it."

Ophelia, a character from Shakespeare's *Hamlet,* sets the theme in psychologist Mary Pipher's book that sent shock waves through families across the country in the mid-1990s and for some time afterward. As a girl, Ophelia is happy and free, but with adolescence she falls in love with Prince Hamlet. At that point, she loses her sense of her own value and lives only for his approval and that of her father. When Hamlet spurns her, she goes mad with grief. Weighed down by her elegant clothes, she drowns in a stream filled with flowers.

The story, down to the fancy clothes, made an impression on many parents when Pipher used it to lay open the effects of what she calls our "girl-poisoning culture." Citing health department surveys that show, for example, that 40 percent of all girls in her hometown of Topeka, Kansas, considered suicide in a single year, she elaborates with story after story from her private practice. Adolescence has always been hard, she says, but it's harder now because of cultural changes in the last decade. Because of the media, "girls all live in one big town—a sleazy, dangerous tinsel town with lots of liquor stores and few protected spaces." As women have become "sexualized and objectified" by the culture, their bodies "marketed to sell tractors and toothpaste, soft- and hard-core pornography everywhere," Pipher says, girls are more vulnerable than ever. She concludes that the combination of old and new stresses is destroying our young women.[13]

Steve Katz told us, "As we read how so many of those ten- and eleven-year-old girls who are powerhouses of creativity and fun become, in a sense, lame and deformed psychologically, we felt vulnerable. Not because Laure showed any signs of becoming Ophelia, but because there were so many stories in that book about kids who look like complete winners and then took a devastating turn in their lives. We couldn't pretend it couldn't happen to us. We wondered, what do you do at this stage?"

They began to think about initiation rites for kids Laure's age and quickly concluded, as Steve put it, that "the initiation for most kids is more and more time at the mall." Laure, a fresh-faced, likable young woman, burst into giggles as her father apparently put his finger on a familiar topic. Steve laughed, too, but he had a point to make. "There's a certain momentum to a girl reaching puberty and the peer pressure that goes on. We had a sense that we have some time here that we can really use well—but it's not a lot of time. The bat mitzvah was a perfect target date to build toward."

Laure was already sure that she wanted a bat mitzvah. Her love of Hebrew and appreciation of her heritage were evident when we spoke with her. But Steve and Iris wanted a lot more. Steve was quite frank in describing what he called "a sense of mistrust in leaving Laure's rite of passage to the culture—even to the Jewish culture itself." Part of this came from his massive disappointment at his own bar mitzvah. His large family traveled to New York for the occasion, but very few of them were present at the synagogue on Saturday morning when Steve was called to the Torah. "What struck me more than anything else was that my cousins and extended family came for the party later that day, but they weren't there to hear me read the Torah portion. They missed what I had ridden five subways for every week for a year. They weren't present for the whole *reason* for the celebration. And I remember thinking as a thirteen-year-old, 'This is a bunch of crap!'"

He laughed with a short, angry explosion. It was clear that the memory still burned. "So even for me, where I had gone through superpreparation, it didn't seem to be enough. Iris and I have touched lots and lots of things that are of value, that inform us and enrich our lives, and we really felt compelled to make sure we could share these things with Laure."

A YEAR OF CHALLENGES

The inspiration to create a new "menu of possibilities" came from Iris, too. As an acupuncturist with a busy practice, she's an expert at juggling seeing her patients, being a mother to college-age Ariana and to Laure, running a house, and occasionally finding time to do the gardening she adores. But one day she just stopped and wondered, "What if my kids grow up and never learn the things I want to teach them? Even if it is sewing. Anything that you learn from your own parents means so much later on. One day I want them to be able to say, 'My mother taught me how to do this' or 'My father taught me how to do that.'"

Laure jumped in at this point, apparently eager to get on with the story. "They came to me with like twenty different choices," she explained, "and said I could choose twelve. They made them all really fun and interesting so it wasn't at all an issue of whether I was going to do it or not. They were very excited and optimistic, and they really wanted me to do it, so I said yes."

Laure's year of challenges began in May 1996 with, appropriately enough, a ladder. We could hear Steve's expertise as a chiropractor behind this first project. He explained that they were creating a physical structure that would be the symbolic scaffolding for the rest of the year. Laure did about 95 percent of the work. She handled the power tools and took all the measurements, and when her ladder was finished, she painted it chocolate brown and decorated it with beads and hearts. (When the interview was over, we all marched out to the garage to see the ladder. It was brown, and decorated, and very substantial indeed.)

In June, Laure and her parents attended a Teen Meditation Day at a nearby retreat center. It included an Indian sweat lodge in the morning, sitting meditation, and then drumming. We asked Laure how she liked it. "I don't really know whether I actually meditated or not," Laure said. "I was experimenting with the whole idea, just kind of sitting there and wondering what was going on. It was fun, especially having a look into more of my parents' world." In July, Laure's sister, Ariana, drove home from Stanford to join the family on a night hike to the top of Mount Tamalpais. They climbed together seven steep miles, with owls and coyotes calling through the dark. "I think we got to the peak about two in the morning and slept at the top for about two hours. And then we got up and watched the sunrise!" Laure reported with evident delight. "It was a hard climb, but I've never been afraid of the dark, so the night part of it was really fun. I was suffering with blisters at the end, and my sister was singing me songs, and we were all telling stories. We made it and kept each other happy."

Nine other "challenges" followed, some quite arduous and others just interesting and new. One month Laure and Iris took a class in women's self-defense. Another time Laure learned some of the traditional arts of a Jewish woman: making matzoh ball soup and baking a challah for Shabbat dinner. Sometime in the middle of the year, Laure learned how to give and receive a massage. "So she begins to learn something about giving and receiving pleasure," Iris explained. Around Christmas, Laure planned to spend one hour for three weeks working in a homeless shelter, doing art with children. But she enjoyed it so much that she continued for the next year and a half.

On Yom Kippur, the Jewish day of atonement, Laure and Steve and Iris not only fasted but kept silence. "I wasn't listening to music or watching TV, and we couldn't talk," Laure recalled with awe. "It was very quiet. It was really nice. We didn't have to spend energy on talking and were just very relaxed." As with each of the other days, a great deal of careful thought went into this day of silence. "The idea of Yom Kippur is to deny the usual pleasures at some level, and the big focus is on denying food. But that is just one level where we distract ourselves from real inner listening, the true prayer. With my yoga background, I felt a strong addition would be a period of silence and solitude, because otherwise you can fast and at the same time you can blab and complain the whole day long."

Throughout the year, on Tuesday afternoons, the roles of guide and student were reversed. Iris wanted to read the Torah portion accompanying Laure's part at the bat mitzvah, but she couldn't read the ancient script and didn't want to just memorize it. So once a week Laure taught her mother to read Hebrew. "It changed our relationship a bit," Iris said, "because she was the teacher, preparing me for something I needed to do."

By the time we had heard the story of the whole year, we began to understand how thoughtfully it had been arranged. The "challenges" clearly had a cumulative effect, becoming more demanding as Laure's confidence and independence developed. "It was really important that we did this year together," Steve explained, "so each day was a challenge but a supported challenge. The idea was to stretch with support. It was like a yoga stretch. You go into a place that's uncomfortable and find where you can handle it, where you can do it. But it's not necessarily what you think you can do to begin with."

Late in the year, Laure rode in a ninety-mile bike-a-thon for breast cancer research. Iris and Steve were "definitely more the support crew," as Iris put it. "It was beautiful to see her momentum," Steve said, beaming. "Laure's often like this—maybe not so sure starting out, but then she lets herself begin to really experience something and gives herself to it, and her energy builds. She started slowly and conservatively, and then she found this strength. On the second day she was just flying! Flying! Down to Sacramento, out to Folsom Dam, and back to Sacramento again. She just kept pouring it on." Laure was laughing with pleasure as Steve described it. He paused and then said softly, "I was proud of her." When Laure collected a whopping $2,500 from her ride, Iris and Steve arranged for her to go down to San Francisco and present all the checks to the executive director of the fund.

The final step of Laure's initiatory year was joining her family and the congregation of Rodef Shalom in becoming a *bat mitzvah,* a daughter of her people, a young woman honored and bringing honor to her community.

CROSSING THE BORDERLAND

How do you judge the success of such a year? Can one assess a rite of passage?

At the end of the interview, Iris asked Laure whether the "year of the challenges" had any effects that she could see. Laure paused to reflect. "I don't think each actual little experience had that much effect," she said, "but I think just the fact that you guys were devoted to me, loved me, and wanted to pass things on to me—that shaped me. I just felt so cared about and loved."

She told us sadly that a number of her closest friends "went downhill," over the last year, and were "getting into bad scenarios." She didn't elaborate, and Steve added only that these girls were "basically playing out Ophelia." Laure told us, "I had a lot of opportunities to do bad, too, but one of the major things I got out of this year was that I felt I owed something to my family. I couldn't disappoint them that way. I felt like we had a good solid thing going, and I didn't want to be the reason it broke up."

The Between offers powerful lessons to those who complete it. Whether one departs for new territory, embarks on a pilgrimage, or is guided through a carefully supported year of challenges, completing the passage means making a fundamental change in identity. You are no longer who you thought you were. When you return to your daily life, you need a period of integration. As we've seen, Elisabet Sahtouris and Will Keepin took several years to bring what they learned to fruition. Elisabet has become a speaker and writer, and Will is continuing to develop and expand his training institute for social activists. Laure, too, is growing into the lessons of her year of challenges.

We could call this final period of the rite of passage by its traditional name, Integration, or Return as it is also termed. But we could just as well name it something like "the reaping of wisdom." Because the final step is metabolizing the experience of the Between, digesting it so well that you embody what you've learned in your mind, heart, and belly. This is no thin mental understanding that the initiate is reaping. It is the getting of wisdom, the knowing that comes from the core of the Mystery. The more open one is, the deeper the potential for experiencing this truth. A greater altruism, a deeper compassion, and fuller trust in life itself are the fruits that seem to come as people go through this process.

Traditionally, the Return was the time of bringing the gifts of the initiation back to the community. Like the earlier stages, it was performed under the guidance of the wisdom keepers of the society, the elders. But in our time, when our culture itself is at the brink of the Between, where will we find the wisdom to guide us through to a new integration? As we'll see, answering this question is part of the exploration that Cultural Creatives are engaged in now, as they develop places and occasions for a new mythos for our time.

chapter ten

a wisdom
for our time

COYOTE WAS WALKING DOWN the road one day, thinking only of food. It had been several days since he had last eaten, and he felt so sorry for himself that he sobbed with his face against his arm. His stomach was making noises like boiling water, and his head hurt. And then, near where the sumac grows, he saw great clusters of delicious-looking red berries! Coyote grew very excited as he ran over to grab them. Just as his hand touched the berries, his mind remembered a talk he had had with the Wise Old Man. During one of their many conversations, Coyote had asked, "Tell me, Old Man, where did we get this land? Was it given to us by our ancestors?" And the Wise Old Man replied, "Of course not, Coyote. We are borrowing this land from our great-great-great-great-grandchildren. We must take good care of it because it belongs to them. To remind us of this, the children of the future have put bunches of red berries near where the sumac grows. These berries are theirs, so no matter how hungry you get, you must never eat them. They are only to remind you that the land belongs to the children yet to come."

"What will happen to us, Old Man, if we do eat the berries?" asked Coyote.

And the Wise Old Man replied, "I am sorry, Coyote, but if you eat those berries, your behind will fall off."

This is what Coyote remembered as his hands touched the berries. He stopped and thought a moment. Sweat was running down his face, and he said to himself, "I have always known the Wise Old Man was a fool. What does he know? He is just trying to keep the berries for himself. Besides, how could I owe something to people who are not even here yet?"

So Coyote ate the berries. He ate as fast as he could and as many as he could. Coyote felt fine! He looked behind him, and his behind had not fallen off. He laughed very loudly and began skipping down the road. He had not gone far when his stomach began to hurt something awful. And then he began to get diarrhea, first a little and then a great stream. Coyote was sick, the sickest he had ever been! Coyote felt terrible! He thought about the children who were yet to come, and he thought about the Wise Old Man, and he was very embarrassed. Coyote walked slowly to the river where he got a drink of water, and then he went to hide himself in the deep bushes. He didn't want anyone to know that he had forgotten the children yet to come and that his behind had fallen off![1]

That trickster Coyote! Asking our worst questions, holding up a mirror to our smallest, most foolish selves. He's sure that the Wise Old Man wants to keep those delectable red berries all to himself. How hard it is for Coyote—and for us—to understand the Wise Old Man's vision of the children yet to come. But there is no question that we need that wisdom now.

We call upon Coyote because, as everyone knows, he manages to create disasters for himself and for anyone around him who joins in his brand of unconsciousness. We humans often behave like Coyote, and all too often we think like him, too. But we cannot afford to do this as a culture, because we're almost up against the wall. The world population is 6 billion at the millennium—at least double, perhaps triple, the long-term sustainable population of the Earth. Given the age structure of populations in the third world, the population can't level off before 8 to 8.5 billion people and possibly not before 10 or 11 billion. At 10 billion, the destruction of the natural areas of the world might well be complete, and the only ecosystems left would be under human cultivation. So many species of plants and animals would die off by then that it is reasonable to predict an ecological and population collapse. After billions die off, what would remain would be a ruined world.

The overconsumption of world resources shows just how unsustainable human consumption is today. Our global ecological footprint would need two or three Earths to be sustainable over the long run, and the American ecological footprint is ten times its world share of resources.[2] At this point, we are already beyond the limits to growth. If we don't completely change our ways within the first few decades of the twenty-first century, we'll be watching the catastrophe from front-row seats.

The problems beggar our reason. We need to go further than the facts to take in the emotional impact of what we know. For this, we'll need to connect with our hearts as well as our minds. And we can't ignore our greedy "Coyote" selves either, because we're already consuming our children's future.

In this chapter, we'll look at three traditional sources of wisdom that Cultural Creatives are turning to now: elders, community, and mythos. Because many of the resources of the past are lost or are no longer appropriate for us today, Cultural Creatives are calling for and in some cases becoming the wisdom carriers, elders, and storytellers that are needed for our time.

THE MAKING OF ELDERS

In ages before our own, and in some indigenous cultures today, wisdom was carried by elders. They guided the initiations and told the stories that gave meaning and connection to life. Because they were old, they knew how long it takes to create something beautiful and good, and how carefully that growth must be protected. Elders took a long view and also a wide view, caring not just about their own children and grandchildren but about all the children. And they knew that wisdom was not mere information. Though not all old people were wise, wisdom was the province of age and experience.

But what of our own time?

Mutombo Mpanya is a professor from Zaire, a man of princely bearing and impeccable manners. He was in his forties, he told us, when he started looking for elders in America. "Ever since I arrived in this country, I have approached old people when I could. 'Excuse me,' I say. 'May I ask you a question? In my country, elders are venerated, and I know that from having lived so long, there must be many things you can teach me. I would like to know what you would answer to a question that your grandchild might ask you. Suppose your grandchild says, "Grandmother, this is such a complicated world. Every day I have difficult choices to make. From what you have learned in life, can you tell me how you determine what is most important?"'"

Mutombo paused to take off his glasses. His eyes were glistening. "They tell me two things," he says. "First, there is always a commentary. It is always something like this. 'My grandchild would never ask me such a question,' they almost always reply. It is clear that they never expect to be asked to pass on their wisdom, and this makes them very sad. And then they will tell me something unique, something that comes from their own life experience that I regard as deep, as essential." He shook his head slowly, perplexed at the strangeness of what he was describing. He could not understand how Western society imagined it could function wisely without elders.

Of course he is right. Our culture is not wise in that combination of compassion and intelligence that is elders' traditional function. Modern culture is set up for adults in their productive years—economically productive years at that. We have only to look around to see how devalued elders are in our society and how little they contribute to its direction. We have no strong cultural story today that tells us the value of aging. What we have is a partial myth, a fragment of the story of the hero or, more recently, modified just a little, a heroine. To age is to fall out of that story and become invisible. "Just how many gray hairs do you need to drop out of the human race?" Old Woman rages in Naomi Newman's "Snake Talk."[3]

No Scaffolding, No Blueprint

We need elders for the children and their concerns. We need them for the young people, who need initiations themselves. And we need them for adults in the middle of their lives who, imagining that there is nowhere further to go, stay in middle age or try to be like the raw, uninitiated adolescents that they feel inside. One woman in her forties told us, "I need the elders in my life—the grandmothers, I call them. They help me more than they know. Each one says to me in her own way: Keep on going. Don't give up. You're on the right track. We need you to speak, to teach, to write." Middle-aged people, she said, need elders to encourage them, "to let us know that our deepest selves have to come into everyday life. But there are so few true elders today."

But if all of us need elders, what about the ones who are coming into elderhood now? Who initiates them? Are there elders for the elders?

"There's no scaffolding, no blueprint for becoming an elder today," Marilyn Ginsberg told us on the eve of her sixty-second birthday. "Those of us who are past sixty have a lot to say, a tremendous spirit. But we don't know what form to give it. It's as if we're each in our own cocoon, unable to see what is unfolding. We're in the process of birthing the membrane that holds the new elder. We're going through for the first time, making our way toward a new way of aging and maturing that most of us have never seen before."

Elders need to be willing not to know what this will look like, she said. To be open. In effect, to go into the Between. "Underneath the glitz of ads for houses on golf courses and happy white-haired couples in tennis clothes lies the terror of the grave," Marilyn told us. "Become elders? Keep on maturing into old age? Forget it! We feel like failures, like dummies. If we had only taken more vitamins or exercised more or spent less time in the sun or not eaten red meat, then we'd still be resilient and strong and wrinkle-free and, most importantly, young."

She's furious at the lack of honest support from the culture. "All that junk we're inundated with about youth, pep, productivity, all the adulation of power and wealth . . . how do you find the courage to realistically face the decline in your ability to function, to be honest with yourself about the memory failures, the trouble hearing, the fact that you can't earn what you once could? It's the anticipation of helplessness and uselessness that is so terrifying, and who wants to talk about that?"

Birthing the New Elders

Part of the problem is Modernism's headlong flight from aging and death. To not run away, to face instead into the loss of what you've taken to be the essence of yourself, is, as T. S. Eliot put it, "to be explorers/ . . . moving into another intensity/ . . . a deeper communion."[4] Aging is the Between that life provides. It's available to everyone who grows old and can bear to be conscious through the passage. It's what initiates elders so they then have the wisdom to guide others through the Between and to guide their communities.

But when the elders themselves have had no initiation, they have very little basis for trusting the process of change. They have not found or even experienced that point of absolute, internal security that tells the Caribou Eskimo shaman, "Do not be afraid of the universe," or that informs Elisabet Sahtouris that "a larger intelligent system surrounds us and works for us." Without support from within, from the Mystery itself, and without a scaffolding or blueprint from the culture, it is almost impossible to trust the process of aging. It is not at all surprising that we have so few real elders today.

But our fear of aging and death is only part of the problem. In fact, the wisdom from the past, when elders were wary of strangers and remembered the wounds and the enemies who inflicted them, is not the wisdom we need. The task of our time is to find our own wisdom and to develop elders who can carry it.

Where will the new elders come from? In the logic of the rites of passage, the answer is clear: the elders will be the ones who go through the Between and return to help their people. By this logic, Elisabet Sahtouris is an elder now, and her vision of the whole planet is an outcome of her initiatory passage. Will Keepin is on his way there, as he works with his colleagues to train conscious activists after his journey through the Between. And Willis Harman, Joe Kresse, Sandra Mardigian, Betty Friedan, Vincent Harding, Adrienne Rich, Thomas Berry, and the "ancestors" like William Kent and Rachel Carson and John Muir and Martin Luther King, Jr.,[5] have all become elders through their own individual rites of passage, creating the new path by walking it. And for each one we have named, there are hundreds of thousands, perhaps millions who are finding their way alone or with the help of friends through their own transformational journeys. But this is not ideal. Walking with friends at your side is not the same as having elders who have made the journey before you and who can offer guidance and support.

An Elder's Perspective

We've told most of the stories so far through the voices of initiates who leave their old way of life, go through the Between, and gradually find a way to bring their gifts to people who want them. We haven't told the stories from the perspective of the elders because that is so much less familiar and less available. But it is a perspective that Cultural Creatives are learning to develop, as more and more of them go through their own passages.

One way of becoming an elder is by invitation. All across the country, Cultural Creatives are asking their friends and relatives to participate in new kinds of initiations, or they are being asked themselves. A group of young and middle-aged women in Portland, Maine, invited one of their members to become an elder when she turned fifty-six. "I don't know *how* to be an elder," the woman objected. "Well, learn!" her friends insisted.

Another example is what happened with Laure Katz, whose yearlong initiation we described in Chapter Nine. As part of that initiation, Laure and her mother, Iris, invited fifteen women friends and relatives to participate in a wisdom ritual. As in every story we've heard where an invitation like this is extended, there is a most surprising consequence: the guides themselves are initiated.

The Women's Wisdom Circle

Most of the women making their way across the sand of Muir Beach, California, on a cool spring evening in 1997 were heading into an event that was totally new to them, and several were a bit edgy. The youngest was Laure's sister, Ariana, who had entered a similar circle seven years earlier when she turned thirteen. The eldest were Iris's two cousins, women in their late fifties who had traveled from Manhattan. Everyone carried a small gift, and everyone brought a story.

The circle began with one of the women beating out a slow rhythm on a drum. The cousins from Manhattan, old pros from their experience in Ariana's circle, smiled benignly. A few of the Californians looked uncomfortable. The woman who was drumming asked the circle to call the names of their own mothers and daughters, and of Laure's family line—ancestors and friends who loved Laure and would want to witness her passage into womanhood. Something about calling the familiar names, invoking the trustworthy connections, grounded the process and made everyone relax. As the drumbeat continued, the women told their stories. Some talked about what they had learned about being a woman; others told anecdotes about Laure as a little girl. A few read poems or pieces from their favorite books. The details didn't seem to matter. The women said later that welcoming a girl into their midst seemed like such a natural thing to do. Laure, alternately radiant and shy, basked in the welcome.

At sunset Laure slipped off her clothes, climbed into a wetsuit, and sprinted down to the cold ocean. She paused a moment and then dove in, surfaced, dove back into the waves again, and surfaced with her arms raised high, laughing triumphantly like some Olympian crossing the finish line. The women jumped to their feet, clapping and yelling encouragement. Laure bounded out of the waves and back to the circle, as her mother enveloped her in a large white towel.

Afterward, over paper cups of espresso and small fruit tarts, the women agreed that there had been two initiations. One was Laure's, of course. But the other, the one that took them by surprise, was their own initiation as . . . women? Elders? They weren't sure what name to give it. But they knew that they had stepped into a new sense of their own significance. They had thought this was all about Laure, that they were drawing on wisdom they weren't sure they had to help Laure into the next step of her life. But what they discovered was something else—an encompassing affection and tenderness, not just for Laure but for their own daughters and granddaughters and all girls everywhere who would become women. And they discovered a new appreciation for themselves as mature women with gifts to share. As they thought of this, they remembered their own mothers and grandmothers and aunts and teachers and felt how far their lineage extended.

They spoke of these things with each other, quietly. Like Laure, they were almost shy, the way one is in speaking of something intimate and true. As they left, many of them said that they intended to create occasions like this for their own children, and for their friends. Because, they said, every initiation is a double blessing. It blesses the ones who receive, and it blesses the ones who give. It means stepping into the fullness of your maturity—whether you're thirteen or thirty or sixty—and letting everybody see you in that fullness. Not hiding. Not pretending to be less than you are. It means standing, like Laure did, in the midst of a circle of others who are overjoyed to be your witnesses and basking in that welcome. It is a blessing, the women concluded, and all too rare.

A HOLE IN THE CULTURE

In every age, elders have one fundamental task to do for the culture. Their work is to carry the wisdom function: to speak for it, protect it, preserve it, and convey it forward for future generations. If no elders are recognized as wise, or if no elders are willing to come forward, the culture loses its wisdom function. There is literally a hole in the culture.

Modernism lives with a hole where wisdom ought to be. We know this. We know that we haven't yet caught up with the speed of our technology, with the genius of our inventions. We make jokes about it. A *New Yorker* cartoon shows two yogis sitting cross-legged on a mountain peak. They've obviously been interrupted in their meditation by a 747 flying by. The older one says to the younger, "Ah, they have the know-*how* but do they have the know-*why*?"

We know that our culture lacks wisdom when we see our children without the clear air or clean water that we had when we were young. Mary Ford told us that when she told her son Daniel about the thousands of tiny sand crabs that used to live on the eastern shore of Maryland but now are gone, he burst into tears. "I'll never get to see them!" he yelled. "It's not fair!"

We need elders who will care about Daniel and the sand crabs and the oceans and beaches, elders who will ask the big, long-term, hard questions for the sake of all the children. The Cherokee question that guided its decision makers—"Will it be good to the seventh generation?"—is joined today with another question: "Will it be good for the planet?" Without elders who will raise these questions, and a community that will hear them and work to develop answers, we lack wisdom.

Michael Meade, a writer and storyteller who works with men across the country, is worried about what the lack of elders and procedures for initiation means for young men and women. "If we don't produce elders, real elders with inner resources and authority, we'll lose the coming generation and the one after that." But producing elders is difficult, he admitted. It means developing people "who can make peace with disappointment, who know how to mourn, who have learned how to listen." He said frankly that he wanted to be like this himself "but the automatic reactions keep pulling me back to the old adaptations: being tough, cynical, having it all together. How do you find the courage to let the hero die so the elder can be born?"[6]

Whenever life gets stuck or reaches a dead end, whenever people are caught in addictions or pulled apart by grief and loss, Meade sees it as evidence of this lack of elders. When rites of passage disappear, they surface in the society "as misguided and misinformed attempts to change one's own life. They become miscarriages of meaning, tragic acts or empty forms," he says.[7] Some psychologists and social workers agree. From their studies of gangs in the inner cities and prisons, and teens in the shopping malls, they say that young people hunger for initiations, and that pseudo-initiations don't work. One observer calls our overcrowded prisons "houses of failed initiation."[8]

The connection between the lack of elders and the increasing numbers of poor young men in prisons is not surprising to Sylvia Maracle, a Mohawk elder. Her people trace relationships on the medicine wheel. Elders are located directly opposite adolescents. "When one part of the wheel is in trouble or disrespected in the culture," she explains, "you know that its opposite is soon going to be falling apart too." When elders are dishonored in our modern world, she says, very soon the young people will be in trouble. If that is not remedied, then the segments on either side of the elders and the youth will begin to fail. And that includes all of the segments: the children and the grandparents and adults in the prime of their lives. "You must not allow this to happen," she warns. "Every part of the wheel depends on every other part for its life."[9]

A feature of earlier wisdom cultures appears in the Mohawk explanation: the network of mutual obligation and caring that is part of a living system. If any part of that fabric is harmed, all suffer. But the reverse is also true: if any part of that network is healed, all benefit.

GETTING A HEART OF WISDOM

> *The days of our years are threescore and ten,*
> *Or even by reason of strength fourscore*
> *Yet is their pride but travail and vanity;*
> *For it is speedily gone and we fly away . . .*
> *So teach us to number our days,*
> *That we may get us a heart of wisdom.*

PSALMS 90:10–12

Sister Miriam MacGillis, a Dominican sister who founded Genesis Farm in Caldwell, New Jersey, knows the value of story in providing hope and vision through the dark times. The story we are living now, she says, is the "story of the Earth coming off remote control," coming out of a five-billion-year process that human beings had no part in shaping. And in this story we are like adolescents, "with these extraordinary powers but without the life experience to integrate those powers into a larger context." The question she asks is this: "Have we arrived at anywhere near the level of maturity to make the decisions that will sustain life?"

Finding that level of maturity cannot be approached simply from knowing the facts. If we cannot find our connection to each other and to the larger life of our planet, we don't know what the facts mean. We only think we know, which is not the same at all. This is what Joanna Macy discovered in 1978.

Joanna was a graduate student when her three college-age children invited her to a daylong conference on the biosphere sponsored by the Cousteau Society. Though she learned nothing new that day, she told us, the cumulative effect was devastating. "People were talking about the arms race and oil spills and the demolition of the rain forests. It broke through to me, somewhere in the middle of the afternoon, that this could really be curtains for us all. I saw this fact so clearly that I didn't know how I could stand it." What shocked her was not the information but the concentrated implications of that information for everything she loved.

"For the next year, I lived with despair. Working at home at my desk, I'd suddenly find myself on the floor, curled up in a fetal position and shaking. In company I was more controlled, but even then in the beginning, the sight of an egret lighting by the edge of a marsh or the sound of Bach from a nearby piano would unexpectedly pierce my heart, as I wondered how long it would be before that piece of beauty faded forever."

Over that year, Joanna went through a searing initiation. Living through her feelings of helplessness and rage and letting them go, allowing the next layer of feelings to roll through and letting them go, she was grieving alone for what was happening to all of us. She would say later that until you can let suffering in, you're paralyzed. "You're afraid of feeling the fear, the grief, the remorse, and you can't take the next step. You can't feel your pain for the world, for other human beings or yourself. But if something happens that lets the psychic numbing crack, then your own deepest responses break through the layers of ice. Your human feelings can flow freely, and you bring yourself to life."

No elders were present to support this passage. Joanna's professors in the graduate department of religion were mystified at the intensity of her emotions. Several seemed embarrassed, and one suggested that she might need psychological help. She did see a therapist, who was equally puzzled. "You have beautiful children, a wonderful husband, a lovely home. Why can't you be happy?" she asked.

That was thirty years ago, before the convergence of consciousness and social activism we discussed in Chapter Seven. The sacred was not supposed to be relevant to emotions, and neither was thought to have much to do with social activism. But today, among Core Cultural Creatives, there is no doubt that a deeply emotional response about the fate of the Earth is an appropriate, intelligent, and probably essential foundation to engagement in the world.

Joanna was one of the pioneers in this understanding. The facts could not remain, as she put it, "mere information." They were connected to everything she loved and everything she hoped for. And when those facts were put together, they broke open the story line that had guided her life. "We're the first generation to have lost the certainty that there will be a future," Joanna told writer Stephan Bodian. "[E]very generation throughout recorded history has lived with the assumption that other generations would follow and that the work of their hands, their heads, and their hearts would be carried on by their children and their children's children. That assumption gave meaning and a sense of continuity to their lives. Failures, sufferings, even personal deaths, were ever encompassed by that vaster assurance of continuity."[10]

Joanna went on to do what initiates have done through all times: she prepared a way for others to come after her. She offered workshops called "Despair and Empowerment in the Nuclear Age." Many wondered, "Why would anybody go to something like that? Who wants to feel despair?" But soon Americans, and later Canadians and Germans and French and Australians, and others around the world who were barely holding off their despair and sick of living with denial, found their way to those workshops. There they told personal, soul-level stories, stories they'd never told anyone because they doubted that they could bear to say what they felt—and because they could not imagine that anyone would listen.

Having lived through her own anguish, Joanna could help others. The first step was to move beyond what she calls "the greatest danger"—the deadening of mind and heart. Helping people to express and move through what they had considered unbearable, Joanna led exercises and meditations in weekend workshops. Later she wrote books about the process so that anyone who wanted to guide the process could follow the instructions and do likewise.[11]

Even today, unless you've been through the process or something of similar depth, it's hard to fathom that tens of thousands of people have been through it and its further developments, going together into the Between for an afternoon or a day with people they've never met before. Not telling themselves to get over it and get on with their lives, but cutting through their psychic numbing to move toward a wisdom of the heart. It seems nothing short of amazing. But it isn't amazing, Joanna insists. The grieving and the fear are not merely private matters. They are sensitive responses to what is happening to all of us. To know that the pain you bear is part of a shared pain, to discover that your hope for a better world is a shared hope—it makes all the difference. What doesn't make sense is to have to make that passage alone, as so many Cultural Creatives do today.

The process of reworking and reformulating that happens in workshops and seminars like Joanna's takes years to complete. No single ritual, no single despair and empowerment workshop, will be enough to carry someone through the process. For each person, the way will be unique. More uncovering and discovering will follow. But what is important is the beginning in a cultural context. Because Joanna and her colleagues are assisting that beginning, we believe that they are doing the work of elders for our time. One part of that work is to provide support and guidance for this cultural rite of passage for each person. Another part is to call forth the stories that need to be spoken and heard now. These stories are maps to a territory that almost everyone thought would lead off the edge of the world, into a chasm of hopelessness. But in fact, they turn out to be life-giving, leading people beyond the boundaries of the old story to make a commitment to a different future.

WEAVING A NEW MYTHOS

On a bitterly cold November day in 1982, we sat drinking coffee with the mythologist Joseph Campbell in his hotel room in Montreal. We were preparing a documentary for the CBC about the paradigm change we thought was starting to happen in the West. We hoped that Campbell would give us an overview of where our culture was heading, and maybe a mythic story or two to provide a context. He began the interview by reaching into his briefcase to pull out an article he'd been reading in *Foreign Affairs,* "The Care and Repair of Public Myth."[12]

A society without a shared myth can't function coherently, the author argued. Without an accepted set of beliefs about nations and the cosmos, a society just goes to pieces. Campbell agreed with this premise, but he said that it was missing two parts, parts he thought were critical to what our culture had to face. "You do not have a myth unless you have an opening into transcendence. The first function of a mythology is to open the mind and heart to the absolute mystery of being in the universe," he said. The article omitted this part, which Campbell considered a big mistake. If we cannot recognize the universe and the nations and ourselves as manifestations of "the grounding mystery of all being," he said, we have nothing we can really trust.

The second part Campbell thought was missing was "the pedagogical function of myth: educating the individual, giving clues to the stages of life from infancy to maturity and self-responsibility and finally through the final gate. If the myth doesn't carry you all the way through those stages," he told us in a gravelly baritone, "it isn't working."

We were new to these ideas, and we argued energetically with the eminent and exceedingly patient professor. How could he claim that myths were so important to the coherence of a society when it was clear that, as a culture, we no longer had such myths? Certainly no guiding story was carrying our generation through the stages of life and opening us to a sacred connection, we said.

"That's exactly the point," he agreed genially.

"Well, where do we get one?" we wanted to know.

"The panorama of possibilities has made it impossible to mythologize," he announced calmly. "The individual is just going in raw. All you can do is follow your own inward life and try to stay true to that."

"That's not very helpful."

"I'm not able to correct the world," he replied. "I can tell you what a mythology is, but when you ask me how we're going to get a new one, you've gone past my level of incompetence." And then he rocked back in his chair and laughed with great amusement.

TRUE ON THE INSIDE

Mythos carries the soul-level truth of a culture. When that truth begins to change, we thirst for new stories and images: not only to help us make sense of the changes, although that is immensely important, but to help us find our connections to each other, to the natural world, and to our past and our future. Without these stories and images, we lose our connections. It is as if we are chopped into fragments with our worlds broken apart, the physical separated from the imaginal. Jungian analyst Marion Woodman told us, "At that point, we lack the cosmos that keeps us in touch with the universal reality. Without stories, we have no way to recollect ourselves when our personal world shatters."[13]

Is this right? Could our modern sense of disconnection, our lack of continuity with the past and lack of responsibility for the future, be caused by lack of a *story*? Or even more unbelievable, a *myth*? Any schoolchild will tell you that myths are stories that aren't true. But, as storyteller Erica Meade says, a myth is a story that's true on the inside. And it's a storyteller's work to reveal the inside truths of a culture.[14] It's a natural part of what Cultural Creatives want and value: a way to remember that they do not stand alone, a way to weave new patterns into the social fabric, spinning lifelines that link the generations.

BECOMING THE NEW STORYTELLERS

In times past, elders were storytellers precisely because they were wisdom carriers. To carry wisdom meant to tell how things had always been done and why, and to help people at each stage of life understand their role and their responsibilities to the community. As Campbell put it so forcefully, Modernism has no shared myth that gives it coherence, no guiding story that educates the individual in the stages of life and grounds the community in the great mystery of being. We are, as he said, just going in raw.

There's another way to see this situation, however. It's not just that we have lost our story, but that we *had* to lose it, because every age needs its own wisdom. Clinging to old stories is not only dangerous and foolish, it keeps a culture stale and without imagination. Because we are living in the time of the Between, we dare not be lulled into listening to the old stories over and over again. And that means that those who carry the wisdom for our time cannot be simply storytellers. They'll have to be story-listeners, story-evokers, artists and teachers of every sort who can call forth the stories we need now.

When an individual loses his story, Jung observed in the wake of the conflagration of World War II, confusion and disorientation result; but when a people lose their story, the entire culture suffers from strange pathologies.[15] We have been living in the aftermath of that loss for centuries. At the beginning of a new millennium, our landscape is still like the first season after a forest fire. But out of the ashes, sharp green shoots are sprouting everywhere, growing up between the blackened stumps.

One of the marvels of our time is precisely this new growth that has never been seen before. After the holocaust of the Nazi *Reich* and Hiroshima and Nagasaki, and the tragedies of the native peoples of North and South America, many wisdom traditions were destroyed. But the dead wood of the feudal system, the absolute power of the Church and the agrarian empires, has also been burned away. From all our grave losses and all our fortunate releases, a space has been cleared for innovation and creativity.

This fertile soil is where the Cultural Creatives are working, preparing the way for a new culture. The new growth, as we have seen, includes the large social and consciousness movements of the last forty years. But it also includes one of the oldest and most powerful forms of human social life: mythos. Its fruits are story and image, visual and performance arts, theater and song, music and metaphor and ritual. New forms of the mythos are springing up today, cultivated by a variety of artists and experimenters of all sorts. In addition, a world culture of music and story is growing as moderns understand ancient teachings in a new way.[16] And everywhere that harbingers of a new mythos are appearing, Cultural Creatives are preparing the way.

LIFELINES

"I'm interested in plays that come from people who have been outside of the core," director George C. Wolfe said about Tony Kushner's Broadway play *Angels in America*. "[I'm interested in] people who have had to stay in touch with their strength and have had to go on journeys of self-examination because they were not, as I like to say, invited to the party. So they've had to stay in touch with a whole series of truths, and muscles, that those in the party didn't have to because they were of the power base." These people and their stories, Wolfe said, are not only witnesses and sources of understanding for who we are and where we are going. They are lifelines.[17]

Some of those lifelines are coming from dreams. Women discover sacred texts filled with blank pages, waiting for the new stories to be inscribed. Children initiate elders, because they need elders and the old people do not know the new way. Photographs are taken of what has never been seen before, but the fluid that can develop the film has not yet been invented. New software is written and waiting in storehouses for the time when hardware is built to run it.

These nighttime images tell of the need to go beyond traditional roles and rules and hierarchies of power. Be more like water than steel, they counsel. Be flexible and curious rather than armed for battle or paralyzed by fear. Don't be afraid not to know, they say. In a beginner's mind, there are a thousand possibilities. In the expert's mind, there are few.

THE HOME PLANET

People everywhere carry fragments of the new mythos, bringing impressions and memories, visions and metaphors. Of all these treasures and shards, one set of images seems to have a special enchantment for us now. It is the photographs of the Earth from space. Futurist Barbara Marx Hubbard has an explanation: we find these pictures so fascinating, she says, because they're our first baby pictures.

Every photograph of the Earth from space and every story of the men and women who have actually traveled into space casts us into what astronaut Rusty Schweickart called "the overwhelming experience of a new relationship." What requires no scientific analysis or laborious processing, Schweickart says, is the overwhelming contrast "between bright colorful home and stark black infinity" and "the unavoidable and awesome personal relationship, suddenly realized, with all life on this amazing planet . . . Earth, our home."

This understanding has quickened many creative, innovative actions. One was the publication of a book that experts considered impossible to produce for economic and political reasons. It was initiated because a man named Kevin W. Kelley could not get the photographs of Earth from space out of his mind's eye; nor could he forget the stories of the astronauts and cosmonauts who had been transformed by their voyages. After years of wondering whether those experiences, portrayed in a book, could transform others, and doubting his ability to create such a book; and after deciding to go ahead and try; and after three more years of intricate negotiations and phenomenal cooperation between the Association of Space Explorers, the Institute of Noetic Sciences, Mir Publishing of Moscow, Addison-Wesley Publishing, and a host of translators, Kelley brought out *The Home Planet*. Published simultaneously in Russian and English, it is the most extensive collection of photographs of Earth from space ever published, with words from the space explorers written in their native languages, including Arabic, Chinese, Vietnamese, Hindi, and Mongolian. The sense of "one planet, our home" is inescapable.

We spoke of being more like water than steel, the counsel of some of the dreams that were described to us. But when we met Kevin Kelley in 1999, an image of water did not spring to mind. A plainspoken, muscular man, he reminded us of tough old leather, someone who could endure the hard knocks of life and might be just flexible enough to get a big job done—if he wanted to do it. There was nothing in his life that he ever wanted more, Kevin told us, than to make a book magnificent enough to evoke the way that Earth looked from space.

Why this passion for seeing the Earth? we asked. What difference did you think it would make? He told us that overviews are very important and quoted the astronomer Fred Hoyle: "In 1946, the year I was born, Hoyle said that when the first picture of the Earth from space is shown, it will change the world." That's what Kevin really wanted: to change the world by giving it new pictures of itself. When you see the planet as a whole, he explained, without man's boundaries dividing it up and separating each country from every other, it can open a different sense of who you are. "I wanted to create a clearer picture, a more informed picture, a more highly defined image of the Earth, and I wanted to raise this as a context in people's consciousness. I thought the world needed this." He paused for a moment. "Desperately."

But there was a problem with this grand vision. "Look, I was a thirty-eight-year-old handyman with no credentials," Kevin explained. "I'd been a boat builder, a general contractor, a wild rice farmer, a fisherman, and every time I got to the end of a project, I'd say to myself, 'This isn't what I want to do with the rest of my life.' I felt like I'd wasted my entire life, like a dog on a chain that had worn the ground bare." The fact was, he said, that nobody would believe that someone who had never gone to college, never been an editor, never accomplished anything big and impressive, could produce a book involving millions of dollars and the cooperation of Soviet and American publishers, the space agencies, and the most celebrated heroes of the world's superpowers.

He was right. Hardly anyone did believe it. Kevin was turned down many times by many people, and some of his closest friends advised him to drop the project completely. His perseverance—his critics would certainly call it stubbornness or worse—was phenomenal. If ever someone was stretched and strengthened by following through on what he believed, it was Kevin Kelley. Not only was he learning new things, but the parts of himself that he was embarrassed by, the ones he thought got him in hot water too much of the time, unexpectedly turned out to be advantages. He was funny, and very honest, about how this worked:

"Through the process of writing the book, I was concerned that I wasn't an ideal person to do the book. I felt like I was too brash, too harsh, too impetuous. At one point, one of the astronauts wanted to take the book away from me.

He said, 'Why don't we just go out and get a normal editor, someone who's done this before?' When it was all over, our lawyer said, 'Kevin, a normal editor wouldn't have done this book. After the first hurdle or two, he would've said screw this and been out of there.'

"At times I felt like I was a Stone Age man with an ax trying to do modern surgery and I didn't have a scalpel. But I wouldn't give up. Everybody that got in the way of getting the book done, and having it done beautifully, just got worn out because I wouldn't give up."

At the end of the interview, as we were saying good-bye, Kevin said, "Tell people not to give up. If I can do it, anyone can." We thought about his words often as we were writing this book. They reminded us of something of the greatest importance: the power of ordinary people to make a difference, simply by persevering in what they believe. Many who were caught up in the social and consciousness movements know this: from those who were in the black freedom movement, to demonstrators in the peace and women's and ecology movements, to longtime meditators and travelers on spiritual paths. And not only did their persistence and steadfastness affect the culture, over time the individuals themselves were affected. If some of the Cultural Creatives seem like extraordinary people, they will tell you that it was the process that made them so, not that they were born that way. They started like everyone else.

As the medieval saying had it, "The fool who persists in his folly shall become wise." What convention considers folly is often real wisdom to those who follow it. Jim Lawson, the man who taught nonviolent tactics to the early leaders of the black freedom movement, put it a little differently. "As you act on your conscience," he told his students, "you will be transformed." And often they were.

Most real-life stories don't have conclusions, but this one does, at least for Kevin Kelley and anyone who has fallen in love with the exquisite book he produced with the Association of Space Explorers and their many partners. You hold the book in your hands and look at the barely fathomable beauty of our planet, and you know that Kevin's tenacious resolve has borne excellent fruit.

IN A CONTEXT OF COMMUNITY

How do you tell a tale untold? For many Cultural Creatives, it is by developing places and occasions where such tales will be welcome. It means building the equivalent of new tribal fires where people can sit around and tell the truth about what they've seen, what they've personally been through, and what it means. Telling the stories in the presence of thoughtful listeners was once done in community with the guidance of elders. It is a way of sharing the gifts of what you've learned so far, of integrating the discoveries from the new territory. Cultural Creatives need this kind of integration, and so they are creating settings where it can happen.

Writing circles are one place where the threads of new stories are being knitted together. "When the official chronicles are full of holes and distortions and you still hunger for the truth," one woman asked, "what do you do?" For some, the answer is, you sit down in a circle and you write. You pull off the mask you wear in public and dig down to the place where you can say, *This is how it was. This really happened.* Then you listen to what other people have to say, and maybe you find the courage to read aloud what you've written yourself. In the process you probably change how and what you trust. Genuineness becomes important, and the unique particulars of each person's experience, and anything original and fresh, adventurous or unexpected.

Some gathering places are for those who are facing illness, death, and loss that would be unbearable alone. Story circles for people with life-threatening illness (described in Chapter Six) are one example, and so are twelve-step programs and support groups of all kinds. Some of the "gathering places" are in fact books, collections of stories or poetry, or photographs—witnesses to what cannot be said quickly but must be brought together slowly, over time.

Charles Garfield's *Sometimes My Heart Goes Numb: Love and Caregiving in a Time of AIDS* is like a council of elders sharing their wisdom around the fire. One of those elders, a caregiver named Eric Shifler, could have had Jung's comment about cultural pathologies in mind when he explains why he's a caregiver. "The real pathology is accumulated grief," he says.[18] That's why you have to enter that grief, unfold it and find its meaning. "Because I was in it since the beginning of the epidemic, I feel like a walking archive sometimes. Like a tribal elder." He tells stories to bear witness to what has been lost and to what lives on. "In accounts of the Holocaust, you hear people talk about surviving so they could tell the story. I have all these memories now, all these stories, and I help people with AIDS and their families and friends and lovers survive to tell theirs."[19]

Some of the most important gathering places are not just about the power of words but the power of voice. Reg E. Gains, a cowriter of the Tony Award–winning hit *Bring in 'da Noise, Bring in 'da Funk,* talks about the growing willingness of people to read poetry aloud to strangers. It wasn't until Gains heard the poet Willie Peromo reading at the Nuyorican Poets Café, he said, that he realized "how voiceless I was."[20] This is part of it: not only giving voice to what you know and remember and long for, but finding out what you never said and never believed anyone would want to hear.

These are, of course, just a few examples among thousands, perhaps millions, of places and occasions where people can tell their stories and find their voices. What is impressive, from a cultural perspective, is that this giving and receiving is not simply about individuals. It is about community: in Latin, *cum* and *munis,* "giving together." In a real community, people share their personal life experiences. It is not some PR trope like "the community of agribusiness" or "the pharmaceutical community" or housing developments that call themselves "communities" but where the neighbors don't know each other.

If we are in fact going through a massive cultural rite of passage, then community could not be more important. It is where the essential steps of return take place when a people emerge from the Between. It is where the gifts of the journey are acknowledged and welcomed. If there is no place to give those gifts, the process of reintegration may be halted. The loss would be great for the individual but even greater for the community. It would not benefit from the new learning and would not be revitalized by the fresh energy and inspiration of the ones who return.

CREATING A WORLD I WANT TO LIVE IN

Like a number of Cultural Creatives, Celia Thompson-Taupin is piecing together what she needs for herself and, in the process, shaping the elements of a new kind of culture. She creates environments for improvisation and mythic play in a context of community. Celia T-T, as she likes to be called, is a bridge person, an original who has had to develop her own syntheses in order to preserve her sanity and wholeness. She's a blend of a midwesterner who spent her childhood in the Ohio countryside and a California artist with a studio in San Francisco. She loves to build things with her hands and has a minuscule tolerance for phoniness. She is also, as she grudgingly concedes, a kind of priestess who creates places and occasions for celebrations.

What do these places look like? It depends on when you come to visit. In San Francisco, on almost any Thursday evening for the past sixteen years, if you drove down south of Market Street to where it crosses Cesar Chavez Avenue and parked in front of a former factory-become-artists'-studios, you could follow the sound of drums and flutes and bells humming in improvisational ecstasy to a gathering called Soup and Bread. There you'd find Celia in the midst of twenty to forty sometime musicians, cabdrivers, therapists, multimedia artists, and other drop-ins.

"I loved making improv music and sound," Celia told us, explaining how this weekly event got started. "I started carrying a basket of instruments to parties, hoping I could get a little group of people to go out in the laundry room or some place, to play with me. I was like a child with a bunch of toys. I wanted to do this more often, so I sent everyone a letter. 'I will do this every Thursday night,' I said, 'and I will provide you with soup and bread. You bring whatever else you want, and this is where it will be. And don't phone me. If you come, okay, but don't call and ask if it's happening. It's happening.'"

Celia's no-nonsense tone was mixed right in with her longing for playmates. But what impressed us was the continuity. Soup and Bread has become an institution. When Celia's away, others take it over. People bring their parents, their children, their lovers and friends. Some come every week. Others show up every few months, and a few come every few years. One eighty-year-old man drives up from Santa Cruz, and a number of middle-aged artists drive across the bridge from Berkeley. "A lot of them are artists in their heads even if they don't work as artists," Celia explained. "One of the faithful lives down the hall here. He's a cabdriver and a musician, an artist at heart. We don't mess with who's successful as an artist."

There are many more men than women. They're eccentrics, Celia says. "Without the music, this whole thing wouldn't work at all. The process of making music together and dancing together, the little chitchat that goes around, is fine. But we don't necessarily share ways of looking at things, or politics, or anything. So it's the music that glues us together and the festivals."

It's a Culture

When some of the people from Soup and Bread wanted to go more fully into exploring their inner experience and being witnesses for each other, Celia created a new structure that goes by the name of Improv Arts Weekends. If you arrive at one of these twice-a-year events, you'll find some combination of creative theater mixed with play and sacred ritual, all designed by and for the community members. One of the longtime members told us, "Celia is an absolute master at creating a structure, which in this case asks for a lot from people, and at the same time provides an atmosphere that is extremely nurturing and gentle and kind of easygoing." The weekends begin with people creating an original piece of art and presenting it to the group with ritual expressiveness through spontaneous words or singing or dance. The high point is usually on Saturday night, when each person creates a theatrical presentation.

As we listened to Celia and some of the other members of the group describe these weekends, we were struck by the mixture of structure and spontaneity. To prepare for the weekends, which involve twenty to thirty people, a great deal of planning and meeting goes on, usually by a group of four to six volunteers. At the same time, the process is free-flowing, riffing off a basic theme and turning corners in surprising ways. One weekend began with each person making a large puppet of one of their ancestors. In the evening presentation, there were dialogues between the ancestor puppets and the puppet makers. Each person spoke with his or her own voice and then with the voice of their ancestor. By the end of the evening, the group had an awe-inspiring experience of being in the presence of their collective ancestors. They felt a sense of continuity and appreciation, Celia told us, for all of those who had gone before them and given them life, and a palpable experience of goodwill.

What are people really doing here, in this serious, joking, goofing-off gathering that has been meeting for over a decade? One woman, who called the weekends "a marvelous mixture of depth and fun," explained it this way: "It's a culture," she said. "The experienced ones carry the culture for the new people, and the new people learn not only the theater of it but the importance of kindness with each other, warmth, and taking things seriously, but not too seriously."

We thought of a comment that Scott Peck once made, to the effect that psychotherapy is one of the strangest things our culture has ever invented. It's so odd to expect that healing can happen when you take a person out of their community and put them in a room with some professional, he said. For millennia, healing has taken place in the context of community. It is not surprising that so much healing and real pleasure happens in contexts like Improv Arts and Soup and Bread.

Salamander Camp

Of all the places that Celia T-T has created, the most breathtaking is a place you reach by driving down serpentine Highway 17, which winds from Silicon Valley to the Pacific. Take a sharp right for a mile or two, and park your car at the crest of a hill. Walk a few yards west toward a green expanse of lawn, and you'll be greeted by a sight that seems to come from some medieval storybook. Three large, circular tentlike structures, with flags flying, are set into a clearing at some small distance from each other. Each structure is surrounded by a graceful wooden deck with a railing and is connected to the others by flower-lined paths.

This, you'll discover, is Salamander Camp, ten acres of land that Celia and her partner have set aside as an extremely low-cost retreat facility for artists and other adventurous groups that want to explore new forms of creative gatherings.

The first weekend we arrived, a group of Wicca lovers of the Earth were in residence, drumming and chanting. The next time there were about fifteen women elders, some from the nearby towns and others who had flown in from other parts of the country. The distant members could afford to fly, they explained, because the cost of the retreat was so low. When we joined the elders in the dining yurt, as the structures are called, modeled on Mongolian round tents, we heard their wonder at where they found themselves. Not only is the land beautiful, they said, but the design is full of beauty, and a feeling of abundance and generosity pervades the camp, from the sprung-wooden dance floor in the meeting yurt to the baskets filled with musical instruments to the funny, secondhand, freshly washed bathrobes hanging in the bathhouse.

"It is as if somebody had been preparing for us for a long time," one woman said, "thinking about just what we'd need and what we'd enjoy."

Another added, "It's way more than we ever expected, all of this beauty and wildness just waiting for us."

Seeing what Celia T-T and her friends have created and are continuing to create impressed us deeply. It showed what is possible for Cultural Creatives with imagination and perseverance. Many people have visions, but actually giving that vision a form that is beautiful and gracious is something else. Equally important is what Margaret Mead called "whole process": seeing your dream all the way through to completion and to the new beginning. How the work is done is also important: the process of building and shaping the new form. And finally comes the result—the gathering place or the weekend event or the music making every Thursday night. How do you do it? we asked Celia.

It's a matter of making the kind of place she'd like to go herself, she explained, the kind of party she'd like to be invited to. Designing Salamander Camp, she said, was an organic process, a communal thing, like making improvisational music. "You start with a baseline and know the main ingredients, and then everybody comes in with their instruments and builds the structure that's in them." The contractor and the men who worked on the yurts and land, and the dozens of friends, "became a team of artists," she said, beaming. "That's how Salamander Camp got so pretty."

And then she gave us what seemed the key to it all: "I try to create the world I want to live in," she said simply.

A WISDOM OF CONNECTION

Elders and story and community—if you dip into one, you draw from another. And not one exists without the truth of Spirit linking it to the others. Cultural Creatives who work with one of these wisdom functions inevitably work with the others, though the interweaving is not always obvious. The blending and weaving are unmistakable, however, in the work of an artist named Vijali Hamilton. In 1987 she had a dream of carving stone and creating community rituals in a giant circle that encompassed the planet. Since then, she has been traveling from the cliffs above Malibu to the shores of the Dead Sea to one of China's large national parks and beyond, tracing a great web of connection around the world.

INTO THE BETWEEN

If there is any wisdom running through my life now, in my walking on this earth, it came from listening in the Great Silence to the stones, trees, space, the wild animals, to the pulse of all life as my own heartbeat.

VIJALI HAMILTON, *In the Fields of Life*[21]

Listening in the Great Silence, as Vijali calls it, was a five-year period from 1982 to 1987 when she lived in virtual solitude on Boney Mountain, the highest ridge of the Santa Monica range running east from the Pacific Ocean. She had come there in something close to desperation, after an intense period of spiritual awakening and the emergence of the powerful kundalini energies that Indian mystics have described in detail.

From the time she was fourteen until she turned twenty-five, Vijali had lived in a Hindu convent in southern California. She was the youngest Vedanta nun in North America, and at the time she entered, it was the answer to her prayers for a place of peace and spiritual practice. But by the time she left, she was eager to be in the world. "I'm not allowed to make any mistakes here," she complained to her teacher, Swami Prabhavananda, "and I'm not growing." She wanted to go to college and study art. She headed for Montreal, where her talents won her full scholarships.

Three years later she returned to California, married, and became a stepmother and a full-time artist. And then, when she was in the midst of hosting art shows and poetry readings and keeping up with the life of a very popular artist, everything changed: "One quiet evening while I was visiting with friends and listening to music, a slow heat began rising from my heart. It burned its way up through my spine and on out of the top of my head, melting everything into a great ocean of light."

After that, change swept through Vijali's life. She could see that "there were no boundaries or borders. It was as if my mind had once long ago made up a story about separate objects with boundaries but the story wasn't true. The true story is that there is a luminous, spacious energy that flows through everything all the time. It's within matter, within things as well as within space, and you can tune in to it at any time, just like changing the frequency on the radio. There is no distance between this essence and ourselves. It is not otherworldly. It is right here, closer than our own flesh."

It was utterly bewildering to have energy and consuming light blasting through her body at any time of the day or night. Although the traditional Indian teachings say that this energy release is aroused gradually through yoga or other spiritual practices, for Vijali it wasn't gradual at all. At last, in an effort to integrate and stabilize what she was experiencing and discovering, she sought refuge on Boney Mountain.

It was a time of deep learning, and her life took on a new simplicity. Synchronizing her days to the rhythms of the sunrise and sunset, she greeted the sun every morning from a high plateau near her trailer and returned every evening to bid it farewell. As every act became a ritual, hauling water and bathing outside, gathering wild greens for salad and sage for tea, she told us, she learned that "a sacred space may be *any* place, not just the ones designated by our ancestors, not just some special power spot. We can create sacred spaces as I did on the mountain, by entering into the spirit of a place through simple actions performed in a reverent way."

Her years on Boney Mountain were a period of almost continual bliss. "Sometimes I would sit in the dark for hours and hours," she said, "and I feel a kind of current from my heart that goes out into the universe and then it pauses and comes back into me, and goes out again. There are streams, matrices, lattices of light that must be some universal pattern. Sometimes you see it and sometimes you don't. But when you relax, it's there like a great web connecting with everything. It feels like it has always been there."[22]

THE RETURN

As we've seen, without elders to guide the passage, the Return is difficult for almost everyone. It was awkward for Vijali, too, and it took her a number of years "to figure out how to walk with knowing that I was really part of this ocean of consciousness and light." But at the end of five years, dreams began to come, calling her back into the world. One dream was particularly compelling. "I saw myself making this giant mandala around the world, carving, and I was with people who spoke languages I'd never heard, and who had these unusual faces of people I had never seen before. We were working at creating community and creating ceremony together."

She decided she wanted to create "a Theater of the Earth." In each new country, she hoped to find a cave or part of a cliff or a mountain or even the Earth itself where the spirit of the land called to her. If the people of that place had an interest in creating a ritual connected to the Earth, Vijali planned to settle there for several months to help create a ceremony for the entire community.

But where could she begin? How can someone call forth the mythos that is particular to each place and each community, especially when she is a stranger? Vijali's solution was simple and direct. In every place she went, she would ask three questions: Who are the people who live here? What is it that ails you? What will heal you? The answers would guide the work, revealing the essence of each community's story. And as for the setting, she would listen for the spirit of each place as she carved the stone.

This all might sound vaguely workable if the artist planning it were wealthy or very well connected or perhaps conversant in a few languages other than English. Vijali was none of these. Her anxious friends in California urged her to stay home. But here is the power of a truly authoritative experience in the Between: you trust the truth of what you know directly. Vijali told us that she wanted to return to the world "with my own priorities, not with society's priorities." It no longer seemed enough to sit on a stone and feel the interconnectedness by herself, she said. She wanted people around the world to know the sacredness of the Earth. That was her priority, and it made her virtually unstoppable. Over the next several years, she began to create beautiful, moving performance rituals in community after community around the world.

THE WORLD WHEEL

She started close to home, in Malibu, on land that was offered by Frank Lloyd Wright's grandchildren. From there the World Wheel went to the Seneca Reservation in upstate New York, followed by Alicante on the Mediterranean coast of Spain, and then the Umbrian forest outside of Gubbio, Italy. The wheel rolled on through the island of Tinos in Greece and to the banks of the Dead

Sea in Israel and Palestine. In a tiny village in West Bengal, Vijali built a community house with the help of the whole village, and in a cave northeast of Lhasa, Tibet, she carved an exquisite feminine Rainbow Bodhisattva. Great mountain carvings remain in Xisan, a national park in K'un-ming, China, from her communal rituals there. Performances were held on the shores of Lake Baikal in Siberia, and finally, in October 1993, the World Wheel was completed in an ancient Shinto shrine in Japan.

The world had become Vijali's studio. And as she had dreamed, art had become a living, communal, sacred endeavor. With almost no money and no "connections," she made connections everywhere. We spoke with her in 1998, after she had returned from her circle of the Earth and settled in Castle Valley, Utah. Through creating sculptures in the Earth and new dance, music, and ceremonies, she told us, the World Wheel communities are "creating a new mythology for our time. We always go back to the earliest rituals of the country that can be found, but we transform them in a way that addresses contemporary concerns. Not staying only with the tradition, but using it as a root, we're allowing the new mythology for our times to come forward." In each place, all the work came together on one weekend when friends and neighbors and family in the nearby villages were invited to act out their story. The mythos was evoked from the people for the sake of the people and for the land, for the ancestors, and the children of the future.

But this weaving of great complexity and skill did not end there. Vijali carried soil from each place on the World Wheel to each new site, and she carried the stories, too, and photographs of the people and the sculptures they built together. It is a conversation, Vijali says, between the voice of the Earth and the voice of the community, between the traditions of the ancestors and the environmental and social problems of the people today. But it's also a conversation between people of different countries "so the process has a chance to mature in a way that an isolated person thinking or going through some ritual could not." That conversation is continuing now, as Vijali begins the second turning of the World Wheel, which she now calls Earth Mandala, in the Otavalo Valley of Ecuador.

In every country, Vijali told us, people long to be connected to others around the Earth. A good example is what happened on the tiny Greek island of Tinos. Friends in Athens had urged her not to "bother going to the little islands, because the people are so provincial. No planes land there. The people only go to church and to church festivals." But Vijali did go to Tinos, and she loved it. She worked with the people of the island and other artists for months to create a ritual. Everyone came, she told us. The mayor and both the Greek Orthodox priest and the Catholic priest, who had been feuding for years. "After the ceremony, the people were so touched. Their cheeks were wet with tears. And they created another ceremony for me to express their gratitude. They wrote poetry, and they danced. What moved them most, they said, was that they were now a part of a planetary connection, part of a global family."

When someone asked the Vietnamese Zen poet Thich Nhat Hanh, "What do we need to do to save our world?" his questioner expected him to identify strategies for social and environmental action. But he answered: "What we most need to do is to hear within us the sound of the Earth crying."[23] When the Canadian geneticist David Suzuki met E. O. Wilson, he had one big question for the eminent biologist: "What can we do to stop the catastrophic level of extinction that's going on around the world?" Wilson surprised the younger man with his reply. "We have to discover our kin," he said simply. "We have to discover our relatives, the other plants and animals who are related to us through our DNA. Because to know our kin is to come to love and cherish them."[24]

Right now over 70 percent of the world population is convinced that something serious has to be done about the dangers facing the planet. Conditions are right for a sharp turn in the direction that elders like Wilson and Thich Nhat Hanh recommend. Most of humanity wants to know how to make the change. It's one of those tipping-point times where things can change unbelievably fast— once some leadership for the change emerges, and some opportunity for it.

As we've seen, it's not a matter of having better information, nor of having the right politics. It's a matter of moral imagination, a wisdom of the heart. This is where many Cultural Creatives are headed now; directly into the core of the problems of our common world.

chapter eleven

inventing
a new culture

*Every few hundred years in Western history there occurs a sharp trans-
formation. Within a few short decades, society—its world view, its basic
values, its social and political structures, its arts, its key institutions—
rearranges itself. And the people born then cannot even imagine a world
in which their grandparents lived and into which their own parents
were born. We are currently living through such a transformation.*

PETER DRUCKER, *Post-Capitalist Society*

looking at the dank and dreary medieval towns that existed before the turn of the first millennium, who would have predicted soaring Gothic cathedrals at the end of the era? In
1705, looking at windmills or even Newcomen's first steam engine for pumping water from
mines, who would have foreseen the industrial revolution a few generations later? In 1890,
when the biggest public health problem in New York City came from the manure of the million or so horses used for transportation, who could have foreseen the coming of the automobile, the hollowing out of cities in favor of suburbs, the interstate highway system, massive air
pollution, or a dependence on imported oil so great that we fought a war to protect our source
of it? In 1960, when mainframe computers were monstrosities that weighed tons and filled several floors of a building, and you accessed them with punchcards, no one dreamed that the

Internet and vast global commerce and communications networks would grow out of a combination of the personal computer and the telephone by the year 2000.

These are all examples of social plus technological inventions that carried their cultures in unpredicted directions. They rested on trends, and they jump-started more trends. But more than trends, they were transformative. Challenging trends in population, ecology, and technology can bring forth responses that create a new culture. Many such changes are already in motion. In this chapter we'll see some of the big trends that Cultural Creatives are involved in, and some surprising developments that Cultural Creatives are creating as responses to those trends.

When enough trend effects accumulate and pressures have grown sufficiently, social transformation results. The word *transformation* signals a change in social structures and cultural beliefs. When people get creative under pressure, they often create new communities and new commerce (like the Internet), new politics, or a new set of political institutions (like turning the thirteen British colonies into the United States). Technological advances may be used in startling new ways, like space exploration, that no one imagined even a few decades earlier. And new cultural meanings, symbols, and worldviews, especially in renaissance periods in the arts and literature, may change beyond recognition in the space of a lifetime. In our unique period in history when humanity is facing a whole string of crises across the planet, we must invent changes of this magnitude with ever more intelligent and compassionate solutions. That is a social transformation.

The need for creativity immediately casts us into the realm of the unknown. What comes next is not mechanically predictable in the manner of laying a ruler on a graph and extending a line farther into the future. At each stage, the future is hard to anticipate, because it hasn't been invented yet. We can regard that as frightening, or see it as part of the adventure of the Between. In fact, most of the positive developments we cite in this chapter will come as a big surprise to those with standard Modern expectations.

In the twenty-first century, a new era is taking hold. The biggest challenges are to preserve and sustain life on the planet and find a new way past the overwhelming spiritual and psychological emptiness of modern life. Though these issues have been building for a century, only now can the Western world bring itself to publicly consider them. The Cultural Creatives are responding to these overwhelming challenges by creating a new culture. With responses directed toward healing and integration rather than conflict and battle, they may be leading the way.

The issue at the center of these challenges is growth. For the past two hundred years, economic and technological growth has been considered an unqualified good. It is the central dogma of modern economics and business. But growth is a large part of the problem we face. It's not just growth in size but the rate of growth that's a problem. Wall Street financiers demand that profits increase above 10 percent or more each year, and they will throw out an executive who doesn't produce that. But nothing in the physical world can match such growth rates for long—they simply cannot be sustained.

Modernism believes numbers of people and amounts of money are the full story of social or economic life. Discussions of growth trends appear in every publication, as if growth were the most fascinating, most real fact of daily life. Behind such discussions is the powerful, usually unrecognized assumption that the social structure will remain largely unchanged. It is comforting to assume that somehow the world we grew up in will continue in most of its familiar patterns. But it almost certainly will not.

Some trends are leading to new structures altogether. As we write, Internet businesses show every sign of replacing ordinary brick-and-mortar stores in commerce. As dollars are spent on the Internet, existing stores will die. The quality of life of your town could change substantially, as it's changing now with the disappearance of independent hardware stores and bookstores. It may be hard to imagine, but what is near and familiar—local stores and cafés, and the people who gather in them—may be erased by trends that are abstract and far away.

Similarly, advances in medicine and biotechnology promise to give us longer life spans within a generation. But will the people who live to one hundred be frail senior citizens who must be supported by a shrinking population of workers? Or will the seniors live healthy and productive lives into their eighties and nineties and not leave the labor force—perhaps preventing younger people from taking their place? Will we be a society of Struldbrugs, like those described by Jonathan Swift in *Gulliver's Travels,* where the dead hand of the past simply lives longer and nastier, and people are ever more greedy and rapacious in their gated communities? Or perhaps, just perhaps, the Cultural Creatives will usher a wisdom culture into being, where a large population of wise elders insists on new values and a longer-term view of what is needed into the seventh generation.

BIG TRENDS THAT CHALLENGE OUR CIVILIZATION

Some of the most significant trends of our time may have the twofold effect of creating social stresses and opening opportunities, especially technological change, globalization, ecological crises, the culture war, and the weakened justification for Modernity. There are many other trends, of course, but these are the ones where Cultural Creatives are likely to be involved. The continued advance of technology has revolutionary implications that are far more hopeful than most activists—and most experts—have yet realized. New technologies may give us solutions to many global problems, if they are brought to life in settings with cooperative, constructive values. Similarly, although globalization enhances the power and wealth of big business, big media, and big finance and threatens the viability of local economies and indigenous people around the planet, it can be a very hopeful development, if the people of the whole planet begin to agree on ecological and other cooperative values. The problem is, again, to institutionalize these newer values.

For now, past growth trends are likely to continue. As stresses on society mount, the justification for modern culture will become ever more tortured. Many Modern technologies and businesses will probably be quite useful to the next culture, but they would have to be servants, not masters. If Cultural Creatives play a major role in shaping the new culture, technology and the economy will be put to the service of cleaning up ecologies, reducing inequality, and supporting the integration of communities and the planet.

If Modernism becomes unjustifiable, then the composition of the three subcultures will change. The size of the Traditional population will shrink steadily, as their young people are recruited to Moderns and Cultural Creatives. Its elderly members will continue to die off and not be replaced. Though Moderns would recruit new members from the Traditionals, they would lose more older members to the Cultural Creatives. The net effect is that Moderns' numbers will shrink more noticeably, precisely because Modernism no longer looks like a winner. The hope of the culture would be transferred to the Cultural Creatives, and their numbers and influence would continue to grow.

If this trend continues, what would be likely to result? Here are some developments that have already started. (We'll highlight them as if they had come to completion.)

challenges and opportunities of the coming decades

Continued acceleration of technological change in five areas—information technology, communications, materials technology, biotechnology, nanotechnology—leading to:

- Information society, with better communications worldwide

- Enhanced globalization of markets and threats to many indigenous economies

- Change in the material basis of civilization:

    Easier invention of new solutions to many global problems
    Potential for industrial-technological disasters on an unprecedented scale

Globalization of big business, big media, big finance

- Market takeover; markets and self-interest; removal of constraints on corporations

- Growing power of big media, big corporations, big finance, combined with shrinkage of big government

- Vastly more unequal incomes

Ecological crisis, heading toward an overshoot of the carrying capacity of the Earth

- Environmental destruction and species extinctions worldwide

- Global climate change

- Damage to health of humans and ecosystems from man-made chemicals

- Overpopulation in poorer countries and overconsumption in richer ones

Intensified culture war between Traditionals and Moderns

- Neotraditionalism and fundamentalism strengthened in reaction to Modernism

- Loss of Traditionalism's credibility in the larger culture

- Conservative attempts to reverse new-social-movement trends, especially social safety net, human rights, feminism, and new spiritualities

- Revivals of ethnic nationalism, as a counter to globalizing culture

Increasing difficulty of justifying dominant Modern culture

- Destruction of ecologies and species worldwide

- Growing inequality of rich and poor, everywhere

- Growing secularization, anomie, and cynicism

Emergence of the Cultural Creatives

All across the Western world, the increasing visibility of the Cultural Creatives would be a major outcome. Knowing that their views are shared by millions of others, they would see those views as more legitimate and normal. Others would know that the Cultural Creatives exist and have positive intentions for the culture. While some might object, others might join. Businesses would be created in massive numbers to serve the Cultural Creatives, civic associations would be created or changed to reflect their views and concerns, and politicians would undoubtedly seek them out as constituents. Artists creating literature, nonfiction, mass media, and other traditional and new forms are likely to start expressing the Cultural Creatives' values and symbols. A spiral of creative expression and reactions is likely to develop. The need for a more sustainable way of life and developing supports for a deeper spirituality are likely to be important. But the impact of the Cultural Creatives wouldn't stop there.

Any big cultural trend that takes off in the West is likely to be pumped out across the planet at the speed of light. So Cultural Creatives' values, concerns, and awareness would be spread around the planet as a planetary communications network emerges. Women are likely to have more of a presence on the world scene, and NGOs also will be important. By creating a big tent politically and coordinating their efforts, movement organizations can gain broad support. If this broad basis is established, we're likely to see networks of organizations then civic associations that carry forward Cultural Creatives' values.

Mainstreaming and Merging

In 1999 the Episcopal Church, under the leadership of the Reverend Sally Bingham, was working in San Francisco and Los Angeles to get all its churches and congregations to adopt Green Power. "Concerned about global climate change and their collective responsibility to future generations, [they] are now buying clean, renewable, electric power. The reliance upon spiritual values to guide decisions in purchasing electricity is breaking new ground. Churches are learning how to educate their members about the complex business of generating, transmitting, distributing, and consuming electricity and, in the process, are re-examining their roles in modern society." At the same time the National Council of Churches set up a series of ecojustice working groups on global warming.[1]

Religious environmentalism locks the environmental ethic into the sacred belief systems of the culture. Today both mainline Protestant churches and conservative evangelical and fundamentalist churches are looking for a basis for action so as to better live their faith. The National Association of Evangelicals and the U.S. Conference of Catholic Bishops are both endorsing environmental issues. Conservative denominations have parted company with the corporate establishment over environmentalism. The vast majority of Cultural Creatives are members of conventional religious denominations, like all other Americans. They've had a leading presence on environmental issues for over a generation— and that's what it takes to get results.

Some religious groups are moving toward psychological counseling, meditation and concern for the inner life, downplaying an exclusive emphasis on personal salvation. Amalgams can easily be developed, combining traditional liturgies and doctrines with what would once have been condemned as New Age—because that's what the people want. Ever greater spiritual and psychological sophistication, covering ever more walks of life, is likely to be introduced. Old doctrines are likely to bend to the new cultural reality, rather than break.

Modernism, in our view, will likely shift its consumption-and-success-oriented culture toward the values and worldview of today's Core Cultural Creatives. Concerns for the planet, for ecology, and for spirituality will become as normal and "natural" as motherhood and apple pie. And in the process, much of the religious side of Western culture is likely to be transformed.

CULTURAL HYBRIDS

Can the visions, concerns, and values of the Cultural Creatives really become a permanent, ordinary, taken-for-granted part of social life—in other words, a new culture?

Probably the change will not happen in a sharp shift to the new values. Rather, cultural hybrids will emerge, strange and upsetting to twentieth-century eyes. These hybrids would be networks of organizations that are neither public nor private but unfamiliar mixtures of moneymaking and vocation. They could fuse together a variety of discrete social and consciousness movements. Many of the hybrids would be part of the "social sector," as Peter Drucker calls it, combining the service orientation of the church, charity, nonprofit, and NGO worlds with a dash of the entrepreneurial as well. Others could be planetwide advocacy groups and also communities of the faithful, who will find new ways of making money.

THE NATURAL STEP

Suppose the day arrives when scientists come to a consensus on the roots of our environmental problems. They define the "nonnegotiable conditions" for human survival. They name the kinds of actions that need to be taken. Educational packets are sent to every school and every household in the country, explaining their views. The hottest celebrities and artists go on TV to promote the effort, and the head of state endorses it. Dozens of multinational corporations then adopt the program.

Does this sound like a dream? Well, check your raised eyebrows at the door, because it has already happened. The project is called The Natural Step. It started in Sweden in 1989 and has spread as a new educational movement to practically every advanced industrial country in the world, including the United States. Karl-Henrik Robért, a physician and scientist who is a leading cancer researcher in Sweden, is the founder of The Natural Step.

Explaining how the project got started, Dr. Robért described what seemed like an impossible hurdle: he got scientists to agree on a set of principles that could guide society "toward a just and sustainable future."[2] Much of the environmental debate, he says, has been like "monkey chatter amongst the withering leaves of a dying tree—the leaves representing specific, isolated problems." People were focusing too narrowly on these isolated problems, like whether catalytic converters are a boon or a menace to the air and whether economic growth is harmful in itself or is necessary to solve environmental problems.

What works, says Robért, is to look at the whole system: "the trunk and roots of the environmental tree are deteriorating as a result of processes about which there was little or no controversy. There has been a basic scientific agreement about the causes of that deterioration for nearly half a century," he notes, "and it should be possible to anchor key decisions affecting society in that scientific consensus. We must learn to deal with environmental problems at the systemic level; if we heal the trunk and the branches, the benefits for the leaves will follow naturally."[3]

First in Sweden and then in other industrial nations, Dr. Robért persuaded people to look at the whole system, not just the details. He got them to agree on first principles that ordinary citizens can use as a basis for their action. He wanted to unify the fragmented knowledge that existed in the field, and he worked to get everyone to agree on "the ethical insight that destroying the future capacity of the earth to support life is wrong."

With persistence and ingenuity, Robért patiently built a consensus among his scientific colleagues by sending out twenty-one successive versions of the principles for comment and correction. Then he persuaded Sweden's business and community leaders to come together around four basic principles that any ecosystem must meet if it is to survive. These have become the basis for defining, for the first time, a common set of goals for the future that no one can disagree with. To everyone's surprise, citizens groups, industrial and business organizations, government, and scientists have been able to use these principles in full discussions without getting tangled in the morass of details of various specialties or the arguments of political ideologies.

The four conditions boil down to these. If we want life to continue on the planet: (1) We must recycle all minerals and fossil fuels from under the Earth's crust, or cut their use to zero. (2) We must do the same with all long-lasting "unnatural" man-made substances. (3) We must stop causing the deterioration of Nature, whether it is by depleting fish and forests, or polluting, or making deserts, or creating extinctions of other species. (4) And we must ensure that conditions (1) to (3) are met by (a) being more efficient in our use of resources, and (b) promoting justice for all the people of the planet. (See the sidebar on page 324.)

Robért argues that if humanity fails to come together to meet these conditions, then life on the planet will fail. Our modern industrial processes will continue to destroy the structure of life that communities of living organisms provide. We will become impoverished and finally go extinct as a species. In Robért's searingly direct words: "Since [these conditions are] nonnegotiable, there are only two alternatives: either we choose to close the material cycles in society with high heads and in pride, or we do it crawling on our knees later on. But we will still have to do it."[4]

The key to The Natural Step is its insistence that every bit of waste needs to be "food" for some other process, and that no one but business can do it. Unlike many environmental groups, The Natural Step is not antibusiness. The first American firm to sign on was the carpet manufacturer Interface, whose leader Ray Anderson you met in Chapter One. (Europeans are well ahead of Americans so far.) Firms have joined because they said they could already see signs that their own industries were about to hit a wall, but they had no good way to focus on the problem. These principles were the jump start they needed to get going.

Third-world countries cannot be expected to come up with the new technologies by themselves, Robért argues. The handful of advanced industrial

the four "system conditions" that have a scientific consensus

- Nature cannot withstand a systematic buildup of dispersed matter mined from the Earth's crust (e.g., minerals, oil, coal, etc.).

    Because: They harm nature and must not be extracted and spread about as waste any faster than their slow redeposit and reintegration into the crust of the Earth. Otherwise the level of those substances on the planet is certain eventually to reach some limits—often unknown—causing irreversible damage. It's not just threatening our prosperity. It threatens all life.

- Nature cannot withstand a systematic buildup of long-lasting compounds made by humans (e.g., PCBs).

    Because: This too harms all life. We cannot keep producing artificial substances faster than they can be broken down and recycled, or faster than they can be absorbed into the Earth's crust. Otherwise the amount and concentration of long-lasting unnatural substances on the planet is certain to eventually reach some limits—often unknown—causing irreversible damage. It's not just threatening our prosperity. It threatens all life.

- Nature cannot take a systematic deterioration of its capacity for renewal (e.g., harvesting fish faster than they can replenish, or converting fertile land into desert).

    Because: Our health and prosperity depend on nature's capacity to turn our wastes into new resources with processes that recycle everything, rather than letting nature deteriorate. The longer we wait to start renewal, the more painful and costly it will be, and failure to correct the deterioration means our death and the death of countless other species.

- Therefore, if we want life to continue, we must (a) be more efficient in our use of resources, and (b) promote justice.

    Because: Humanity, and indeed all life on the planet, requires a resource metabolism that meets the prior three system conditions. To achieve the changes that we need in time, both social stability and cooperation are needed. Ignoring poverty will lead the poor, for short-term survival, to destroy resources that we all need for long-term survival (e.g., the rain forests).

Source: *The Natural Step*[5]

nations must develop the appropriate technologies. Otherwise "the Chinese and the Indians will start to pollute as we do, the rainforests will be destroyed, and that will knock out the possibility to survive." He says, "Industries must move from defending themselves to being heroes, ahead of everyone else, fighting for tomorrow's market and tomorrow's technology. In ten years the market will be about *nothing else* but sustainability.

"That is what we are teaching industry," he explains, "and they buy it. We give them a crystal ball by talking about thermodynamics, the building up of structure, how the structure is the basis for our economy, and how the tearing down of structure is deteriorating the economy. We also tell them in practical terms how the costs appear, and they agree—they have seen all those costs already."

When the insurance industry starts to insist, with genuine fear, that it can't survive the weather damage that will accompany global warming (as many are now saying), then Moderns clearly have to change their ways. In 1999 *Harvard Business Review* published a major article on how to make industrial production sustainable. Many large companies already agree: really big multinational corporations like Electrolux, ABB, and Mitsubishi Electric, which belong to The Natural Step, are already convinced that they must change, or they'll hit that wall and die. So they're changing toward sustainable practices.[6]

Notice that industries accept a wiser view if it is framed for them in the name of self-defense. The good of the whole system over the long run becomes an essential part of their new focus, but ultimately their motivation is self-interested: a more realistic new way to find continued profits and avoid instability. As our modern knowledge about society and the planet has grown over the past generation, we have discovered that for all its dynamism and profitability, modernization has been a very unstable wave of change. From the elder wisdom viewpoint, the exclusive focus of stock markets and corporations on short-term profits at the expense of everything else cannot be good for our grandchildren's future. And when industries pay more attention to what is going on around the planet, they soon become aware that this short-term focus is also spreading devastation in many developing nations. Today's tightly linked global markets and communications mean that "whatever goes around, comes around"—circling the globe incredibly fast—right back to the developed world. The industries that adopt The Natural Step principles have accepted them as the structure of our new global reality and adapted accordingly.

Natural Capitalism

In 1999 a stunning book came out called *Natural Capitalism,* a work that is destined to set a pattern for business innovation in the twenty-first century. It focuses on the same issues as The Natural Step, but it shows how to redesign every business process to be ecologically efficient and to protect the biosphere—and still be profitable for business. Numerous technological and business trends are already in motion to do just that, say the authors, and all that is needed is to put them together in a single coherent system. Authors Amory B. Lovins and L. Hunter Lovins are well known for their energy-efficiency strategies; we described Lovins's work on the hypercar and the new bank design in earlier chapters. The other author, Paul Hawken, created the Smith and Hawken high-quality gardening tools company and wrote *The Ecology of Commerce,* linking the long-term success of business with ecological principles.

The authors start with "the idea that the world economy is shifting from an emphasis on human productivity to resource productivity," which amounts to using natural resources four, ten, or even a hundred times more efficiently. They show an amazing array of inventions that already do this, which are "real, practical, measured and documented." Those inventions include hydrogen fuel cells for cars, instead of the gasoline engines we use today; the same kind of fuel cells can also be plug-in generators for electricity in every home and neighborhood. "Buildings already exist that make oxygen, solar power, even drinking water." By going to innovative ways to use fiber, along with new kinds of paper and ink, "we could enable the world's supply of lumber and pulp to be grown in an area about the size of Iowa. Weeds can yield potent pharmaceuticals; cellulose-based (versus petroleum-based) plastics have been shown to be strong, reusable and compostable; and luxurious carpets can be made from landfill scrap. Roofs and windows, even roads, can do double duty as solar-electric collectors, and efficient car-free cities are being designed so that men and women no longer spend their days driving to obtain the goods and services of everyday life."[7]

Four big strategies are key to keeping our world livable, saving the ecology, and doing good business all at the same time.

Radical Resource Productivity   This means making industrial processes and most of what happens in buildings and transportation from four to a hundred times more productive, mostly based on better principles of design, using technologies that already exist. Radical resource productivity would slow resource depletion, cut pollution, provide a basis for increasing employment, and cut costs to business. Scientists and engineers today are really talking about making all these changes.

Biomimicry   Today, too many materials and too much energy are used to support human activities. Easily 94 percent of what American industry does is waste. Only 6 percent of what we process winds up as products. *Durable* products are only 1 percent of what we process. Eliminating the very idea of waste is the key; instead, every material used should be reused somewhere else when we're finished with it. It should be "food" for some other process. That means not making or using toxic chemicals, and it means using processes that mimic nature. Competitive pressures are already pushing businesses to start practicing biomimicry, but if we also take away hidden subsidies to waste, then the change in costs will drastically speed up the transition.

Service and Flow Economy   In such an economy, a business doesn't sell an object; it leases the use of it. Then it takes the object back when the customer is finished with it, or when it's used up, and recycles it. This economy is based on the idea that people don't really value TV sets, for example, for themselves but only for the services they give—like providing TV programs. You could lease a car for its transportation services, while the physical car itself is the manufacturer's responsibility. This shift to service would be an incentive to make TV sets and cars quite differently. It fits the emerging culture and the values of Cultural Creatives: instead of affluence in the form of goods, a certain quality of life and well-being is desired. Ecological sustainability becomes much easier when we're less attached to "stuff." Some businesses have already started down this path, which all businesses using natural capitalism will follow.

Investing in Natural Capital   Such investing is about "reversing worldwide planetary destruction through reinvestment in sustaining, restoring and expanding" the whole living world. From a business viewpoint, natural capital is the aspect of the environment that produces all the services and resources we have.

Amazingly, *Natural Capitalism* lists solutions for topics like reinventing the automobile, getting rid of industrial waste, redesigning housing, optimizing entire systems rather than just the parts, using fibers more efficiently for things like cloth and paper, improving the way we grow food, and solving water problems. It even summarizes practical approaches to making economic markets work better. In short, it's a practical compendium for sustainability, as seen from the business side. Businesses that want to deny environmental problems are warned that doing so will endanger their financial viability. Activists who are used to thinking of all business as the enemy must now see many businesses as potential allies.

For most people who have heard about environmental problems their entire lives, the idea that all the technologies and business approaches necessary to create ecological sustainability already exist sounds too good to be true. "How is it that we have created an economic system that tells us it is cheaper to destroy the earth and exhaust its people than to nurture them both?" the authors ask. They answer that our current economics is based on poor design approaches and obsolete reasoning. "To make people better off," they argue, "requires no new theories, and needs only common sense. It is based on the simple proposition that *all* capital be valued. . . . If there are doubts about how to value a seven hundred year old tree, ask how much it would cost to make a new one. Or a new atmosphere, or a new culture."

ANOTHER HYBRID: CONSCIOUS COMMERCE

Here's an example of how commerce can mix successfully with consciousness. In 1998 and 1999, the top-selling movie video, *The Lion King,* was outsold by a video of another category—an instructional video for, of all things, yoga. That particular tape sold more than a million copies. In fact, among Amazon.com's ten top-selling videotapes for those two years were two other yoga videotapes as well. It's the kind of commercial success that modern business prizes. But the people who make and sell those videos aren't Moderns. They are among the idealistic new breed of companies started by Cultural Creatives that base their entire business strategy on marketing to Cultural Creatives. The videos are made by Living Arts, and when their parent company, GAIAM, made a stock offering, it proclaimed to Wall Street that its goal is "consciousness in commerce."

This example is not just about one successful company. It grows out of the way the business and the spiritual practices of yoga are intertwined, and each drives the other forward. In the 1950s and 1960s, yoga was "under the radar . . . and *health nut* was a derogatory term," says Phil Catalfo of *Yoga Journal.* The mainstream saw yoga as a passing fad. Now yoga is on television at 6 A.M. each day in nearly every city in North America, and a plethora of books, magazines, videos, and, of course, classes are available. There are even training institutes that offer teacher certification courses, plus at least one course, "The Business of Yoga: Earning a Living through Teaching." Offered in gyms, health clubs, and community centers, yoga is regarded as a normal, healthy activity that is part of the lifestyle of many people—most of them Cultural Creatives. After three decades of steady, unspectacular growth, yoga had about four million users in 1990 and six million in 1994. Then the growth curve shot up to eighteen million users in 1998. Twenty-eight million users are projected by 2002.[8]

The business of consciousness is growing at a rate that surpasses almost everything else in today's economy, except perhaps computers and the Internet. As a result, Cultural Creatives are becoming more and more attractive as potential customers—the "new natural consumer," some observers call them—to businesses who could supply products and services. Contrary to the moans and groans that crass commercialism is ruining everything (some of which are quite justified), the confluence of the consciousness movement and business is spiraling into a feedback loop that drives the growth of both. Furthermore, in most cases, the result seems to be a high standard of quality.

One indicator of how much change has happened since the 1970s is the growth of the industry that supports "lifestyles of health and sustainability." A large study of the industry found the results summarized in the box.[9]

the new "lohas" industry in the united states

LOHAS stands for Lifestyles of Health and Sustainability.

SEGMENT	SALES FOR YEAR 2000
Sustainable economy	$76.5 billion
Ecological lifestyles	$81.2 billion
Healthy living	$32.0 billion
Alternative health care	$30.7 billion
Personal development	$10.6 billion
Total	$230 billion

(est. at $500 billion for the whole planet)

Source: *Natural Business*

Such numbers would all have been much smaller in the 1960s. Here's the kicker: the only category that represents business-to-business sales is "sustainable economy." The other four categories represent consumer sales. The analysts who put this data together explicitly see the Cultural Creatives as the primary market for that $154.5 billion of goods and services. These figures are by no means a perfect indicator of cultural change, because they really correspond to the demand for goods and services. But when we put this chart next to the actual beliefs, values, and lifestyles of Americans, we see it's telling a similar story. Just as we might expect, the material culture of Americans is shifting toward their beliefs, but with a time lag.[10] New ways are penetrating into American life, carried by a very successful commercial culture and growing fast. This change toward lifestyles of health and sustainability is vastly underestimated in the popular press, so that most people are unaware of its scope.

In the 1990s, most of the industries within the "healthy living" category (natural, organic, and healthy products, which include foods, vitamins, and personal care products) grew at a rate of over 20 percent a year, about five times as fast as the national economy, in a smoothly accelerating curve.[11] The interest in natural and healthy living is by no means confined to the United States. In 1999, the global market for natural, organic, and health food products was $65 billion—36 percent of it in the United States, plus 31 percent in Europe, and 16 percent more in Japan.

As for the "alternative health care" category, a pair of Harvard studies shows a growing percentage of Americans visited alternative health care providers, going from 61 million persons (33.8 percent of adults) in 1990 to 83 million (42.1 percent of adults) in 1997. They increased their number of visits from 427 million to 629 million, and their spending from $14.6 billion to $21.2 billion. That represents a 47.3 percent increase in visits and a 45.2 percent increase in spending over those seven years, for growth rates of a little over 5 percent a year. That doesn't sound like much until you hear that in the same period, total visits to establishment physicians actually declined from 388 million to 386 million. The standard medical model has some serious competition.

As of 1997, 85 percent of Americans had used one or more of the twenty-three kinds of alternative health care studied. A new demand for true health care is emerging here, not just for disease-oriented medicine: over half the alternative remedies used were intended not to cure illness but to prevent it. Furthermore, Americans were not substituting alternative health care for standard medical care, but using one in addition to the other.[12] This is not a turning away from scientific medicine, as some Modernist medical experts would like to claim, but a search for health. As we said earlier, Cultural Creatives are much more likely to be both users and providers of alternative health care than are the other two subcultures.

While much of the "ecological lifestyles" category is about ecological consumer products, a new up-and-coming area is *ecotourism,* a development of the 1990s that seeks to correct the old pattern of Western tourists exploiting the natives and the land. It is a nature-and-culture-based form of specialty travel defined by The Ecotourism Society (TES) as "responsible travel to natural areas which conserves the environment and sustains the well-being of local people." American LIVES did a 1996 survey of frequent vacation travelers. Twenty-five percent wanted ecotourism vacations, but even more dramatically, 64 percent of Cultural Creatives want it; in fact, Cultural Creatives are a majority, 53 percent, of all ecotourism vacation travelers.[13]

Travelers who want ecotourism want the following kinds of vacation activities on some (not all) of their vacations:

Nature and camping	69 percent
Personal/spiritual growth	65 percent
Exotic locales/activities	61 percent
Health, body care, sports	54 percent
Minimalist (do/spend little)	53 percent
Intense experiences	51 percent

Ecotourism is typical of industries done *by* Cultural Creatives *for* Cultural Creatives. You can hear the voice of the subculture in the way ecotravel businessman Will Weber describes his work: "This is a great business. We have the privilege of connecting intelligent, curious, caring travelers with friendly, responsible local hosts in a spirit of goodwill and sympathetic inquiry. The more authentically we present destination cultures and natural habitats, the more our travelers appreciate and value the experience. I can't imagine a business with more potential for aiding environmental preservation and cross-cultural understandings."[14]

These trends are less interesting for what they say about growth in consumer spending than for what they show us about the growth of a lifestyle. Ecotourism has the kind of steeply uptilted growth curves you see for use of personal computers. But even though it's growing very fast and getting to be very large, ecotourism as a trend is underreported in the press, even the business press.

Modernist businesses are often interested in Cultural Creatives as a market, if not as people. But they get very frustrated because the Moderns' tried-and-true techniques of advertising and selling turn off most of this population. Moreover, the Moderns are trying to sell them "stuff," discrete consumer objects, when Cultural Creatives are much more interested in trying to make their lives work better.

The growth of the "lifestyles of health and sustainability" industry comes from the demand of Cultural Creatives and others for its products and services. But it also comes from the supply side, too. Many Cultural Creatives are developing businesses that let them go beyond earning a living to have "right livelihood." Some formulate it explicitly in Buddhist terms, while others call it "walking your talk," just like those movement activists we met earlier. They want to make their living in a way that supports their larger sense of purpose and their fundamental values, which moves their work in the direction of a true vocation. Many of the skilled professionals who work in these businesses, we saw, were sacrificing a fair amount of income to do what's more important to them. And in many cases, they try to make the workplace a more caring place.

Spike Anderson, of Monday Technology Solutions, is a headhunter in Silicon Valley. He described the job-seekers he works with this way: "Almost everyone I talk to who is looking for a job would rather have a job that has meaning and has some altruistic purpose than one that doesn't and pays more. They'll even make some sacrifices. Some, not much. If they can find something where they feel like they're doing some good, that's where they'll go."

COLLISIONS OF PRINCIPLE

When you venture into the Between, a lot of the old signposts disappear and those that remain may not have the old meanings. There are new signposts here, made by scouts who have found or are making new paths. And everyone who travels through this unmapped territory has opinions about which paths are trustworthy and which are not, and which ones *should* work and which ones aren't even worth considering. Yet everyone is a traveler here, and all of them have left the old culture for a new way of life.

This is how it is with Cultural Creatives now. They share a set of common values and a worldview, but they don't agree on how to put their values into practice. As with the Jews making their exodus from Egypt and finding their way through the desert, Cultural Creatives' old categories and paradigms are in collision. This is a sure sign of a people in the midst of a significant change in their culture. Real innovations are bound to elicit strong reactions, some of them decidedly negative.

There is not much conflict about the cultural hybrids that deal with green products and services. So long as the companies are not faking it ("greenwashing"), most Americans see these businesses as positive, if not terribly exciting. Toilet paper, detergent, recycled paper products, and water filters—they're all just fine. In contrast, almost everything in the "business of consciousness" sparks controversy.

The consciousness business is based on selling experiences, and products and services are secondary. It ranges from vacation travel to psychotherapy and weekend workshops, from book publishing to producing audiotapes and videotapes to a booming profusion of Internet companies. The new businesses seek to uplift your spirits, educate your mind, soothe or delve into your feelings, engage your inner artist (or child), and enlighten your consciousness, sometimes all in one well-hyped weekend.

SHADOWS AND TRAPS IN THE BUSINESS OF CONSCIOUSNESS

American culture is good at business. So when institutional supports for the consciousness movement were lacking, business was the source of inventiveness that flowed right in to fill the hole. When the business of consciousness started developing, nobody was ready for it. The real love-hate issues of major cultural change start here.

As we have seen, the trend to a convergence of business and consciousness makes a lot of people unhappy. It offends those on the left who believe that business must be greedy and cynical, and those on the right who hate the new paradigms and want "all those counterculture people" kept in their place. It upsets the meditation, yoga, and health practitioners who didn't want to run a business, and it upsets actual counterculture hippies who only wanted a natural food cooperative. Here they were having to do yucky things like advertising and promotion and keeping books and hiring and firing people. But when we innovate, as in nearly all aspects of human culture, we unreflectively carry a lot of old practices forward as "the way it's done."

Traditionally, monastery walls separated spiritual seekers from the hurly-burly of the marketplace, but today most of our walls have been torn down. In our present landscape of materialism and consciousness, an aching wish for renewal of body and soul can be most bewildering.

Consider, for example, the daily mail. Many Cultural Creatives return from their mailbox every day with catalogs promising deep satisfaction from natural-fiber clothing and accessories, and gifts made in the third world, right alongside brochures promising to reveal the deep truths of the world's spiritual traditions if you will only purchase a dozen tapes or sign up for a weekend seminar. (The bonus gifts are "yours FREE without obligation.") How different are these spiritual and psychological offers, really, from the dozens of mainstream clothing and gift catalogs that also come every month? They even use the same slick graphics and pitches. Madison Avenue calls it "aspirational advertising." The trap here is letting modern materialism do the business of the soul. This is the shadow to the success of the business of consciousness.

Another problem is also poisoning the well of community. When successful Cultural Creative authors or speakers aim for national recognition and a chance to rally people, they turn to "experts" in direct mail marketing, or public relations, or advertising. They may even get an infomercial made to broadcast on cable TV. Why? Because they feel helpless. Because as children of Modernism, they turn things over to experts, who say, "This is how it's done. You want to reach a lot of people? Then do it this way." At that moment, the automatism of modern culture takes over. The process is a form of unconsciousness, running on rails and following standard procedures.

How does this affect Cultural Creatives who receive the direct mail? The same way they've been affected since the 1970s, when national good causes sent them direct mail soliciting contributions. Too many direct mail pieces from good causes produce a vague sense of betrayal. Whatever initial connection or interest they felt slowly diminishes, along with the hope that what they care about will be addressed honestly. The genuine connection, the sense of being recognized as a member of a shared community, is lost.

ALTRUISM OR SELF-INTEREST?

There's likely to be outrage that old boundaries are being crossed as some Cultural Creatives make new ways of life. The hard part about making a new culture is getting untangled from the mass of unconscious assumptions you grew up with. You really know an innovation belongs to a new culture if you can't decide whether you love or hate it. The love-hate response arises not just because something you dislike is mixed in with something you enjoy, but because the invention is making a mess of your old categories and paradigms. Real cultural innovations are bound to elicit some strong negative reactions.

The new cultural network is likely to include not just professionals in alternative health and in consciousness disciplines, and not just spiritual teachers and seekers, but managers who help people get organized and make sure the organizations are self-supporting. The Internet will probably come to dominate these outreach efforts. Some elements of a for-profit business model are almost inevitable, although instead of businesses as we have known them, some public-private hybrid will become the norm, doing both commerce and community service and maintaining a strong relationship to a clientele.

Many church-related community groups are already linking together and helping out small support groups, such as seniors groups, youth groups, substance abuse groups, and groups that provide job development and support and life-threatening illness support. Many nonchurch groups are doing the same. In the future they may be partly paid by the members and partly subsidized by churches or government. New institutions may mix research and training programs, on the one hand, with a variety of community and support groups on the other. The programs at Commonweal follow this pattern. The Internet will help replace the canned broadcasts of twentieth-century mass communication with new forms of public communication that have participatory aspects.

The use of business models and managers is likely to provoke outrage. Something feels ethically compromised—but what? Suppose you expect a new institute to be part of the old "begging for money" culture of the foundation-supported NGOs, but instead it's making its own money, with some mix of altruism and self-interest. Maybe it's part of a network of for-profit and not-for-profit groups, and they all help each other. What kind of an enterprise is this? you want to know. Is there a conflict of interest, and are the people compromising their integrity?

It might just be a *vocation,* an old concept that secular Modernism discarded a century ago. A vocation says that you follow a higher calling in your profession and simultaneously operate very much in the world. It's both self-interested and altruistic, and the two cannot be disentangled. In the nineteenth century and still in many small towns today, the lawyers, dentists, doctors, and architects were completely embedded in their communities and had to do mutual back-scratching and business with everyone. Now in an urban setting, the same behavior is often condemned by professional associations as self-dealing or a conflict of interest. But of course, in a small-town environment nothing but embeddedness will do, because that's the entire basis of trust for professionals. Suppose we succeed in bringing community back, or succeed in making organizations that are a mix of public service and private gain. Maybe the known professional standards will be fine, and maybe they won't. The idea sounds fine, but our familiar categories may break down. Someone will be upset. Someone will be sued.

Old distinctions will be muddied or mixed together, like: public and private, religious and secular, church and business, left and right, spirituality and psychotherapy. In each of these cases, Modernism has said there's supposed to be a clear dividing line. Blurring that line can cause confusion and disorientation.

But in the chasm between public and private, a huge variety of not-for-profit groups and nongovernmental organizations are actually neither public nor private and always have had a third status. Suppose they become a "social sector" that is given public responsibility and public money to deliver services that government isn't competent to do, and that business is too profit-oriented to do. Lines will be erased, especially if some of the groups are church affiliated. Someone is certain to complain about the business aspect. And if it's religious (or secular). Now there's upset all around.

At this moment, more people refuse to be labeled as left or right than identify with either side. Color the left as red, and the right as blue. But a new political direction is emerging that wants nothing to do with the old right-left spectrum. Color it green. When the newspaper reporter or the politician wants to know, "Are you liberal or conservative or just in the mushy middle?" their answer is still "No!" Suppose a strong Green party emerges. When reporters insist on labeling each of its platform planks as liberal or conservative, calling the platform inconsistent, are the Greens justified in cussing them out?

And what shall we do with the psychotherapist who also has a spiritual practice and does some spiritual counseling? Should the insurance company refuse to pay? Is the spiritual tradition being compromised? Is the scientific basis for the counseling a complete sham? Should the other members of the American Psychological Association complain?

Another source of dismay may be that the innovators look amateurish in public and seem not to have gotten their act together. But what's new is genuinely hard to do. Many times novices don't get to practice before they have to go to prime time. It's the equivalent of taking your show onto Broadway without a tryout in New Haven (and a chance to rewrite half the script). Many times the newbies onstage don't look like movie or TV stars either, but just ordinary people with all the surface flaws. Should the media rate them like performers?

THE MOVEMENTS GET RESPECTABLE

For at least two centuries in American life, associations have done the work of civil society. Associations are families, neighborhoods, communities, friendship groups, unions, churches, and various nonprofit organizations that operate in that indistinct area between business and government. As de Tocqueville pointed out in 1835, associations are what Americans create to get things done, instead of depending upon an aristocracy or a government. But many respectable civic associations today started out as controversial movements similar to those we described in Part Two. Today many Cultural Creatives are clothing their heartfelt desires in the flesh of concrete organizations, like alternative health care clinics, yoga studios, environmental consulting companies, new political parties, and new NGOs. Supported by organizations that can live a long time, they gain the courage to hang in for the long term and the wisdom not to overestimate what can be done in the short term. This is probably a sign of what's coming in the future.

For over a century, civic associations have turned citizen involvement from sporadic social movement demonstrations and gatherings into a regular part of everyday life: lobbying groups, political parties, civic clubs, think tanks, institutes, foundations, charities, unions, clinics, and churches. Some of those associations were successful enough that they went on to become institutions of American life, with all the benefits, and the traps, that that implies. Their innovations then became part of the new mainstream, often making society more self-consciously pluralistic.

Many left-wing activists mistakenly believe that creating associations and institutions is a cooptation, a sellout. In reality, creating associations solidifies temporary changes and provides the continuity that keeps movement volunteers from burnout. Many associations carry the cultural changes introduced by the avant-gardes into the everyday life of the middle class. Civic associations are at their best in maintaining past gains—a serious achievement in the face of a conservative backlash that tries to roll back the gains of, say, the women's movement, the civil rights movement, the peace movement, the environmental movement, the gay liberation movement, and the movements for organic and natural foods and alternative health care.

The second generation of the consciousness movements introduced a seeming paradox: the nonprofit and NGO status of an established good cause constantly appealing for funds is not necessarily the desired outcome. The natural food and alternative health care movements went directly toward being businesses and professions. Anything that uses the market and makes money can make many left-wing activists profoundly suspicious. A socially conscious business may be idealistic, but it sure isn't "power to the people." Interestingly, right-wingers who want to believe that none of these movements could be up to any good don't like these businesses any better. In reality the American penchant for commerce is being elaborated here, in the direction of "conscious commerce," as one Cultural Creatives' company labels it.

Slowly a lesson has been drifting in on one movement organization after another. At some point, opposing something bad ceases to be enough, and they must stand for positive values, or produce a service that is important to their constituency.

Now What Do We Do?

Hurrah, we've won the hearts and minds of the people!
. . . pause for celebration . . . Omigod, now what do we do?

With 70 to 90 percent of the population supporting even the strongest pro-ecology statements, the environmental and ecology movements have won the battle for the hearts and minds of the Western world. But now they must face a difficult fact. It's no longer enough to tell people how bad things are or to raise awareness. Not only do people already know it, but they pretty much agree with the movement's views, too. Agreement must now be turned into practice.

Our studies show that huge majorities of Americans want ecologically sensible "green" products and services, but most aren't willing to pay a premium to get products that should not have been destructive in the first place. Similarly, they want business to stop inflicting environmental damage, and they believe that a better use of technology could do the job without destroying the economy. (As *Natural Capitalism* argues, they're right.) They want actual leadership and proactive initiatives from all levels of government that aren't sellouts to big business. And they want practical proposals on how to change their behavior and lifestyle. But nobody's delivering.

Certainly big money and some big industries (oil, gas, coal, nuclear, utilities, chemicals, autos, agribusiness) use their control over big media and big government to paralyze attempts at concrete action. But that's only part of the problem. Additionally, no institutions have been set up to translate public sentiment favoring ecological sustainability into practical action (including the work of lining up all the elites and power groups, and facing down the financiers). Green activists, accustomed solely to raising awareness, have not constructed those institutions.

We know a strongly pro-environment scientist who works for a major utility. He's on many committees that link industry, government, and environmentalists, and he has been bothered by this problem. "I've worked for years trying to get all these groups to agree, and it's finally succeeding. A lot of business who once backed off from honestly admitting the need for action are now willing to adopt the ecologists' platforms. But you know what? At this point, the environmental groups are backing off, scared. They're afraid of what will happen if business just says 'You're right. Now what?' They seem to feel that business could just take over their positions and their movement would collapse. I'm afraid the environmentalists are not set up to keep pushing businesses to take the next step—because the next step involves making detailed analyses of what actually works in business practice, and making big changes in people's lifestyles. They haven't a clue how any given industry works, they don't know how to make and sell products for a new lifestyle, and they haven't thought about how [ecological sustainability] changes the culture."

Ecological sustainability and commerce must come together, as Green businesses often see, even though the two have been at each other's throats for years. A change in consciousness is needed, so that "conscious commerce" can be a reality, unifying the inner and the outer. But the ones who know how to do business are often the ones who scorn consciousness, and the ones who know how to work with consciousness avoid spreadsheets and profits. Who can trust the businessman to be honest, or the environmentalist to be practical? All sides must learn to build trust within a new sense of community.

New Online Communities

The Internet is a phenomenon of the global information society, creating connections across the globe. The media companies are pushing it for commerce and entertainment, but its potential for creating online communities and education is opening up almost as fast. Soon we will be able to see each other's faces and hear our voices over the Internet, not just send text and still pictures. The quality of personal relationships on the Internet will go way up, because a much more nuanced personal connection will be possible.

The Internet's potential for global integration is remarkable. Once these connections are in place, often by satellite, whole libraries of valuable information can be made available across the world, cheaply and in a few minutes. Direct person-to-person connections among ordinary people take the authorities and the experts out of the place of control. The consequences are just barely imaginable.

All of these developments depend on very fast cable modems and other high-speed, high-capacity Internet connections. Wiring up the world or connecting all of the world by satellite will be one of the big projects of the twenty-first century. When all of humanity regards all the rest of humanity as real human beings, not as dangerous Others or faceless ciphers, then the next era will have begun. If we add connectivity to the spread of conflict negotiation skills and solutions for health and ecology, then vast inequalities and old enmities will be harder and harder to maintain.

What might this connectivity look like in the near future? Imagine a Web portal that is an online community and also a business. It gives seminars and workshops and scans the World Wide Web for information to share. It also has a business district, with a variety of e-commerce "stores" that share the values and worldview of the community. To make money, the businesses must give away information, services, and support to anyone who enters the Web portal, as well as to their customers. It's worth it, because the "stores" are hoping to buy the loyalty of their community members.

Is this scenario a business or a community, profit or not-for-profit, self-interested or altruistic? It is all of these. The old distinctions are breaking down—again. In January 2000 there are about a dozen Web sites and portals that want to fit the above description and are in different stages of planning and development, and several print magazines and cable channels as well. All are designed with the Cultural Creatives in mind. And all of them want to promote both community and commerce and support the kind of changes introduced by the social and consciousness movements. Some will not make it off the ground, and others will no doubt turn out to have business flaws. But it is very likely that some will succeed. Building a community from an electronic base will not replace face-to-face community, but it could go a long way toward making the Cultural Creatives aware of one another.

If the Cultural Creatives of the future form real online communities, then a new politics cannot be far behind. And perhaps an education movement. What else can you imagine?

A POSITIVE IMAGE OF THE FUTURE

We are a future-creating species, the great futurist Fred Polak wrote in 1955. Our future is not merely something that happens to us but something that we participate in creating. If we do this consciously, we can create a world that works. With a positive image of the future, we'll invest in our children's education and upbringing, build schools, roads, ports, bridges, and sewer, water, gas, electric, and communication lines, and establish new businesses and institutions. Even if we turn out to be quite mistaken on the details of what we imagine, the result will still be quite positive.

Polak demonstrated the power of a culture's images of the future in a two-volume magisterial survey of fifteen hundred years of Western beliefs about the future. He showed that society's image of the future is a self-fulfilling prophecy and helped initiate the discipline of future studies. His enormous, painstaking study was no mere academic exercise. Polak was a Dutch Jew who spent the entire war in hiding from the Nazis. His work is the result of wrestling with the most necessary, urgent question of our time: how can humanity create a better future?

If a culture lacks a positive vision of the future, Polak showed, its creative power begins to wither and the culture itself stagnates and eventually dies out. Negative images are even more destructive, leading to hopelessness, helplessness, and failure to provide for the future. The collective pessimism results in "endgame" behaviors, with people snatching and grabbing to secure something for themselves before everything falls apart. This behavior brings about the very collapse they fear.

Today as we are besieged by planetary problems, the risk is that we will deal with them in just the pessimistic and unproductive style Polak decried. Transfixed by an image of our own future decline, we could actually bring it about. A positive vision of the future, according to writer and philosopher David Spangler, "challenges the culture to dare, to be open to change, and to accept a spirit of creativity that could alter its very structure."[15]

There is nothing inevitable about the kind of life we have now in Modern society, and nothing inevitable about the kind of future that lies before us. Cultural Creatives are quite clear that they do not want to live in an alienated, disconnected world. Their guiding images refer again and again to a sense of wholeness. They say that each of us is a living system within a greater living system, connected to each other in more ways than we can fathom. If we focus on that wholeness, we can begin to imagine a culture that can heal the fragmentation and destructiveness of our time. The appearance of the Cultural Creatives, we suggest, represents a promise that a creative vision of the future is growing. It is a resurgence of hope, of imagination, of willingness to act for the sake of a better civilization. The work toward a reintegration of, and design for, a new culture can have great power in our collective imagination. What we want and what we choose can shape our future.

the ten thousand mirrors

NO ONE TODAY CAN remember the time when Amaterasu Omikami, the Great Mother Sun, hid herself deep in the Cave of Heaven and refused to come out. But to those who know the story, every mirror is a reminder that there once was a time when all the spirits of living things had to join together to bring life back to the Earth.

In those very early times, the spirit of every living thing was called its kami. *The kami of the mountain was lavender and long. The kami of trees was great and green. Animals' kami was smooth as silk. The kami of rocks and rivers was silent as the moon. All the strength of these kami poured forth from Amaterasu Omikami, and in her honor the great pattern of the seasons of planting and harvest was woven.*

One day it happened that Amaterasu Omikami fell into despair because of the actions of her jealous brother Susanowo. Some say he betrayed the Great Goddess by tearing through the rice paddies in a drunken fit of rage, until every plant in every field was broken and dying. Others remember Susanowo heaving a calf through the windows of the celestial weaving house, smashing the looms and breaking the sacred threads of connection between every living thing. But though some say this and some say that, everyone agrees on what happened next.

Amaterasu Omikami fled to the Cave of Heaven and locked herself inside. Without her light, all the realms of heaven and earth were plunged into darkness. The kami of the rice withered. The kami of the birds and animals and mountains and trees and fishes turned into frail gray ghosts. The Earth and all that was of it began to die.

Eventually, and none too soon, the kami gathered together to discuss what to do. "We must moan and weep outside her cave," some said. "That will never work," said others. "Who wants to join a crowd that's moaning and weeping?" Finally someone said, "Let's have a celebration with songs that make us laugh and music that sets our feet tapping. And let's have dances with lots of stomping and whirling. Surely that will bring the Great Sun out of her cave."

Everyone agreed, but they decided that one more thing was needed: a huge mirror. "If we reflect Amaterasu's radiance back to her," they said to each other, "maybe she'll take heart and remember us. Maybe she'll return to the Round of Life."

But as soon as they thought of the need for a great mirror, their courage failed. Because not one of them had the strength to lift such a mirror. Then someone whispered, in a voice so feeble everyone had to strain to hear, "Let's each bring a tiny piece of mirror and hide it in our clothes. As soon as Amaterasu Omikami peeks out of her cave, we'll all hold up our shards at the same time—and our tens of thousands will make a single mirror."

And that is precisely what they did. The very next day, all the kami in the world collected outside the Cave of Heaven and slowly, almostly inaudibly, started to sing. In time their voices rose high and rich into the night. But even while the kamis' drums beat their irresistible rhythms, and even while the kamis' feet stomped and tapped in splendid whirling dances, no one forgot to watch the door of the Cave of Heaven. Finally, very late in the evening, the cave door cracked open, and a single beam of light slipped out. Instantly, the kami lifted their slivers of mirror to Amaterasu's radiance.

The goddess gasped in amazement. Fascinated, she took a step forward. And another. Soon she had stepped all the way out of her cave. Laughing and clapping her hands to see herself reflected in so many thousands upon thousands of forms, the Great Mother Sun danced all the way out of her hiding place and all the way into the wide blue sky.

Once again the kami of the mountains grew lavender and long. The kami of trees was great and green. Animals again had kami as smooth as silk. The kami of rocks and rivers and fish and flowers once more poured forth from the Great Mother Sun. And in her honor the pattern of the seasons of planting and harvest was again woven. And so it is to this very day.[1]

Sometimes a primal story like this Japanese sun goddess myth can evoke a reality so immediate that it touches a core longing in our soul. The story's images resonate with the truth of our own time. Amaterasu Omikami's story is one of those ancient resonators. Maybe the betrayal that leaves every plant broken and dying recalls the way our ecology is being ruined. Maybe the tearing apart of the sacred threads of connection reminds us of how, in the name of progress, we are using up what belongs to our children. Or maybe the kami's lack of strength and wisdom to stop the Earth from dying touches our own sense of helplessness to invent a future that will sustain the generations who will come after us.

But, as the story says, whether it's this or whether it's that doesn't really matter. What everyone remembers is the solution: the countless beings who come together to create a collective mirror to save the Earth. Imagine them all, arrayed like some giant dish antenna facing the cave of heaven, singing and dancing and waiting for the exact moment to focus the creative fire of the sun goddess back to her. This is no passive mirroring. When the sun finally comes out to play, she's moving fast. The kami need to be alert and sensitive so they can track her movements precisely. Otherwise, she'll dance out of their focus. The spirit of everyone is needed here: to be awake, to sing their songs and dance their dances, and to help create this splendid, necessary emergence that will reweave the threads of connection for all of them.

There's a place in the Arizona desert where this millennium-old story comes to life. It's an Israeli-built solar collector made of an immense array of freestanding mirrors. Every mirror reflects the sun's light onto a single collector tower that heats water to over a thousand degrees to drive turbines for electricity. Each mirror is slightly curved and pivots independently under sensitive computer control to track the sun's beams and keep them focused on the tower. All of them taken together make the equivalent of a gigantic parabolic mirror.

In the ancient story and in its high-tech analogue in Arizona, the same powerful solution is given: focus tens of thousands of individuals on the creative fire and let them move independently but with a common purpose, and the life-giving energies will be beyond belief. The power that can be focused by compound mirrors is vast, while that reflected by uncoordinated individual actions has little effect. An individual's work may be personally satisfying and a testimony of great value, but like mirrors pointed in a hundred different directions, isolated actions can't make the kinds of changes that are needed now. In a culture as individualistic as ours, the implications are clear.

Today, our fast-moving world requires that we make dynamic, sensitive responses and not repeat the old stories of our past. Certainly the Cultural Creatives are focusing on such responses, but their efforts alone will not be enough. All of us with our diverse capacities and deepest insights, our lively curiosity and compassion and all our intelligence, are needed. One grand mirror won't do it. Our new story is one that requires ten thousand tellers and ten times more to be inspired by it. Our new face needs ten thousand mirrors, each with a unique angle of vision to catch the creative energy available now. And as the new stories and vision are coordinated into action, the new designs and new technologies have an enormous leverage that makes possible a sustainable world.

But technologies and cleverness alone will not save us. In today's world, each of us needs to take a dual viewpoint. We invite you to consider the story of Amaterasu Omikami from two viewpoints: that of the ten thousand kami of life on the planet, and that of the sun goddess herself. If we only see from the perspective of the kami, we are like the initiate in the midst of the Between— teetering between fear and trust, uncertain of who he is or where she is going. But if we also see from the perspective of the sun goddess, our shining, life-giving completeness will be reflected in every living thing. We will reflect the personal and the eternal truth of who we are.

In every age where people have come through a time of immense change, they have done so with a wisdom tradition with elders, a community, and a guiding story to focus their energies toward life and hope. In the Exodus story, "the Dusty Ones," as Thomas Cahill calls them, wandered "through Sinai's lunar landscape, denuded of the ordinary web of life, baked in absolute heat and merciless light,"[2] sustained by a vision of a land flowing with milk and honey. In the New Testament, it is the city shimmering on the hill that calls to people. In Tibetan Buddhism, it is Shambala, and in Japanese Buddhism, it's the Pure Land. Athens, Venice, and Byzantium were images of the ideal cities to Mediterranean peoples. And in every instance, the vision of the possible was a beacon and a resting place, a sustenance through times when the flow of life was hard to trust and life's goodness hard to remember.

When the age of Modernism has ended and we have prepared the way for a new culture to take its place, our vision of the world we can create will help us through the deserts of the Between. We can begin right now to imagine a culture wise enough to make this passage and imagine our part in it. That is the first step in making it so.

OLD AND LOST RIVERS

Slow, sludged-in, mud-bound rivers
Old rivers, sand rivers carved into dust
Louisiana, Mississippi, Oklahoma
We are digging out the lost rivers and it seems we have been digging
for a thousand years.

Alberta, Montana, Idaho
Mountain rivers iced dry
Color of steel, color of bone
Frozen rivers defeat us. Implacable rivers, dead rivers
We are helpless here.

Nothing is left now.
Impulse of nerve rises. Drops. Rises.
What if . . . No. Nothing can be done.
Slow rivers. Lost rivers. Rivers iced dry.

Days go by. Weeks.
Our defeat certain,
heralds
arrive in the mountains.

We have given up listening.
We do not hear
the occasional
cracking.

Within days
Whether we listen or not
watch or not
Hold ourselves still, rapt, anxious and waiting,
or not
there is a thin
spilling
onto stone,
trickling under matted leaves,
pooling through—through!—ice floes.

Where the eye looks and where it does not,
where streams ran and where they never ran before
where there has been a place season after season
and where there never was a place before
pools puddles eddies
open before us
overflow from hidden ponds

Rushing spinning sighing singing tumbling
celebrants
are running before us
shouting:
What was lost is found,
What was frozen, melted.
What was bound, free.
The warfare is accomplished.
The voice of the turtle is heard in the land.

SHERRY RUTH ANDERSON

appendix a

survey results

The survey data reported in this book come from two kinds of "values and lifestyle" surveys, most of which used mail questionnaires. One kind of survey is American LIVES, Inc.'s thirteen years of consumer surveys for private companies or public opinion polls for nonprofit groups. These results are summarized in a general, qualitative way in the lifestyle discussions of Part One. No statistics are given, because these tend to be small, highly tailored, proprietary surveys of particular demographic groups (for example, people with incomes over $25,000, only homeowners), particular regions (such as Southern California), particular behavioral groups (for instance, all people who bought a home in the last year, all people who gave money to an environmental cause in the last two years), or some combination of those (such as recent homebuyers in Southern California, or people over age 55 and with incomes over $25,000 in the larger Detroit region).

Over thirteen years, these surveys have covered every region of the United States, except New England, and have included such topics as home and community preferences, home decorating and remodeling, food and beverages, automobiles, "green or natural" product use, consumer electronics, personal computers, shopping, financial services, adult education, alternative health care, media use (television, books, magazines, Internet), vacation travel, leisure and sports behavior, giving to good causes, environmental and urban growth attitudes, retirement and nursing home attitudes, relations among ethnic groups, and health attitudes and behaviors. These surveys have yielded a wealth of insights into all three subcultures discussed herein—the Moderns, the Traditionals, and the Cultural Creatives.

The second kind of survey reported in this book is the representative national survey. All statistics provided here are from two such surveys: the January 1995 Integral Culture Survey, sponsored by the Fetzer Institute and the Institute of Noetic Sciences, and the January 1999 Sustainability Survey sponsored by the Environmental Protection Agency and the President's

Council on Sustainable Development. Both of these were demographically balanced, representative national samples, using mail panels—that is, people who had previously agreed to answer several surveys over the course of a year. Both included American LIVES, Inc.'s proprietary battery of values items that are used to identify the three subcultures.

The Integral Culture Survey was executed by National Family Opinion of Toledo, Ohio, using a mail questionnaire designed and analyzed by Paul H. Ray. It had a sample return of 61 percent, with 1,036 respondents. The Sustainability Survey was executed by Market Facts of Chicago, Illinois, using a mail questionnaire designed and analyzed by Paul H. Ray, and by Mark Epstein, Eric Zook, and Purnima Chawla of Porter Novelli, Inc. It had a sample return of 51 percent, with 2,181 respondents.

IDENTIFICATION OF THE SUBCULTURES

The three subcultures are identified using a battery of seventy questions and a statistical methodology proprietary to American LIVES, Inc. The questions are values statements designed to elicit what is most important in people's lives, and answers are scaled as degrees of importance, or degrees of agreement or disagreement. People are classified into subcultures by combining those responses into fifteen values measures, plus a measure of socioeconomic status. The measures are further analyzed into orthogonal dimensions, using factor analysis and multidimensional scaling. A special version of K-means clustering derives the subcultures, which amounts to grouping people by the similarity of their values profiles. The accuracy of the subculture identification is then validated using statistical modeling.

Over thirteen years, this approach has yielded highly reliable subculture groupings, survey after survey, year after year. The results are very stable and slow changing. For more detailed statistics on the survey results, the interested reader may go to our Web site at www.culturalcreatives.org. We can also be contacted at that site.

notes

PREFACE

1. Don Edward Beck and Christopher C. Cowan, *Spiral Dynamics: Mastering Values, Leadership and Change* (Cambridge, MA: Blackwell, 1996). Brian P. Hall, *Values Shift: A Guide to Personal and Organizational Transformation* (Rockport, MA: Twin Lights Publishers, 1995). Willett Kempton, James S. Boster, and Jennifer A. Hartley, *Environmental Values in American Culture* (Cambridge, MA: MIT Press, 1997). Ronald Inglehart, *Culture Shift in Advanced Industrial Society* (Princeton, NJ: Princeton University Press, 1990) and *Modernization and Postmodernization: Cultural, Economic and Political Change in 43 Societies* (Princeton, NJ: Princeton University Press, 1997). Paul R. Abramson and Ronald Inglehart, *Value Change in Global Perspective* (Ann Arbor, MI: University of Michigan Press, 1995). Alberto Melucci, *Challenging Codes: Collective Action in the Information Age* (New York: Cambridge University Press, 1996). Manuel Castells, *The Power of Identity,* vol. 2 of *The Information Age: Economy, Society and Culture* (Cambridge, MA: Blackwell, 1997).

CHAPTER ONE. WHO ARE THE CULTURAL CREATIVES?

1. Jean Houston quoted in "Changing Our Minds." *Ideas,* CBC (1984).

2. As this book goes to press, Patte Mitchell writes to us: "I am not sure these statistics hold true today as the program has adapted to the constraints of managed care. There have been no recent studies. It is a real miracle Peninsula Village is still in operation. Most of the adolescent programs in this area of the country have closed out of financial necessity."

3. John Leonard, *Smoke and Mirrors: Violence, Television, and Other American Cultures* (New York: The New Press, 1997).

4. Prathia Hall, videotaped interview at the Gandhi-Hamer-King Center for the Study of Religion and Democratic Renewal, Iliff School of Theology, Denver, CO.

5. Michael Oneal, "Who Speaks for America?" *Business Week,* May 8, 1995.

6. Thomas Moore, "Does America Have a Soul?" *Mother Jones,* Sept./Oct. 1996.

7. Barry Lopez, *Crow and Weasel* (New York: Farrar, Straus and Giroux, 1998), p. 59.

8. Ibid.

CHAPTER TWO. BECOMING A CULTURAL CREATIVE

1. Janet Kalven, "Respectable Outlaw," cited in Elisabeth Schüssler-Fiorenza, *Bread Not Stones* (Boston: Beacon Press, 1984), dedication.

2. Sherry Ruth Anderson and Patricia Hopkins, *The Feminine Face of God* (New York: Bantam, 1992), p. 48.

3. Rick Fields, "Evolution," *Inquiring Mind* 16, no. 1 (Fall 1999).

4. Matthew Fox, interview by authors, Toronto, 1985.

5. Molly Ivins, *Molly Ivins Can't Say That, Can She?* (New York: Vintage, 1992), p. xiv.

6. Daniel Quinn, *Ishmael* (New York: Bantam, 1995), pp. 36–37.

7. K. Robert Schwarz, "A Young Composer Leaps Ahead of a Promising Pack," *New York Times,* January 18, 1998.

8. Nicolas Dawidoff, "The Pop Populist,"*New York Times Sunday Magazine,* January 26, 1997.

9. Quinn, *Ishmael,* p. 91.

10. Kenny Ausubel, *Restoring the Earth: Visionary Solutions from the Bioneers* (Tiburon, CA: HJ Kramer, 1997), pp. 71–84.

CHAPTER THREE. THE THREE AMERICAS

1. Paul Weyrich quoted in *Washington Post,* February 18, 1999.

2. Henry Hyde quoted in Thomas B. Edsall, "Key Conservative Surrenders in Culture War, but Fight Continues," *Washington Post,* February 18, 1999.

3. Robert H. Bork, *Slouching Towards Gomorrah* (New York: Regan Books, 1996).

4. James Davison Hunter, *Culture Wars: The Struggle to Define America* (New York: Basic Books, 1991), p. 52

5. Quotes from Hunter, *Culture Wars,* p. 232.

6. Ibid., p. 245.

7. Ibid., p. 63.

8. Richard Eder, "Don't Fence Me In," *New York Times Book Review,* May 23, 1999.

9. Ibid.

10. Nicholas Lemann, "The New American Consensus: Government of, by and for the Comfortable," *New York Times Sunday Magazine,* November 1, 1998.

11. Joint conference of the American Psychological Association and the National Institute for Occupational Safety and Health, reported by Patrick A. McGuire in *APA Monitor* 30, no. 5, May 1999.

12. Steven Sauter (chief of the applied psychological and ergonomics branch of the National Institute for Occupational Safety and Health), quoted in "Worker Stress, Health Reaching Critical Point," *APA Monitor* 30, no. 5, May 1999.

13. Ruben Nelson, interview by authors, "Changing Our Minds," *Ideas,* CBC (1984).

14. Ibid.

15. Some churches rang their bell as few as three times, others as many as seven.

16. Allegra Goodman, *Kaaterskill Falls* (New York: Dial Press, 1998).

17. Laurie Goodstein, "Hundreds of Thousands Gather on the Mall in a Day of Prayers," *New York Times,* October 5, 1997.

18. Quoted in Michael Oneal, "Who Speaks for America?" *Business Week,* May 8, 1995.

19. In colonial America, nearly all settlers were actually Moderns—early modern Europeans from the first rustlings of the industrial revolution. The colonialists were well beyond feudalism and the medieval worldview when they landed in the New World. By the time the American Revolution began, the Modern world was just hitting its stride. A good description of the origins of all fundamentalisms in the midst of Modernism is found in Karen Armstrong, *The Battle for God* (New York: Alfred A. Knopf, 2000).

20. Ibid.

21. Laurie Goodstein, "Reviving Labyrinths, Paths to Inner Peace," *New York Times,* May 10, 1998.

22. The Labyrinth Project is described in *Veriditas,* available from Grace Cathedral, 1100 California Street, San Francisco, CA 94108. The meditation and wellness centers at Beth Israel and Sloan-Kettering are described in Leslie Berger, "A Therapy Gains Ground in Hospitals: Meditation," *New York Times,* November 11, 1999.

23. Beck quoted in Jon Pareles, "A Pop Post-Modernist Gives Up on Irony," *New York Times,* November 8, 1998.

24. Thomas Berry, *The Dream of the Earth* (New York: Sierra Club Books, 1990), p. 123.

25. Gerda Lerner, *Why History Matters* (New York: Oxford University Press, 1997), p. 110.

CHAPTER FOUR. CHALLENGING THE CODES

1. Denise Levertov, "Making Peace," in Daniella Gioseffi (ed.), *Women on War: Voices from the Nuclear Age* (New York: Simon and Schuster, 1988).

2. British sociologist Anthony Giddens, an adviser to Prime Minister Tony Blair, writes: "Social democratic parties originally began as social movements in the late nineteenth and early twentieth centuries. Today, in addition to undergoing their ideological crisis, they find themselves outflanked by new social movements and, like other parties, caught up in a situation where politics has apparently been devalued and government apparently drained of power." *The Third Way* (London: Polity Press, 1998).

3. See Eric Foner, *The Story of American Freedom* (New York: Norton, 1998), chap. 12.

4. Vincent G. Harding, interview by authors (1998), and interview by Rachel E. Harding, "Biography, Democracy and Spirit: An Interview with Vincent Harding," *Callaloo* 20, no. 3 (1998), pp. 682–98.

5. Foner, *American Freedom,* pp. 275–76.

6. Vincent Harding, *Hope and History* (Maryknoll, NY: Orbis Books, 1990), pp. 6–7.

7. See Václav Havel, *Open Letters: Selected Writings, 1965–1990* (New York: Vintage Books, 1992.) See also Paul Berman's thoughtful essay "The Philosopher-King Is Mortal," *New York Times Sunday Magazine,* May 5, 1997.

8. David Halberstam, *The Children* (New York: Random House, 1998), pp. 5–9.

9. Anne Braden, videotaped interview at Gandhi-Hamer-King Center for the Study of Religion and Democratic Renewal, Iliff School of Theology, Denver, CO.

10. See Vincent Harding, *There Is a River: The Black Struggle for Freedom in America* (San Diego: Harcourt, Brace & Co., 1981), chap. 6.

11. The white supremacy that white southerners saw as God given was a European invention from the 1600s. The codes that supported it spread worldwide with the expansion of modern Europeans into North and South America, Asia, and Africa, as they sought to justify both slavery and colonialism. Before this time, racism had been nearly indistinguishable from the ordinary ethnocentrism that claimed "my people are better." In the Roman and Byzantine empires, one's skin color was considerably less important than one's ethnicity, language, or protector. Not until around 1800 were biological racial theories proposed.

12. King quotes are from Clayborne Carson et al., eds., *The Eyes on the Prize Civil Rights Reader* (New York: Viking Penguin, 1991), pp. 48–51. Background information is from Taylor Branch, *Parting the Waters* (New York: Touchstone, 1998), chap. 4.

13. The background relies on Halberstam, *Children,* chap. 4. James Lawson is quoted on p. 62.

14. John Lewis quoted in Halberstam, *Children,* pp. 139–40. See the photograph of John Lewis facing p. 344.

15. Paul Begala is quoted in "Hero?" *Esquire,* November 1998, p. 108.

16. Betty Friedan, *The Feminine Mystique* (New York: Dell, 1984); quoted in Foner, *American Freedom,* p. 295.

17. Mary Daly, *Gyn/Ecology* (Boston: Beacon Press, 1978), pp. 386–87.

18. Ibid. Our account of the women's movement relies in part on Carol Mueller's meticulous "Conflict Networks and the Origins of Women's Liberation," in Enrique Laraña, Hank Johnston, and Joseph R. Gusfield, eds., *New Social Movements* (Philadelphia: Temple University Press, 1994), pp. 234–63. We disagree with Mueller's interpretation that the invisible, submerged networks are mainly important during the latency phases of a movement's development. The women's movement continued to depend on learning and growing outside the public eye and is continuing to do this still.

19. Marge Piercy, in Robin Morgan, ed., *Sisterhood Is Powerful* (New York: Random House, 1970).

20. The number of movement periodicals leaped from two in 1968 to about sixty in 1972.

21. Nelle Morton, "Beloved Image," paper delivered at the National Conference of the American Academy of Religion, San Francisco, December 28, 1977.

22. Carol Lee Flinders, *At the Root of This Longing* (San Francisco: HarperSanFrancisco, 1998).

23. Gerda Lerner, *The Creation of Feminist Consciousness* (New York: Oxford University Press, 1993), p. 275.

24. Lyn Mikel Brown and Carol Gilligan, *Meeting at the Crossroads* (Cambridge, MA: Harvard University Press, 1992).

25. Carolyn Heilbrun, *Writing a Woman's Life* (New York: Norton, 1988), pp. 24–25.

26. See Charles Garfield, *Sometimes My Heart Goes Numb: Love and Caregiving in a Time of AIDS* (San Francisco: Jossey-Bass, 1975); and Charles Garfield, Cindy Spring, and Sedonia Cahill, *Wisdom Circles* (New York: Hyperion, 1998).

27. Carol P. Christ, "Nothingness, Awakening, Insight, New Naming," *Diving Deep and Surfacing* (Boston: Beacon, 1980).

28. Mueller, "Conflict Networks," p. 253.

29. Wendy Wasserstein quoted in Mervyn Rothstein, "After the Revolution, What?" *New York Times,* December 11, 1988, sec. 2.

30. Richard Flacks, *Beyond the Barricades: The Sixties Generation Grows Up* (Philadelphia: Temple University Press, 1990).

31. *Fear and Favor in the Newsroom,* produced by NorthWest Passage Productions in association with KTEH San Jose Public Television. Directed and co-produced by Beth Sanders, 1997.

32. Todd Gitlin, *The Whole World Is Watching* (Berkeley, CA: University of California Press, 1980), p. 28.

33. Manuel Castells has a trenchant discussion of these issues in *The Information Age: Economy, Society and Culture,* volume 2, *The Power of Identity* (Cambridge, MA: Blackwell, 1997), chap. 6.

34. Charlene Spretnak, preface to *The Politics of Women's Spirituality* (New York: Doubleday, 1994), p. xi.

35. Harding, *Hope and History,* p. 111.

CHAPTER FIVE. TURNING GREEN

1. Alice Walker, "We Have a Beautiful Mother," *Her Blue Body Everything We Know: Earthling Poems 1965–1990* (New York: Harcourt Brace & Company, 1991).

2. Duane Elgin and Colleen LeDrew give an excellent summary of cross-national surveys on environmental issues in *Global Paradigm Change,* Research Report of the Institute of Noetic Sciences and the Fetzer Institute, 1997. The twenty-four-nation study of attitudes toward the environment is the Health of the Planet survey conducted in 1993 by Gallup International. The survey director, Dr. Riley E. Dunlap, concluded that it "demonstrates virtually world-wide citizen awareness that our

planet is indeed in poor health, and great concern for its future well-being." In nearly all nations, over 70 percent, ranging up to 90 percent, expressed either "a fair amount" or "a great deal" of personal concern about the environment, and in the developing nations the numbers were more consistently high. (The United States was at 85 percent.) The level of concern was even higher for the loss of plant and animal species across the world; those who believed the problem is "very serious" or "somewhat serious" were consistently in the range of 85 to 95 percent (with the United States again at 85 percent). In a major blow to the main project of modern capitalism, large majorities of people say they would choose protecting the environment over economic growth. In the industrialized nations, the proportions ranged from 53 to 77 percent (the U.S. was at 58 percent), and in the developing nations the proportions ranged from 53 to 71 percent (except for India, Turkey, and Nigeria).

3. David Suzuki, Untitled, in Roberts and Amidon, *Prayers,* p. 212.

4. Cited in Steve Van Matre and Bill Weiler, eds., *The Earth Speaks* (Warrenville, IL: Institute for Earth Education, 1983), p. 67.

5. Aldo Leopold, *A Sand County Almanac, With Other Essays on Conservation from Round River* (New York: Oxford University Press, 1981).

6. John Muir, "My First Summer in the Sierra," in Van Matre and Weiler, *Earth Speaks,* p. 53.

7. William Kent's story is based on his biography, by Elizabeth T. Kent, "William Kent, Independent," undated. It is available at the Marin County Public Library Archives. An appallingly incorrect version of this story appears in Galen Rowell, *Bay Area Wild* (San Francisco: Sierra Club Books, 1999).

8. Annie Dillard, *Pilgrim at Tinker Creek* (New York: Harper and Row, 1974), p. 201.

9. Joanna Macy, Untitled, in Roberts and Amidon, *Prayers,* p. 158.

10. Rachel Carson, *Silent Spring* (New York: Fawcett, 1962), p. 262.

11. Quotes about the reception of *Silent Spring* are from Robert Gottlieb's outstanding treatment of the American environmental movement, *Forcing the Spring* (Washington, DC: Island Press, 1993), pp. 85–86.

12. Susan Griffin, *Woman and Nature* (New York: Harper Colophon, 1978), p. 219.

13. Mark Dowie, *Losing Ground* (Cambridge, MA: MIT Press, 1996), p. 5.

14. Ibid.

15. By the 1980s, as might have been expected, a major conservative backlash to the environmental movement had formed. First, the religious right generated a cultural backlash against all the new social movements. Second, escalating movement demands—for safer factories, less pollution, healthier products, limits on logging and mining, reduced risks of oil spills and chemicals release—threatened to cut profits and send costs through the ceiling, or so big business feared. It looked like polluting industries would soon be sued for millions *and* be regulated by government.

A third factor was the emergence of the new conservative movement, created when the old radical right (like the John Birch Society), Barry Goldwater's Sunbelt Republicans, and the silk-stocking Taft Republicans of the Northeast all joined forces with the industries most likely to be regulated—and called in volunteers from the Traditionals. The movement was financed by the same kind of worried reactionary wealth that had opposed William Kent and Teddy Roosevelt at the end of the Gilded Era. When all these forces were joined and industries were able to buy legislators at both the state and federal levels, the forces lined up against environmentalism were great indeed. By the Reagan 1980s, they could often neutralize the national environmental organizations.

The parties at the Washington conference tables included: big corporations who were damaging the environment, the conservative movement (financed by the same corporations), government officials (often linked to the same corporations by campaign contributions or by the hope of future jobs through the revolving door), and big environmental organizations (often linked to law firms that hoped to get business from those corporations, or funding from foundations whose boards had ties to those corporations). Not surprisingly, the compromises tended to favor the corporations. The grassroots movement was merely a sideshow, out of sight of the star players and the main event.

16. Mark Dowie documents this shift well in *Losing Ground*. See also Gottlieb, *Forcing the Spring*, pp. 117–61, 316–19.

17. Donella H. Meadows, Dennis L. Meadows, and Jorgen Rangers, *Beyond the Limits* (Post Mills, VT: Chelsea Green Publishing Company, 1992).

18. Willett Kempton, James S. Boster, and Jennifer A. Hartley, *Environmental Values in American Culture* (Cambridge, MA: MIT Press, 1996).

19. By "theme," we mean a distinct group of questionnaire items that we identified using factor analysis and multidimensional scaling, then transformed into a measurement scale. Each scale is far more reliable than any single questionnaire item.

20. We capitalize the word *Ecologist* to distinguish these political activists and thinkers from scientific ecologists. We avoid calling them *Greens* here to avoid confusing them with the Green Cultural Creatives or the Green parties in various countries.

21. William McDonough, "The Next Industrial Revolution," in *Collective Heritage Letter* (publication of the Collective Heritage Institute, Santa Fe, NM) 1, no. 2, 1998.

22. Amory Lovins, "Designing with Biology," *Collective Heritage Letter* 1, no. 2, 1998.

CHAPTER SIX. WAKING UP

1. John Moyne and Coleman Barks, *Open Secret: Versions of Rumi* (Putney, VT: Threshold Books, 1984), quatrain 91.

2. Elizabeth Lesser, "Wisdom and Folly: The New Age Comes of Age," *New Age Journal* (January–February 1997). For a much fuller exposition, see her book *The New American Spirituality* (New York: Random House, 1999).

3. Joan Tollifson, *Bare-Bones Meditation* (New York: Bell Tower, 1992), pp. 26–27.

4. Ibid., p. 31.

5. Our account of the early years of Esalen depends on Walter Truett Anderson, *The Upstart Spring: Esalen and the American Awakening* (Reading, MA: Addison-Wesley, 1983), and on our 1984 interview with Michael Murphy in Mill Valley, CA.

6. Ibid., p. 69.

7. Ibid., p. 80.

8. Ibid., p. 66.

9. John Davis is a senior teacher of the Diamond Approach. These quotes are from the introduction to his book, *The Diamond Approach: An Introduction to the Teachings of A. H. Almaas* (Boston: Shambhala, 1999), pp. xix–xxxii.

10. *Natural Business,* no. 41 (October 1999).

11. Lance Morrow quoted in Lesser, "Wisdom and Folly," p. 27.

12. Amy Hertz quoted in *Publishers Weekly,* December 6, 1993.

13. Chogyam Trungpa Rinpoche, *Cutting Through Spiritual Materialism* (Boston: Shambhala, 1987).

14. Lesser, "Wisdom and Folly," p. 30.

15. People who value some of these items tend to value nearly all of them. (That is, statistically, all these items are highly intercorrelated.)

16. Caroline Myss, *Anatomy of the Spirit* (New York: Harmony, 1996), p. 17.

17. David E. Rosenbaum, "The Gathering Storm over Prescription Drugs," *New York Times,* November 14, 1999.

18. Zeev E. Neuwirth, M.D., "The Silent Anguish of the Healers," *Newsweek,* September 13, 1999.

19. Ibid.

20. Larry Dossey, *Meaning and Medicine: A Doctor's Tales of Breakthrough and Healing* (San Francisco: HarperCollins, 1992).

21. Rachel Naomi Remen, presentation to the conference "Helping Heal the Whole Person and the Whole World," Kalamazoo, MI, June 25, 1988; cited in Barbara McNeill and Carol Guion, *Noetic Sciences Collection, 1980–1990: Ten Years of Consciousness Research* (Sausalito, CA: Institute of Noetic Sciences, 1991), pp. 60–65.

22. For more information, write to Voices of Healing, at voicesofhealing@infoasis.com, or 33 Millwood Avenue, Mill Valley, CA 94941.

23. Thomas Berry, lecture at Santa Sabina Convent, San Rafael, CA, February 21–23, 1992.

24. See the Commonweal Web site: *www.commonweal.org.*

CHAPTER SEVEN. A GREAT CURRENT OF CHANGE

1. Mark Satin, *New Age Politics* (New York: Delta, 1978), preface.

2. George B. Leonard, *The Transformation* (New York: Delacorte, 1972), pp. 1–3.

3. Robert Kuttner, "The Seattle Protesters Got It Right," *Business Week,* December 20, 1999.

4. Elsa C. Arnett, "Seattle Protests Put a New Activism in Play," *San Jose Mercury News,* December 3, 1999.

5. Open letter on the Internet from Starhawk, December 10, 1999. For an Internet video produced by the Independent Media Center and Beth Sanders's forthcoming "This Is What Democracy Looks Like," see *www.indymedia.org.*

6. Aruna Uprety quoted in China Galland, *The Bond Between Women* (New York: Riverhead Books, 1998), p. 28.

7. Ralph H. Turner, "Ideology and Utopia After Socialism," in Enrique Larana, Hank Johnston, and Joseph R. Gusfield, eds., *New Social Movements* (Philadelphia: Temple University Press, 1994), pp. 79–81, 89–97.

8. For this analysis, we scored each person as *agreeing* with a particular movement, *neutral* (not caring one way or the other), or *disagreeing* with it. We then counted up how many of the five movements they were in broad agreement with. This gave us an indication of how many moral publics they belong to. (We don't have evidence for all twenty movements, but indications are that the overlap is about the same.) In case you were wondering, none of the variables we measured here were used to determine who belongs to the Cultural Creatives population. That was based on an entirely different battery of measures.

9. But only sometimes do core activists of one movement become core activists in several others.

10. Michael Lerner, "The Age of Extinction and the Emerging Environmental Health Movement," unpublished paper, Commonweal Institute, Bolinas, CA, March 12, 1999; available on *www.commonweal.org.* Cited with permission of the author.

11. Ibid., p. 5.

12. Ibid.

13. From "#2 Censored: Chemical Corporations Profit Off Breast Cancer," in Peter Phillips and

Project Censored, *Censored 1999* (New York: Seven Stories Press, 1999), p. 35.

14. Barbara A. Brenner, "Seeing Our Interests Clearly: Follow the Money II," Breast Cancer Action (1998); available at *www.bcaction.org/news/9902-02.html.*

15. Samuel Epstein quoted in Sharon Batt and Liza Gross, "Cancer, Inc.," *Sierra* (September–October 1999).

16. Ibid. See also Barbara A. Brenner's articles "Cash and Cancer: An Unholy Alliance" and "New England Journal of Industry?" Breast Cancer Action (1997); available at: *www.bcaction.org/news/index.html.*

17. Audre Lorde, *Sister Outsider* (Freedom, CA: Crossing Press, 1984).

18. Political scientist Charles Lindblom named it "disjointed incrementalism."

PART THREE. MAPS FOR THE JOURNEY

1. Karl Polanyi, *The Great Transformation* (Boston: Beacon Press, 1944).

2. James Cowan, *A Mapmaker's Dream* (Boston: Shambhala, 1996), pp. 6–7.

CHAPTER EIGHT. INTO THE BETWEEN

1. John Naisbitt, *Megatrends* (New York: Warner Books, 1984), pp. 249–50.

2. Ibid., p. 250.

3. Naomi Newman's character is from her play written with Martha Boesing, *Snake Talk: Urgent Messages from God the Mother* (produced by A Traveling Jewish Theatre, San Francisco, 1988).

4. Suzi Gablik, *The Reenchantment of Art* (London: Thames & Hudson, 1992), p. 3.

5. Peter Schwartz, "The Art of the Long View," *Wired* (July 1997).

6. Bruce Wallace, "One Member's Views," submitted to the University Forum on Liberal Education, Virginia Polytechnic Institute and State University, Blacksburg, VA, June 1990; quoted in Lester R. Brown et al., *Saving the Planet* (New York: Norton, 1991), pp. 17–18.

7. Margaret J. Wheatley, "I Once Was Blind But Now I See: The Amazing Grace of Y2K," unpublished manuscript, 1999.

8. Interview with Christine Nüsslein-Volhard, *New York Times Sunday Magazine* (October 12, 1997), p. 45.

9. See, for example, Matthew Fox, *Illuminations of Hildegard of Bingen* (Santa Fe: Bear & Co., 1985).

10. This idea is inspired by Marion Woodman's description of death and rebirth in *The Pregnant Virgin* (Toronto: Inner City Books, 1988), p. 14.

11. William Ury quoted in Jane Lampman, "Challenging the 'Necessity' of Conflict," *Christian Science Monitor,* January 20, 2000, p. 15.

12. Arnold Toynbee, *A Study of History* (New York: Oxford University Press, 1972).

13. Pitirim A. Sorokin, *Social and Cultural Dynamics,* vols. 1–4 (New York: Bedminster Press, 1937–41). Unfortunately, Sorokin's work fell out of favor in the 1950s and 1960s. Many academics hated it for what it said about their own preoccupations. Sociologists said Sorokin thought too big and not rigorously enough, and besides, he was rude about the value of their research methods. But in those years, all of the social sciences were deeply committed to the project of Modernism and its vision of material, secular progress, while Sorokin wasn't having any of it. He was thoroughly out of step with his time. (He thought current sociology was dealing in trivia, and in retrospect, he was right. It's hard to tell which offended his colleagues more: his later writings on "fads and foibles in the social sciences," or his later research on "the ways and power of altruistic love.") Today he'd probably be a cult hero.

14. Ervin Laszlo, *The Choice: Evolution or Extinction?* (New York: Tarcher, 1994); *Evolution: The General Theory* (Cresskill, NJ: Hampton Press, 1996).

15. Richard Tarnas, "The Great Initiation," *Noetic Sciences Review,* no. 47 (1998), p. 57.

16. Barbara Marx Hubbard, *Conscious Evolution* (San Francisco: New World Library, 1997).

17. T. S. Eliot, "East Coker," *Four Quartets* (New York: Harcourt Brace Jovanovich, 1971), ll. 138–39.

18. Daniel Quinn, *Ishmael* (New York: Bantam, 1995), p. 214.

19. At the NGO Forum in Beijing in September 1995, the women's singing group Sweet Honey in the Rock quoted Tubman as they were teaching women to sing "Wade in the Water." Quoted by Fran Peavey and Tova Green in the newsletter *Crabgrass* (1996).

20. Jews are proud that one of their daughters, the poet Emma Lazarus, wrote the words inscribed at the base of the Statue of Liberty, which stands as a symbol of welcome to immigrants "yearning to breathe free."

21. Today the many ways to tell this story include E. M. Broner's *The Telling* (San Francisco: HarperSanFrancisco, 1994), about Jewish women who celebrate the Passover through community and ceremony; and Judith Plaskow's classic *Standing Again at Sinai* (San Francisco: HarperSanFrancisco, 1990).

CHAPTER NINE. CATERPILLAR, CHRYSALIS, BUTTERFLY

1. Recounted originally by the Caribou Eskimo Igjugarjuk to the scholar and explorer Knud Rasmussen in the 1920s, this quote is taken from Richard Tarnas, "The Great Initiation," *Noetic Sciences Review,* no. 47 (1998).

2. Marion Woodman, *The Pregnant Virgin* (Toronto: Inner City Books, 1988), p. 13.

3. Victor Turner, "Betwixt and Between: The Liminal Period in Rites of Passage," in Louise Carus Mahdi, Steven Foster, and Meredith Little, eds., *Betwixt and Between: Patterns of Masculine and Feminine Initiation* (LaSalle, IL: Open Court, 1987), p. 8.

4. Ibid., p. 9.

5. Elisabet Sahtouris, *Earthdance: Living Systems in Evolution* (Alameda, CA: Metalog Books, n.d.). The book can be downloaded from her Web site, *www.ratical.org/lifeweb.*

6. See *www.ratical.org/lifeweb.*

7. Sahtouris's 1998 books are *A Walk Through Time: From Stardust to Us,* with Sidney Liebes and Brian Swimme (New York: Wiley); and *Biology Revisioned,* with Willis Harman (Berkeley, CA: North Atlantic Books).

8. Bill Keepin and Brian Wynne, "Technical Analysis of IIASA Energy Scenarios," *Nature* 312 (December 20–27, 1984), pp. 691–95.

9. Joseph Campbell, *The Hero with a Thousand Faces* (Princeton, NJ: Princeton University Press, 1972), p. 58.

10. Annie Dillard, *American Childhood* (New York: HarperCollins, 1998), p. 243.

11. Sherry Ruth Anderson and Patricia Hopkins, *The Feminine Face of God* (New York: Bantam, 1992), pp. 148–49.

12. Mary Pipher, *Reviving Ophelia* (New York: Putnam, 1994), p. 44.

13. Ibid., pp. 27–28.

CHAPTER TEN. A WISDOM FOR OUR TIME

1. Anonymous Native American story, told on the cover of the CD *Lou Harrison: A Portrait* (Uni/London Classics, 1997). The text of story 3 of "Three Coyote Stories" appears in Harrison's Symphony no. 4 ("Last Symphony").

2. William Rees and Mathis Wackernagel, *Our Ecological Footprint* (Gabriola Island, BC: New Society, 1995).

3. Naomi Newman in collaboration with Martha Boesing, "Snake Talk: Urgent Messages from the Mother" (1986), A Traveling Jewish Theatre, San Francisco.

4. T. S. Eliot, "East Coker," *Four Quartets* (New York: Harvest/HBJ, 1971), ll. 202–206.

5. Martin Luther King, Jr., did have elders who blessed him and spoke frankly to him, and he also had elders who criticized him and counseled others not to follow him. But he had no circle of those who had directly gone before him, except for the generation a hundred years earlier. That is a lot, more than most have today, unless they reach back to make their own direct connections.

6. Michael Meade, at a workshop in northern California, 1967.

7. Michael Meade, in Louise Carus Mahdi, Steven Foster, and Meredith Little, eds., *Betwixt and Between: Patterns of Masculine and Feminine Initiation* (LaSalle, IL: Open Court, 1987), p. 29.

8. Louise Carus Mahdi, introduction, ibid.

9. Sylvia Maracle, lecture in Toronto, 1996.

10. Joanna Macy, interview by Stephan Bodian, "Visions of a Peaceful Planet," in his *Timeless Visions, Healing Voices* (Freedom, CA: Crossing Press, 1991), p. 9.

11. The earliest book, the one Joanna said was "harder than anything I have ever undertaken," was *Despair and Personal Power in the Nuclear Age* (Philadelphia: New Society Publishers, 1983). In a section of Joanna's book with Molly Young Brown, *Coming Back to Life* (Gabriola Island, BC: New Society, 1998), the guides are told, "Be sure you have done a good measure of your own despair work before attempting to facilitate others." One translation of that, in rite-of-passage terms, is: You cannot become an elder until you have passed through your own initiation.

12. William MacNeill, "The Care and Repair of Public Myth," *Foreign Affairs* 61 (Fall 1982), pp. 1–13.

13. Marion Woodman, author interview in Toronto, 1985.

14. Erica Helm Meade, *Tell It by Heart* (LaSalle, IL: Open Court, 1995).

15. Thomas Berry, address at Santa Sabina Convent, San Rafael, CA, February 22, 1992.

16. See Sobonfu Somé, *The Spirit of Intimacy* (New York: William Morrow, 1997), and Malidoma Patrice Somé, *Ritual* (Portland, OR: Swan/Raven & Co., 1993), for two profound and detailed discussions of these interconnections.

17. George Wolfe, interview on public television, 1995. We are grateful to Dirk Velten for this reference.

18. Charles Garfield, Cindy Spring, and Doris Ober, *Sometimes My Heart Goes Numb* (San Francisco: Jossey-Bass, 1995), p. 24.

19. Ibid., pp. 15–16.

20. Reg E. Gains quoted in Michel Marriott, "From Rap's Rhythms, a Retooling of Poetry," *New York Times,* September 29, 1996.

21. Vijali Hamilton, *In the Fields of Life* (Castle Valley, UT: Earth Mandala Press, 1999), prologue. Also see www.rocvision.com /vijali.htm.

22. Vijali Hamilton, interview by Sherry Anderson and Patricia Hopkins, Boney Mountain, 1987.

23. Thich Nhat Hanh, quoted in Macy and Brown, *Coming Back to Life,* p. 91.

24. David Suzuki, "Listening to the Elders," *New Dimensions* tape no. 2359 (Ukiah, CA: New Dimensions Foundation, undated).

CHAPTER ELEVEN. INVENTING A NEW CULTURE

1. Peter Asmus, *EarthLight* (Fall 1999), pp. 8–10.

2. *The Natural Step News,* no. 1 (Winter 1996).

3. Karl-Henrik Robért, "Educating a Nation: The Natural Step," *In Context,* no. 28 (undated).

4. Karl-Hendrik Robért, interview, *In Context,* no. 28 (undated).

5. The Natural Step, The Presidio, Thoreau Center for Sustainability, P.O. Box 29372, San Francisco, CA 94129-0372.

6. Amory B. Lovins, L. Hunter Lovins, and Paul Hawken, "A Road Map for Natural Capitalism," *Harvard Business Review,* May/June 1999.

7. Paul Hawken, Amory Lovins, and L. Hunter Lovins, *Natural Capitalism: Creating the Next Industrial Revolution* (Boston: Little, Brown, 1999), p. 20.

8. Numbers are from *Yoga Journal.* Their sources are a 1990 and 1994 Roper Starch study commissioned by *Yoga Journal;* a June 1998 *Wall Street Journal*/NBC Poll; and 1999 Mind Over Media research, including interviews, list analysis, and trend analysis.

9. The term *lifestyles of health and sustainability* was developed by Natural Business Communications, Inc., and by GAIAM, Inc. It seems to have been enthusiastically accepted by Wall Street analysts.

"Sustainable economy" includes:

- Environmental management solutions, audits, and services

- Renewable energy—solar, wind, and geothermal

- Energy conservation products and services, including resource-efficient products and alternative energy processes

- Sustainable manufacturing processes

- Recycling and goods made from recycled materials (paper, textiles, plastics, rubber, glass, metals)

- Related information services: Web sites, CDs, videotapes, for both consumers and businesses

- Related books, audiocassettes, manuals: educational tools requiring time and money of users

"Ecological lifestyles" includes:

- Natural and ecoproducts: environmentally friendly cleaning supplies, garden and lawn care, nonfood products made of natural and nontoxic materials, and ecological appliances, for both consumers and businesses (e.g., hotels)

- Ecotourism: responsible travel to natural areas that conserves the environment and sustains the well-being of local people—about 7 percent of all tourism, led by Cultural Creatives

- Related information services: Web sites, CDs, videotapes for both consumers and businesses

- Related books, audiocassettes, manuals: educational tools requiring time and money

"Healthy living" includes:

- Natural products: natural and organic foods, dietary supplements, personal body care products

- Related information services: Web sites, CDs, videotapes

- Related books, audiocassettes, manuals: educational tools requiring time and money of users

"Alternative health care" includes:

- Health and wellness solutions: air and water filtration, fans, heaters, air purifiers and humidifiers, back care products, vision solutions, injury remedies that are part of the alternative health care package

- Natural health services: alternative noninvasive treatments: massage, chiropractic, acupuncture, acupressure, biofeedback, aromatherapy, etc. Estimated at $27 billion in 1997. See David Eisenberg et al., "Trends in Alternative Medicine Use in the U.S., 1990–1997," *Journal of the American Medical Association* 280, no. 18 (November 11, 1998), pp. 1569–75.

- Related information services: Web sites, CDs, videotapes
- Related books, audiocassettes, manuals: educational tools requiring time and money of users

Note: This category is more concerned with the health of the entire person, and with prevention and healing, not just intervention, in catastrophic illness. Survey data show that most users of alternative health care are using it in addition to other medical treatment, not as a substitute. (Sources: Eisenberg, "Trends"; Paul H. Ray, The Integral Culture Survey, Institute of Noetic Sciences, 1996.)

"Personal development" includes:

- A wide range of personal experiences, solutions, products, information, and services relating to mind, body, and spiritual development, such as yoga, meditation, relaxation, spirituality, and realizing human potential
- Equipment, tools, and clothing
- Studios and clubs
- Lectures, instruction, and seminars
- Related information services: Web sites, CDs, videotapes
- Related books, audiocassettes, manuals: educational tools requiring time and money of users

10. Such time lags often result from the inability of businesses to do a good job of meeting people's needs, rather than from an absence of change.

11. *Natural Foods Merchandiser* and *Natural Business* #41, October 1999. The natural products industry is growing at a rate of 21 percent a year (calculated in constant dollars), from about $5 billion in 1991 to $15 billion in 1997. Similarly, organic product sales are growing at 22 percent a year, from $1.2 billion in 1991 to $4.8 billion in 1998 (same accelerating curve). Natural personal care sales are growing at 28 percent a year, from $0.8 billion in 1991 to $4.2 billion in 1998 (same accelerating curve). Dietary supplements are growing at "only" 13.3 percent a year.

12. Eisenberg, "Trends."

13. The sample size was 753. Only 21 percent of Moderns wanted ecotourism, and only 34 percent of Traditionals. Moderns were 60 percent of frequent vacation travelers, Cultural Creatives were 30 percent, and Traditionals were just 10 percent. Even so, Cultural Creatives were 53 percent of those who want ecotourism.

14. Will Weber, *Journeys,* highlighted on the Ecotourism Society's Web site: *www.ecotourism.com.*

15. David Spangler, *Emergence: The Rebirth of the Sacred* (New York: Delta, 1984), pp. 9–13.

EPILOGUE. THE TEN THOUSAND MIRRORS

1. The Amaterasu story is adapted from Jalaja Bonheim, *Goddess: A Celebration in Art and Literature* (New York: Stewart, Tabori, and Chang, 1997), and Carolyn McVickar Edwards, *The Storyteller's Goddess* (San Francisco: HarperCollins, 1991). It is based on eighth-century Japanese Shinto and Buddhist texts.

2. Thomas Cahill, *The Gifts of the Jews* (New York: Nan Talese/Doubleday, 1998), p. 142.

index

action, engaged, 9–10
activism, 10–11; *see also* social movements
adaptive response, 240
adolescence, difficult years of, 281–85
aging, as the Between, 291–94
AIDS, 215, 305
Alaracón, Francisco X., 62–63
Ali, Hameed, 182–83
alienated Moderns, 73, 300
Alioto, Caroline, 174
Allport, Catherine, 9–10, 145–47, 149
alternative health care, 221, 330
altruism, 15–17
Amaterasu Omikami, 343–46
America LIVES, Inc., 349–50
American consensus, environment and, 157–61
Anatomy of the Spirit (Myss), 193–94
Anderson, Marian, 89
Anderson, Ray C., 10–11, 163, 323
Anderson, Sherry Ruth, 348
Anderson, Spike, 332
Anderson, Walter Truett, 176
Angels in America (Kushner), 301
Aquarian Conspiracy, The (Ferguson), 207
Armstrong, G. W., 91
Artress, Lauren, 87, 89
associations, in civil society, 336–38
AstraZeneca, 224–25
Audubon Society, 142, 154
Auh-Ho-Ho, Choqösh, 277
Ausubel, Kenny, 62
authenticity, 8–9, 130
authority, inner, 277–78

Balboa, Rocky, 203
Bare-Bones Meditation (Tollifson), 175–76
BCA (Breast Cancer Action), 223–24
Beck (pop singer), 91–92
Begala, Paul, 125
behavior, values as predictors of, 7–14
Berke, Jerry H., 225
Berkeley, University of California at, 225
Berlin Wall, fall of, 245
Berry, Thomas, 92, 201, 202, 292
Between, the, 235–61
    aging as, 291–94
    birth and death in, 243–44
    challenge and response of, 245–46
    evolutionary change in, 248–50, 253–54
    Exodus and, 254–61
    gazing into, 236–44

mapping beneath the surface of, 248–54
metabolizing, 285
metamorphosis and, 269–70, 276–77, 279–80, 285
preparation for, 269
rites of passage in, 252–54, 269
scenarios of, 237–40
third way in, 244–45
uncertainty of, 235–36, 276–77, 332
wisdom in, 310–12
Beyond the Limits (Club of Rome), 152
Bingham, Rev. Sally, 320
biomimicry, 327
birthright, sense of, 173
black freedom movement, 81, 112–14, 117–25, 216
Blake, William, 226
Blueprint for Survival, 152–53
Bodian, Stephan, 297
bonds, breaking of, 75–76
Boney Mountain, 310–11
Bonhoeffer, Dietrich, 213
books, as silent allies, 277–78
Bork, Robert, 65
Borysenko, Joan, 195
Braden, Anne, 117–18
Breaking the News (Fallows), 134
Breast Cancer Action (BCA), 223–24
Brenner, Barbara, 225–26
bridges, personal, 89–90
Brown, Lyn Mikel, 129
Bucke, Richard, 171
buildings, whole-systems, 164–65
Burck, Doug, 52, 53
business
    big, 227, 229
    of consciousness movement, 328–34, 338
    corporate cancer links, 224–26
    corporate pressure, 221–23, 225–28
    ecotourism, 331
    natural capitalism, 326–28, 338
    radical resource productivity, 326–27
    service and flow economy, 327
    and survival of the Earth, 152, 325
business as usual, 152, 227–28
business conservatives, 71–72, 84

Cahill, Thomas, 346
California Institute of Integral Studies, 278
Campbell, Joseph, 51, 277, 298–300
cancer
    breast, 223–26
    corporate arena of, 224–26

Capra, Fritjof, 207, 278
Carson, Rachel, 110, 150–51, 225, 292
Carver, George Washington, 242
Cash, Eugene, 90–91
Catalfo, Phil, 328
celebrities and leaders, 37–39
change
    evolutionary, 248–50, 252–54
    great current of, 205–30
    planetary transitions, 250–54
    in values, 17–20
chemoprevention industry, 224–25
children
    healing of, 201
    sex trade in, 215
Chopra, Deepak, 195
Christ, Carol, 131
Ciba Geigy, 163–64
civil rights movements, 81, 112–25
    black freedom, 112–14, 117–25
    women's liberation, 126–33, 216, 217
Civil War, 81, 84
Clinton, Bill, 65
Clive, Margery Anderson and Mark, 89–90
Club of Rome, 152
Commonweal, 202–3, 335
community, context of, 304–6
consciousness movements, 108, 169–204
    analogies from the past in, 186–88
    business of, 328–34, 338
    convergence of social movement with, 206–7,
        210–15, 221, 237
    Esalen Institute, 176–77, 178–80
    first generation of, 174, 175–84, 187
    going the distance in, 203–4
    growth of, 185, 188, 203–4
    healing in, 193–204
    meditation in, 176
    New Age and, 188–89, 192
    new people vs. longtime practitioners in, 185–86, 189
    origins of, 171–74
    premise of, 173–74
    psychology and, 180–81, 210
    second generation of, 174–75, 184–88, 337–38
    spiritual materialism in, 189
    support structures for, 187–88, 338
    use of term, 171
    values and beliefs in, 190–91
    waking up to, 169–71, 174–75
    yoga, 328–32
consciousness-raising groups, 128–29
conservation, use of term, 142
conservation movement, 150
conservatives
    backlash of, 153
    business, 71–72, 84
    international, 88
    see also Traditionals
constituency, of healing, 201, 202

conventional Moderns, 72
convergence of social movements, 210–21
Core Cultural Creatives, 14–15
    consciousness movement and, 172, 182, 189,
        192–93, 203–4
    healing and, 201, 202, 203
    planet Earth and, 297
Cosmic Consciousness (Bucke), 171
Coyote, 287–88
creating outside the box, 58–61, 301
creation stories, 99–105, 205–30
    of Cultural Creatives, 107
    current of change, 205–30
    social movements and, 103
critics, confronting, 54–58
Csikszentmihalyi, Mihaly, 170
cultural conditioning, 129
Cultural Creatives
    becoming, 43–64
    changing a worldview, 17–19, 217–18
    creation story of, 107
    demographics of, 22–24
    as departure from Modernism, 86, 92–93
    disenchantment of, 17
    emergence of, 320
    first step of, 48–49
    fourth step of, 58–64
    leaders and celebrities, 38
    lifestyles of, 33–37
    moral publics of, 217, 219, 238
    as new country, 40–42
    new social inventions of, 40
    as ordinary people, 19–21
    promise of, 39
    second step of, 49–52
    social movements and, see social movements
    survey, xiv, 349–50
    as third alternative, 33, 87, 89
    third step of, 54–58
    two wings of, 14–15
    values of, 8–13, 15–17, 28–29
culture
    change of heart in, 279–80
    collapse of, 65
    future challenges, 318, 319
    hole in, 186–88, 294–95
    macroview of, 66–67
    new, 93–94, 315–41
    outsiders in, 102–3, 301
    reframing old problems in, 128
    transformation of, 315
    values of, see values
    vernacular, 166
    worldviews and, 7, 93
culture wars, 33, 66–67
    feedback in, 84–86
    getting beyond, 92, 94–95
    uniting for, 84, 86
Culture Wars (Hunter), 67

Daly, Mary, 128
Danielpour, Richard, 55
Davi, Ray, 47
Davis, John, 182–84
de Leña, Dixon, 56
demographics, 22–24
    numbers of women, 23
    use of term, 23
denial, 57–58
Dickinson, Emily, 171
Dillard, Annie, 148, 277
Direct Action Network (DAN), 208
distorted mirrors, 55
Dossey, Larry, 195, 196
Dowie, Mark, 154
dreams, creation stories in, 301–2
Drucker, Peter, 315, 321

Earth
    business and, 152, 325
    carrying capacity of, 152, 157, 288–89, 322–23,
      327–28, 338
    concern about, 297; *see also* environmental
      movement
    as Gaia, 148, 167, 221
    growth and, 156, 161–63
    interconnectedness of life on, 63–64, 167
    photographs from space, 153, 302–4
Earth Day, 151–53
Ecologist, The, 152, 166
ecology
    globalism and, 11–12, 209–10
    interconnectedness and, 63–64, 167
    sustainability and, 152, 157, 288–89, 322–23,
      327–28, 338
    see also environmental movement
ecology movement, 156–61, 165–67, 216
Ecology of Commerce, The (Hawken), 10, 326
ecotourism, 331
Eddy, Mary Baker, 171
Eder, Richard, 72
Edwards, Jonathan, 81
Einstein, Albert, 155
elders, wisdom of, 289–94
Eliot, T. S., 253, 291
Emerson, Ralph Waldo, 148, 171
enantiodromia, 78
Energy Foundation, 276
engaged action, 9–10
environment, use of word, 150–51
environmental health, 219, 221
environmental movement, 139–67
    against the death of nature, 150–53
    collective sense of the future in, 148–49, 157–58,
      338–39
    consensus and, 157–61
    conservative backlash against, 153
    cultural shift of, 148, 156
    design assignment in, 163–64

    Earth Day and, 151–53
    ecology movement in, 156–61, 165–67, 216
    economic growth and, 156–57, 161–63
    EPA/PCSD survey in, 157–59
    forest preservation, 142–50
    four segments of, 150, 320
    global warming and, 156–57
    impact of, 140–41
    integrated design process in, 164–65
    lawsuits and legislation in, 154
    obstacles to, 153–56
    other movements converging with, 206, 221
    religious, 320–21
    resource utilization economics in, 155
    Silent Spring and, 110, 150–51
    survival as theme of, 151–52, 322–23
    system conditions for, 324
    whole-systems building and, 164–65
    WTO and, 207–10, 213
EPA/PCSD survey, 157–59
Episcopal Church, 320
Epstein, Samuel, 224–25
Erhard, Werner, 179–80
Esalen Institute, 176–77, 178–80
Eskimo shamans, 263, 291
ethnic feuds, 69, 84, 87
ethnic-pressure-group politics, 119
evolution, design and, 165
evolutionary change, 248–50, 252–54
Exodus, story of, 254–61, 346
extinction response, 155
eye on the big picture, 62–63

Fallows, James, 134
family, outsider in, 100–103
fears, social, 114
feedback, positive vs. negative, 83–86
Feminine Mystique, The (Friedan), 126–27
feminism, 128, 131–32
    and consciousness movement, 206
    and spirituality, 134–35
    see also women
Ferguson, Marilyn, 207
Findhorn, Scotland, 177, 278–79
Flacks, Richard, 133, 209–10
Foner, Eric, 113
Ford, Mary, 21
forest preservation, 142–50
Fox, Matthew, 47
freedom
    individual, 74–75
    social movements toward, 113–25
    women's movement, 126–33
Free Speech movement, 125
Friedan, Betty, 126–27, 151, 292
Frum, David, 30
Fuller, Margaret, 171
fundamentalism, 84, 88
future, positive image of, 340–41

Gablik, Suzi, 236
Gaia, 148, 167, 221
Gains, Reg E., 305–6
Gandhi, Mohandas K., 122, 208
Garfield, Charles, 305
Gary, Tracy, 13–14, 146–47
Gennep, Arnold van, 251
Getting to Peace (Ury), 244
Gilligan, Carol, 129
Ginsberg, Marilyn, 133, 290–91
Gitlin, Todd, 133
globalism and ecology, 11–12, 209–10
global warming, 156–57, 320
Gold, Rabbi Shefa, 255–61
Goldsmith, Edward, 166
government, big, 227, 229
Grand Canyon, 148
Great Depression, 114, 171, 245
Green Cultural Creatives, 14–15, 172, 193
Green parties, 152–53, 166, 336
green products, 332–33, 338–39
Griffin, Susan, 153
Grof, Stanislav, 278
Gulliver's Travels (Swift), 317

Halberstam, David, 117
Hall, Prathia, 21
Hamer, Fannie Lou, 113
Hamilton, Vijali, 310–14
Harding, Vincent, 21, 113, 114, 116, 135–36, 292
Harman, Willis, 44–46, 292
Harvard Business Review, 325
Harvard University, School of Public Health, 225
Havel, Václav, 64, 116
Hawken, Paul, 10, 326
healing, 193–204
    of children, 201
    compassion and common sense in, 196–97
    constituency of, 201, 202
    health and, 196
    holistic, 108, 216
    medicine vs., 194–95
    miracles of, 197–201
    multipliers of, 201–3
    new healers in, 195–96
    personal responsibility for, 224
    as transformative, 200
    use of term, 195
heart path, 52–54
Heidi Chronicles, The (Wasserstein), 132
Heilbrun, Carolyn, 129
Henderson, Hazel, 207
Hider, Chip, 62
Hildegard of Bingen, 243
holistic healing and health, 108, 216
Holocaust, 114, 305
Home Planet, The (Kelley), 302–4
hope, reasons for, 40, 340–41
Houston, Jean, 9, 234

Hoyle, Fred, 303
Hubbard, Barbara Marx, 251, 302
Hudson River School, 148
human potential movement, 206, 216
human rights issues, 214–15, 216
Hunter, James Davison, 67
Huxley, Aldous, 169, 181
Hyde, Henry, 65
hypercar, 11–12

idealism, 10–11
ideals, nonhierarchical models, 95
information age, social movements in, 213, 214–15
inner authority, 277–78
Inner Critic, 54
inner departure, as first step, 48–49
integrated design process, 164–65
Integration, 285
InterBeing, 221
interconnectedness of life, 63–64, 167
International Institute for Applied Systems Analysis
    (IIASA), 273–76, 278
International Monetary Fund (IMF), 209
Internet, online community of, 339–40
Ishmael (Quinn), 49, 57, 254
Ivins, Molly, 48, 54

James, William, 171
Jan (outsider story), 100–104
Jewish Renewal movement, 255
Jim Crow, 81, 84, 117–21
Johnson, Lyndon B., 126
Joyce, James, 169
Jung, Carl Gustav, 300

Kalven, Janet, 43
Katz family, 280–85, 292–94
Keepin, Will, 272–76, 277–80, 285, 292
Kelley, Kevin W., 302–4
Kempton, Willett, 157
Kent, Martye, 145
Kent, William, 142–45, 146, 147, 148, 292
Kimble, Sage, 186
King, Martin Luther, Jr., 113, 120–21, 126, 151,
    213, 292
Kresse, Joe and Barbara, 50–52, 54, 292
Krishnamurti, 277
Ku Klux Klan, 81, 84, 87
Kushner, Tony, 301
Kuttner, Robert, 209

labor union movement, 216
La Casa, 13–14
land preservation movement, 150
Laszlo, Ervin, 248, 249, 252, 253
Lawson, Rev. James, 122–23, 124, 304
leaders and celebrities, 37–39
Lemann, Nicholas, 76–77
Leonard, George, 207

Leopold, Aldo, 141
Lerner, Gerda, 129
Lerner, Michael, 203, 219, 222
Lesser, Elizabeth, 171, 189
Levertov, Denise, 107
Lewis, John, 124–25
Lewis, Michael, 87
Lewis, Rob, 21
Limits to Growth, The (Club of Rome), 152
Linden, Anne Kerr, 126–27
Living Downstream (Steingraber), 225
LOHAS industry, 329–33
Lopez, Barry, 40
Lorde, Audre, 223–26
Lovins, Amory B., 163, 164–65, 326–28
Lovins, L. Hunter, 326
Luce, Gay, 186
lynchings, 114
Lyons, Chief Oren, 57

McDonough, William, 163–64
MacGillis, Sister Miriam, 64, 296
Machado, Antonio, 54
McLuhan, Marshall, 57
Macy, Joanna, 148–49, 296–98
maps, 233–34
    beneath the surface of the Between, 248–54
    from history, 246–48
    into the Between, 235–61
    metamorphosis, 263–85
    of a new culture, 315–41
    of wisdom, 287–314
Maracle, Sylvia, 295
Mardigian, Sandra, 52–53, 54, 292
market economy, 77–78
Marshall, Thurgood, 119, 127, 154
Marty, Martin, 88
Maslow, Abraham, 181
materialism, spiritual, 189
Mazeaud, Dominique, 48
Mead, Margaret, 9
Meade, Erica, 300
Meade, Michael, 294–95
Meadows, Donella, 152
media
    advertisers, 133, 223
    audience ratings as goal of, 133–34
    big, 227, 229
    blind spots of, 228–29
    corporate interests of, 222–23, 225–28
    and freedom movement, 123, 126
    movies, 227, 328
    and women's movement, 126
    WTO meeting and, 207
medicine vs. healing, 194–95
medieval world, 78–79
meditation, 176, 178, 278
Megatrends (Naisbitt), 235–36
Merton, Thomas, 148

metamorphosis, 263–85
    Between and, 269–70, 276–77, 279–80, 285
    preventing Ophelia in, 280–85
    return and integration in, 271–72
    rites of passage in, 263–64
    separation of, 267–69
    story of, 266–67
    transformation as, 264–66
    trusting the unknown in, 272–77
Milne, Paul, 91
mirrors, distorted, 55
Mitchell, Patte, 15–17
Moderns, 25–30, 70–78
    alienated, 73, 300
    clinging to the past, 237–38
    conventional, 72
    in culture wars, 33, 66–67, 84, 92
    departure from, 52–54, 81, 83–87, 88–89, 92–93
    as dominant culture, 102–3
    downside of, 75–78
    dream of success, 47–48, 76–77
    economic growth and, 152, 162, 317, 321
    emergence of, 70
    fragmentation of, 92
    hole in culture of, 294–95
    and individual freedom, 74–75
    leaders and celebrities, 38
    market takeover of, 77–78
    self-interest of, 76–77
    subgroups of, 71–73
    successes of, 71, 73–75
    values of, 28–29, 68, 69
moral publics, 217, 219, 238
moral values, 66, 67, 68, 120, 238
moral witness, tradition of, 213
Morrow, Lance, 188
Morton, Nelle, 129
Mpanya, Mutombo, 289–90
Muir, John, 142, 144, 148, 171, 292
Muir Woods National Monument, 142–45, 147, 149
multipliers, of healing, 201–3
Murphy, Michael, 176
Myss, Caroline, 193–94, 195
Mystery, core of, 285, 291
mythos, new, 298–300

NAACP, 119, 127
Naisbitt, John, 235–36
Nash, Diane, 117
National Council of Churches, 320–21
Natural Capitalism (Lovins and Lovins), 326–28, 338
Natural Step, The, 322–25
Nelson, Ruben F. W., 56, 77–78
neotraditionalism, 88–89
New Age, 188–89, 192
new country, exploring, 40–42
New England Journal of Medicine, 225
New Left movement, 125, 128
new life path, creating, 46–47, 49–52, 86

Newman, Naomi, 236, 290
nonviolence, 122–23, 124
Northrup, Christiane, 195
Novartis, 225
nuclear weapons, 110
Nüsslein-Volhard, Christine, 242

occupational health and safety movement, 150, 221
"Old and Lost Rivers" (Anderson), 347–48
Oliver, Mary, 169
Olmsted, F. E., 143
Omega Institute, 189

Palmer, Parker, 20
Paramahansa Yogananda, 60
Parks, Rosa, 112
PCSD/EPA survey, 157–59
peace movement, 135, 214
Peninsula Village, 15–17
people of the parenthesis, 234
Peromo, Willie, 305–6
personal bridges, 89–90
Person/Planet (Roszak), 207
Piercy, Marge, 128
Pinchot, Gifford, 143
Pipher, Mary, 280–81
Poe, Edgar Allan, 103
Polak, Fred, 340–41
Polanyi, Karl, 233
politics, as spectator sport, 134
Politics of the Solar Age, The (Henderson), 207
pollution, cancer-causing, 224–25
poverty, devastation of, 215
Prabhavananda, Swami, 310
Pred, Elenore, 223–24
Price, Richard, 176
principle, collisions of, 332–33
productivity, radical resource, 326–27
Prohibition, 84
protest movements, 81
    black freedom, 112–14, 117–25
    convergence of, 210, 213
    moral witness of, 213
    nonviolence in, 122–23, 124
    reframing of, 121–22
    transformation in, 124–25
Pruden, Wesley, 81
psychology, 180–81, 210, 216
public health movement, 150

Quinn, Daniel, 49, 57, 254

rap groups, 67–68
Rathbun, Richard, 50
Reconstruction, 81, 118
Redl, Maureen, 198–200, 226
Redwood Canyon, 143–45
religion
    and community groups, 335

and environment, 320–21
    male viewpoint in, 129
    values and, 69–70
Religions of Man, The (Smith), 277
Remen, Rachel Naomi, 195, 196, 198–99, 202, 226
Reviving Ophelia (Pipher), 280–81
Rich, Adrienne, 130, 292
Rinpoche, Chogyam Trungpa, 189
rites of passage
    adolescence and, 281–85
    cultural, 306
    elders in, 292
    Integration, 285
    metamorphosis, 263–85
    planetary, 250–54
    stages of, 252–54
Robért, Karl-Henrik, 322–24
Rocky Mountain Institute, 12, 163, 276
Roosevelt, Theodore, 142, 143–45
Roszak, Theodore, 207
Rumi, Jelaluddin, 169

Sacred Grove, 9–10, 145–49
Sahtouris, Elisabet, 57–58, 63, 265–72, 279, 285, 291, 292
Salamander Camp, 308–9
Salick chain, 224–25
Satin, Mark, 206–7
Schumacher, E. F., 278
Schwartz, Peter, 236
Schweickart, Rusty, 302
science, as corruptible, 151
self-actualization, 15–16, 181, 217
self-interest, 76–77
separation stage, 252–53
setting out, as second step, 49–52
Shavano Institute, 279–80
Shifler, Eric, 305
Siegel, Bernie, 195
Sierra Club, 142, 154
silence, about what matters, 56
Silent Spring (Carson), 110, 150–51, 225
Small Is Beautiful (Schumacher), 278
Smith, Adam, 78
Smith, Huston, 277
SNCC, 117
social codes
    as belief systems, 122
    challenges to, 130–31
    cultural conditioning in, 129
    Jim Crow, 81, 84, 117–21
    lies in, 129–30
    male viewpoint in, 129
social inventions, 39–40
social justice, 221
social movements, 81, 107–38
    activists of, 103–4, 107–8, 154–55, 210, 213, 229
    associations and, 336–38
    black freedom, 112–14, 117–25, 216

blind spots of, 229
civil rights, 81, 112–25
collective identity of, 210, 213
conservative backlash to, 153
convergence of, 206–7, 210–17, 218–19, 221–23, 226, 237
creation stories and, 103
cultural arms of, 128, 134–35, 212
Cultural Creatives at center of, 217–18
elitism in, 154–55
environmental, *see* environmental movement
extinction response in, 155
for freedom, 113–25
grassroots groups, 132–33
impact of, 110–12, 131–32, 135–38, 221–22
important to Cultural Creatives, 137
in information age, 213, 214–15
interdependence of, 166, 214–16, 222–23, 226–29
kinds of, 115–16
mainstreaming of, 135
media coverage of, 123, 133–34
moral publics of, 217, 219, 238
new kind of, 219, 221–22
new territory of, 229–30
political arms of, 128
political parties and, 109
separateness of, 218–19
size of, 108–10
specialists in, 229
submerged networks of, 134–35
survey of, 111
transformation in, 124–25, 189, 207, 233–34, 239–40
values and beliefs of, 218, 220
walking your talk, 123–25
where did they go?, 131–35
women's liberation, 126–33, 216, 217
Sorokin, Pitirim, 246–48
Soup and Bread, 307–8
space, Earth photographed from, 153, 302–4
Spangler, David, 188, 341
spirituality, 15–17
consciousness movements and, 108, 171
health and, 225–26
new, 171
other movements converging with, 206, 210, 213
women's movement in, 134–35
spiritual materialism, 189
Spretnak, Charlene, 134
Springsteen, Bruce, 55
Starhawk, 213
Steinberg, Saul, 70
Steingraber, Sandra, 225
stories
Amaterasu Omikami, 343–46
in community context, 304–6
Coyote, 287–88
creation, 99–105, 205–30
in dreams, 301–2
Exodus, 254–61, 346

guiding, 222
mythology, 298–300
new tellers of, 300–301
official, 92–93
Titanic, 240–41
striving center, Moderns, 72–73
Students for a Democratic Society (SDS), 209
subcultures
in culture wars, 33, 66–67, 84, 92
diverging paths of, 82
identification of, 350
leaders and celebrities from, 37–39
moral publics of, 219
signposts in, 37, 39
survey results, 349–50
values and beliefs among, 25, 28–29, 68–69
see also Cultural Creatives; Moderns; Traditionals
success
changing the dream of, 47–48
illusion of, 32–33
opportunity for, 76–77
sun, myth of, 343–46
Supreme Court, U.S., and civil rights, 119
survey, xiv, 349–50
sustainability, ecological, 152, 157, 288–89, 322–23, 327–28, 338
Suzuki, David, 140–41, 314
Swift, Jonathan, 317

tamoxifen, 224–25
Tao of Physics (Capra), 278
Tar Babies, 127, 129–30
Tarnas, Richard, 251
technology
evolution of, 315–17
for survival, 325
Teilhard de Chardin, Pierre, 51
Thich Nhat Hanh, 221, 314
Think on These Things (Krishnamurti), 277
Third Wave, The (Toffler), 207
Thompson, William Irwin, 237
Thompson-Taupin, Celia, 306–9
Thoreau, Henry David, 148, 171
tikkun (healing), 195
time, measurement of, 79
Titanic, story of, 240–41
Toffler, Alvin, 207
Tollifson, Joan, 175–76
Toynbee, Arnold, 239, 245
Traditionals, 24, 30–32, 80–81
as counterculture, 81, 83
in culture wars, 33, 66–67, 84, 92
fundamentalism and, 84, 88
imaginary past of, 88–89
leaders and celebrities, 38
memory and, 80
as neotraditionalism, 88–89
split from Moderns, 81, 83–87, 88–89, 92
values of, 28–29, 68–69

Transcendentalists, 171
transformation
	of culture, 315
	of healing, 200
	journeys into space, 302
	metamorphosis as, 264–66
	in social movements, 124–25, 189, 207, 233–34,
		239–40
	technological, 316
Transformation, The (Leonard), 207
truth, explorations of, 129–30
Tubman, Harriet, 255
Turner, Ralph H., 216
Turner, Victor, 269
Turning Point, The (Capra), 207

unconscious life systems, 249–50
United States, subcultures in, 24
Uprety, Aruna, 215
upward mobility, 72
Ury, William, 244, 245

values
	activism and idealism, 10–11
	altruism, 15–16
	authenticity, 8–9, 130
	changing, 17–19
	in consciousness movement, 190–91
	ethnic, 69
	globalism and ecology, 11–12
	importance of women, 12–14
	moral, 66, 67, 68, 120, 238
	and new way of life, 58–64
	as predictors of behavior, 7–14
	protest movements and, 120
	relativism vs. pluralism, 68–70
	religious doctrine and, 69–70
	self-actualization, 15–16
	social movements and, 218, 220
	spirituality, 15–17
	of subcultures, 24, 28–29, 68–69
	whole process learning, 9–10
van Gelder, Sarah, 93
Vivian, Rev. C. T., 123–24
vocation, 335
Voices of Healing, 200–201

Walker, Alice, 139–40
walking your talk, 123–25
Wallace, Mike, 227
Warrick, Brooke, 8
Wasserstein, Wendy, 132, 207
waste, recycling vs., 327
Weber, Will, 331
Web of Life, 221
Weil, Andrew, 195

Welwood, Jennifer, 173–74
West, Mariquita, 196–200
Weyrich, Paul, 65
White, Lovell, 143
whole process learning, 9–10
whole-systems buildings, 164–65
Wilson, E. O., 314
wisdom, 287–314
	of connection, 310
	in context of community, 304–6
	creating a world, 306–9
	Earth from space, 302–4
	of elders, 289–94
	heart of, 295–98
	hole in culture and, 294–95
	into the Between, 310–12
	lifelines of, 301–2
	new mythos of, 298–300
	new storytellers, 300–301
	women's circle of, 292–94
	World Wheel, 312–14
Wolfe, George C., 301
women
	adolescence and, 281
	consciousness-raising of, 128–29
	cultural conditioning of, 129
	as Culture Creatives, 23–24
	importance of, 12–14
	poverty of, 215
	rights of, 92, 126–33
	second-class status of, 110
	spirituality movement and, 134–35
	wisdom circle of, 292–94
	younger branch of, 128, 131
Women's Foundation, 13–14
women's movement, 126–33, 216, 217
women's nonhierarchical models, 95
Woodman, Marion, 264–65, 300
Woolf, Virginia, 131
World Trade Organization (WTO), 207–10, 213
worldviews
	changing, 7, 17–19, 110–12, 217–18
	culture and, 7, 93
World War II, 114, 171, 300
Worldwatch Institute, 152
World Wheel, 312–14
WRECS, 135
Wynne, Brian, 274–75

Yes! (van Gelder), 93
yoga, 328–32
Youngblood, Mark, 58–61, 62

Zen
	and meditation, 176, 178, 278
	suchness of, 170